America's Economic Way of War

How did economic and financial factors determine how America waged war in the twentieth century? This important new book exposes the influence of economics and finance on the questions of whether the nation should go to war, how wars would be fought, how resources would be mobilized, and the long-term consequences for the American economy. Ranging from the Spanish–American War to the Gulf War, Hugh Rockoff explores the ways in which war can provide unique opportunities for understanding the basic principles of economics as wars produce immense changes in monetary and fiscal policy and so provide a wealth of information about how these policies actually work. He shows that wars have been more costly to the United States than most Americans realize as a substantial reliance on borrowing from the public, money creation, and other strategies to finance America's war efforts have hidden the true cost of war.

HUGH ROCKOFF is a professor of Economics at Rutgers, the State University of New Jersey, and a research associate of the National Bureau of Economic Research. His publications include numerous papers in professional journals, *The Free Banking Era: A Re-examination* (1975), *Drastic Measures: A History of Wage and Price Controls in the United States* (1984), and a textbook, *History of the American Economy* (2010, with Gary Walton).

NEW APPROACHES TO ECONOMIC AND SOCIAL HISTORY

SERIES EDITORS

Nigel Goose, *University of Hertfordshire*
Larry Neal, *University of Illinois, Urbana-Champaign*

New Approaches to Economic and Social History is an important new textbook series published in association with the Economic History Society. It provides concise but authoritative surveys of major themes and issues in world economic and social history from the post-Roman recovery to the present day. Books in the series are by recognized authorities operating at the cutting edge of their field with an ability to write clearly and succinctly. The series consists principally of single-author works – academically rigorous and groundbreaking – which offer comprehensive, analytical guides at a length and level accessible to advanced school students and undergraduate historians and economists.

America's Economic Way of War

War and the US Economy from the Spanish–American War to the Persian Gulf War

HUGH ROCKOFF

CAMBRIDGE
UNIVERSITY PRESS

CAMBRIDGE UNIVERSITY PRESS
Cambridge, New York, Melbourne, Madrid, Cape Town,
Singapore, São Paulo, Delhi, Mexico City

Cambridge University Press
The Edinburgh Building, Cambridge CB2 8RU, UK

Published in the United States of America by
Cambridge University Press, New York

www.cambridge.org
Information on this title: www.cambridge.org/9780521676731

First published 2012

Printed in the United Kingdom at the University Press, Cambridge

A catalogue record for this publication is available from the British Library

Library of Congress Cataloging-in-Publication data

Rockoff, Hugh.
America's economic way of war : war and the US economy from the Spanish–American War to the Persian Gulf War / Hugh Rockoff.
p. cm. – (New approaches to economic and social history)
ISBN 978-0-521-85940-0 – ISBN 978-0-521-67673-1 (Paperback)
1. War–Economic aspects–United States–History–20th century. I. Title.
HC110.D4.R58 2012
330.973′091–dc23

2011046107

ISBN 978-0-521-85940-0 Hardback
ISBN 978-0-521-67673-1 Paperback

Contents

Figures

Boxes

Tables

Chronologies

Acknowledgements

My first and largest intellectual debt is to Larry Neal who suggested that I write this book, and took upon himself the task of keeping me focused on the important issues. Michael Edelstein talked with me at length about the book and awakened my interest in a number of questions that I had not previously thought about. Robert Higgs was an important influence through conversations about war economics, and through his provocative writings. Mira Wilkins graciously took time to answer questions about American foreign investment at the turn of the century. Stanley Engerman read the entire draft at a later date and saved me from many errors, large and small. My Rutgers colleagues, Michael Bordo, Eugene White, Carolyn Moehling, and John Landon-Lane, were smart and patient sounding boards for ideas. Sung Won Kang provided diligent and thoughtful research assistance. Michael Watson at Cambridge University Press provided sound advice and firm but polite reminders about when things were supposed to be done. My wife, Hope Corman, provided emotional support without which this book would never have been completed. None of these fine people, however, is responsible for what I am sure are a large number of remaining errors.

1 *A century of war*

The sinews of war are infinite money.

Roman statesman and philosopher, Cicero

This book is about the economic causes and consequences of the wars that the United States fought in the twentieth century. Although the general public and professional historians focus considerable attention on wars, economists tend to neglect them. To be sure, there is a small group of economic historians who have diligently worked to increase our knowledge of the economics of war – one of the purposes of this book is to bring their findings to the attention of a larger audience – but it is fair to say that economists as a whole tend to think of peace as the norm and war as an exception to be ignored. But the idea that war can be regarded as a rare outlier belies the truth: America was at war somewhere in the world during a significant portion of the twentieth century.

The wars that opened the century, the Spanish–American and Philippine–American wars, required relatively small fractions of the nation's resources. The two world wars that followed required much larger fractions, and brought in their train far-reaching networks of government control. The post-World War II conflicts in Korea, Vietnam, and Iraq again were "limited wars," similar to the wars that opened the century, rather than to the world wars. Indeed, there is a sense in which we have come full circle: the wars which America is now fighting in Iraq and Afghanistan bear a strong and often unsettling likeness to the Spanish–American and Philippine–American wars. Each war presented unique military, political, and economic challenges, but there were many common elements. In this volume I will try to summarize these elements by answering some of the most familiar questions about the economics of America's wars, starting with questions about how the country got into the wars, moving on to questions about how they were fought, and ending with questions about their legacies. The answers to most of these questions cannot be laid down with certainty. In this chapter I will provide only a few facts to illustrate the nature of the issue and to suggest my main conclusion. Hopefully, the discussions of individual wars in subsequent chapters will provide more compelling evidence.

Were America's wars fought for economic reasons?

Economic forces were not the main cause of America's involvement in wars, but economic forces often played an important secondary role in pushing the nation toward war. Special interests that definitely favored war, or at least had an economic interest in doing so, could be identified for every war. These interests frequently added their voices to the chorus demanding war, often offering economic justifications. Before the Spanish–American War, for example, some Americans with business interests in Cuba were deeply concerned about the ongoing insurrection on the island and called for an American intervention to restore order. Once the United States was engaged militarily in the Philippines merchants concerned about access to China called for American control of the Philippines – "an American flag only 500 miles from China." Special economic interests, however, were never enough to push the United States into war. For one thing, some special interests opposed wars. Many bankers, for example, opposed the Spanish–American War because they thought it would produce inflation (as had happened in the Civil War and earlier wars) that would hurt bank balance sheets and, conceivably, undermine the gold standard, which had just been firmly ensconced after the long battle with the bimetallists. Indeed, important segments of the banking community were opponents of most wars.

Determined groups in the executive branch, typically in the State Department or Department of Defense, with allies in Congress, who believed that it was in the interest of the United States to use its military power to achieve foreign policy goals were more important to the launching of wars than were special economic interests. During the Spanish–American and Philippine–American wars, Theodore Roosevelt in the Navy Department and his allies in Congress, especially Senator Henry Cabot Lodge, saw the ability of the United States to project its naval power by building ships, constructing an isthmus canal, and acquiring colonies and naval bases, as crucial to American prosperity in an increasingly imperialist world. They were willing to take bold actions to push America into war and into taking possession of the Philippines and other colonies. US entry in World War I was pushed in some quarters because the neutral trading rights of the United States were being violated by the German submarine campaign, but also because its long-time allies, Britain and France, were nearing exhaustion. US entry in World War II was the result, of course, of the Japanese attack on Pearl Harbor, but the path of conflict between the USA and the Axis had been taken not only for economic reasons, narrowly understood, but also because of opposition to the depredations of Japan in China and Germany in Europe. The Korean War was entered to protect South Korea from North Korean aggression, but that aggression was part of the worldwide struggle by the United States to contain Communism, an economic system violently opposed to its own. Similarly, in Vietnam, a long list of State Department and government officials argued that letting the Communists succeed in that country would lead to Communist takeovers throughout Southeast Asia (the domino effect), and weaken American influence throughout the world.

However, even the power of special interests and foreign policy experts combined was limited. In the end, going to war required massive public support. That meant appealing to America's sense of honor and justice, and usually that entailed some dramatic event that was, or could be portrayed as, a direct military attack on the United States or its allies, a *casus belli*. The Spanish–American War required an American public outraged by Spanish attempts to suppress the Cuban independence movement and the explosion of the battleship *Maine* in the harbor at Havana. The Philippine–American War required the outbreak of fighting between Americans and Filipinos in Manila. World War I required German submarine attacks. World War II required Pearl Harbor. The Korean War required the North Korean invasion of South Korea. The Vietnam War required the naval battles that produced the Tonkin Gulf Resolution. The Cold War required attempts at a Communist takeover in Greece. The Persian Gulf War required the Iraqi invasion of Kuwait. And the Afghan and Iraq wars required the attack on the World Trade Center on September 11.

How did America fight its wars?

Inevitably, whatever the initial intentions, wars became cruel as financial costs and casualties mounted. When the war in the Philippines began, few Americans would have believed that the "water cure," forced concentration of the population, burning of crops, and other brutal tactics would be used by the United States. When World War II began, few Americans would have believed that it would lead to the firebombing of cities, to two nuclear bombs, and to millions of civilian deaths. Mass bombing of civilian targets was used again in the Vietnam War, and few Americans would have thought that a likely outcome when the war began. Of course, most nations fight wars ferociously. But the number of casualties America inflicted on its enemy's civilian population was often high because America's armed forces employed a high ratio of capital to labor. In other words, the United States at war behaved much like a private firm faced with low interest rates relative to wages and substituted capital for labor.

The twentieth century saw the development of many new capital-intensive weapons, but above all it was the airplane that allowed the United States to exploit its lead in capital and technology. World War I saw the beginnings of air warfare, but aircraft could play only a supporting role; after all, that war began in August 1914, just eleven years after the Wright brothers' first successful flight at Kitty Hawk. But progress in utilizing this new technology was rapid. By the end of the war, as we will see, the United States was producing airplane engines at a rate approaching 50,000 per year. In World War II, of course, the airplane became a major component in America's campaigns against Germany and Japan, and then it was a mainstay of US forces in Korea, Vietnam, and the Persian Gulf War. Unmanned drones have become a major tool in the ongoing wars in Afghanistan and Iraq. The airplane is the ultimate expression of America's capital-intensive way of war and the destruction of civilian populations that was a consequence.

How did America finance its wars?

There are many ways of financing wars. For example, civilian spending can be cut or the government can rely on gifts: contributions by America's Mideast partners defrayed a substantial part of the costs of the Persian Gulf War. Indeed, one of the purposes of this book is to explore the ways in which the financing of wars influences and is influenced by almost every aspect of a war economy. Policies that at first sight seem far removed from finance, such as price and wage controls and the draft, I will try to show, are closely tied to the process of war finance. Nevertheless, economists tend to focus on three methods – taxes, borrowing, and printing money – because, typically, these were the most important. Printing money, of course, has a bad name, because it produces inflation. But in World War I, World War II, and during the Vietnam era, America relied in part on the printing press. There were several reasons. One was simply that the wars were costly and the government was reluctant to push tax finance and bond finance to the extent necessary to finance the entire war. The establishment of the Federal Reserve, moreover, hid the process of money creation. In the nineteenth century the connection between the printing press and inflation was visible to the naked eye because new forms of currency were introduced. In the twentieth century the connection was much harder to see: the Federal Reserve would purchase government bonds, creating new balances for the Treasury. When these were spent the additional competition for goods would bid up prices. But it was harder for the public to see the connection. Inflation might well be blamed on war profiteers rather than monetary policy. It was not always necessary to resort to inflation to finance the war. Most of the smaller wars – the Spanish–American, Philippine–American, Korean, and Persian Gulf Wars – were financed without inflation.

Debt finance was an important source of financing for the world wars and the Vietnam War. The American capital market was sufficiently broad, and the credit of the US government sufficiently good, for it to finance smaller wars without having to pay significantly higher interest rates. But in the world wars interest rates might have risen if the Federal Reserve had not stepped in and created additional liquidity in financial markets. Rising interest rates would be a sign to the public that the war was costly. They also might be a sign to enemies that the war was straining the country's resources.

In the world wars the government tried to encourage private purchases of bonds with patriotic campaigns that included bond rallies and now famous posters: "Get in the Scrap, Buy War Bonds Now." How much the campaigns really contributed in terms of broadening the market for bonds and holding rates on them below what they otherwise would have been is debatable. However, they must have had some effect, and they strengthened support for the war, and eased anxieties, by giving people a way of demonstrating their support. They also helped suppress the increase in interest rates that might have signaled the cost of the war.

Finally, the cost of each of the United States' wars was, until the most recent war in Iraq, defrayed in part by raising taxes. It was an honorable tradition. Raising taxes, of course, communicated the cost of the war to the public. So most governments did what they could to mitigate the political fallout. One strategy was to press for a tax bill as soon as a war began. In this way the government could take advantage of the early enthusiasm for the war. In the Spanish–American War the government relied in part on "sin" taxes, such as those on alcohol, tobacco, and chewing gum. In the First World War it increased income tax only for the very wealthy. In World War II and Korea, however, a combination of liberal administrations and broad-based support for the war led to broad-based increases in taxes. Indeed, a kind of high point was reached during the Korean War, when under the indefatigable Harry S. Truman the government financed most of the war with taxes. The Vietnam War, however, was a different story, and marked a return to an earlier form of war finance. President Lyndon Johnson was deeply concerned that a tax increase would reveal the cost of the Vietnam War to the public and undermine support for his Great Society program. Despite rising inflation and recommendations from his economic advisors Johnson refused, for a long time, to call for higher taxes. Eventually, however, he relented and called for a limited tax "surcharge."

Did wars stimulate the economy?

The idea that in economic terms wars are "good" because they stimulate the economy derives mainly from the US experience in World War II. However, while the mobilization did play a part in returning the economy to full employment, the idea that it took a full-blown world war to lift the United States out of the Depression is an exaggeration. By December of 1941, when the United States entered World War II, unemployment was close to the 1929 level and falling steadily: 1942 would have been a boom year even in the absence of Pearl Harbor. Other forms of spending, moreover, could have taken the role played by spending on armaments in the late 1930s and early 1940s. And the highly expansionary monetary policies followed during World War II could have been followed in any case.

Does economics have anything useful to say about wars?

Many scholars, including some economists, reject the idea that economics – based on self-interested consumers, profit-maximizing firms, supply and demand, and so on – is of much value at any time. For them it is obvious that wartime economies are even less susceptible to traditional economic analysis. They would argue that the idea that people are simple, self-interested, and rational calculators surely does not apply in wartime when national interests borne on waves of patriotism take center stage.

Indeed, in empirical studies wars are often treated as "outliers," periods that can be neglected because they have little in common with peacetime. This attitude, I believe, is a mistake. Wars often provide better evidence about how the economy works than peacetime experiences. Milton Friedman put it this way:

> The widespread tendency in empirical studies of economic behavior to discard war years as "abnormal," while doubtless often justified, is, on the whole, unfortunate. The major defect of the data on which economists must rely – data generated by experience rather than deliberately contrived experiments – is the small range of variation they encompass. Experience in general proceeds smoothly and continuously. In consequence, it is difficult to disentangle systematic effects from random variation since both are of much the same order of magnitude.
>
> From this point of view, data for wartime periods are peculiarly valuable. At such times, violent changes in major economic magnitudes occur over relatively brief periods, thereby providing precisely the kind of evidence that we would like to get by "critical" experiments if we could conduct them. (Friedman 1952, 612)

To be sure, waves of patriotism were important. They were important in the decision to go to war and in the willingness of people to bear the costs of war. One would not begin to think about the economics of war without putting patriotism center stage. But the student of the economic history of America's wars cannot fail to be struck by how often the basic tools of economics help us understand how America's wartime economies worked. Whether it's bankers opposing the

Spanish–American War because the war might produce inflation and weaken their balance sheets, or candymakers in World War II adding fillers to candy bars in order to evade price controls, the traditional economist will find plenty of grist for his or her mill.

Economics, moreover, is inevitably brought into the fray when public debate moves on from whether to go to war, an issue often debated in lofty ethical and philosophical terms, to the practical issue of how to pay for war. Economists approached the Spanish–American and Philippine–American wars with the tools and values of classical economics. War was a matter of public finance; and public finance, like private finance, meant balancing the budget. The problem for economists was to recommend the fairest and most efficient way of raising the money the government needed. The view of the economists was widely shared. Taxes, such as sin taxes were raised, but little thought was given to monetary policy or explicit wage and price controls. There was no central bank that could stealthily finance the war by purchasing government bonds, and no reason to engage in the actual printing of new money, the policy adopted during the Revolution, the War of 1812, and the Civil War.

The financing of World War I was very different. Taxes were raised, including income tax, which was now in place as a result of a recent constitutional amendment. But despite higher taxes, deficit spending produced a rapid increase in the public debt. The newly established Federal Reserve was able to finance the purchase of a substantial portion of that debt by printing new money. Perhaps most at variance with classical ideas of war finance, the United States instituted a far-reaching set of price and wage controls. All of these policies were quickly abandoned after the war ended. Although some economists began to embrace this mix of policies as appropriate in peacetime, most regarded them as a temporary departure from sound policy forced on the United States by the exigencies of war.

The Great Depression, and the analysis of it in John Maynard Keynes's *General Theory* (1936), profoundly changed macroeconomics: deficit spending was no longer anathema in peacetime, a rising money stock and low interest rates were desirable, and wage and price controls could be used to stem inflation. Keynesian economics was, to some extent, war economics. The difference was that in World War I most mainstream economists had viewed this mix of policies as an aberration – something that had to be tolerated during the war, but then would be removed afterwards. Keynesian economics, although it was seldom explicitly acknowledged, was simply the argument that these policies would be useful in peace as well as in war.

This mix of policies was adopted again in World War II. And the speed with which they restored full employment helped convince most economists of the correctness of Keynesian economics. The influence of Keynesian economics during the Korean War, however, was limited. President Truman held traditional views about finance and demanded and got tax increases that went a long way toward financing the war. And the Federal Reserve, concerned about a temporary surge in inflation, was able to assert its independence, including the right to raise interest rates as an anti-inflationary measure.

World Wars I and II helped establish Keynesian economics, but the Vietnam War undermined it. To be sure, Keynesian economists, including those at the Council of Economic Advisors, recommended tax increases to fight the inflation that began to emerge in the late 1960s as the Vietnam War intensified – tax increases that had been delayed and then limited mainly for political reasons. But inflation still posed a major theoretical problem for Keynesian economics, which by that decade had been augmented by the Phillips Curve, the idea that there was a stable negative relationship between unemployment and inflation. But in the late 1960s inflation began to rise without unemployment falling to the low levels that had prevailed in World War II and the Korean War. Macroeconomists now began to listen more to Milton Friedman and his monetarist colleagues who argued that there was no permanent tradeoff between inflation and unemployment, and that controlling the money supply, a policy considered of secondary importance in Keynesian macroeconomics, was in fact the key to controlling inflation.

In the ensuing years a third school of economics, what might be called the Minnesota School, came to prominence. Sometimes also called the Freshwater School to differentiate it from the Neo-Keynesian views dominant on the coasts, the Minnesota School emphasized the potential negative effects of tax increases on work effort, even in wartime. Lee E. Ohanian (1997) importantly drew the conclusion that the heavy reliance on taxes to finance the Korean War was a mistake. It would have been better to "smooth" taxes over time, that is, increase taxes less and rely more on debt finance during the war. In that way productivity during the war years would not be discouraged by high taxes. By the time of the wars in Iraq and Afghanistan the tradition of raising taxes in wartime had largely disappeared.

Did the United States rely on central planning to reallocate resources in World War I, World War II, and the Korean War?

It is sometimes assumed that wars prove that central planning is a more efficient mechanism for allocating resources than the incentive system used by the market, at least in national emergencies. In both World War I and World War II, and to a lesser extent during the Korean War, the United States imposed a comprehensive system of wage and price controls, and created federal agencies charged with controlling and maximizing war production. In fact, for better or worse, the United States relied mainly on incentives, "throwing money at the problem," to achieve the desired reallocation of resources from the civilian sector to the military sector. In both World War I and World War II the most celebrated attempts to impose a more centralized system for allocating resources, such as the Controlled Material Plan of World War II, came too late to have much effect on the crucial reallocation of resources.

Did wars alter the financial system?

Wars have produced the most important reorganizations of the world's financial system. The major industrial nations, with the exception of the United States, left the gold standard during World War I. Most returned during the 1920s. But the major industrial nations, including the United States, abandoned gold once again during the Great Depression. After World War II a new financial system, the Bretton Woods system, was established, with fixed exchange rates and the dollar as the world's central currency. As part of this agreement, the International Monetary Fund and World Bank were established to help maintain global financial stability and promote growth. This system appeared to work well for a time. But increases in US inflation and deterioration in its balance of payments, in part consequences of the Vietnam War, led to America's decision to abandon the Bretton Woods system and to adopt the modern system of fluctuating exchange rates.

How costly were America's wars?

The wars of the twentieth century were extraordinarily costly. World War II, the most expensive, cost the United States more than 400,000 lives and almost one and one-third years of GDP. Smaller wars, of course, were less costly, although expenditure did mount up. The Philippine–American War cost nearly as much as the Spanish–American War. The long period of heightened military spending after the Philippine War – what President Theodore Roosevelt called a "large policy," and what his critics called imperialism – proved to be even more expensive in resources if not in lives. Expenditure on the Cold War was greater than that on World War I and nearly as great (in terms of resources) as World War II.

Ultimately, this book is about war finance, but war finance conceived more broadly than is usually the case. There are discussions of taxes and bonds and Federal Reserve policy, as one might expect in a book on such a subject, but there are also discussions of the draft, price controls, and veterans' benefits. The discussion of all of these issues takes us back to questions of war finance. The draft, to take one example, is a moral and philosophical issue, but it is also a form of war finance. The draftee is taxed, this sum being the difference between what the draftee could earn in the private sector and what he or she earns in the armed forces. Price controls are another example. To the extent that controls suppress inflation, they also suppress one of the indicators that the government is involved in an expensive enterprise. True, controls may produce irritating side-effects, such as black markets or quality deterioration. But the public's ire may be directed at the black marketeers or the firms engaged in quality deterioration, rather than at the government that made the decision to wage war. The ancient Roman statesman and philosopher Cicero put it this way: "the sinews of war are infinite money."

Does America reward its veterans generously?

Veterans' benefits are the largest long-run cost of America's wars, one that is hard to take into account during the march to war. Usually America tries to do the right thing by its veterans, but sometimes concerns about the budget have had a major impact. The veterans of the Spanish–American and Philippine–American wars were well rewarded in comparison with the veterans of past wars in part because their small number posed few fiscal problems. The veterans of World War I, on the other hand, found many of their claims for a bonus blocked repeatedly because of fiscal considerations. World War II veterans were rewarded more generously. Their benefits included the education provisions of the famous GI Bill. However, the latter were reduced for veterans of the Korean War.[1]

[1] There are, of course, many other important questions about the impact of wars on the American economy. It has been suggested, for example, that wars have produced important scientific and technological breakthroughs, that they have improved the status of women and minorities, and that they have fundamentally expanded the role of the federal government in the economy. In this book, in the discussions of individual wars there is considerable material that relates to these questions, but they are not covered in detail.

2 *The economics of war*

Economics is a very unsatisfactory science. But it would have to be much more unsatisfactory than it is if such an event as a war, however extensive and destructive, sufficed to upset its teaching.

Schumpeter 1954, 1146

Before beginning the discussion of individual wars, it will be helpful, at least for some readers, to review the ways in which the basic principles of economics can be applied to war economies.[1] As the quote above by the distinguished Austrian and American economist Joseph Schumpeter indicates, there is a tendency to assume that economic ideas don't apply in wartime, perhaps

[1] Here I am concerned with how economics can be used to describe the impact of wars on the economy. The book does not address, except in passing, the question of how resources were or should have been allocated within the military – whether, for example, more resources should have been allocated to the army and less to the navy or air force during particular conflicts – although this issue will be raised on occasion. And it is not about how to achieve an efficient allocation of resources within a service – whether, for example, weapons should have been made in government arsenals or purchased from the private sector, and if purchased from the private sector whether they should have been purchased with cost-plus or through competitive bidding – although again these issues will be raised on occasion. And it is not about war strategy – should the enemy forces be ground down with an aerial bombardment before a ground attack begins? Economists have analyzed these issues using their fundamental tools, and have a great deal to say about them. Indeed, a whole division of economics, defense economics, has arisen to deal with these issues. Defense economics now takes its place alongside other branches such as international economics and agricultural economics, as well it should. Total US exports in 2008 were 12.7 percent of GDP, exceeding the 5.1 percent of GDP generated in the defense sector. But the latter figure was considerably more than the 1.1 percent accounted for by agriculture, forestry, and fisheries (*Economic Report of the President* 2010, Tables B-1, B-12, and B-24). However you look at it, defense is a major component of the economy. Keith Hartley and Todd Sandler (1995) provide an overview of the field of defense economics and a selection of the key papers.

because non-pecuniary motives for human action, such as patriotism, take precedence over mere maximization of income. But as I will try to show here, and in more detail in subsequent chapters, the principles of economics can be extremely helpful in understanding the important economic and financial questions posed by America's decisions to go to war.

The economic causes of America's wars

Untangling the complex forces that have propelled Americans into war has perplexed political scientists, historians, and economists. Nevertheless, it is frequently argued that wars were the result of economic forces. These arguments are usually versions of one of three recurring ideas.

1 One argument is that America was driven into foreign wars by the need to capture foreign markets. John Maynard Keynes (1964 [1936], 381–3), looking back on the experience of Europe in the nineteenth century and World War I, concluded that a combination of free trade and fixed exchange rates under the gold standard had forced nations to a battle for foreign markets. The gold standard deprived the central bank of the use of the rate of interest as a tool for combating unemployment. The only tool left open for attacking unemployment, then, according to Keynes, was to fight for a balance of trade surplus (exports exceeding imports) by creating exclusive foreign markets for a nation's products (for example by establishing colonies) and by denying domestic markets to its rivals (for example by raising tariffs). A balance of trade surplus would create jobs because the positive rounds of spending produced by sales of exports would exceed the negative rounds of spending produced through expenditures on imports – the Keynesian multiplier applies to the trade surplus. A balance of trade surplus, moreover, would mean an inflow of gold, and thus an increase in the money supply that would decrease interest rates, stimulate investment, and push the economy toward full employment. Colonialism, in this story, was simply the nineteenth-century version of a decision by the Federal Reserve to lower interest rates. Competition for a balance of trade surplus, and the resulting competition for markets, Keynes claimed, set

countries on the road to war. Keynes's argument that the search for full employment, imperialism, and war were intimately bound together was widely shared in broad outline, although not in detail, by various heterodox thinkers: Vladimir Lenin, John A. Hobson, Rosa Luxemburg, and so on. We will return to Keynes and the others when we discuss the origins of the Spanish–American War, the Philippine–American War, and World War I. In World War II and in subsequent wars the United States went to war to combat first Fascism and then Communism. There were clearly underlying non-economic concerns – democracy and protection of individual rights – but there was also an economic dimension. In World War II Germany, Italy, and Japan were clearly attempting to establish empires that would have set up barriers to American economic penetration. And the Communists whom Americans fought for decades were bent on destruction of capitalism itself.

2 Sometimes the argument that special interests push the United States into wars takes on an even darker cast. Manufacturers of arms will benefit from a conflict, and it is natural to look to them as the instigators of wars. In the aftermath of World War I there were charges that arms manufacturers, the "merchants of death,"[2] had lobbied for and thus helped push the United States into the war. The resonance of this argument with the American people is the reason that Dwight Eisenhower's warning in his farewell address (January 17, 1961) has become such a favorite:

> This conjunction of an immense military establishment and a large arms industry is new in the American experience. The total influence – economic, political, even spiritual – is felt in every city, every Statehouse, every office of the Federal government. We recognize the imperative need for this development. Yet we must not fail to comprehend its grave implications. Our toil, resources and livelihood are all involved; so is the very structure of our society.

[2] The term, or at least its popularization, can be traced to a book of that name by H. C. Engelbrecht and Frank Cleary Hanighen (1934). Although not as sensational as one might infer from the title, it tells some fascinating stories about the industrial origin of modern weapons. Molander (1976) traces the history of the "merchants of death argument." George Bernard Shaw's play *Major Barbara*, premiered in 1905, created the iconic portrait of an immoral arms merchant.

> In the councils of government, we must guard against the acquisition of unwarranted influence, whether sought or unsought, by the military-industrial complex. The potential for the disastrous rise of misplaced power exists and will persist.

3 As Eisenhower's classic statement reminds us, special interests that favor war may include segments of the public sector as well as the private sector. Members of the armed services have good reason to assume that promotion to higher rank will be expedited by service in war, and this provides them an incentive to lobby for the continuation of old wars or the launching of new ones. Other segments of the public sector may also benefit. Experts on foreign policy may benefit when wars they have promoted are launched in parts of the world where they are experts. In a provocative but convincing paper, Gregory D. Hess and Athanasios Orphanides (1995) showed that the United States in the twentieth century was more likely to go to war when the President was in his first term (and thus could stand for reelection) and the economy was doing badly (and the President needed to show his competence in war-making to compensate).

Financing wars

Once the decision to go to war has been made – a decision often made in the heat of what is rightly called a war fever – policymakers soon realize that the war will be costly, sometimes far more costly than the initial estimates based on the premise of a quick and easy victory. Soldiers must be paid, munitions must be purchased, and armies must be transported to the field of battle. All this costs a great deal. In other words, the question "how will we pay for the war?" usually follows on the heels of "should we go to war?"

There are many ways of financing wars, but economists, as we noted in the first chapter, tend to draw attention first to three: raising taxes, borrowing from the public, and printing money. Typically, tax finance means simply raising taxes that were already in place before the war, for example tariffs or income taxes. But at times new taxes are introduced to take advantage of wartime patriotism, for example, an excess profits tax. Borrowing from the public also may mean simply issuing more of the type of security that the government used before the war; but at times new securities may be issued to take advantage of patriotism.

While taxes and borrowing from the public are easy to understand, the idea of financing a war by "printing money" requires a bit of explanation. In the Civil War, the term printing money could be understood literally. The United States simply printed the famous greenbacks, declared them to be "legal tender" – acceptable for the payment of taxes (except tariffs) or other debts – and used them to pay soldiers. After the establishment of the Federal Reserve in 1913, however, the process was more complex. The Treasury would sell bonds to the public, acquiring cash. The Federal Reserve would then buy some of those bonds on the open market by writing checks on itself. When these checks were deposited in banks the money supply, defined as the sum of currency and deposits, rose. Not literally printing money – although more paper money would get into circulation if people withdrew some of their deposits – but having the same economic effect: the government has more money on hand with which it can pay soldiers and buy munitions.

The latter method of finance tended to conceal the costs of war. If inflation resulted from printing a new form of money, such as the greenback, it was relatively easy to see that the inflation, and the destruction of value it brought, was a cost of the war, although even in this case, some people might be persuaded that the government was printing more money, and adding more zeros as it did so, because prices were rising. In any case, if the Federal Reserve was purchasing bonds on the open market, the source of monetary expansion and inflation was much harder to see.

The purchase of bonds by the Federal Reserve set in motion a multiple expansion of bank deposits. After the initial purchase of government bonds by the Federal Reserve, banks found themselves with increased reserves. They needed to keep only a fraction of these new reserves against the initial deposit; they could use the rest to make loans or purchase additional government bonds. The amount of government bonds purchased in the first round by the Federal Reserve is usually designated finance through direct monetary creation, the subsequent purchases by the banking system as indirect money finance. Box 1, "The mathematics of the printing press," explains the process in more detail.

1. The mathematics of the printing press

Define the following terms.

Cb = currency held by banks
Cp = currency held by the public
Dp = deposits held by the public in banks
M = money = Cp + Dp
Db = deposits held by commercial banks at the Federal Reserve (bank reserves)
H = high-powered money = Cp + Cb + Db
c = the currency ratio = Cp/Dp
r = the reserve ratio = (Cb + Db)/Dp
Bf = government bonds owned by the Federal Reserve
Bb = government bonds owned by the commercial banks
Bp = government bonds owned by the public
Lb = loans to the private sector held by commercial banks
b = the bond ratio = Bb/Lb
R = the revenue from creating money
Rh = the revenue from creating high-powered money
Rl = the revenue from creating low-powered money
P = the price level
V = velocity
y = real income

The relationships among the assets defined above are based on highly simplified balance sheets of the Federal Reserve, the commercial banking system, and the public.

Federal Reserve

assets	liabilities
Bf	Cp
	Cb
	Db

Commercial banks

assets	liabilities
Cb	Dp
Db	
Bb	
Lb	

Public

assets	liabilities
Cp	Lb
Dp	
Bp	

If there was no banking system, or with a banking system that held 100 percent reserves, then all of the revenues from creating money would flow directly to the government.

(1) $R = \Delta M = \Delta H$

With a fractional reserve banking system, however, the revenue from creating money comes from two sources: the flow from creating high-powered money (sometimes known as "base money") and the flow from the expansion of bank money and the investment by the banking system in government bonds, or the investment by its borrowers in government bonds.

(2) $R = Rh + Rl$

With the help of a money supply equation we can gain a sense of the relative magnitude of Rh and Rl. Combining the definitions of M and H and rearranging terms yields the following money supply equation:

(3) $M = H[(1 + c)/(c + r)]$

Assuming c and r are constant, assuming all the additional resources of the banking system are invested in government bonds, and combining the derivative of (3) with (1) and (2) yields the following:

(4) $R = Rh + Rl = \Delta H + \Delta H[(1 - r)/(c + r)]$

Note that if the banking system holds 100 percent in reserves ($r = 1$) then equation (4) reduces to equation (1): there will be no additional money creation or revenues from a secondary expansion of the banking system. But normally the secondary effects will be larger than the primary effects. For example, if the reserve ratio of the banking system was 10 percent, and the currency ratio was 5 percent, the amount of revenue flowing from the increase in bank money would be six times as large as the amount created by the direct action of the Federal Reserve: $(1 - r)/(c + r) = 6$.

The banking system, however, will not necessarily invest all of its new deposits in reserves and government bonds. It may invest part in new loans to the private sector that may or may not be invested in government bonds. In the case in which none of the additional loans to the public were reinvested in government bonds, the government's share of the additional deposits created by the banking sector would be given by the following equation:

$$(5)\quad Rl = [b/(1 + b)][(1 - r)/(c + r)]\Delta H$$

The quantity theory of money helps us understand the ultimate sources of these revenue flows. It can be written as follows:

$$(6)\quad MV = Py$$

In percentage change terms it is written as follows:

$$(7)\quad \Delta M/M + \Delta V/V = \Delta P/P + \Delta y/y$$

From equation (1) we can write the revenue from creating money in real terms as the product of the amount of new money created and the existing amount of real money balances.

$$(8)\quad R = \Delta M/P = (\Delta M/M)(M/P)$$

Combining equations (7) and (8) yields the following:

$$(9)\quad R = (\Delta P/P)(M/P) + (\Delta y/y - \Delta V/V)(M/P)$$

The first term on the right-hand side is the revenue generated by the inflation tax: inflation forces money holders to increase their nominal money holdings to maintain the real value of their money holdings. The second term on the right-hand side is a voluntary loan to the government (or partly to the private sector if the revenues from inflation are shared) arising from the public's desire to increase its money holdings. This desire may arise either because real income is rising ($\Delta y/y$ is positive) or for other reasons ($\Delta V/V$ is negative).

What is the appropriate mixture of taxes, borrowing, and money creation? What percentage of war expenditures should be financed by taxing, what percentage by borrowing, and what percentage by simply printing the money? Economic opinion about the ideal mixture has changed over the years.

Generally, however, economists through the years have agreed that printing money to finance wars, except in desperate circumstances, is unwise because it produces inflation. The Civil War, when prices more than doubled, and the experience in other wartime economies, shows the danger of the printing press. There are reasons, economists understand, why governments might use the printing press to finance wartime expenditures in certain circumstances. The printing press can be pressed into service quickly, and the administrative costs are low compared with conventional forms of taxing, which requires setting up an administrative network, or borrowing, which requires dealing with the financial community.

Some reliance on printing money has been justified from time to time on the grounds that printing money is simply another form of taxation. Just as an income tax reduces the taxpayer's income or the estate tax reduces the value of the taxpayer's estate, inflation reduces the purchasing power of the money in the taxpayer's pocket or bank account. The inflation rate is the tax rate. Real (adjusted for inflation) money balances are the tax base. During the Revolutionary War Benjamin Franklin made this argument as a way of defending the Continental Congress's heavy reliance on the printing press. Indeed, Franklin argued not only that inflation was a tax, but that it was a very fair tax because almost everyone held money, and the tax was applied for exactly the length of time that the money was in taxpayer's possession (Grubb 2007).

Despite Franklin's ingenious argument, economists have usually regarded printing money with distaste. In *The Economic Consequences of the Peace*, John Maynard Keynes, writing about Germany and other countries in central Europe at the end of World War I, described the evils of using the printing press to finance wars:

> Lenin has declared that the best way to destroy the Capitalist System is to debauch the currency. By a continuing process of inflation, governments can confiscate, secretly and unobserved, an important part of the wealth of their citizens. By this method they not only confiscate, but they confiscate

arbitrarily; and, while the process impoverishes many, it actually enriches some. The sight of this arbitrary rearrangement of riches strikes not only at security, but at confidence in the equity of the existing distribution of wealth. Those to whom the system brings windfalls, beyond their deserts and even beyond their expectations or desires, become "profiteers," who are the object of the hatred of the bourgeoisie, whom the inflationism has impoverished, not less than of the proletariat. As the inflation proceeds and the real value of the currency fluctuates wildly from month to month, all permanent relations between debtors and creditors, which form the ultimate foundation of capitalism, become so utterly disordered as to be almost meaningless; and the process of wealth-getting degenerates into a gamble and a lottery. (Keynes 1920 [1919], 298)

Keynes went on to explain why governments nevertheless adopt inflation as a means of finance: it hides the cost of government.

Lenin was certainly right. There is no subtler, no surer means of overturning the existing basis of society than to debauch the currency. The process engages all the hidden forces of economic law on the side of destruction, and does it in a manner which not one man in a million is able to diagnose. (Keynes 1920 [1919], 298)

While economists tend to agree that financing by printing money is bad, the choice between taxes and borrowing has been the subject of changing opinions. The "classical" tradition favored taxes over borrowing.[3] As originally set out by David Hume (1970 [1770], 91–2)[4] and Adam Smith the case for taxes was political rather than economic. In the following passage Smith explains how bond finance encourages war by hiding the true costs of war.

In great empires the people who live in the capital, and in the provinces remote from the scene of action, feel, many of them, scarce any inconveniency from the war; but enjoy, at their ease, the amusement of reading in the newspapers the exploits of their own fleets and armies. To them this amusement compensates the small difference between the taxes which they pay on account of the war, and those which they had been accustomed to pay in time of peace. They are commonly dissatisfied with the return of peace, which puts an end to their amusement, and to a

[3] The philosopher Immanuel Kant (1917 [1795]) also insisted on tax finance as a way of reducing the likelihood of a war.

[4] Although Hume's essay first appeared in 1752, the argument against bond finance was not included until an edition published in 1770.

thousand visionary hopes of conquest and national glory from a longer continuance of the war. (Smith 1976 [1776], 1080)

Later economists in the classical school such as David Ricardo continued to favor financing one hundred percent by taxation. Ricardo believed that there was a risk that wartime government debt would "crowd out" private savings and reduce the capital stock. Ricardo acknowledged that if people were well informed and rational they would recognize the higher future taxes implicit in current debts and increase their savings accordingly – this is the basis of so-called "Ricardian Equivalence" – but he thought that in practice people were unlikely to recognize the full future tax costs of wartime government borrowings (Dooley 1989). John Stuart Mill, as might be expected from his centrist image, took a more moderate position. Mill emphasized the dangers of borrowing, but thought that some borrowing would be tolerable. The rate of interest was the test: a stable rate would show that borrowing has been held to a prudent level; an increase would be the sign that borrowing had reached an excessive level (Mill 1936 [1848], 873–6).

By World War I concerns about equity had begun to play a major role in the thinking of economists. However, these concerns again pointed to taxes as the most desirable means of financing a war. With bond finance a soldier drafted into the army would suffer doubly, once when he was drafted and again when he paid higher taxes imposed to pay off wartime debt after the war. With tax finance the soldier would make the greater sacrifice, possibly his life, but the man who stayed home would pay for the increase in government expenditures.

Economists had always understood that higher taxes in wartime could discourage work effort, especially because they were temporary. Why spend long hours at one's desk or in the factory, if the government was simply going to tax away the financial gain? It might be hoped that patriotism would offset the effects of higher taxes, but if patriotism could not be relied on, it would be better to raise taxes only a little during the war, by enough to assure payment of interest on the debt, and then keep them higher after the war to fund the gradual retirement of the debt. If taxes were plotted against time, they would show a gradually rounded swelling, rather than a sharp peak during the war. Debt should be employed, to use the economists' favorite term, to *smooth* taxes. Robert J. Barro is the economist most closely associated today with the view that debt should be used to smooth wartime increases in taxes in order to moderate the impact on production (Barro 1987, 1989). As we will see as we explore America's wars in detail, all of the ideas about war finance developed by economists – from Adam Smith's idea that debt finance encourages war by hiding its true costs to Robert J. Barro's idea that debt finance smoothes taxes – have shaped the actual financial decisions of the United States as it has fought its wars.

The draft and other veiled means of financing wars

The three typical forms of finance – taxing, borrowing, and printing money – are, as I have noted, by no means the only ways that a nation can acquire resources for a war. Resources can also be acquired, for example, through voluntary contributions. The families who brought blankets to their soldiers during the Revolutionary War are an early example. The scrap drives of World War I and World War II, and the financial contributions made to the United States by Saudi Arabia to offset US costs during the Persian Gulf War, which we will discuss below, are twentieth-century examples.

In some cases resources can be taken from the enemy. In the nineteenth century armies often focused on capturing artillery so that it could be turned against enemy troops. In the twentieth century the specialized ammunition and training that would be needed to make use of captured weapons made this a less useful tactic. There were still many ways, however, to make use of resources captured from the enemy. Ships and railroad cars, for example, can be confiscated and used to transport troops and supplies. Once the enemy has been defeated new governments can be installed that impose taxes that can defray the costs of occupation. This was the case in the Philippines, a case we will explore below, and it was a hoped-for result in the Iraq War. In some cases formal reparations can be imposed, as was done with Germany after World War I. Acquiring resources from the enemy reduces the cost of war to the American people. Exaggerated hopes for resources from this source, however, may hide, for a time, the ultimate cost of the war.

Another way to acquire war resources is to reduce government spending on non-military categories or even on military categories not directly related to the war. Governments can reduce the amounts spent on maintaining roads, subsidizing the production of agricultural products, undertaking scientific research, and so on. Delayed maintenance of roads and other means of transport is another hidden cost of war. Taxpayers being asked for money to repair roads and highways in the postwar period, sums that may have been magnified because scheduled maintenance was delayed, are unlikely to understand that the sums they are paying are part of the cost of the war.

Resources can also be commandeered, that is taken directly from their owners without full compensation. Any type of resource may be commandeered – land for building military facilities, mines that produce raw materials necessary for producing arms, even patents for chemical processes important to the war effort. In practice the draft has been the most important form of commandeering, indeed, the most important non-financial means of acquiring resources. The Spanish–American, Philippine–American, and Persian Gulf wars were fought with volunteer armed forces, but in World War I, World War II, the Korean War, and Vietnam War soldiers were drafted.

The draft can be compared to a tax. The individual who is drafted pays the tax which is the difference between what the draftee would earn if he or she chose to serve in an all-volunteer army and what he or she actually receives in a draft army. The idea of a draft as a tax appeals to economists because it forces one to think about the opportunity cost of the resources used in a war, but the concept seems alien to the average citizen. If the opportunity cost of a soldier is the same whether he or she is drafted or induced to serve through high wages and benefits, why do governments resort to the draft? One reason is that the draft hides the cost of the war. We tend to think of the cost of the war simply as the tax bills we pay – income taxes, gas taxes, property taxes, and so on – and not the more exotic taxes conceived by economists.

One of the best ways of understanding the economics of the draft during the twentieth century is to consider the draft used in the Revolutionary War and in the North during the Civil War when draftees were allowed to hire substitutes to fight in their place. One of the most famous examples is Grover Cleveland who served as President in 1885–9 and 1893–7. Cleveland was drafted in the Civil War, but although only twenty-six, he was already a successful lawyer and chose to hire a replacement. Indeed, this was not difficult, aside

2. The draft and the supply and demand for soldiers

Figure 2.1 illustrates the economics of the draft. The supply curve shows the number of soldiers who would serve voluntarily depending on the wages and other benefits offered by the government. The demand curve is "inelastic," meaning that the government would not reduce its demand for soldiers "much" even as the cost in terms of wages and benefits rose. This assumption is probably more nearly correct for the major wars, when there was a sense that war must be won at all costs, than for the minor wars. The government could hire all the soldiers it wanted by paying AG. But instead it chooses to pay only AD. This decision may reflect the conviction that the higher taxes associated with AG would undermine support for the war. At wage AD, however, there will be a shortage of EF soldiers; DE will be willing to serve, but the government wants DF. A draft can be the answer; EF soldiers can be forced to serve whether they want to or not.

The draft lowers the nominal (budgetary) cost of the war. Each soldier is paid only AD. But each soldier in the draft army is in fact paying a tax, DI, which is the difference between the amount that the soldier would be paid in an all-volunteer armed force, AI, and what they are paid as draftees, AD. To the public the military labor budget looks to be ADFC, but properly measured it is AIJC.

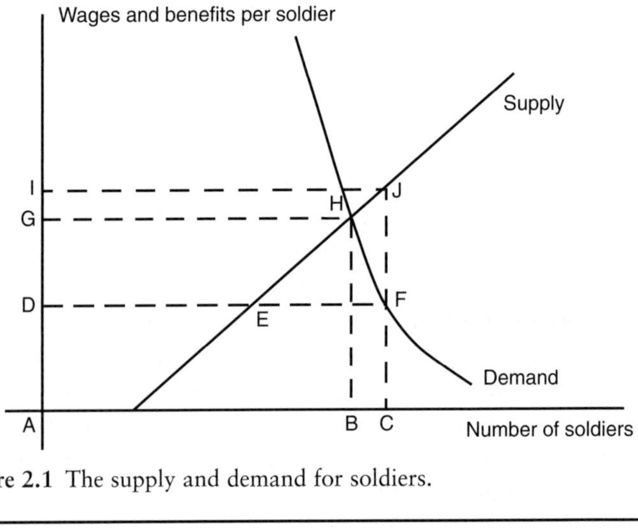

Figure 2.1 The supply and demand for soldiers.

from the cost involved, because a well-functioning market for substitutes evolved during the Civil War. For an economist concerned about efficiency the system of allowing draftees to hire substitutes seems eminently sensible. The draftee pays the tax directly to the substitute. If the draftee has a high income because he or she is highly skilled – Grover Cleveland is an example – the economy is more efficient than it would be if the draftee was forced to serve. But one can, of course, think of a different kind of example: the prodigal son of a rich landowner. Why should the prodigal son avoid the fight just because he can draw on the resources of a wealthy father? Or as the saying went in the Civil War, why should it be a "rich man's war and a poor man's fight"? In 1917 after the declaration of war, the United States passed the Selective Service Act, creating a very different sort of draft to raise the huge army needed for World War I. The use of enlistment bounties to attract volunteers and the hiring of substitutes were explicitly prohibited. The mistakes of the Civil War were not going to be repeated.

Mobilizing resources

The crucial decision for the United States, as indeed for any nation at war, regards how much of its resources to devote to the war effort. Our first reaction is to say that we need to devote as much as necessary to win. But that idea seldom provides a guide for practice. Estimates of how much is needed will differ, and absolute commitment to victory is a seldom realized ideal. Typically, a political group favoring vigorous prosecution of the war will have to contend with other groups that favor compromise or even the admission of defeat. The government's plan for mobilization then will be to allocate enough resources to the war effort to move the country in the direction of victory, but not so many resources that political support for the war erodes.

Economists like to describe the tradeoff between war goods and private sector goods, the tradeoff between "guns and butter," with a production possibilities curve such as the one shown in Figure 2.2. Guns, measured along the vertical axis, stands for the output of military goods: tanks, planes, ships, the food, clothing, and shelter for the army, and so on. Butter, measured along the horizontal axis, stands for the output of all other goods: food, clothing, and shelter for civilian workers, entertainment, housing, and so on. If all production was for the civilian and none for the military, in other words if the

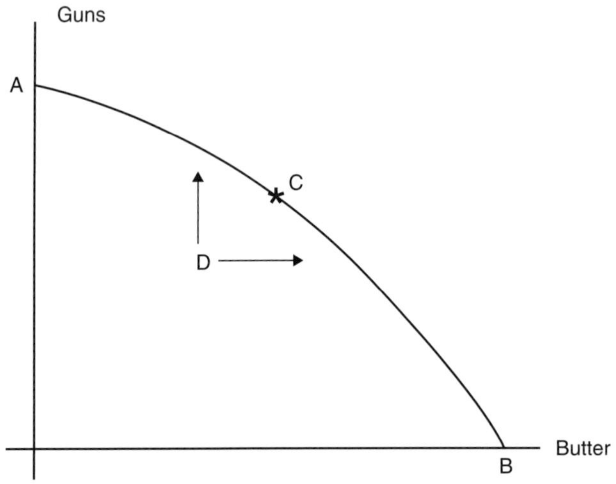

Figure 2.2 The tradeoff between guns and butter.

economy produced only butter, then the economy would be at point B, maximum production of butter and zero production of guns. If, on the other hand, the economy were at maximum production of guns it would be at point A. To be sure, it is hard to imagine an economy that literally produced only guns. Therefore, it makes more sense to regard the vertical axis as measured net of some bare minimum production of civilian goods necessary to maintain production. Once the economy reaches full employment – all the workers have jobs and all the factories are humming – the economy will be on the production possibilities frontier, the curved line between A and B. If the economy is at C, for example, production of more war goods can only be achieved by moving along the production possibilities curve toward A. That is production of more guns can be achieved only by reducing consumption of butter. The production possibilities curve is curved. Why? The curve reflects the idea of diminishing returns. As production of munitions rises it becomes harder and harder to squeeze out more. Workers have to work overtime, machines have to be pushed and repaired more often, raw materials must be brought from more distant sources. All this means that the amount of butter that must be sacrificed to obtain one additional unit of guns rises.

One value of this analysis is that it shows how macroeconomic conditions affect the tradeoff between guns and butter. If the economy is at less than full employment, as represented by point D, then mobilization can take place relatively easily. The economy can move toward the production possibilities curve as shown by the vertical arrow above D, increasing production of guns without reducing production of butter. The most famous case was the United States on the eve of World War II when it could (to some extent) increase production of guns without reducing production of butter simply because there were still unemployed resources resulting from the Great Depression. Indeed, if the economy is at less than full employment when the war begins, the fiscal and monetary stimulus from government spending is likely to push the economy toward the production possibilities curve. The experience in World War II, and in several other cases, of a wartime boom gave rise to the idea of "wartime prosperity," the idea that war is good for the economy. We will explore this idea in more detail as we discuss the histories of individual wars.

Given that a decision has been reached about the total amount of resources to be devoted to the war effort, how much will be in the form of labor and how much in the form of capital? The United States has always been a country with a high ratio of wages to the cost of capital compared with other countries, and so, following good economic principles, the United States has always used a relatively high ratio of capital to labor: more cannons, tanks, ships, and airplanes per soldier than in nations with lower wages and higher costs of capital. A large manufacturing sector with the capacity to turn out large amounts of capital for war is likely to have, and in the American case has had, the ability to innovate. Not only have Americans gone to war heavily armed, but they have been able to refine existing weapons and develop new ones, on more than one occasion even as the war has progressed. To be sure, politics has worked to reinforce economics. A democratically elected government is not likely to survive for long if it is not minimizing casualties and magnifying the enemy's casualties with massive firepower. Capital intensity, in short, constitutes an important component of the "American Way of War."

In a market economy prices and profits are the incentives that produce the reallocation of resources to the war sector, that move the economy along the production possibilities curve away from B and toward A. As the order books of munitions makers fill with profitable contracts they are able to bid resources away from firms producing for civilian markets. For a variety of reasons, however, governments may intervene to prevent market mechanisms from working and by substituting alternative mechanisms. This was particularly noticeable in World War I and World War II when elaborate systems of price controls and rationing were introduced.

Why did the United States, a traditionally free market economy, turn to government controls during some of its wars? Several factors were at work. First of all, ideology played a role. World War I, World War II, and the Korean War were fought under presidents who were deeply skeptical about the efficiency and fairness of free markets. The prominence of the military in wartime worked in the same direction. The military is organized in a hierarchical fashion. When the general commands, soldiers obey. It is understandable that when the military comes to the fore, and when military purchasers become one of the leading purchasers in the economy, they would want the private sector to be organized in the same fashion.

Second, sometimes it was hoped that patriotism could substitute for the financial incentives of the marketplace. It was hoped, for example, that workers could be persuaded to work longer and harder for the good of the nation, rather than simply for the reward of higher wages.

A further reason may have been that it was easier, or at least appeared to be easier, to manage the economy centrally, because the ultimate goals of economic activity were clearer in wartime. One of the great strengths of the market system is that it reveals consumer preferences. If people lose interest in movies about cowboys and become more interested in movies about hardboiled detectives, the box office receipts will soon reveal the change in preferences, and induce the appropriate change in output. When the nation is at war, especially when it is involved in the life and death struggle of a world war, consumer preferences are already known. The overarching goal is to win the war and the economic problem is how to allocate resources in the most efficient way to achieve that end. In wartime, moreover, time is of the essence. In peacetime we can afford the luxury of allowing people to delay the performance of a task while we negotiate and cajole them into performing it. In wartime we cannot afford to wait; people must be compelled by government to act immediately. The famous British economist Lionel Robbins explored this argument in *The Economic Problem in Peace and War*, a book based on his experiences in Britain in World War II (Robbins 1947, 85).

Finally, centralized controls may be another way of hiding the cost of the war. One way for the government to deprive a citizen of his or her resources is to raise taxes. Then, as Adam Smith pointed out, the cost of the war will be obvious. Consider a different story. The amount of good X that a consumer is allowed to purchase is strictly rationed. This allows the government to purchase a portion of the amount produced of X at a lower controlled price. Will the consumer recognize that it is the government's prosecution of the war that has limited purchases of X? Or will they blame the "shortage" of X on profiteers or, best of all, on the enemy?

Economics also comes into play when we move from the amount of war goods produced to the more specific question of the kinds of munitions. One example is the choice between airpower and ground power. Relying on air power makes sense for a nation, such as the United States, that is capital rich, namely where the cost of capital is low relative to the cost of labor. But what about the choice between tactical bombing (bombing in support of ground forces) and strategic bombing (bombing aimed at crippling the enemy's economy)? This choice will depend upon military considerations, but also on the assessment of the economic effects of the bombing and the connection between the economic effects and the military capacity of the enemy. Our production possibilities curve is useful in analyzing some of the effects of strategic bombing. A campaign aimed simply at the mass destruction of the enemy can be thought of as an attempt to shift the enemy's production possibilities curve in Figure 2.1 to the left, so that it cuts through D rather than C. But, as the figure makes clear, the enemy can attempt to offset the effect of bombing on the position of the curve by moving along it, by shifting from production of butter toward production of guns.

The costs of wars

The most important costs of war from the point of view of the American people were the deaths and non-mortal wounds suffered by the fighters, their fellow citizens. Appendix 2 shows deaths – distinguishing between those in combat and those that occurred while the individual was in the armed forces, but for other reasons such as accident and disease. The table also shows non-mortal wounds by war. Economists have tried to place monetary values on these losses. We could, for example, think of an individual killed in battle as an amount of human capital, the discounted value of future earnings, and add that value to other costs. And in our calculations of the cost of wars we will include an estimate of veterans' benefits which includes monetary compensation to veterans for wounds suffered and compensation paid to the families of veterans who died. Most people, however, view the loss of life and the grieving of families who have suffered the loss of loved ones in a different light – one that reflects a wide range of philosophical, religious, and political values – from the loss of civilian output when resources are devoted to the production of war goods. As much as we economists might want to reduce all of the costs of war to a single dollar value. It makes more sense to view loss of life and limb, on the one hand, and economic costs, on the other, as distinct and at times incommensurate costs of war.[5]

The economic cost of war may be defined as what the resources employed in the war could have produced had they been employed for alternative purposes. The list of alternatives is endless; it is the whole range of goods that could have been produced by the civilian economy (bridges, coffee cups, productions of *Macbeth*, medical research, butter, and so on) and other goods that could have been produced by the government (lighthouses, highways, medical research, and so on). Perhaps the most important distinction here is between investment goods and consumption goods. To the extent that wars employed resources that would have produced investment goods, then our current standard of living has been affected by past wars. If research in medicine or agriculture was slowed, if plans to build new dams and bridges were shelved, if workers went into the army rather than to technical school, then we are the worse for it. On the other hand, if it was mainly consumption that was reduced then our current standard of living may be much the same as if no war was fought. This

[5] Even when we adopt the economic approach there are philosophical choices that must be addressed. Is the goal of economic life to maximize GDP, in which case we would include in the cost calculation the value of all of the output that would have been produced by the fallen soldier; or is the goal to maximize per capita income, in which case we would include only the decrease in the income of the survivors – the externalities that would have been generated by the fallen soldier? This issue is further complicated by the possibility of immigration. If we focus on the income of the survivors, how do we measure the loss of life in the war when the income of the survivors can be restored by admitting an immigrant with the skills of the fallen soldier?

was part of what the Nazi leaders Hermann Goering and Joseph Goebbels were getting at in the 1930s when they said that Germany should have guns instead of butter (Birchall 1936, 1). Butter was a consumption good, a luxury. In the long run the standard of living would not be reduced if in the short run people switched to a less expensive substitute.

The opposite problem arises when the war-related spending creates capital that is valuable in peacetime. The synthetic rubber plants created in World War II are a good example. Although the rubber they produced contributed to the war effort, the plants were mainly employed after the war to produce synthetic rubber for the civilian market. In a case like this we may want to deduct the value of the flow of postwar civilian products from the wartime cost of the capital to get at the true cost of the war. In practice, however, such a calculation is hard. For a variety of reasons plants that were sold to the private sector were sold at a price below the discounted value of future profits. One reason was that the private firm that had been operating a plant during the war had an inside track when it came to purchasing the plant. Even when an auction was held, there were few outside bidders.

Human capital may also be created in wartime. A worker may learn new skills that make him or her more productive after the war. For many farm workers, for example, work in war factories in World War I and World War II provided skills that made it possible to continue in factory work after the war. To be sure, many agricultural workers would have made the transition from farm to factory even if the nation had remained at peace. But the high demand for industrial labor during the war may have tipped the balance in favor of making the transition. Similarly, moving can be an investment. Many American laborers made the trek to California during the depressed 1930s, but the ease of finding a job in California during World War II persuaded many others that the 1940s was the right time to make a move they had long contemplated. The cost of moving to do war work should be counted as part of the cost of a war, a cost not included in conventional estimates. But omitting this cost is probably not a major problem because a worker typically recaptured some of those expenses in the form of higher wages or more enjoyable living conditions after the war.

A major issue encountered in any attempt to measure the costs of war, but especially the costs of "minor" wars, is whether we should include all the costs of the military, or only the additional costs produced by the decision to go to war. It is the classic economic problem of how to allocate fixed costs. There is no single "right way" to make the calculation. As is often the case in economics, the decision about how to allocate the fixed costs of the military spending depends on the question we are asking. Looking at the marginal cost of the war – ignoring the fixed costs of the military establishment altogether – may lead to sensible conclusions about whether to engage in a particular war, given that past spending is a sunk cost. On the other hand, looking at only marginal costs would produce bad decisions about whether maintaining large armies and navies ready to engage in wars makes sense. To answer the latter question looking at the average cost of wars is more useful. Setting the share of fixed costs at zero and computing only the marginal costs of wars, in other words, makes imperial war-making appear less costly than it is. All this is clearer if we take a less politically charged example: the fire department. The marginal cost of fighting a particular fire given the expenditures already incurred to buy equipment, build firehouses, employ firefighters, etc. is normally small. This small marginal cost is the right one to look at if the question is: Does it pay to put out the fire on Mulberry Street in Springfield? However, if we add up the marginal costs of fighting the ten fires that occur annually in Springfield, we will greatly underestimate the annual cost of maintaining the fire department. To address the question of whether Springfield needs a fire department we are better served by looking at the average cost of maintaining the fire department.

When we turn to the interest on the government debt, which in some ways is analogous to veterans' benefits, there is more agreement among economists that to count both the expenditures on the war itself and the interest and principal payments made subsequently is double counting. Again, it helps to consider a less emotionally charged example. When we pay \$300,000 for a home, we say that is the cost whether we reduce our bank account by \$300,000 or take out a mortgage at 8 percent interest for thirty years. True, the total payments are different. If we pay cash, we write a check for \$300,000; if we take out a thirty-year mortgage at 8 percent, we will write checks that total about \$790,000. But if we claimed that we were living in a \$790,000 home because that was the sum of all the interest and principal payments we would rightly be accused of exaggerating.

The same is true of civilian government spending. We say that a program to finance medical research is the $50 billion we pay now; we do not count future interest payments as part of the cost. To do so would mislead someone who assumed that the normal conventions were being followed.

There is an extreme case worth considering. In Britain it was once a common practice to finance government deficits by issuing consols, or perpetuities, as they were sometimes known. The principal of a consol need never be repaid: a consol promised a fixed amount of interest each year forever. If a war or other government program was financed by issuing consols, and the cost of the program was measured by adding all future interest payments, the conclusion would be that the cost was infinite. After the war taxes must be raised to pay for the interest on debt. Therefore, some citizens have more income and others have less, but leaving aside the distorting effect of the taxes, the size of the economy is not affected. Evidently, it would be misleading when measuring the costs of wars to include interest payments because it means adopting an accounting practice different from the one normally used in measuring costs in the private sector or the civilian government.

As we explore the costs of war in the twentieth century we will need to compare the costs over time. The cost of the Spanish–American War (before adding veterans' benefits) was about $274 million (see Appendix 3). But we want to know how much that is in today's money. Prices and wages have changed a great deal since 1898, so it will not do to simply compare the number of dollars spent on the Spanish–American War with the amount spent on wars being fought today. We must, to use the economists' term, "inflate" the costs of the Spanish–American War to make them comparable to costs incurred today. As usual in economics, there is no single measuring rod that is always the right one to use. We use different measuring rods depending on the question we want to address. A price index is the most commonly used measuring rod. The consumer price index in 2010 was about twenty-seven times as high as it was in 1898 (Officer and Williamson 2011). So using the consumer price index to inflate the costs of the Spanish–American War would mean that the cost of the war was about $7.4 billion ($274 million × 27.01) in today's money. This figure tells us how much money it would take today to buy the goods and services that Americans used to carry out the war in 1898. There are a variety of price indexes one could use. If the cost of the Spanish–American War was inflated using the GDP deflator the figure would be smaller, at \$6.5 billion (\$274 million × 23.6). The GDP deflator is broader than the consumer price index; it includes, importantly, investment goods as well as consumption goods. It is probably a better deflator in terms of describing how much it would cost to outfit a similar force today.

One could also use an index of the costs of war goods (labor and munitions), although as far as I am aware there is no index currently available that extends back to the turn of the century. In the case of weapons, technological progress becomes important. The cost of modern weapons has risen greatly since the turn of the century. Rifles, artillery, machine guns, and battleships all cost more than did similar weapons in 1898. Inflating the amount spent on weapons by a price of weapons index that was not adjusted for quality would yield a much larger figure for the amount that would be needed today to equip the military as it was equipped in 1898. Modern weapons, however, are far more lethal than their turn-of-the-century counterparts. To equip an army today that was of equal lethality to the army of 1898, which could, for example, fire the same number of bullets per minute, might require a smaller sum than was spent in 1898. What really matters is the firepower of one army relative to its enemy. We might want to ask how much it would cost today to create an army that had the same edge over the Spanish military as did the US army and navy of 1898.

Wages are another commonly used inflator. The use of wages has a long and distinguished history. This is how Adam Smith justified using wages to compare values at different points in time:

> Equal quantities of labour, at all times and places may be said to be of equal value to the labourer. In his ordinary state of health, strength and spirits; in the ordinary degree of his skill and dexterity, he must always lay down the same portion of his ease, his liberty, and his happiness. The price which he pays must always be the same, whatever the quantity of goods he receives in return for it ... Labour alone, therefore, is alone the ultimate and real standard by which the value of all commodities can at all times and places be estimated and compared. (Smith 1976 [1776], 50–1)

In 2010 the wages of unskilled labor were about 124 times higher than they were in 1898 (Officer and Williamson 2011). So using this inflator, the cost of the Spanish–American War would be $34.0 billion ($274 million × 124.01). This computation answers a somewhat different question than the previous computations: how much would it cost today to acquire the same amount of labor that was employed in the war in 1898, both as actual combatants and as civilian workers producing goods for the military?

GDP is still another, and very different, inflator often used to compare wars. GDP in 2010 was about 810 times what it was in 1898 (Johnston and Williamson 2010). Thus, if we use GDP we find that the cost of the Spanish–American War in today's money would be about $221.9 billion ($274 million × 810). Now we are talking about real money! This is what the United States would have to spend today to say that it was making the same effort that it made at the turn of the last century. There is, to sum up, no one right answer to the question of how much a past war costs in today's money. Instead, there are an array of estimates, each illuminating a different question.

Perhaps one of the most important costs of wars is one of the least visible: the moral cost. Few wars are fought according to rules laid down by philosophers. When people are desperate for victory, savagery often wins out. Typically, a few courageous voices oppose attacks on civilians during war, but opposition is often muted by the overwhelming desire for victory and the fear of reprisals from supporters of the war. In retrospect many people find the means adopted to fight a war troubling. Indeed, the moral costs of the war may grow over time, even as other costs, such as the cost of caring for veterans, diminish. In retrospect, for example, many Americans are troubled when they learn about the savage tactics used against civilians during the Philippine–American War that will be described below. It is natural, and to some degree justified, to be cynical about such feelings. There was considerable opposition to America's use of savage tactics in the Philippine–American War, even as the war was being fought, but support was widespread. Theodore Roosevelt, who after the assassination of McKinley was President while much of the war was being fought, went on to be elected President in his own right, and to win the Nobel Peace Prize (although for his role in ending the Russo-Japanese War – not for his role in the Philippine–American War). In retrospect, to take another example, many Americans are troubled by the use of strategic bombing during World War II. The use of firebombing against Hamburg, Dresden, and Tokyo, and the use of atomic bombs against Hiroshima and Nagasaki, which will also be described below, are viewed today by many Americans, including some of our best young historians, as among the most shameful episodes in American history. But at the time the goal of minimizing the costs of victory created irresistible pressure for attacks on civilians.

The tendency for sympathy for others to disappear in wartime is, of course, nothing new and nothing uniquely American. As Adam Smith pointed out 250 years ago our sympathy for others declines as our social distance from them increases. In wartime we are concerned mainly with how our fellow citizens feel about our behavior, and so opposition to war or to the more savage methods of waging war is likely to be of little significance. This is how he put it in *The Theory of Moral Sentiments* (Smith 1976 [1759], part III, chapter 1):

> In the most unjust war, however, it is commonly the sovereign or the rulers only who are guilty. The subjects are almost always perfectly innocent. Whenever it suits the conveniency of a public enemy, however, the goods of the peaceable citizens are seized both at land and at sea; their lands are laid waste, their houses are burnt, and they themselves, if they presume to make any resistance, are murdered or led into captivity; and all this in the most perfect conformity to what are called the laws of nations.[6]

Smith would have recognized American behavior in World War II. Sympathy for the plight of German and Japanese civilians (who were often vilified in American propaganda), although voiced by a few individuals, was generally missing. Only after the war, as the fears and passions generated by the war faded, and as America developed productive economic and diplomatic relations with Germany and

[6] Smith (1976 [1759], part III, chapter 1) also noted that our lack of sympathy for our enemies is likely to produce a breakdown in the niceties of international affairs:

> When two nations are at variance, the citizen of each pays little regard to the sentiments which foreign nations may entertain concerning his conduct. His whole ambition is to obtain the approbation of his own fellow-citizens; and as they are all animated by the same hostile passions which animate himself, he can never please them so much as by enraging and offending their enemies ... In war and negotiation, therefore, the laws of justice are very seldom observed. Truth and fair dealing are almost totally disregarded. Treaties are violated; and the violation, if some advantage is gained by it, sheds scarce any dishonour upon the violator. The ambassador who dupes the minister of a foreign nation, is admired and applauded.

Japan, did large numbers of Americans come to be disturbed by the attacks on civilians carried out during the war. Evidently, it is easier to be upset about actions taken in the past, when all that is called for in response is moral indignation, than to oppose attacks on civilians when war is ongoing and the risks of defeat are real. Nevertheless, even if we are entitled to discount expressions of sympathy and moral indignation that come long after the fact, we must still count the shame produced when war crimes are finally uncovered, as one of the important, if hidden, costs of war.

The economic legacies of wars

Wars produce many long-term changes in the economy. The tax system is almost always changed during a war, and these changes persist. The federal alcohol and tobacco taxes levied during the Civil War are still with us, as is the federal inheritance tax imposed during the Spanish–American War. Partly, the long-term effects on the tax system are a reflection of the long-term burdens of interest payments and veterans' benefits that follow wars. Wars have also left their marks on the monetary system. The Federal Reserve's reliance on open market operations was a result of World War I; the collapse of the international gold standard during the Depression and World War II led to the Bretton Woods system adopted after the war.

One of the most frequently cited, and most frequently debated, effects of wars is on the status of women and minority workers. The increased demand for labor produced by wartime mobilizations and the decrease in the supply of male workers resulting from expansion of the armed forces, and (in some cases) the decreased supply of immigrant labor, leads to increases in the employment of women and minorities. The question is to what extent these temporary changes become permanent changes. Do they open opportunities in the postwar economy by changing the attitudes of employers, coworkers, and the women and minority workers themselves? Or does the status quo reassert itself after the war is over?

As the last point suggests, wars are often alleged to produce economic benefits as well as costs. Better access to job markets for women, the elderly, and minorities may increase productivity. Defense of the principle of free trade may increase access to world markets. Suppression of Communist revolutions may protect American property. But in each case the benefits are hard to measure. The non-economic benefits of wars, such as protection of human rights, moreover, lie along a dimension different from the economist's usual profit and loss calculations. In the end, when it comes to putting numbers to wars, we will stick, as economic historians usually do, to measuring mainly the fiscal costs of wars. We will address the other economic costs and benefits, but acknowledge our limited ability to measure them.

One of the most important economic legacies of wars was in the realm of economic ideas. The opinions of economists and economic policymakers are strongly influenced by their past experiences: by booms and depressions, inflations and deflations, stock market bubbles and busts, and so on, that occurred when they were forming their basic ideas. With the exception of the Great Depression, no experience has shaped economic opinion as much as war. World War II, as we will see, had an enormous impact on the way economists see the world. Many economists were attracted to the case for spending on public works to cure unemployment in a depression laid out by John Maynard Keynes in the *General Theory* (1936). But it was the rapid transition from depression to full employment, powered by military spending before and during World War II, that seemingly provided conclusive evidence for the theoretical case made by Keynes. Most centrist economists followed Keynes in believing that the government's role could be limited to maintaining sufficient aggregate demand. Once full employment was achieved through fiscal policy, Keynes argued, conventional economic thinking that stressed the costs of government intervention in individual markets came back into play. Some prominent economists on the left, however, went further than Keynes, basing their case on the war experience. For John Kenneth Galbraith, who was a major figure in the government agency controlling prices in World War II, and a major public intellectual after the war, the wartime experience was proof that the economy could be run better with a combination of heavy demand produced by expansionary fiscal policies and price controls to contain inflation (Galbraith 1952, 81).

The economics of veterans' benefits

Veterans' benefits are the expenditures paid directly to men and women who have served in the military, or paid for services provided to them, after their service has ended. Veterans' benefits were an important part of the fiscal cost of every war in the nineteenth and twentieth centuries, and constituted the largest component of the costs of the smaller wars, except Korea. The vexing problem for economic historians is how to treat veterans' benefits when computing the "opportunity costs" of wars. Almost no one doubts that payments made to the dependants of military personnel killed while in service, or payments made to surviving veterans for medical care for disabilities incurred while in the service, or to compensate veterans for earnings lost after the war as a result of their war-related disabilities, are true opportunity costs of war. Clearly the output of the economy as a whole is lower if a veteran was killed or his or her productivity was reduced by injuries – including, we have finally recognized, psychological injuries. Measures to provide for the care of maimed and sick soldiers and sailors in England date from the first Elizabeth's reign, and were widely adopted in colonial America (Glasson and Kinley 1918, 9–18). Similarly, one can see that a veteran whose post-service earnings are reduced because he or she, while serving in the military, lost time that could have been spent developing skills useful in the postwar economy, also represents a true opportunity cost of war. The postwar economy is poorer just as if the veteran had been physically injured. In all of these cases – physical and psychological injuries and time lost that could have been invested in education or skill-building work in the private sector – there is an opportunity cost of war and that fact cannot be changed whether we make the burden of that loss fall on the veteran by denying a benefit, or whether the public as a whole shoulders the burden and compensates the veteran for his or her loss.

However, payments to veterans who are just as productive in the postwar economy as they would have been had they not volunteered for or been drafted into military service, or perhaps more productive, are less clearly part of the opportunity cost of war. The income of veterans is higher than it would otherwise be in the postwar era, and the income of taxpayers is correspondingly lower, but if the output of the economy is unaffected should we regard the payment to the veteran as a transfer or as an opportunity cost of the war? Because of this ambiguity some students of the cost of war have treated veterans' payments as a separable "fiscal cost" of war (from the point of view of the government budget) (Clayton 1972, 375–95), leaving it to the users of the estimates to decide for themselves whether they want to include veterans' benefits as a part of the economic cost of war. Thus we can treat veterans' benefits as analogous, to some extent, to social security benefits, an item that affects the federal budget and through it taxes and other financial variables, but does not represent a using up of GDP in the same sense as current military expenditures.

But it is also important to recognize that veterans have come to anticipate post-service benefits. Benefits, from this point of view, are a form of deferred pay, a bonus for dedicated service. If that bonus had not been offered, the veteran might not have served, or if forced to serve by a draft, might not have served with the same commitment. Without the implicit or explicit promise of veterans' benefits, additional resources would have been needed during the war to fight with the same effectiveness, or the war might not have gone as well as it did, and the postwar product of the economy might have been lower. For that reason, I have followed the practice of including all veterans' benefits as true opportunity costs of war, although also showing them separately so that someone who views the matter differently can see the costs net of veterans' benefits. This focus on injuries and losses, and wages, I should note, ignores the undeniable fact that some veterans acquired important skills, including leadership skills, that increased their productivity in the peacetime economy. In those cases veterans' benefits can be regarded as similar to the subsidies that firms sometimes pay workers for attending school and learning new skills.

Since veterans' benefits are paid over a long period of time we are faced with the problem of how to take the element of time into account. The most natural approach for an economist, and the one usually followed, is to discount veterans' benefits back to the period of the war itself. In effect, this approach asks the following question: suppose the nation was to purchase a bond, the interest from which would have paid the future veterans' benefits, how large would that bond have to be? But, of course, veterans' benefits are never funded in this way. They are, to use the modern jargon, an unfunded liability, another hidden cost of war.

America's nineteenth-century and colonial wars

America's twentieth-century wars were the offspring of the wars that it fought in the nineteenth century and, on occasion, of wars that it fought during the colonial era. Military technology, of course, changed a great deal, but the similarities in the political and economic context are striking. In some cases, similarities reflected continuity in underlying political or economic institutions: similar institutions faced with similar challenges produced similar results. In other cases, the similarities between the earlier wars and the wars of the twentieth century reflect the lessons of history – this is what we did last time, so this is what we should do this time – and in some cases the similarities simply reflect the personalities involved: the same generals and the same politicians met the challenges of a new war in the same way they had met the challenges of an earlier war. Space prevents us from considering these similarities in detail, but we can identify the major continuities in the way America fought its wars.

Throughout the colonial era and most of the nineteenth century the United States fought wars to drive Native Americans from land that white Americans wanted as white America expanded westward, and to subdue or destroy the Native Americans who remained. The tactics were often brutal. The Philippine–American War (1898–1902), which we will explore below, was in some ways a continuation. Indeed, many of the officers and men who fought in the Philippines had fought in the Indian Wars. General Leonard Wood won a Medal of Honor in the campaign to capture the Apache chief Geronimo (*New York Times*, March 19, 1916, SM1), helped organize and lead the Rough Riders in Cuba, fought against the Moros in the Philippines, and eventually became commander of the department of the Philippines. Williams (1980, 828) studied the backgrounds of the thirty generals who served in the Philippine War from 1898 to 1902 and found that twenty-six "had experience with Indians in the West." Wood's friend Theodore Roosevelt wrote that colonial expansion was "precisely parallel between the Philippines and the Apaches and Sioux. My doctrine is what I preached in my *Winning the West* ... to withdraw from the contest for civilization because of the fact that there are attendant cruelties, is, in my opinion, utterly unworthy of a great people" (quoted in Williams 1980, 826).

The brutal tactics employed against Native Americans and against the native populations of the Philippines were partly the product of racism. Many Americans felt little sympathy for peoples whom they considered different and inferior. Cruelty, however, also was demanded by the economics of war. During the colonial era and the nineteenth century American settlers occupied small homesteads spread over thousands of miles. Protecting all of them from surprise attacks by concentrated forces of Native Americans was prohibitively expensive. It was possible to assemble small armies of volunteers in response to particularly violent attacks or increases in the level of attacks, but how could Native Americans be brought to battle? What was to prevent them from melting into the forest when faced with a concentrated force, only to return later for guerilla attacks? The answer was the punitive campaign. By burning the crops of Native Americans, by destroying their villages, and by killing men, women and children, white armies could intimidate Native Americans, and perhaps bring them to battle where superior numbers and firepower would deliver victory. These were the tactics, for example, that brought success to General "Mad Anthony" Wayne in his campaign against Native Americans in Ohio, where in August 1794 he won a decisive battle against a confederacy of Native American tribes at the Battle of Fallen Timbers.

But cruelty toward civilians, we should remember, is a commonplace of war, and not confined to wars against people of other races or people who employ inferior military technologies. Americans have used brutal tactics against white as well as Native American populations when the cost of alternatives was prohibitive. When Union General William Tecumseh Sherman planned his "march to the sea" during the Civil War, he did not tell his superior, General Ulysses Grant, that he would win the "hearts and minds" of the people of Georgia and persuade them to give up slavery and rejoin the Union; he told Grant that he would "make Georgia howl." The logic was unavoidable. Deep within the Confederacy, faced with an enemy who could retreat for hundreds of miles or turn to guerilla warfare, Sherman needed some way to intimidate the South or bring Southern armies to battle. In World War II, faced with distant well-entrenched enemies the United States turned to aerial bombardments of civilian targets, including nuclear attacks. The purpose was much the same.

Mexico, unlike Native American tribes, could field a European-style army with units of field artillery. But Mexico was simply too small and too poor to defeat a determined United States. The Mexican War (1846–8) ended with Mexico ceding large areas in the Southwest, including California. The Mexican War was in many respects similar to the Spanish–American War that would follow fifty years later. In both cases the United States relied on an army of volunteers to win a quick and decisive victory over a second-tier power. And in both cases the United States won significant colonial concessions. Hunger for land, it is true, was advertised more nakedly in the Mexican War than in the Spanish–American War. President James K. Polk made no secret of his goal of wresting California from the Mexicans. The Spanish–American War, as we will see below, was pushed in part by public concerns about Spanish atrocities committed in the course of suppressing the Cuban independence movement. But the partisans of imperialist expansion, such as Theodore Roosevelt and Henry Cabot Lodge, had their hand in the war as well. Both wars, moreover, spawned opposition by American foes of imperialism. Ulysses Grant, who fought in the Mexican War, regarded it "as one of the most unjust ever waged by a stronger against a weaker nation" (Grant 1885, 53). John Sherman, the brother of Grant's principal lieutenant, William Tecumseh Sherman, as we will see, opposed the war to conquer the Philippines. During the Vietnam War, opposition to it would force President Lyndon Baines Johnson to give up his quest for reelection.

During the colonial period and the nineteenth century the United States also fought wars against major powers. The French and Indian War was the American branch of the Seven Years War, in many ways a world war. The War of 1812 was fought against Britain, the leading military power of the age. The British blockade of the European continent during the Napoleonic Wars, and the resulting interference with what America saw as its right as a neutral to trade wherever it was profitable, was a major cause. The rallying cry was "Free trade and sailors' rights." The same issue would help propel the United States into World War I. Germany's submarine blockade of Britain, in part a response to the latter's surface blockade of the continent with conventional ships, brought Germany into direct and violent conflict with the United States.

America was a rich nation by world standards in the eighteenth and nineteenth centuries. Wages were relatively high and interest rates low. Heavy reliance on capital made economic sense when America went to war. Firepower, historian David Hacket Fischer tells us, was one of the basic principles of George Washington's army. At the First Battle of Trenton the ratio of guns to soldiers in Washington's army was twice that of the Hessian army it faced (Fischer 2004, 374). Heavy reliance on capital was a feature of the armies that Lincoln and Grant constructed in the Civil War to subdue the South. Grant relied on the telegraph to coordinate his forces striking simultaneous blows at widely dispersed points in the South. And both sides relied on the railroads to move troops. A high ratio of capital to labor would be even more characteristic, as we will see, of the American approach to war in the twentieth century.

The wars of the eighteenth and nineteenth centuries raised many of the same financial problems that were encountered in the twentieth century. The Revolutionary War was largely financed with "Continental dollars" and the Civil War was financed in the North, initially, with greenbacks and in the South, throughout the war, with Confederate dollars. "Financed by printing money" was more than an informative analogy; it was the literal truth. Governments also relied on increased taxes and borrowing to finance wars. During the Civil War the United States introduced a personal income tax and a corporate income tax along with "sin taxes" on alcohol and tobacco. The United States also borrowed large amounts of money during the Civil War, turning as it did so to the investment banker Jay Cooke, who marketed war bonds to the middle class. When World War I began the Secretary of the Treasury turned, naturally, to the history of the Civil War for lessons about war finance.

The problem of whether to prosecute a war to victory or negotiate a compromise was felt most strongly during the Civil War. With casualties mounting Lincoln was urged repeatedly to negotiate a settlement with the South. But despite some gestures, in the end Lincoln stuck to the policy of unconditional surrender. This policy, undoubtedly, prolonged the Civil War and cost many lives. Once defeat was on the horizon the South might well have agreed to many Northern demands in exchange for an end to the fighting. But the policy of unconditional surrender laid the basis for "reconstruction" of the South. The South was occupied and the slaves were freed. The Radical Republicans wanted to go much further. They wanted to break up the plantations and give the former slaves the land – forty acres and a mule. They wanted, moreover, to give the former slaves the vote: a democratic society would replace rule by the "slaveocracy." Lincoln and Grant's policy of unconditional surrender had made such reforms possible. The costs of unconditional surrender, in other words, could be seen as an investment in a democratic future based on reconstruction.

Of course, things did not go as far as the Radical Republicans had hoped. Land reform was blocked; the Ku Klux Klan, the product of unreconciled Confederate soldiers turning to guerrilla tactics, used terror to maintain white power; and the project of turning the South into a democratic society would have to wait until the second half of the twentieth century. Reconstruction, of course, had and continues to have a contentious reputation. For some, the failures of reconstruction were proof that Lincoln should have negotiated an end to the war. For others, the right conclusion to draw from the failures of reconstruction was that there was a missing ingredient: Lincoln's policy of charity toward the defeated South. Had Lincoln lived, the policy of unconditional surrender followed by "charity for all, and malice toward none" could have proved to be the right policy. In any event, America's conflicted views of unconditional surrender and reconstruction would play important roles in determining the response of the United States to the challenges posed by World War I and World War II.

3 *The Spanish–American War*

It has been a splendid little war, begun with the highest motives, carried on with magnificent intelligence and spirit, favored by that Fortune which loves the brave.

Secretary of State John Hay to Theodore Roosevelt, July 27, 1898

A chronology of the Spanish–American War

1896		
February	10	General Valeriano Weyler arrives in Cuba to suppress an insurgency. His cruel tactics arouse indignation in the United States.
1897		
June	7	Secretary of State John Sherman complains to Spain about General Weyler's brutality.
July	7	The Dingley tariff raises taxes on imports to new heights; the tariff on sugar is raised to 97 percent, a level that will hurt sugar producers in Cuba.
1898		
January	25	The US battleship *Maine*, dispatched by President McKinley to show the American flag in Cuba, reaches Havana.
February	15	The *Maine* explodes under mysterious circumstances. "Remember the *Maine*" will become a rallying cry for those advocating war with Spain.
March	9	Congress appropriates an additional $50 million for defense.
April	19	Congress adopts a war resolution that includes a demand that Spanish armed forces leave Cuba.

	22	The Volunteer Army Act authorizes a volunteer cavalry, the Rough Riders. Cuban ports are blockaded by the US navy.
	23	President McKinley calls for 125,000 volunteers.
	24	Spain declares war on the United States.
	25	The United States declares war on Spain.
May	1	The Spanish fleet protecting the Philippines, a Spanish colony, is destroyed by an American fleet under the command of George Dewey.
June	6	US navy captures Guantanamo Bay in Cuba.
	13	The War Revenue Act provides new taxes and a bond issue.
	14	Seventeen thousand US troops depart Tampa, Florida for Cuba.
July	1	After fierce fighting, in which Theodore Roosevelt distinguishes himself, Fort San Juan Hill is taken by American forces.
	17	Santiago de Cuba surrenders. The US army takes 24,000 prisoners.
	26	Spain requests peace terms.
October	1	Peace negotiations begin in Paris.
December	10	The Treaty of Paris is signed. Spain gives up all claims to Cuba. Spain also cedes Puerto Rico, Guam, and the Philippines to the United States. For the last-named Spain receives $20 million.

Sources: Linton (1975), Schlesinger and Bowman (1993), Morris and Morris (1996), other chronologies of American history, the *New York Times*, and the *Wall Street Journal*.

The Spanish–American War lasted only about three months. The United States formally declared war on April 25, 1898; an expeditionary force departed for Cuba on June 14; the most famous battle took place on July 1; and Spain asked for peace terms on July 26. The war did not suddenly make the United States into an imperial power; the many wars against Native Americans, the Mexican War, and the forcible "opening" of Japan are clear examples of American imperialism in the years before the Spanish–American War. Nevertheless, the war substantially increased America's commitment to controlling territories beyond its borders. The treaty of peace signed in December 1898 transferred Puerto Rico, Guam, and, in exchange for $20 million ($16 billion would have been the same share of GDP in 2008), the Philippines to the United States.[1]

The origins of the war

Cuban independence had been on the American political agenda for several years prior to the outbreak of the war. In 1896 and 1897 sympathy for revolutionaries trying to win Cuba's independence from Spain rose to a fever pitch. In attempting to suppress the revolutionaries Spain had turned to General Valeriano Weyler. Weyler, who took command of Spanish forces in Cuba in February 1896, attempted to crush the rebellion by adopting harsh tactics including the use of concentration camps to separate the general population from the revolutionaries. Stories about Spanish atrocities in Cuba, some accurate, some exaggerated, filled the American press.

The Democratic Party platform of 1896 asserted the party's support for the Monroe Doctrine, and declared that: "We extend our sympathy to the people of Cuba in their heroic struggle for liberty and independence." Similarly, the Republican platform, after asserting the party's respect for the right of European powers to maintain their colonial possessions, declared: "We watch with deep and abiding interest the heroic battles of the Cuban patriots against cruelty and oppression, and best hopes go out for the full success of their determined contest for liberty." It went on to argue that diplomatic actions were justified: "The government of Spain, having lost control of Cuba, and being unable to protect the property or lives of resident American citizens, or to comply with its Treaty obligations, we believe that the government of the United States should actively use its influence and good offices to restore peace and give independence to the Island" (Wooley and Peters 2008).

Years later the poet Carl Sandburg, who volunteered for service in the war, recalled how he felt at the time.

[1] The annexation of Hawaii on July 6, 1898, although not a direct result of the war, owed something to the imperialist emotions stirred up by it.

I read about ... the people of Cuba who wanted independence and a republic ... I read about Gómez, García, the Maceos, with their scrabbling little armies fighting against Weyler. They became heroes to me. I tried to figure a way to get down there and join one of those armies ... I was going along with millions of other Americans who were about ready for a war to throw the Spanish government out of Cuba and let the people of Cuba have their republic. If a war did come and men were called to fight it, I knew what I would do. (Quoted in Perez 1999, 356)

Despite this outpouring of sympathy for the Cuban people, war was by no means inevitable. Chance events also played a role. The most important was the mysterious explosion and sinking of the battleship *Maine*. The *Maine* had been dispatched to Cuba by President McKinley as a warning to Spain. It sank in the harbor of Havana in February 1898 with the loss of 260 men. Spain was blamed for the explosion, although the true source remains a matter of controversy. As a result, "Remember the *Maine*," sometimes "Remember the *Maine*, to Hell with Spain," became the rallying cry that accelerated the march to war. Indeed, as James A. Field Jr. (1978, 668) has pointed out, the name of the ship itself was an important historical accident. Had a vessel with a less alliterative name been sent, let alone one that rhymed with Spain, say the *Texas*, the resulting slogan would have been far less effective.

As we will see in subsequent chapters, this event was not unique in the history of America's wars. A galvanizing event, a clear and understandable affront to America's honor, was a part of each march to war. Sometimes, the events were just as they seemed at the time; sometimes subsequent investigation would show that the interpretation of the event that dominated the headlines at the time was in error.

But what of economic motives? Was the war fought, for example, to open markets for American businesses? As is often the case, it is difficult to arrive at firm conclusions because lines of influence are difficult to trace. We can be fairly certain, however, that in general the American business community was opposed to the war at the end of 1897 and in the opening months of 1898, despite the rise of sympathy in the United States for the Cuban revolutionaries. The classic analysis is by Julius Pratt (1934). Pratt based his conclusion on a close and wide-ranging reading of the business press. Most historians before Pratt, many of whom tried to show that the business community led the march to war, relied on selected and possibly unrepresentative quotations.[2] The business press, Pratt found, generally denied that the economy as a whole would benefit from a war. The most likely result would be higher taxes and inflation. As Jonathan Kirshner (2007, 44–51) has recently shown, opposition to the war was especially strong in the financial community. There was little concern that the war would be long or that the United States might lose, it being widely assumed that the United States could defeat Spain rather easily. The main concern of the financial community was that a war would produce inflation and, possibly, a temporary or permanent abandonment of the gold standard. Less than two years earlier William Jennings Bryan had won the Democratic nomination for President after declaring "thou shall not crucify mankind upon a cross of gold" and then conducted a vigorous campaign based on replacing the gold standard with a bimetallic standard. Although Bryan was soundly defeated, the financial community was by no means certain that the cheap money forces had been banished forever. Many advocates of intervention were also advocates of free silver, who welcomed the financial demands of a war precisely because they might lead to a silver or even a paper-based inflation.

Opposition to the war follows to some degree directly from the balance sheet of financial institutions. Banks and other financial intermediaries, typically, are net monetary creditors: their assets fixed in dollars (reserves, loans, bonds, and so on) exceed their liabilities fixed in dollars (deposits); they will lose from an unanticipated inflation.[3] This is not true of all businesses. Farmers, for example, are usually net monetary debtors. Their assets (land, equipment, and livestock) are not fixed in dollars and their real value can remain constant or rise in the face of inflation, while their liabilities (mortgages) are fixed in dollars and their real value will decline in the face of inflation.[4]

Pratt and Kirshner also mentioned some movements in the stock market to support their readings of the financial press. We can follow

[2] Kirshner (2007, 38–44) summarizes the more recent literature, which is generally supportive of Pratt.

[3] Alchian and Kessel (1959) provided some of the first data on the adverse effects of inflation on banks.

[4] Once inflation is anticipated interest rates on dollar-denominated assets will rise and offset the effects of inflation on bank balance sheets. There would also be some offset through the "sharing of the seignorage:" the increase in bank reserves resulting from an increase in government-issued paper would permit banks to make additional loans. In general, however, the evidence is that banks suffer some damage from wartime inflation.

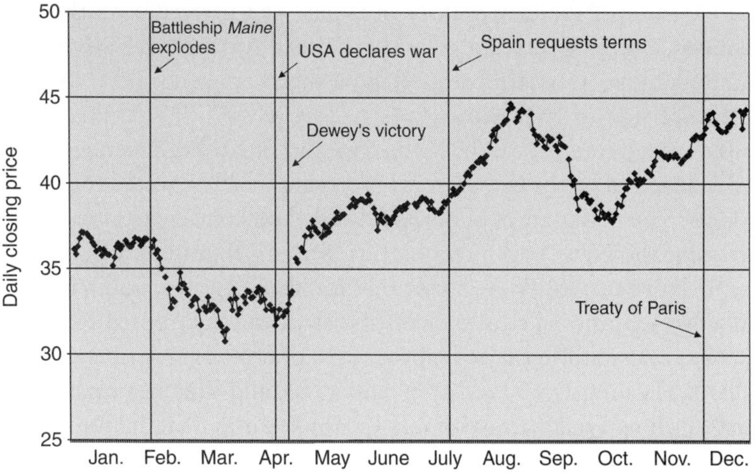

Figure 3.1 The Dow Jones Industrial Average in 1898. The gaps occur on days when the market was closed.
Source: Global Financial Data.

their lead by looking at the Dow Jones Industrial Average, which is plotted in Figure 3.1. Notice that during the interval between the sinking of the battleship *Maine* and the declaration of war, the stock market slumped and exhibited a high variance from day to day. This is consistent with Pratt's argument that business was generally opposed to the war. Once war was declared, however, and Admiral Dewey won his famous victory at Manila, the market surged. Again, this finding reinforces the argument based on the business press that business became favorable to the war on the heels of favorable war news. The market hesitated during the period of ground combat in Cuba, but then surged again after Spain requested terms on July 26. The break in the market in September, however, does not seem to have been closely tied to war news. Indeed, by September the war, from the market's point of view, was stale beer. Fears of tightness in financial markets may have played a role and some unfavorable dividend announcements, but the war seems to have been forgotten as a factor that could influence the market (*New York Times*, October 3, 1898, supplement, p. 1).

What about special interests that may have profited from a war? Perhaps the war was not the result of general support from the business community, or the financial community, but rather the result of pressure from individual businesses or sub-sectors that stood to profit from an American victory in Cuba. The literature on the war mentions several special interests that pushed for the war, although it is impossible to estimate precisely how much influence each exerted on the decision to go to war.

One special interest can be divined in Carl Sandburg's recollections: he was inspired by the Cuban revolutionaries when he *read* about their exploits. The newspapers of the day dwelled on conditions in Cuba. In particular the New York press barons William Randolph Hearst and Joseph Pulitzer, who were notorious for their "yellow journalism," published sensational stories about the atrocities committed by Spain in Cuba. These stories, based on the work of famous reporters such as William Harding Davis and Stephen Crane, and sketches by famous artists such as Frederick Remington, captured the imagination of the American people. Other newspapers were more circumspect (Auxier 1940), but it is hard to resist the conclusion that the sensational accounts of the war for the independence of Cuba that appeared in Hearst's *New York Journal*, Pulitzer's *New York World*, the *Chicago Tribune*, and other papers did much to inflame public opinion – and increase circulation.[5]

Mass circulation newspapers had arrived in Britain at the same time, and profited from the contemporaneous Boer War (1899–1902) in much the same way that the American press barons profited from the Spanish–American War. When one of the editors of the British *Daily Mail* was asked what sells newspapers, he replied:

> The first answer is "war". War not only creates a supply of news but a demand for it. So deep rooted is the fascination in a war and all things appertaining to that . . . a paper has only to be able to put up on its placard "A Great Battle" for its sales to go up. (Ferguson 2004, 213)

Owners of property in Cuba and their workers also stood to benefit from the war. The revolution, which Spain was unable to crush, disrupted business and lowered property values. The intervention of the United States would restore order and do so under the control of a government committed to the preservation of private property rights, especially American private property rights. As I noted above, the Republican platform of 1896 identified the failure of the Spanish

[5] But the story that Hearst told Remington "You furnish the pictures and I'll furnish the war" may be apocryphal.

government to protect "the property and lives" of American citizens as a reason for aggressive American diplomacy, if not for war. In May 1897 a group of citizens doing business in Cuba presented a petition to Secretary of State John Sherman asking for United States government involvement in restoring peace in Cuba. One of the firms signing the memorial was August Belmont and Company, a prominent investment banking house. A similar memorial was presented by a group of New York executives to President McKinley in February (Pratt 1934, 175–7).

There were also interests that stood to lose from a successful American intervention. Before Congress adopted the declaration of war against Spain it insisted on the so-called "Teller Resolution," according to which the United States disavowed any intention of exercising "sovereignty, jurisdiction, or control" over Cuba. The resolution was sponsored by Senator Henry Teller, a Republican of Colorado. Teller's resolution expressed the strong anti-imperialist sentiment in Congress, but it also expressed, as historian Walter LaFeber (1993, 143–4) pointed out, the interests of Colorado's sugar beet growers who did not want competition from cheaper Cuban sugar. (Cuban sugar might be admitted duty free if Cuba became part of the United States.) There were even businesses in Cuba, such as American-owned iron mines, that had managed to keep going despite the insurrection and opposed American intervention because they feared that it would mean increased military activity that would finally damage their businesses (Pratt 1934, 177).

Robert Zevin (1972, 353–8) has argued that the military itself constituted an interest group that benefited from the war and the colonialism that followed. Spending on the army and navy, and the number of service personnel ratcheted upward as a result of the Spanish–American War (Figure 3.2). The war, in other words, meant more bases to command and more ships to captain, not just during the short period of the war itself when promotions could be won, but for years to come. In the months leading up to the war the navy under Secretary Theodore Roosevelt began to ponder how George Dewey's Pacific squadron could be used. A variety of options were considered, even an attack on the Canary Islands (Field 1978, 665–6). In the end, however, they settled on the Philippines. The great victory at Manila served to make Dewey's career – at one point he was considered a likely candidate for President – and to promote the interests of the

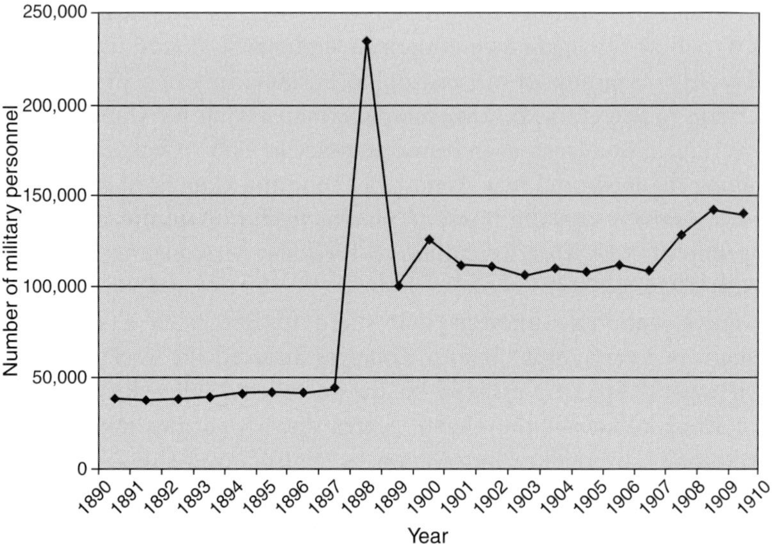

Figure 3.2 Total number of military personnel on active duty, 1890–1910. The Spanish–American War produced a permanent increase in the size of the armed forces.
Source: Carter *et al.* (2006, series Ed26)

navy. The army also saw its role in the world increased by the Spanish–American War. General Leonard Wood, who commanded occupation forces in Cuba, supervised the construction of transportation facilities, hospitals, and schools. Wood even wrote a book about investment opportunities in Cuba, as he also did about the Philippines when he became military governor there. The war had created opportunities.

In the end the decision for war was up to President McKinley. And his understanding of and response to the pressures we have outlined above must to some degree remain beyond the reach of the historian, partly because McKinley did not leave voluminous and revealing records, and partly because the interior process by which motives and fears become policy is never fully observed even by the decision-makers themselves.[6] Certainly the historian Walter LaFeber's (1993, 144) conclusion that McKinley acted out of a combination of motives – to end the revolution in Cuba that was stirring American passions, to

[6] A well-known story about McKinley reaching his decision after a prayer session with visiting clergymen may be apocryphal.

protect American property on the island, and to extend American power in the Pacific in order to maintain the Open Door policy in China – is a defensible reading of the evidence.

Financing the war

Shortly after the outbreak of the war Congress unanimously appropriated $50 million. The equivalent today, as a percentage of GDP, would be about $40 billion. On June 13 Congress passed the War Revenue Act that raised taxes and authorized the issue of debt to finance the war. Davis Rich Dewey (1931, 465–6) in his classic financial history of the United States concluded that the "action of the treasury and of the Congress in this conflict was alike commendable." The reason was simply that Congress had levied additional taxes that were adequate to finance a substantial part of the war. Nevertheless, a reading of the tax schedule suggests that Congress was well aware that patriotic support for the war would not translate automatically into a willingness to pay higher taxes. Congress still had to be very careful about who got stuck with the bill. At the time, the tariff was the source of about one-half of federal revenues, so raising the tariff had to be considered. But Congress had passed the controversial Dingley tariff in July of 1897 – widely denounced by Democrats as a punishing increase in protection – and neither the President nor the Congress was prepared to revisit the issue. Instead, internal taxes were imposed or increased on a long list of items.

Walter LaFeber (1993, 145) has suggested that it was the ability to tax goods produced in the "Second Industrial Revolution" that made higher taxes possible. But the list of goods taxed suggests that other considerations were more important.[7] Personal failings came in for particular attention. Taxes on tobacco and fermented liquors – taxes first imposed in the Civil War – were doubled. Distilled spirits were omitted, an omission Dewey (1931, 466) approved because it left "a fruitful source of revenue in reserve for a future emergency." Taxes were imposed, however, on "banks, brokers, proprietors of theaters, bowling alleys, billiard and pool

[7] The following description of the tax bill is based on the schedule published in the *New York Times* (June 27, 1898, 1).

rooms, and amusement places in general." Stamp taxes were imposed on a wide range of financial transactions – the sort of tax that had so outraged Americans on the eve of the Revolution – and on "toilet articles, chewing gum and wine." A citizen could, in other words, avoid many of the costs of the war by being virtuous – no wine, tobacco, or chewing gum, no frequenting of theaters or pool rooms. Sin and luxury taxes are always an attractive option for legislatures. But war adds an extra reason to tax these activities. It is not simply that one is hurting oneself by drinking wine, chewing gum, and frequenting pool rooms; one is also hurting the war effort.

There was a small exception to the rule that the tariff could not be touched: the levying of a small tax on imported tea. This duty may have been imposed partly to finance the Board of Tea Experts, which was established on March 2, 1898, to test the quality of imported tea. In any case, the tax on tea like the taxes on chewing gum and pool halls could be avoided, if one had the will power.

There were also taxes that reflected progressive-populist concerns. The taxes on banks and brokers, mentioned above, fall into this category as do the taxes levied on sugar refining and petroleum refining. For many contemporary critics of big business the sugar trust and Standard Oil were the iconic examples of the cartels exploiting the public. Taxing them would be popular. Congress may have been counting on the idea that the public believes that taxes stay where they are placed. A tax on oil pipelines might increase the price of kerosene, but the newspaper reading public might assume that the tax was simply reducing the profits of the oil companies, leaving kerosene prices unchanged: John D. Rockefeller would pay the tax, not John Doe. If the price of kerosene did rise the public might miss the connection between the higher prices they were paying for kerosene and the war.

Another progressive-populist measure was the inheritance tax, a revival of a source of finance used during the Civil War. It was graduated with respect to both the relationship with the deceased and the size of the estate. The surviving husband or wife was not taxed. Lineal descendants and ancestors, and siblings, however, were taxed at a rate of 0.75 percent on their interest in estates ranging from $10,000 to $25,000. This rate increased, according to the size of the estate, up to 2.25 percent for interests in estates over $1 million. The rates were higher for descendants of brothers and sisters; higher still for aunts, uncles, and their descendants; and highest for persons with a low degree of consanguinity or "strangers in blood." For the last category, the rate reached a maximum of 15 percent for interests in estates valued over $1 million. If we use the consumer price index as our inflator, $10,000 would be about $250,000 in today's money and $1 million about $25 million. If we used, say, personal income the amounts would be much larger. These were, in short, large estates, and the revenues generated were small.

Table 3.1 shows the increase in expenditures attributable to the war, about $274 million, and the part played by taxes and debt in financing it. Here I computed the cost of the war in a simple way. I took total spending by the army and navy in 1898 and 1899 and subtracted twice army and navy spending in 1897, adjusting for inflation. This is probably close to the way contemporaries thought about the cost of the war when they considered how to finance it.[8] There were some additional expenditures undertaken by other government agencies, but these were rather small. Below I will consider some of the longer-run costs of the war, in particular veterans' benefits.

The revenues from the wartime tax levies were somewhat less than expected. Congress had anticipated about $140 million in the first year and the take was actually about $100 million. This rose to about $125 million in the second year, still below initial hopes (Shultz and Caine 1937, 452). Some overstatement of the emergency revenues was, perhaps, to be expected. Some of the enthusiasm for the war would have dissipated if the war had to be financed with hard-hitting taxes. Nevertheless, the increase in tax revenues – driven mainly by the alcohol, tobacco, and stamp duties – was sufficient to pay for about 80 percent of the marginal costs of the war, and to provide ongoing revenues sufficient to retire the debt created during the war itself, although not sufficient to fund future expenditures on behalf of veterans.

That the Congress did as well as it did in raising taxes may have been partly a matter of timing. The tax bill was passed about fifty days after the declaration of war, when patriotic enthusiasm ran high. Had

[8] Studenski and Krooss (1952, 235) give a similar estimate, "approximately $250 million," without explaining how they arrived at this figure (Carter *et al.* 2006, series Ed170).

Table 3.1 *The Spanish–American War: cost of the war and sources of finance*

Category of expenditures	$000	Percent
Cost of the war	274,083[a] (6.30)[b]	100.0
Increase in tax revenues	225,838[c]	82.4
Customs	2,595[d]	0.9
Alcohol taxes	71,028[e]	25.9
Tobacco taxes	27,304[f]	10.0
Inheritance taxes	1,235[g]	0.5
Stamp taxes and other revenues	123,676[h]	45.1
Borrowing and money creation	48,245[i]	17.6

Source: Carter *et al.* (2006), series as given in individual notes.

Notes:

[a] Spending by the army and navy in fiscal 1898 and 1899 less (in each year) spending in 1897 adjusted for inflation (Carter *et al.* 2006, series Ea638, Ea639, and Ca13).

[b] The sum in billions of year 2008 dollars.

[c] Series Ea588.

[d] Series Ea589.

[e] Series Ea600.

[f] Series Ea601.

[g] Series Ea598.

[h] Increase in tax revenues less revenues raised through customs and alcohol, tobacco, and inheritance taxes.

[i] Cost of war less increase in tax revenues. The rate of interest on the bonds issued to finance the war was lower than it would otherwise have been because the bonds could be used to issue national bank notes. A rough estimate of the proportion of the costs of the war that were indirectly defrayed by money creation is 4.7 percent. See text.

the administration found it necessary to come back later for higher taxes, it is far from clear that the public or the Congress would have been receptive. There is perhaps a hundred-day rule here: Congress must pass a tax increase in the first hundred days following a declaration of war if it expects to capitalize on enthusiasm for the war to overcome the public's normal reluctance to support higher taxes. It was possible, moreover, to rely on sin taxes and taxes on the targets of progressive-populist ire because the resources employed in the war represented only a small fraction of the total economy, 1.29 percent of average GDP for 1898 and 1899. The much larger wars to follow could not be financed in the same way.

Although Congress did finance the major part of the war with increased taxes, it also covered about a fifth of the cost, $48 million, by issuing debt. The government, however, borrowed more: $200 million. This was through 3 percent bonds redeemable in ten years (the government *could* pay the principal in ten years if it chose) and payable in twenty years (the government *must* pay the principal in twenty years). Bond denominations were low, presumably to attract wide support from the general public. And the bonds were popular. Subscriptions (offers to purchase) amounted to $1,400 million, seven times the amount put on sale. The enthusiasm for the bond issue, Shultz and Caine (1937, 454) suggest, was "partly a reflection of the popular support for the government's war policy, partly a reflection of the anxiety of the national banks to obtain federal bonds as a backing for increased note circulation."

The latter consideration arose from the nature of the national banks. These banks could issue hand-to-hand notes, that is paper money, provided that they were backed up by government bonds. Bonds that bore the "circulation privilege" sold at a premium, so part of the war was financed by money creation, although it is difficult to say exactly what proportion. In 1898 New England municipal bonds were yielding about 3.35 percent, while US government bonds were yielding about 2.50 percent (Carter *et al.* 2006, series Cj1192 and Cj1194). The New England municipals yielded more because they were riskier (although they were relatively low risk compared with corporate debt) and because they did not have the circulation privilege.[9] Thus 25 percent (3.35 less 2.50 divided by 3.35) would be an upper bound on the amount of the bond issue that was financed by money creation.[10] Since about 17.6 percent of the war was financed through bond issues, this means that overall an upper bound estimate of the share of the cost of the war financed by money creation would be 4.4 percent.

Borrowing more than proved necessary for the immediate prosecution of the war was prudent, but created technical problems.

9 Tax considerations, important today, were probably not very important at the time since there were no federal income tax.

10 Another way to think of this calculation is the following. The annual interest costs would be the same whether 100 percent of the gap between spending and taxes was financed by borrowing at 2.50 percent or 75 percent by borrowing at 3.35 percent and 25 percent by printing money.

The sale of the bonds raised Treasury balances, which tended to reduce the stock of money in circulation. The Secretary of the Treasury, Lyman J. Gage, offset this effect by prepaying interest and maturing principal on federal debt and depositing funds in national banks (Friedman and Schwartz 1963, 145, n. 12). Eventually, continuing war-related expenditures reduced the Treasury balances. In any case, the effects of Treasury money market operations were small compared with the effects of the rapid increase in the stock of monetary gold, which rose 24.4 percent between June 1897 and June 1898, and 13.0 percent between June 1898 and June 1899 (Cagan 1965, 340). The money stock, responding to this increase in the monetary base, rose 13.7 percent and 15.7 percent over the same years (Friedman and Schwartz 1982, 6–8). I will discuss these increases in more detail below, but note here that the gold stock rose mainly as a result of the accelerating flow of gold from South Africa, Western Australia, and other areas. Thus, the vigorous economic expansion from June 1897 to June 1898 may have been influenced more by the increase in the world supply of gold than by the limited monetary and fiscal stimuli arising from the war.

Mobilization

To fight even this small war, the army had to be expanded in a short time from an active duty force of 27,865 in 1897 to 209,714 in 1898. The navy expanded from 11,985 in 1897 to 22,492 in 1898; the marines from 2,217 in 1896 to 3,806 in 1897 (Carter *et al.* 2006, series Ed9, Ed38, and Ed43). Figure 3.2 shows the trend in the total for all three services. While the armed forces were cut back after the end of the war, once the dust had settled they remained about twice as large as they had been before the war. Much of this increase is explained by the occupations of former Spanish colonies, including especially the Philippines, which we will discuss in the next chapter. Most of the cutback was in the army. By 1902 the navy had more personnel on active duty than during the Spanish–American War.

Paul A. C. Koistinen (1997, 78–88), the historian of American war mobilization, identifies a number of successes and failures and argues that the successes may have been more impressive than the failures because of the difficult circumstances facing military planners. The armed forces had to be expanded rapidly. The overall strategic plan, moreover, kept changing: first a substantial period of training was planned, then an attack on Havana, and finally an attack on Santiago, while separate plans were laid for attacks on Puerto Rico and the Philippines. The mobilization was difficult, moreover, simply because the United States had not mobilized for a long time. Although a number of army officers were Civil War veterans, many of the lessons about how to mobilize a large army had been forgotten.

Nevertheless, Koistinen gives high marks to the ordinance and commissary departments. The stocks of the latest shoulder arms and the smokeless powder ammunition were limited, but were allocated efficiently until larger supplies became available. Under General Charles P. Eagan the army's commissary department bought large quantities of food including, for the first time, refrigerated beef. A great deal may have been wasted, and the diet was boring, but "No one ever complained that there was not enough to eat" (Koistinen 1997, 79). There were charges, it is true, that the army had accepted tainted beef. As a result, General Eagan was forced to resign. But Brandes (1997, 115), no friend of wartime profiteers, concludes that these charges were exaggerated, and that most of the problems resulted from a failure to realize how quickly canned beef would spoil when opened in the tropics.

There were, however, a number of significant problems. The choice of Tampa, Florida as the embarkation point for the major assault on Cuba proved to be a mistake. The facilities, both housing and transport, were inadequate to accommodate a large army, and congestion was a constant problem. The departure for Cuba became chaotic when a rumor circulated that the supply of transport ships was inadequate and the orderly boarding of ships became a mad scramble to avoid being left behind. The troopships, moreover, were crowded and unsanitary, and the disembarkation in Cuba turned out to be as chaotic as the departure.

The largest problem, however, was the slow and inadequate response to the epidemic of tropical diseases – typhoid, dysentery, malaria, and (possibly) yellow fever – that swept through the expeditionary force. The armed forces suffered only about 385 deaths in combat during the war, but perhaps another 5,000 died of disease, most from tropical diseases. Many fell ill aboard ship on the way home and the questions of how to care for the men, and when and where to discharge them from the service, became fraught with controversy. Eventually many of the men were taken to a base at Montauk on Long Island. The facilities there were inadequate, and the army medical service was severely criticized for the conditions under which the army suffered.[11] It was the darkest chapter in "the splendid little war."

The cost of the war

American battle deaths during the Spanish–American War were low compared with those in subsequent wars. As noted above, about 385 men died in battle or of wounds sustained in battle: 369 in the army and 16 in the navy and marines (see Appendix 2). This figure, incidentally, omits the 260 men lost in the explosion of the battleship *Maine*. Deaths from disease (mainly tropical diseases such as malaria, cholera, yellow fever, and dysentery) and injury, however, were much higher: according to Beebe and DeBakey (1951, 21) – who give higher estimates than *Historical Statistics* – some 5,083 men died of these causes. Spanish deaths are not known with any degree of accuracy. Clodfelter (2001, 287) puts "Spanish combat deaths in action against US forces" at about 900, but does not provide an overall estimate of Spanish losses.

The financial cost of the war at current prices – estimated by taking total military expenditures and expenditures on international affairs in 1898 and 1899, and for each year subtracting 1897 spending adjusted for inflation – was about $274 million (Appendix 3). This was about 1.5 percent of average GDP during the war years. The costs incurred in 1898 and 1899, however, were not the largest component of the costs of the war. For one thing, pensions and medical care for veterans came to more than the contemporary costs of the war. We will discuss these costs in the next chapter, on the Philippine–American War, because the veterans of that war, along with the veterans of the Boxer Rebellion, were combined for legislative and reporting purposes with veterans of the Spanish–American War. The Spanish–American War,

[11] Severo and Milford (1989, 187–228) describe the plight of the Spanish–American War veterans who fell ill.

moreover, ushered in a new era of American imperialism, including the Philippine–American War, military actions in Latin America and the Caribbean, and an enlarged navy. I will also consider these costs after discussing the Philippine–American War.[12]

The impact on the economy

The US economy was recovering from a recession when the Spanish–American War began. The National Bureau of Economic Research (NBER) – the organization that has come to be the official timekeeper of America's business cycle – dates the trough of the business cycle in June 1897 and the peak in June 1899.[13] This meant that there was still considerable slack in the economy when the war began and that resources – men, ships, food, and so on – could be shifted to the war effort without squeezing the civilian sector. The economy was at point D in Figure 2.2: it was moving toward the production possibilities curve, and was able to produce more guns and more butter. Despite the mobilization, *civilian* employment grew from 24.4 million workers in 1897 to 26.1 million in 1899, a growth of 6.69 percent in two years. Unemployment dropped from 8.51 percent of the civilian labor force in 1897 to 5.85 percent in 1899 (Carter *et al.* 2006, series Ba470 and Ba475). Industrial production rose in every year from 1893 to 1899. By the time of the Spanish–American War it was nearly 40 percent higher than in 1893, and it would rise another 6 percent the following year (Carter *et al.* 2006, series Cb28).

The statistics show that the expansion of the economy was sufficient to provide for both a war abroad and an expanded flow of civilian goods and services, masking the resource cost of the war from the public. But did the war stimulate the economy or simply ride the wave? In other words, did the increase in government spending stimulate the economy, or would GDP have risen at the same pace in the absence of war spending, but with more production taking place on the civilian side?

12 The Spanish–American War left few institutional legacies. The Army War College established in 1901 by Secretary of War Elihu Root in response to criticisms of the army's organization and performance may be the most important.

13 The National Bureau of Economic Research business cycle dates are available at www.nber.org.

It is hard to be sure, but it seems likely that the macroeconomic stimulus produced by the war was small. To begin, a persuasive case has been made by Milton Friedman and Anna J. Schwartz (1963, 138–9) that two other factors – the increase in the stock of money and favorable developments in agricultural markets – account for the vigor of the recovery. The stock of money, as they note (Friedman and Schwartz 1963, 138), "bounded upward at an extraordinary rate" (by historical standards) during these years: "15 percent from 1897 to 1898, 17 percent from 1898 to 1899, 6 percent from 1899 to 1900, 15 percent from 1900 to 1901, and 9 percent from 1901 to 1902." We might be tempted to associate this rapid increase in the stock of money with the war: war finance through printing money. In this case, however, because the United States was firmly committed to the gold standard – the United States had returned to the gold standard in 1879 and in 1900 it would pass the Gold Standard Act strengthening its legal commitment to gold – there was little room for financing the war by printing money.

There was, as noted above, a way to use the printing press, and the government did take it. Debt issued by the federal government could be given "the circulation privilege." National banks could issue bank notes provided they held a requisite amount of government bonds in reserve to back the notes. By giving banks the right to circulate notes on the basis of the bonds issued to finance the war, the government strengthened the market for government debt, increased the amount of paper money in circulation, and concealed the cost of the war from the public. However, the large increases in the monetary base during these years were driven not by increases in national bank notes, but rather by increases in the amount of gold. Between the beginning of 1897 and the end of 1900 the stock of high-powered money (the monetary base) in the United States rose from $1.399 billion to $1.927 billion, a cumulative increase of 32 percent in four years. Of the increase in the base of $528 million, $414 million, 78 percent, was accounted for by the increase in monetary gold. The increase in national bank notes accounted for only 12.5 percent of the increase in the base, and all other factors only 9.1 percent.

The increase in the stock of monetary gold, in turn, was part of a worldwide increase in the supply of gold: discoveries in the Klondike, Western Australia, and most importantly South Africa (the last made possible by the new cyanide process for extracting gold from ore) were turning the deflation of the 1880s and early 1890s into an inflation. International trade spread these increases throughout the countries on the gold standard. The largest increase in the United States, $163 million, occurred in 1898. Indeed, this was the largest annual increase in the stock of monetary gold between the return of the United States to the gold standard in 1879 and World War I.[14]

This increase in the stock of monetary gold was not so much a product of the war, but rather the result of fortunate (from the point of view of the United States) circumstance: a conjunction of a bad wheat harvest in Europe with a favorable wheat harvest in the United States. This contributed to a favorable balance of trade and an influx of gold.[15] But the amount of gold that flowed into the United States in 1898 is hard to explain on these grounds alone. Net exports of US merchandise moved sharply into the black at this time, and remained so for a number of years, but this was the only year with such a large net inflow of gold (Carter *et al.* 2006, series Ee371, Ee372, and Ee373).

Perhaps the war didn't stimulate the economy through the usual channels, monetary and fiscal policy, but perhaps it did stimulate it over the longer term by winning new markets for American exports in Cuba. Figure 3.3 addresses this possibility. It shows US exports to and imports from Cuba, each as a percentage of GDP, from 1890 to 1915. The main change before the war was a decline in imports that reduced the US balance of trade deficit with Cuba to negligible proportions. After the war, exports to Cuba did increase, although they never rose to as much as 0.25 percent of GDP before World War I. Imports, moreover, rose faster than exports after 1898 and the trade gap widened again. Cuban sugar growers and refiners had been aggressive in adopting new technologies in the nineteenth century, but the new relationship between the US and Cuba encouraged US investment, particularly in the less developed eastern part of the country (Dye 1998). This investment added to the flow of sugar to the USA Anyone who had hoped that Cuba would provide a large market for

14 The figures on the stock of high-powered money and the stock of monetary gold are from Cagan (1965, 333).

15 This conjunction, which had happened a number of times in the nineteenth century, was a chance occurrence from the point of view of the economy. It may well have been the result of recurring meteorological phenomena, and thus, ultimately, predictable.

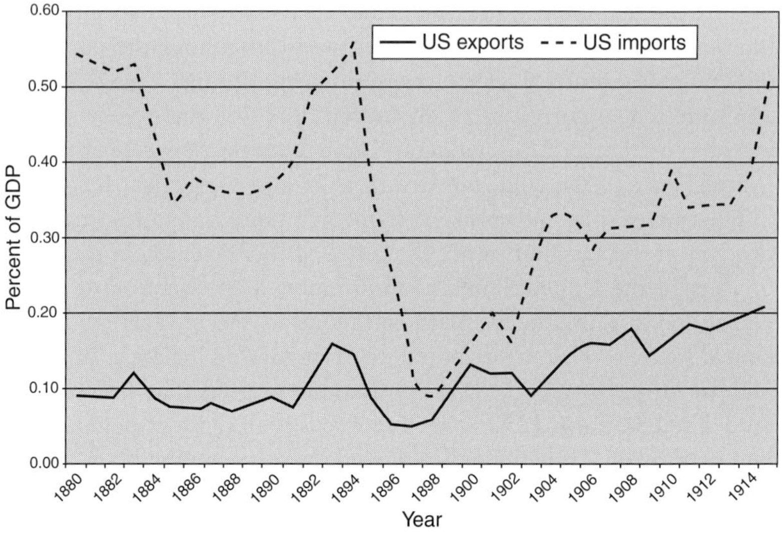

Figure 3.3 US trade with Cuba, 1880–1915.
Source: Exports and imports: Carter *et al.* (2006, series Ee536 and Ee554). GDP: Carter *et al.* (2006, series Ca10).

US exports and would contribute to an improvement in the US balance of payments would have been disappointed.

The main reason for the growing trade gap after 1898 was the increase in sugar imports. In 1901 the United States signed a Reciprocity Treaty with Cuba. This treaty presumably represented the economic fruits of America's military effort on the island. Essentially, the treaty reduced the tariff that applied to sugar imported from Cuba, giving the Cubans a leg up compared with producers outside the American sphere of influence. Stanley Lebergott (1980) argues persuasively that the main beneficiary of the treaty was not the American consumer (since the tariff reduction did not affect the price in American markets), or even the American Sugar Refining Trust (which controlled a large proportion of US production), but rather landowners in Cuba. And they were not primarily Americans. Lebergott (1980, 237) shows that as late as 1902 Americans together controlled only about 16 percent of the Cuban sugar crop. He concludes as follows:

> The prime economic beneficiaries of the Spanish–American War, in sum, were the Spaniards and Cubans who owned Cuban sugar land at the start of

the war. The generous donor of benefits to these gentlemen turned out to be the American taxpayer. For the latter's taxes had to make up for US tariff revenue foregone by the Reciprocity Treaty. (Lebergott 1980, 237)

To say that the war benefited a limited class of Spaniards and Cubans, however, is not to say that this economic interest was not a factor in supporting intervention. Undoubtedly, the "Cuban junta" was important in mobilizing public opinion in the United States in support of intervention in Cuba. By providing information to US newspapers and organizing sympathy rallies the junta magnified support in the United States for the Revolution (Auxier 1939).

4 *The Philippine–American War*

Suddenly came the Spanish War. Dewey's fleet was at Manila and we were the masters of the Philippines. We were an Eastern power. We held the crossroads of the Pacific at Hawaii, and we had our foothold in the island of Luzon. The master of Manila can make terms with every power in the East, and those vast markets must be held open in the interest of our industry and our commerce, of our farmers and our workingmen to the free competition of mankind – a contest in which the genius of American enterprise need fear no rival.

Theodore Roosevelt, speech at Boston, October 31, 1899

A chronology of the Philippine–American War

1898		
May	1	The Spanish fleet protecting the Philippines is destroyed by an American fleet commanded by George Dewey.
May	19	The revolutionary leader Emilio Aguinaldo with the help of the United States returns to the Philippines.
June	12	Aguinaldo establishes a provisional government and declares the Philippines to be an independent democratic republic.
July	26	Spain requests peace terms.
August	12	Spain and the United States sign an armistice.
	13	American ground forces capture Manila.
October	1	Peace negotiations begin in Paris.
December	10	The Treaty of Paris. Spain gives up all claims to Cuba and cedes Puerto Rico, Guam, and the Philippines to the United States. For the last-named Spain receives \$20 million.

1899		
January	5	Aguinaldo, having learned the provisions of the treaty, calls on Filipinos to declare their independence from the United States.
	20	President McKinley appoints a Philippine Commission.
February	4	War breaks out between the US army and Aguinaldo's Army of National Liberation.
	6	Treaty of Paris ratified by the US Senate 57–27.
	12	Rudyard Kipling's poem "The White Man's Burden" is published.
March	31	American forces enter Malolos, the capital of Aguinaldo's government.
November	13	Aguinaldo disbands his army and adopts guerilla warfare.
1900		
January–March		A new phase of the war begins. Small-scale guerilla attacks are launched against American forces.
November	6	William McKinley is reelected President, dashing hopes in the Philippines that the anti-imperialist William Jennings Bryan would win.
1901		
March	23	Aguinaldo captured.
April	19	Aguinaldo issues proclamation accepting American sovereignty.
September	28	Insurgents kill forty-eight Americans and wound many others in a surprise attack at Balangiga on the island of Samar.
1902		
July	4	President Theodore Roosevelt declares an official end to the Philippine–American War. Roosevelt's declaration excludes the Islamic regions of the Philippines where fighting continues.

Sources: Linton (1975), Schlesinger and Bowman (1993), Morris and Morris (1996), other chronologies of American history, the *New York Times*, and the *Wall Street Journal*.

On November 1, 1898 at the Paris peace conference the United States demanded that Spain cede the Philippines to the United States. Spain resisted, but the final treaty, signed on December 10, called for Spain to cede the Philippines in exchange for $20 million.[1] The Philippine–American War that followed was an extension of the Spanish–American War, but it proved to be a very different kind of war. The Spanish–American War was short and decisive. It left many Americans proud of their idealism: they had gone to war to help a poor struggling colony achieve independence. The Philippine–American War, however, dragged on for years, and left the American people divided about its morality.

Initially, the Philippine–American War was fought along conventional lines, and the Americans went from success to success. The Philippine forces led by Emilio Aguinaldo, who had fought for independence from Spain and who were now fighting for independence from the United States, were quickly driven from Manila and then from Aguinaldo's capital at Malolos. The war had its American critics from the beginning, but most Americans probably celebrated these victories. But when the Filipinos turned to guerilla warfare, and a short war marked by decisive American victories became a long war marked by failures as well as successes, Americans became bitterly divided. Some continued to support the war, but others, repelled by the high costs and the use of torture, scorched-earth tactics, and similar policies, turned sharply against it.

In some ways the Philippine–American War followed the same path, and had the same consequences for the United States, as the nearly contemporary Boer War (1899–1902) had for Britain. Initially, the Boer War was fought along conventional lines. The British suffered some early defeats, but when the weight of their forces began to inflict defeats on the Boers, the British rejoiced. They celebrated the relief of Mafeking (May 1900) in the same way that Americans had celebrated the driving of Aguinaldo's forces from Manila and the capture of Malolos a year earlier. But when the Boers turned to guerilla warfare the story changed. Casualties were heavy and the methods used to quell the rebellion, scorched-earth tactics and concentration camps, were repellant. The Boer War would become the point at which the British lost their taste for empire. The Philippine–American War had a less decisive effect on American attitudes, perhaps because the United States was better able to absorb its costs, but in the United States as well the taste for empire soured.

[1] Puerto Rico and Guam were ceded to the United States as an indemnity.

The origins of the American conquest of the Philippines

The American conquest of the Philippines was a part, although not an indispensable part, of the "large policy" being pushed by US expansionists, in particular Theodore Roosevelt, the Assistant Secretary of the Navy in 1897 and 1898, and his close friend and ally Senator Henry Cabot Lodge of Massachusetts.[2] Their program included the annexation of Hawaii, the building of an isthmus canal, and the acquisition of colonies in the Caribbean and the Pacific. All of this was meant to support, and be supported by, the development of a strong aggressive navy. Roosevelt and his fellow expansionists had been influenced in particular by the writings of Captain, later Admiral, A. T. Mahan. Mahan's thesis was that sea power was crucial to achieving international hegemony, a truth abundantly proved, according to Mahan, by history. In his review of two of Mahan's books for the *Political Science Quarterly* (1894), Roosevelt wrote that Mahan had shown that it was not enough for the US navy to rely on mere commerce raiders, a cheap defensive device; instead "we must have a great fighting navy."

Much of the expansionist program was embedded in the Republican platform of 1896. The plank on the navy read as follows:

> The peace and security of the Republic and the maintenance of its rightful influence among the nations of the earth demand a naval power commensurate with its position and responsibilities. We, therefore, favor the continued enlargement of the navy, and a complete system of harbor and sea-coast defenses.

And the plank on foreign territories read as follows:

> The Hawaiian Islands should be controlled by the United States, and no foreign power should be permitted to interfere with them. The Nicaragua Canal should be built, owned and operated by the United States. And, by the purchase of the Danish Islands we should secure a much needed Naval station in the West Indies.

The Democratic platform, by way of contrast, was silent on these issues in 1896 (Wooley and Peters 2008).

[2] Robert Higgs (2008, 305–6) identifies four phases of America's neo-imperialist wars (the Philippine–American, Korean, Vietnam, and Iraq wars): I, upper-echelon plotting; II, outbreak and early combat; III, sustained combat and strategic stalemate; and IV, cessation of combat and workable resolution. While the term "upper-echelon plotting" is deliberately provocative, one has to concede that it fits fairly well.

Was the large policy an economic policy? The expansionists, it is true, offered an economic justification for their program: imperial expansion was necessary to protect and enlarge America's foreign trade. But the expansionist policy reflected at least to some degree a separable interest in national power and prestige for its own sake (Pratt 1932). Arthur Schlesinger Jr. (1986, 152) saw the expansionists as "aristocrats and warriors" who "hoped to redeem the odious plutocratic society by giving it a martial purpose."

In contrast to the expansionists, the American business community appears to have had little interest in colonies, especially in the Far East, prior to the Spanish–American War. However, the confluence of two events in 1898 led to a radical shift in business opinion. First was the heating up of European efforts to carve up China. In late 1897 Germany seized the Chinese port of Tsingtau and by January of 1898 China had agreed to cede the port and rights to economic development in the surrounding area to Germany. Russian warships then entered Port Arthur, and by May 1898 China had agreed to cede territory in the Liáoding peninsula to Russia. It now looked as though America was in danger of being excluded from the China trade by the European powers. The China trade was then a small part of America's foreign trade, but one could imagine that it could be important in the future, *provided* the door to China was kept open. True, in the end the China trade proved to be more myth than reality (Varg 1968), but that did not stop the fear of being excluded from having an important influence on American foreign policy.

The second event that influenced business opinion about the Far East, perhaps the most important, was Dewey's victory at Manila. In prospect the business community might not have seen the value of a war to capture the Philippines, but now that they had (seemingly) fallen into American hands, and now that the Europeans seemed intent on carving up China, an American presence in the Philippines – an American flag only 500 miles from China – seemed too valuable to throw away. In a short time business opinion in the United States turned 180 degrees. Julius Pratt (1934, 195) put it this way:

> Judging opinion as best we can from available expressions of it, it seemed safe to conclude that American business in the winter of 1897 and 1898 was opposed to war and either opposed to colonial expansion or oblivious to the problem. From similar evidence it seems equally safe to conclude that after the battle of Manila Bay American business became definitely imperialistic.

The course of the war

The Philippine–American War went extremely well for the United States – at first. Soon after Dewey destroyed the Spanish fleet in Manila Bay American troops landed near the city, quickly forcing the Spanish army there to surrender. Indeed, the Spanish garrison was ready to surrender – better the Americans than the Filipinos with whom the Spanish had been fighting a bitter and protracted war of independence. The battle with the Americans was largely ceremonial, although not without casualties.[3]

Emilio Aguinaldo, the leader of the Philippine insurrection, had been in exile in Hong Kong as part of a complicated deal with the Spanish. But the Americans had returned Aguinaldo to the Philippines so that he could take up the fight against the Spanish once again, which he did. After the Spanish garrison surrendered, Aguinaldo's Army of National Liberation moved into the suburbs of Manila and deployed opposite the Americans. A truce prevailed, but tensions mounted. Once the insurgents learned the terms of the treaty between the United States and Spain, which apparently denied them their independence, it was inevitable that the two sides would come to blows. There is still some debate, however, about which side was to blame for the outbreak of hostilities on February 4, 1899.

The Americans were triumphant in the battles that followed. The Filipinos, courageous but poorly trained and equipped, could not contain their assaults. Within a short time the Americans drove the Army of National Liberation from Manila. In the following weeks the Americans pressed their offensive, and on March 31, 1899 they entered Malolos, Aguinaldo's capital. Throughout the summer of 1899 American forces pushed into central Luzon and pursued Aguinaldo. Success did not come as easily as it had in the opening phase of the war. Nevertheless, the Americans gradually increased their control of the major agricultural regions of Luzon. By the fall of 1899 it looked to the Americans as though the war was almost over. But it then took a new and disquieting turn. The Filipinos disbanded the Army of National Liberation and began launching small-scale guerilla attacks. American forces were usually successful in setpiece

[3] The cartoonist John T. McCutcheon (1950, 120–1), who watched the battle from Dewey's flagship, provided a vivid depiction of the event.

military encounters – superior equipment and training combined with aggressive tactics carried the day – but they had no similarly effective answer for guerilla tactics.[4] It would not be the last time that the United States found thrilling victories over conventional forces giving way to frustrating guerilla warfare.

The anti-imperialist movement, which opposed the annexation of Cuba, the Philippines, and other territories, arose almost simultaneously with Dewey's victory at Manila Bay (Harrington 1935, 213). It enlisted an impressive group of supporters. Many of the names are still familiar today: former President Grover Cleveland, writers William James and Mark Twain, and industrialist Andrew Carnegie, among others.[5] The leading Republican to oppose the war was John Sherman, the father of the Sherman Anti-trust Act and other legislation. Sherman had served briefly as McKinley's Secretary of State and resigned in April 1898 for reasons of health. He disavowed the notion that he left the cabinet because he was opposed to the war, but nevertheless made his opposition to it and the annexation of the Philippines clear (*New York Times*, May 30, 1898, 3; August 18, 1898, 2). In a letter to the Anti-imperialist League he wrote: "I sympathize with Aguinaldo in his ambition to found a republic in the China Sea near the equator, and hope he may become the Washington of a new nation absolutely free from European and American influence" (*New York Times*, December 8, 1898, 1).

William Jennings Bryan, the titular head of the Democratic Party, had opposed annexation of the Philippines from the start.[6] He inevitably became the leader of the anti-imperialist movement. It was not, however, a match made in heaven: many of the leading anti-imperialists, such as Cleveland, Carnegie, and Sherman, supported the gold

[4] As the war began to sour the newspaper correspondents covering it became convinced that the army was attempting to paint an excessively optimistic portrait of how it was going. The correspondents decided to circulate a joint communiqué describing the situation and calling for more troops, a communiqué that was initially censored (McCutcheon 1950, 141).

[5] Agricultural interests that might have been hurt by the annexation of the Philippines, for example tobacco and sugar beets, supported the anti-imperialist movement, but did not play a prominent role (Harrington 1935, 220).

[6] Bryan, however, had encouraged Senate Democrats to ratify the treaty. Bryan maintained that his position was always that the best course of action would be to ratify the treaty, and then grant independence to the Philippines (*New York Times*, September 7, 1900).

standard, while Bryan was its leading opponent. Bryan, however, was an inspiring leader, and partly because of his leadership, the Democratic Party took a strong anti-imperialist stand (Harrington 1935). On September 4, 1899 at a Democratic meeting in New York the crowd cheered at the mention of Aguinaldo (*New York Times*, September 5, 1899, 3). Although some Republicans, like Sherman, were opposed to the subjugation of the Philippines, most supported the McKinley–Roosevelt policy of annexation. On September 24 a Republican crowd in Ohio heard Theodore Roosevelt, then governor of New York, give a stirring defense of the war: "It is absolutely impossible to save our honor except through victory, and it is equally impossible to win peace, to restore order in the islands, or to prepare the way to self government there, except through victory." For Roosevelt, giving in to Filipino demands for independence would be like giving in to Southern demands for independence in the Civil War or to a demand by the Sioux and Apache to allow them to expel white settlers from the lands these Native Americans had once held (*New York Times*, September 24, 1899, 3).

The Republican platform of 1900 endorsed America's attempt to subjugate the Philippines. The argument it offered was legal and political, not economic: it was America's duty to provide law and order in the islands under the Treaty of Paris (Wooley and Peters 2008). The Democratic Party platform of 1900, on which Bryan ran, unequivocally denounced the war. Economic issues were not the top concern, but the Democrats responded to what they claimed to be the Republican economic case for the war:

> The greedy commercialism which dictated the Philippine policy of the Republican administration attempts to justify it with the plea that it will pay; but even this sordid and unworthy plea fails when brought to the test of facts. The war of "criminal aggression" against the Filipinos, entailing an annual expense of many millions, has already cost more than any possible profit that could accrue from the entire Philippine trade for years to come. (Wooley and Peters 2008)

To be sure, this plank, apparently dictated by Bryan, narrows the question somewhat: the benefits to be compared with the costs are those derived in the Philippines. It ignores the Roosevelt–Lodge argument for a "large policy:" subjugation of the Philippines would pay dividends elsewhere, particularly in China.

The result of the election on November 6, 1900 was a resounding victory for McKinley. Explaining election results is always an uncertain project, but it seems doubtful that the election can be considered a referendum on the war. The key factors may well have been the prosperous state of the economy and the fear that the election of Bryan would bring monetary experiments and, possibly, a financial crisis (Bailey 1937; Harrington 1935, 227–8).[7] Even Andrew Carnegie, a staunch opponent of the subjugation of the Philippines, voted for McKinley and, as Carnegie saw it, continued prosperity (*New York Times*, November 4, 1900, 1). In the Philippines the defeat of Bryan was seen as a stunning setback for the insurgents, who had been counting on his victory to carry them to independence.

The intensity of the resistance to the Americans in the Philippines varied dramatically from place to place, as might have been expected in a chain of islands characterized by enormous linguistic, cultural, and religious diversity. In some areas there was no resistance. In other areas resistance was minimal, and soon gave way to cooperation. But in some areas resistance was bitter, intense, and prolonged. American tactics varied too, depending on the nature of the resistance, the political context, and the character of individual commanders.

Overall, the policy has been described as a combination of "attraction and chastisement."[8] Attraction was the part the army liked to talk about. It meant building schools, digging wells, rewriting the legal system, and, in general, bringing progressive government, as it was then understood, to the Philippines. Similar policies have been part of America's subsequent colonial wars.

Chastisement, on the other hand, was something best kept out of the public eye as far as the military was concerned. Before the election the military was restrained in its use of punitive tactics because of the fear that if their use became widely known it would swing the election to Bryan and end the American project in the Philippines. After Bryan's defeat, however, the army was free to "chastise" the Filipinos. Under General Arthur MacArthur (the father of Douglas MacArthur, the

[7] The economy, according to the NBER chronology (www.nber.org/cycles.html), peaked in June 1899, before the election, but the central political fact may have been the expansion of the preceding two years, which pulled the United States out of the depression of the 1890s.

[8] This phrase became the title of Max Boot's (2002, 99–128) chapter on the Philippine–American War.

World War II hero) these proved to be brutal tactics. American forces, in some areas, arrested and deported guerilla leaders, burned crops and livestock, limited access to food, arrested men of fighting age, and forcibly relocated and concentrated the population.

The island of Marinduque, about a dozen miles southwest of Luzon, witnessed some of the earliest experiments with punitive tactics.[9] In September 1900 US forces on Marinduque had suffered a stinging defeat in which four Americans died in combat and fifty, the entire surviving force, surrendered (Birtle 1997, 262). The American reaction was merciless. The first plan was to arrest all male inhabitants between the ages of fifteen and sixty and deport them to a prison island. This policy, however, proved hard to execute. Many men went into hiding, and when the navy ships patrolling the prison island were withdrawn in order to make them available for other actions, most of the prisoners escaped. The army then turned to tactics reminiscent of General Sherman's during his famous march to the sea in the Civil War: they began systematically destroying homes and supplies in the interior of the island to starve out the rebels and win the grudging support of the civilians, particularly the wealthier civilians who had the most to lose. The analogy between Sherman's tactics and the army's is not a historian's invention: army officers at the time reached back to the Civil War as well as the Indian Wars for examples of how to contend with a determined foe willing to use guerilla tactics in their own territory.

In the final phase of the campaign on Marinduque, the army combined internal devastation of the island with "concentration" – forcing the population to live in designated towns garrisoned by the Americans. In this way the interior became a wasteland that could not support the insurgency. On April 15, 1901, as a result of the direct pressure on the Marinduque insurgents, and of events elsewhere in the Philippines, resistance on the island came to an end with the surrender of the most important guerilla leader, Colonel Maximo Abad. The story on Marinduque remained hidden from the American public. As William Howard Taft was to admit in a letter to Elihu Root, the Secretary of War, "The severity with which the inhabitants have been dealt would not look well if a complete history were written out" (Birtle 1997, 255).

[9] My discussion of tactics on Marinduque is based on Birtle (1997).

Similar events on the island of Samar, however, did come to light. On September 28, 1901 insurgents armed with bolos (large knives similar to machetes) surprised a company of Americans at the small town of Balangiga. It was a brutal battle that left 54 Americans dead and most of the survivors wounded, while estimates of Filipino dead range from 50 to 250 (Boot 2002, 102). It was one of the worst defeats for the United States during the war. The press quickly labeled it the "Samar Massacre."

As on Marinduque, the army's response was brutal. General Jacob H. Smith gave Major Tony Waller, the man who would command his punitive mission in Samar, simple instructions: "I want no prisoners. I wish you to kill and burn; the more you kill and the more you burn, the more you will please me" (Boot 2002, 120). Whether these orders were meant to be taken literally is a matter of dispute, but there is no doubt that a brutal campaign followed. The island was blockaded, the population was forced into zones of concentration – producing malnutrition, unsanitary living conditions, and cholera – villages were razed, animals and crops were burned, and suspected insurgents were tortured and killed (Silbey 2007, 193–201). The story might have remained hidden, but early in 1902 Major Waller decided to execute eleven prisoners without the benefit of a trial. He soon found himself charged with murder. Eventually Waller was acquitted, but General Smith, whose orders came out at Waller's trial, was forced to resign.

The Senate, as a result of these revelations, investigated the campaign in Samar and the conduct of the war in the Philippines more generally, including the use of torture in the form of the "water cure." It was a thoroughly partisan debate: leading Republicans defended the conduct of the war, and the Democrats attacked it. Senator Henry Cabot Lodge, a staunch supporter of the war, rose to defend punitive tactics. He pointed out, according to the *New York Times* report, that similar actions had been taken by Nero against the Christians and by the Tartars against practically everyone in their march across Europe, thus refuting, at least to Lodge's satisfaction, the charge that the cruelties in the Philippines were unprecedented. Senator Rawlins of Utah answered for the Democrats and in a fiery speech blamed not the army, but rather the administration and Senator Lodge himself for the atrocities (*New York Times*, May 6, 1902, 3).

Although the campaign in Samar was the best-known punitive campaign, there were other areas where these tactics were used.

In the Batangas province of southern Luzon, the army again turned to confinement of the population in concentration camps and the destruction of buildings, crops, and livestock outside the camps to crush the resistance. Some 11,000 Filipinos are said to have died in the camps in Batangas, mainly of cholera and malaria. The army attempted to control the diseases, but it is hard to resist the conclusion that the concentration of the population contributed to the epidemics (Boot 2002, 124).

Although the resistance in some areas was stiff, the rebellion began to collapse. On March 23, 1901 an American force captured Aguinaldo, an important symbolic blow, which reflected the deterioration of the rebellion in Luzon. In the latter part of 1901 and the beginning of 1902 more and more of the Philippines was brought under American control. By July 4, 1902 President Roosevelt was in a position to announce an end of the war. With three orders – a general amnesty for Filipinos who had fought against the United States, and orders through the Secretary of War ending the role of military governor and commending the performance of the army in the Philippines – Roosevelt announced that, as far as he was concerned, the war was over. The preamble to the amnesty announced the end of the war, but also contained an important caveat (*New York Times*, 4 July 1902, 1):[10]

> Whereas the insurrection against the sovereignty and authority of the United States is now at an end and peace has been established in all parts of the archipelago except in the country inhabited by the Moro tribes, to which this proclamation does not apply . . .

Indeed, the fighting in the Muslim areas of the Philippines (Mindanao and some smaller islands) would continue for a number of years. Some scholars see this fighting, with some justice, as a different war with different dates, a Moro–American War lasting from 1898 to, say, 1913. Actions in the Moro–American War occurred at irregular

[10] Roosevelt's stirring homage to the armed forces contained an oblique reference to criticisms of the tactics used to suppress the rebellion. "With surprisingly few individual exceptions its [the army's] course has been characterized by humanity and kindness to the prisoner and the non-combatant." It also contains a reference to earlier wars that would be unacceptable today: "Utilizing the lessons of the Indian Wars, it has relentlessly followed the guerilla bands to their fastnesses in mountains and jungles and crushed them."

intervals and were small by the standards of the major wars to follow, but nevertheless involved fierce fighting. In March 1905, for example, fifteen Americans and six Filipino scouts died in action against the Moros. In June 1913 General John J. Pershing, who would lead the American armies in World War I, lost fifteen men from a combined American–Filipino force while defeating a Moro army which lost about five hundred men. All told, it is estimated that the United States suffered 125 deaths and 323 woundings in actions against the Moros. The peak force engaged was about 12,000 (Clodfelter 2001, 272). The ending date for the Moro–American War refers to the time when military operations were transferred from the United States to the central government of the Philippines. Periodic eruptions of fighting, however, continued in this area for many years.

Why was the US effort in the Philippines successful, at least in the sense that armed resistance in most of the archipelago came to an end after about three and a half years? Historians of the war have pointed to several factors.

1 Perhaps the most important factor favoring the Americans, most historians agree, was the naval blockade. This restricted the access of the insurgents to weapons and food, and prevented insurgents on different islands from cooperating, even when differences in language and religion did not. Sometimes the insurgents had to rely on the bolo. Even when they had rifles, perhaps captured from the Spanish or the Americans, their ammunition was often locally made and ineffective.
2 The insurgency had a number of homegrown problems. Aguinaldo had sought to inspire the insurgents by stressing that Bryan and his supporters favored independence for the Philippines. He may well have believed that Bryan's triumph was likely. While this may have been an effective strategy for a time, Bryan's defeat then undermined morale. Many of the leaders in the insurgency, moreover, were drawn from the wealthy landowning class. Therefore, the insurgency lacked the promise, explicit in later Communist revolutions, that a successful war would produce a redistribution of land and an improvement in the standard of living of the peasantry.
3 It also appears that "attraction and chastisement" was effective. It is the latter part of the equation that is the most controversial. Did the United States succeed because it employed brutal tactics such as

concentration, destruction of the rural economy, torture, and execution of civilians without benefit of trial – tactics that would never win approval from the American people – or were these merely exceptions to a more benign policy? The controversies about how widely such policies were used and about how much they ultimately contributed to the pacification of the Philippines are likely to continue.

The cost of the war

The deaths and non-mortal casualties suffered by Americans in the Philippine–American War seem to have been largely forgotten in the United States. Neither the *Historical Statistics of the United States*, nor various US military websites that I searched, reported deaths or non-mortal casualties in the war. Yet the Philippine–American War was more costly in terms of American lives lost and wounds suffered than the Spanish–American War. This tells us something, surely, about the nature of our collective memory and its tendency to reinvent the past in a more favorable light. The war we remember was the "splendid little war" in Cuba in which the United States quickly liberated that island from the yoke of foreign domination – however accurate that characterization of the war may be. The war we forget is the long and bitter war in which the United States conquered the Philippines.

To compare the two wars, consider the figures for the army. In the Spanish–American War, 369 army personnel (or by an alternative estimate 379) were killed in action or died of wounds sustained in combat (Appendix 2). By May 1900, the army was reporting that 656 men had died in combat or of wounds sustained in combat in the Philippines: 267 regulars and 389 volunteers. Many of the latter had volunteered to free Cuba, not to conquer the Philippines.[11] Overall, there would be 1,064 army battle deaths in the Philippines. Again, as in the Spanish–American War, there would be a larger toll from tropical diseases: malaria, cholera, dysentery, and so on. In the Spanish–American War, some 4,795 men died of disease; in the Philippines 4,874. Deaths from injuries also appear to have been higher in the Philippines: 1,063 in the Philippine–American War compared with 288 in the Spanish–American War. Overall, the army lost 5,462

[11] The figures for the US army to May 1900 are from US Senate (1900, 4).

soldiers in the Spanish–American War and 7,001 soldiers in the later war. The number of men wounded was also higher in the Philippines: 2,911 compared with 1,662 in the Spanish–American War (Appendix 2). Losses on the Philippine side, military and civilian, are less certain. The numbers put forward are fraught with political significance (how cruel was the United States?) and have as a result have been the subject of much controversy. Clodfelter (2001, 272), who has a good sense of casuality figures based on his wide reading of the literature on wartime casualties, says that "at least" 16,000 Filipinos were killed in combat and that "possibly as many as" 200,000 civilians died from "disease, starvation, and privation."

What about the financial cost of the war? In early 1902 the Senate called on the naval and war secretaries for estimates of the cost of the Philippine–American War. Both William H. Moody for the navy and Elihu Root for the War Department made determined efforts to comply, and came up with reasonable estimates. The costs for the navy were $20,855,637 at 1897 prices and those for the army $170,408,745.[12] These totals, plus the $20 million the United States paid to Spain for the Philippines, make a total of $211,264,382 (about 1 percent of average GDP), a sum not very different from the cost of the Spanish–American War of, say, $274 million.

The main uncertainty for Moody and Root was how to treat expenditures that might have been incurred even in the absence of the war in the Philippines, for example food and clothing for troops or coal for the navy, which would have been required even if the army and navy forces were stationed in the United States. In other words, to use the economic jargon, how (if at all) should they calculate the marginal costs of the war? The figure of $211,264,382 includes these fixed costs, but it could be argued that they should be excluded. Root simply noted the problem; Moody estimated that perhaps two-thirds of the naval expenditures that he was attributing to the war would have been incurred in any case. It was natural for Root and Moody to raise this issue. Calculating only the marginal cost of the war would make the war look less costly.

[12] The estimate for the army is from US Senate (1902a); the navy estimate is from US Senate (1902b). I adjusted the estimates for price changes using the GDP deflator, and made a small allowance to take the figures through July 4, 1902 – the official end of the war.

I checked the official figures with a calculation similar to the one made previously for the Spanish–American War. In each year from 1900 to 1903 I computed one-half the difference between total military spending and 1897 military spending adjusted for inflation and then summed the results. The figure of one-half was chosen arbitrarily to split additional spending between the Philippines and other areas, mainly the Caribbean. The result of this "outsider's" calculation was almost identical to the official figure.

In 1912 the House asked President Taft to state "the cost which has accrued to the Government of the United States, from the beginning of and as the result of the occupation of the Philippine Islands by the United States." If anyone could do such a calculation it would be Taft: he had served as the chief American civil administrator in the Philippines and as Secretary of War before becoming President. In a testy reply, Taft insisted that there were relatively few expenditures (about $3.5 million) that had not been recompensed in full by the government of the Philippines. Even these small expenditures, according to Taft, were more than offset by monies spent by the Philippine government on behalf of the United States for military purposes during the period 1898–1900. Therefore, all the costs of the occupation, Taft claimed, had been more than offset by monies received from the Philippines except for expenses resulting from "military and naval operations in and about the archipelago and from the construction of fortifications and naval stations therein" (Taft 1912). But the latter costs, Taft explained, could not be estimated because they could not be separated from the overall budgets of the army and the navy. Yes, there was an army in the Philippines, he acknowledged, but it would have to be maintained at home if it were not there (although the army was now larger than it had been before the Spanish–American War). Yes, there was a naval squadron in the Philippines, but the US had had a squadron in the Far East for many years. The right number to calculate, according to Taft, was the small marginal cost of the occupation, and that calculation could not be made. The question of how much the United States had spent in the Philippines was simply not answerable. Neither of the secretaries nor Taft mentioned the veterans' compensation and disability payments that would have to be paid in years to come. These will be considered in more detail below.

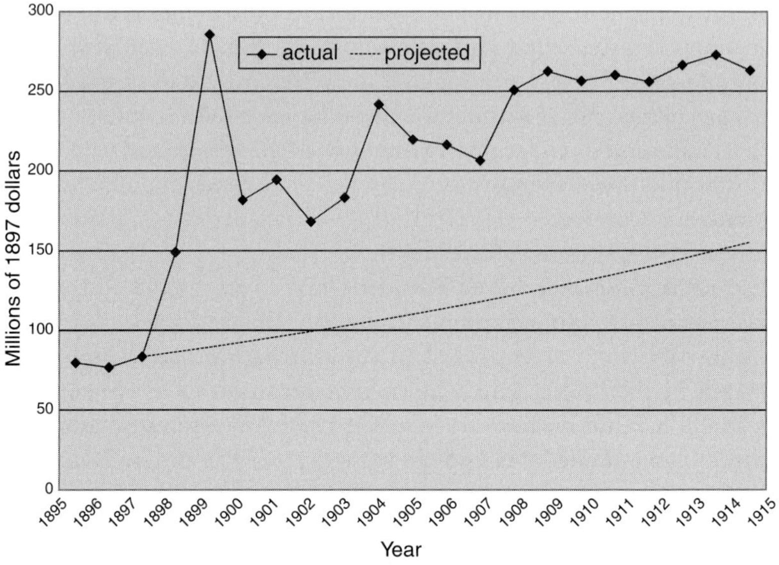

Figure 4.1 US military expenditures, 1895–1915 (millions of 1897 dollars). Military spending, defined as the sum of army and navy spending, was deflated by the GDP deflator (Carter *et al.* 2006, series Ea638, Ea639, and Ca13). The projected series is the actual level in 1897 projected forward at the growth rate observed in the previous five years. Military spending ratcheted upward during the Spanish–American War, and never returned to the prewar trend.

The costs of a "large policy"

While it is hard to measure the costs of specific military operations, as Taft and the Secretaries of War and the Navy argued, it is possible to look at the cumulative impact of imperialism on the military budget. Figure 4.1 plots actual US military spending from 1895 to 1915 and a projection of military spending based on the actual level in 1897 and the growth rate in the previous five years. All sums were deflated using the GDP deflator. Evidently, military spending rose during the Spanish–American and Philippine–American wars, fell back a little after the wars ended, but remained higher for the remainder of the pre-WWI era. Military spending during this era provides a clear example of the "ratchet effect" of wars on spending stressed by Robert Higgs (1987). The difference between the two lines is a measure of the resource costs of the Spanish–American and Philippine–American wars, and of postwar imperialism.

The costs of the Spanish–American War (including veterans' benefits) amounted to about $24 billion in year 2008 dollars, 5.5 percent of average GDP during the war. The costs of the Philippine–American War amounted to about $13 billion (year 2008 dollars), 2.6 percent of average GDP.[13] The costs of both wars and postwar imperialism together, Theodore Roosevelt's "large policy," amounted to about $86 billion, nearly 16 percent of average GDP (Table 4.1).

One way to think about these costs is to compare them with the costs of large civilian government projects. The Panama Canal, the largest government-financed civilian project of the day – which was itself part of America's imperial ambitions – cost about $397 million, including a payment of $25 million made by the Wilson administration to Colombia, about $6.5 billion in year 2008 dollars (Hutchinson and Ungo 2004, 15).[14] Thus the cost of the Spanish–American War was about 3.7 Panama Canals; the cost of the Philippine–American War was about 1.9 Panama Canals; and the cost of both wars and Theodore Roosevelt's "large policy," that is the cost of turn-of-the-century imperialism, was about 13.1 Panama Canals (plus the Panama Canal!). The costs, evidently, were very high. The less visible cost of maintaining a larger military force year after year, moreover, exceeded the costs (excluding veterans' benefits) incurred during the period of active fighting. Another, more conventional, way to look at the costs of the wars is in terms of economic growth forgone. Real GDP grew by

[13] I used the implicit GDP price index as the deflator. This is appropriate because the idea is to measure the opportunity cost (output sacrificed) of military spending. A price index for military goods would address what America bought for its expenditures.

[14] Clearly the Panama Canal could not have been constructed for $6 billion in 2008. The appropriate yardstick for putting historical costs into today's money depends on the question being addressed. A wage index, or an index of construction costs, would yield a more realistic figure, if the goal was to determine what it would cost to produce the same project today. But using a project built closer in time to the war – the Panama Canal was completed about ten years after the end of major fighting in the Philippines – but still in operation today, provides another useful way of putting old values into today's money.

Table 4.1 *The costs of increased military spending after 1897*

	Incremental costs during the period of active conflict (millions of current dollars)	Incremental costs during the period of active conflict in constant dollars (billions of 2008 dollars)	Incremental costs as a share of average real GDP during the war (%)	Veterans' benefits discounted to the midpoint of the war at 4.5% (billions of 2008 dollars)	Total costs (billions of 2008 dollars)	Total costs as a share of average GDP during the war (%)
Spanish–American War (1898–9)[a]	274	6.09	1.56 [1.30]	17.92	24.01	5.54
Philippine–American War (1899–1902)[b]	230 (211)	4.93	1.05 [1.09]	7.58	12.51	2.64
Turn-of-the-century imperialism (1898–1915)[c]	3,073	60.08	11.17 [11.14]	25.50	85.58	15.62

Notes: The dates in parentheses show the fiscal years "affected" by the war. The numbers in square brackets show the sum of the share of war spending in GDP over the course of the war years.

[a] Total military spending in 1898 and 1899 less spending in the corresponding categories in 1897 (Carter *et al.* 2006, the sum of series Ea638 and Ea639). GDP and the GDP deflator are Carter *et al.* (2006, Ca10 and Ca13). Veterans' benefits are from Edwards (2010, Table 2).

[b] The sum of one-half the difference between current military spending in each year from 1900 through 1903 and military spending in 1897 adjusted for inflation. I have also included the $20 million paid to Spain for the Philippines. The estimate in parentheses is US Senate (1902a, 2; 1902b). The figure of one-half was chosen arbitrarily, with the idea that the additional military spending needed to be split in some fashion between the Philippines and the Caribbean. As it turned out, the resulting estimate was quite close to the official estimate. Veterans' benefits are from Edwards (2010, Table 2).

[c] This is an estimate of the total costs of the Spanish–American War, the Philippine–American War, and the higher level of military spending maintained after these wars. It was computed, as described in the text, as the difference between actual military spending and a projection based on pre-Spanish–American War spending. Veterans' benefits are simply the sum of benefits for veterans of the Spanish–American and Philippine–American wars. Thus, it ignores retirement benefits for military personnel serving in peacetime.

about $11 billion per year (at year 2008 prices) from 1897 to 1915. Therefore, the Spanish–American War absorbed about 2.2 years' growth, the Philippine–American War absorbed about 1.1 years' growth, and both wars and postwar imperialism together absorbed about 7.7 years' worth of growth in GDP. War and imperialism came at a high price.

Imperialism and trade

What were the consequences of conquering the Philippines, and more generally of an imperialist military policy, for American trade with Asia and the Pacific? Figure 4.2 shows America's trade with the Asia-Pacific region from 1880 to 1915. Exports and imports are shown as percentages of GDP. Exports did rise after the assertion of American naval power at the turn of the century, from 0.25 percent of GDP to 0.60 percent. This might be counted a gain, albeit a small one, that could be attributed, however tenuously, to the new policy.[15]

This small gain in trade is not, of course, the same as a gain in welfare. For one thing, the increased trade with the Asia-Pacific region may to some extent have been diverted from other areas. Most theories that attribute expansionary effects to foreign trade (for example, a traditional Keynesian model) focus on the balance of payments surplus. The balance of trade with the Asia-Pacific region, however, remained persistently negative after the turn of the century. The deficit narrowed somewhat in the years after the Spanish–American and Philippine–American wars, but increased a little toward the end of the period. Anyone who expected the Spanish–American and Philippine–American wars and the adoption of the Roosevelt–Lodge policy of an assertive navy-based foreign policy to provide a significant fiscal stimulus to the American economy through its effects on American exports would have been disappointed.

[15] Mitchener and Weidenmier (2008) found that being a US colony had a statistically significant positive effect on US investment. The Philippines was the most important colony; the category also included Guam, Puerto Rico, the Virgin Islands, and a few other areas. And investment in the Philippines and other tropical Pacific islands, as shown in Table 4.2, rose substantially in percentage terms. But this investment remained a small part of the overall picture.

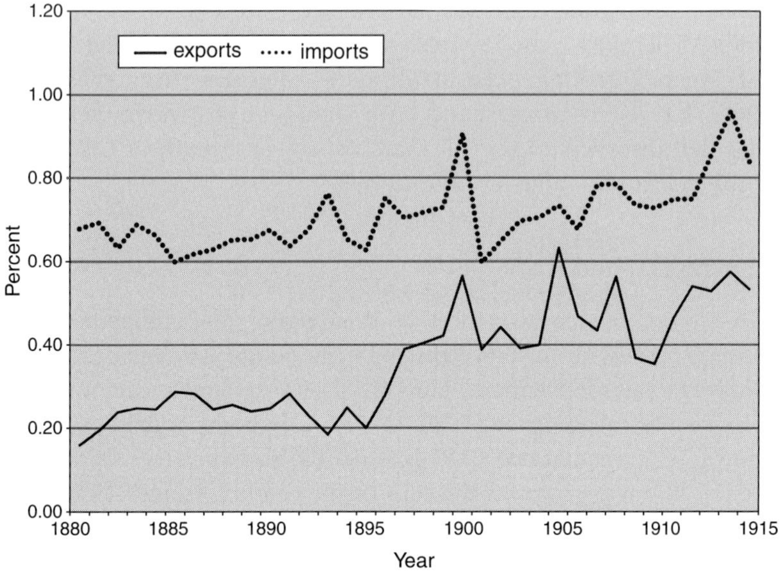

Figure 4.2 US trade with Asia and the Pacific, 1880–1915, as a share of GDP. Exports to Asia and the Pacific rose after the Spanish–American and Philippine–American wars, but never reached 1 percent of GDP, and never completely closed the gap with imports.
Source: Exports and imports: Carter *et al.* (2006, series Ee545, Ee549, Ee563, and Ee567). GDP: Carter *et al.* (2006, series Ca10).

As I noted in Chapter 2, a number of scholars have argued that one factor behind turn-of-the-century imperialism was the desire of financiers to increase foreign investment. Wall Street, in other words, might have benefited from increased commissions from the placing of foreign securities or arranging direct investments, and pressured the United States into imperialist adventures, even if the country as a whole, or even the business community as a whole, did not benefit. What do the numbers show? America's investments abroad did increase dramatically after 1897. Table 4.2 shows America's foreign investments in 1897, 1908, and 1914. Total US foreign investment rose from $684.5 million in 1897 to $3,513.8 million in 1914, a vigorous rate of increase: 9.62 percent per year. During the same period the GDP deflator was rising only about 2.08 percent per year. Increased investment in the areas directly affected by US imperialism, however, account for only a small part of the overall increase. Investment in

Table 4.2 ***America's foreign investments, 1897–1914 (millions of dollars)***

	1897	1908	1914	Share of increase (%)
Direct investments				
Europe	131.0	369.3	573.3	21.92
Canada and Newfoundland	159.7	405.4	618.4	22.73
Mexico	200.2	416.4	587.1	19.17
Central America	21.2	37.9	89.6	3.39
South America	37.9	104.3	323.1	14.13
Africa	1.0	5.0	13.0	0.59
International including banking	10.0	20.0	30.0	0.99
Cuba and the other West Indies	49.0	195.5	281.3	11.51
Philippines and other Oceania	1.5	10.0	17.0	0.77
Asia	23.0	74.7	119.5	4.78
Total	634.5	1,638.5	2,652.3	100.00
Direct and portfolio (total) investments				
Europe	151.0	489.2	691.8	19.11
Canada and Newfoundland	189.7	697.2	867.2	23.95
Mexico	200.2	672.0	853.5	23.09
Central America	21.2	41.0	93.2	2.54
South America	37.9	129.7	365.7	11.59
Africa	1.0	5.0	13.2	0.43
International including banking	10.0	20.0	30.0	0.71
Cuba and the other West Indies	49.0	225.5	336.3	10.15
Philippines and other Oceania	1.5	10.0	17.0	0.55
Asia	23.0	235.2	245.9	7.88
Total	684.5	2,524.8	3,513.8	100.00

Source: Lewis and Schlotterbeck (1938, 606).
Note: Davis and Cull (1994, 81) present a similar table also based on Lewis. The last column is the increase in a row between 1897 and 1914 divided by the total increase, and expressed as a percentage of the total increase.

Cuba and its neighbors accounts for only 10.2 percent of the total increase, investment in the Philippines and its neighbors for only 0.55 percent of the total increase, and Asia (recall that conquering the Philippines was supposed to prop open the door to China) accounted for only 7.9 percent of the increase. Canada, Mexico, and Europe gained the lion's share of increased US foreign investment. It is hard to believe that the new form of American imperialism had much to do with these increases.

Much of the investment in Asia, moreover, was the result of increased investments in Japanese securities. These investments, associated mainly with the Russo-Japanese War, reflected the rise of Japan as a military and industrial power, more than rising US imperialism. The direct investments in Cuba and in the Philippines are linked more directly to US imperialism. But in both cases American economic policies tended to divert investment from other areas. Legislation, as I noted above, lowered the tariff barriers on Cuban and Philippine sugar. It made sense to expand production in Cuba and the Philippines, but the investment may simply have been diverted from regions that did not enjoy the benefits of favored status under the tariffs. Lance Davis and Robert Cull (1994, 80) compared the geographic patterns of American foreign investment in 1897 and 1914 and concluded that "Although, by 1914, the relative role of Mexico had declined by a small amount and the proportion directed towards South America had increased somewhat, overall, the patterns had changed little." The Spanish–American and Philippine–American wars that had created (at a substantial cost) an American empire evidently had little impact on the pattern of American foreign investment.[16]

Still, the surge in US capital exports after 1897, it must be acknowledged, remains something of a mystery. Milton Friedman and Anna Schwartz (1963, 142–8) investigated the question at length, and explored a long list of candidate explanations – uncertainty about the monetary standard, the outbreak of the Boer War, domestic movements in stock and bond yields, and so on – but concluded that none of the candidate explanations they looked at was convincing. The best explanation at the present time would seem to be that

[16] Mitchener and Weidenmier (2005a and 2005b), however, show that America's gunboat diplomacy in the Caribbean and Latin America had a significant impact on the price of sovereign debt, and may help explain the increased investment in the region as a whole.

capital exports were partly a response to the great opportunities that American corporations saw in direct foreign investments, the largest component of US foreign investment at this time. Mira Wilkins (1970, 70–217) shows how company after company found new opportunities in country after country. In at least one case, she shows, the Spanish–American War created headaches rather than opportunities. Singer (sewing machines) was doing a good business in Spain when the war began and it had to scramble to distance itself from America in order to hang on to its Spanish customers. One device was to collect funds for the relief of seamen and their families who had been injured or killed in the war.

There may be non-pecuniary benefits from imperialism that, at least to some, justify the expense. The Republicans continued their support for the Philippine intervention for years, offering such justifications. In 1904 the Republican platform hailed the end of the war in the Philippines:

In the Philippines we have suppressed insurrection, established order, and given to life and property a security never known there before. We have organized civil government, made it effective and strong in administration, and have conferred upon the people of those islands the largest civil liberty they have ever enjoyed.

And suggested a tangible strategic benefit for the United States:

By our possession of the Philippines we were enabled to take prompt and effective action in the relief of the legations at Peking and a decisive part in preventing the partition and preserving the integrity of China.

To be sure, one could debate how important control of the Philippines was to the relief of Peking. It may have been possible to negotiate coaling stations and a naval base in the Philippines without conquering the islands. The strategic value of the Philippines to the United States could not in any case be given a dollar value to set against the cost of the war.

The Democrats in 1904, however, saw only crude attempts by special interests to benefit from American control of the Philippines.

The endeavor of the Secretary of War, by pledging the Government's endorsement for "promoters" in the Philippine Islands to make the United States a partner in speculative exploitation of the archipelago, which was only temporarily held up by the opposition of Democratic

Senators in the last session, will, if successful, lead to entanglements from which it will be difficult to escape.

In their 1908 platforms the parties were at it again.

In the Philippines insurrection has been suppressed, law is established and life and property made secure. Education and practical experience are there advancing the capacity of the people for government, and the policies of McKinley and Roosevelt are leading the inhabitants step by step to an ever-increasing measure of home rule. (Republican platform 1908)

We condemn the experiment in imperialism as an inexcusable blunder which has involved us in enormous expense, brought us weakness instead of strength, and laid our nation open to the charge of abandoning a fundamental doctrine of self-government. We favor an immediate declaration of the nation's purpose to recognize the independence of the Philippine Islands as soon as a stable government can be established, such independence to be guaranteed by us as we guarantee the independence of Cuba, until the neutralization of the islands can be secured by treaty with other powers. In recognizing the independence of the Philippines our Government should retain such land as may be necessary for coaling stations and naval bases. (Democratic platform 1908)

There were similar contrasts in the platforms of 1912 and 1916. The Republican platform falls silent on the Philippine question in the 1920s, but Democratic platforms in the 1920s and early 1930s continued to call for the country's independence.

The costs of an imperial policy after 1898, to sum up, were high; they were the equivalent of net additions to real GDP for six years. Economic benefits in the form of substantial increases in trade with Asia and the Caribbean, the most frequently cited potential benefits, are hard to find. But there were potential benefits along another dimension that must be acknowledged even while they are hard to measure. Imperialism helped build the US military: new ships for the navy were constructed, and men and officers in the army were trained. When the United States entered World War I General Pershing was recalled from the campaign he was leading against the Moros in the Philippines and given command of America's expeditionary force. In 1918 many Americans thought that their military services, especially the army and the army air force, were woefully unprepared, and that the government should have been spending more, not less, on the military in the years before 1918.

The veterans of the Spanish–American and Philippine–American wars

The veterans of the Spanish–American and Philippine–American wars received benefits greater than those received by veterans of earlier conflicts, as might be expected given the rise in per capita income, and, perhaps somewhat more surprising, benefits comparable to those received by veterans of later wars. Indeed, by some measures, the veterans of the Spanish–American and Philippine–American wars were the best rewarded of all of America's veterans.

The veterans of the Spanish–American and Philippine–American wars formed several organizations immediately after the wars (they later merged to become the Veterans of Foreign Wars) that lobbied on behalf of the veterans. Success came in 1920 when a combined disability and service pension bill was passed. Thus, the veterans of the Spanish–American War had to wait only eighteen years for a service pension compared with the veterans of the Civil War who had to wait twenty-eight years, and the veterans of earlier wars who had to wait even longer. Under the 1920 act disabled veterans were entitled to between $12 and $30 per month, depending on their degree of disability. Under the old-age provision, a veteran was eligible for a pension of $12 per month at age 62, rising to $18 at age 68, $24 at age 72, and $30 at age 75 (Weber and Schmeckebier 1934, 53). Monthly per capita GDP in 1920 was $68 (Carter *et al.* 2006, series Ca12), so the maximum pension was more than 40 percent of per capita income.

The case for a pension was based, first of all, on precedent. The soldiers of all previous wars, including the Revolution, had received both disability payments and service pensions. Indeed, the granting of pensions was so well established by 1897 that it could be said that the promise of a pension was implicit in the call for volunteers. The veterans of the Spanish–American and Philippine–American wars, and their supporters, also made a number of additional arguments for a pension that were unique to these wars. The veterans it was claimed, with some justice, had undergone especially terrible hardships while fighting overseas. True, the losses from combat were low compared with the Civil War: deaths averaged 8 per 1,000 for men serving in the Spanish–American and Philippine–

American wars, compared with 165 per 1,000 for Union soldiers and sailors in the Civil War. Death rates were also higher in the Mexican War (Carter *et al.* 2006, series Ed1–5 and Ed2). You would have to go back to the War of 1812 to find a death rate comparable to the rate experienced during the Spanish–American and Philippine–American wars.

Death rates and similar statistics, however, do not tell the whole story. Living conditions in Cuba and the Philippines were often horrible, and many soldiers contracted tropical diseases that the military medical services were unable to recognize and treat. Richard Severo and Lewis Milford (1989, 187–228) provide a powerful description of what befell the veterans of the Spanish–American War. An epidemic of tropical diseases raced through the troops after the close of the campaign in Cuba. The veterans were then transported to Montauk on Long Island where they were forced to live, and in many cases die, while the army seemed maddeningly slow to provide adequate housing and medical care.

The Philippine–American War also took a heavy toll. Again, tropical diseases were the main cause of death and disability. The guerilla war, moreover, added psychological costs that were new to Americans. Soldiers stationed in the "boondocks" – an Americanization of a Tagalog word for mountain – suffered from long periods of boredom interrupted by short and dangerous encounters with the guerillas. And some veterans suffered when they were asked to carry out actions against civilians that violated their ethical values.

Supporters of a pension also pointed to the success of the "splendid little war." Through the efforts of these veterans the United States had gained an empire and become a global power. It was accomplished quickly and at relatively low cost because of the great courage displayed on the battlefield. Shouldn't the veterans be rewarded for accomplishing so much? Does that mean that the pension should have been smaller if the American effort had met with disaster, if the brutal war in the Philippines had failed, and the United States had been forced to leave the Philippines? The question seems to have a simple answer: the pension should not be based on the success of American arms. History, however, suggests that there could be a connection between the success of arms and the willingness of Americans to award a pension. It may be that part of the problem the veterans of the War of 1812 had in securing a pension was the result of the perception that the troops had not performed well. It was also said that the Spanish–American and Philippine–American wars had soothed the psychic scars left from the Civil War because Northerners and Southerners fought on the same side.[17] Finally, it helped that Theodore Roosevelt, a veteran, became the President of the United States.

The small number of troops involved also worked in favor of the veterans of the Spanish–American and Philippine–American wars. Only about 0.42 percent of the population served in the Spanish–American War and only 0.16 percent in the Philippine–American War, compared with 6.87 percent during the Civil War or 4.58 percent during World War I (Carter *et al.* 2006, series AA7 and Ed1). True, the small number of veterans meant that they could offer relatively few votes to politicians who supported their cause. On the other hand, it was possible to satisfy the demands of the Spanish–American and Philippine–American War veterans without significantly raising taxes. The pension for the veterans of the Spanish–American War was debated at the same time as the so-called bonus for the veterans of World War I. But the weighty objection to the WWI bonus, that it would require the maintenance of high wartime taxes, did not apply to a pension for the veterans of the Spanish–American War, and the latter sailed through Congress.

Further liberalizations of the pension for the veterans of the Spanish–American War in the form of relaxation of the eligibility requirements and increases in the pension rates occurred in 1926 and 1930. The liberalization of 1930 was passed over a veto by President Hoover. Hoover objected to eliminating the requirement that a disability not be due to the "vicious habits" of the veteran, objected to a reduction in the minimum service from ninety to seventy days, and objected to the lack of a means test on the grounds that it was unfair to tax the poor in order to pay a pension to a well-off veteran (Weber and Schmeckebier 1934, 236–7). The pension was abrogated by the Economy Act of 1934, but it was quickly reinstated.

The veterans of the Spanish–American and Philippine–American wars, to sum up, were, by some measures, the best rewarded of all veterans. They had everything going for them: these were small wars, so the additional tax burden associated with rewarding the veterans was small, and American arms were successful in

[17] This was truer of the Spanish–American War than of the Philippine–American War. Many of the volunteers who served in the latter were from western states.

producing a new empire and global standing for the United States. According to Edwards's calculations (2010, 35–6) veterans of the Spanish–American and Philippine–American wars received about $84,000 (present value in 2008 dollars) compared with $66,000 for veterans of World War I, $87,000 for veterans of World War II, and $38,000 for veterans of the Korean War. All told, veterans' benefits accounted for nearly 80 percent of the cost of the Spanish–American and Philippine–American wars.

5 *World War I*

The world must be made safe for democracy. Its peace must be planted upon the tested foundations of political liberty. We have no selfish ends to serve. We desire no conquest, no dominion. We seek no indemnities for ourselves, no material compensation for the sacrifices we shall freely make.

From President Woodrow Wilson's message to Congress asking for a declaration of war against Germany, April 2, 1917

A chronology of World War I

1914		
June	28	Archduke Franz Ferdinand is shot.
August		The beginning of the war.
1915		
May	7	The sinking of the British liner *Lusitania*. Loss of American life; talk of war increases in the United States.
September	1	Germany pledges not to attack civilian ships without warning.
November	21	Germany resumes attacking civilian ships without warning.
1916		
May	4	Germany pledges not to attack civilian ships without warning.
June	3	The National Defense Act expands the army.
August	29	The Council of National Defense is established.
September	7	US Shipping Board and Emergency Fleet Corporation.

1917		
February	1	Germany renews unrestricted submarine warfare.
	3	USS *Housatonic* sunk; USA breaks diplomatic relations with Germany.
March	1	The contents of the Zimmermann note proposing a secret alliance between Germany and Mexico are made public.
	17	German submarines sink three American merchant vessels.
April	6	USA declares war on Germany.
	24	Liberty Loan Act.
May	14	First Liberty Loan offered.
	18	Selective Service Act.
July	28	War Industries Board.
August	10	Lever Food and Fuel Control Act.
October	1	Second Liberty Loan offered.
	3	War Revenue Act.
December	18	Prohibition Amendment.
	26	US Railroad Administration.
1918		
January		Maximum Prices for Steel.
March		Germans begin a massive offensive on the western front.
	4	Bernard Baruch heads the War Industries Board.
April	5	War Finance Corporation.
	6	Third Liberty Loan offered.
	8	National War Labor Board established.
May		First independent action by the American Expeditionary Force.
June		Second Battle of the Marne – German offensive stopped.

	18	Wilson presents Congress with a list of "fourteen points" that would provide the basis of a lasting peace. Point fourteen was a League of Nations.
September		900,000 Americans in the Battle of Meuse–Argonne.
	28	Fourth Liberty Loan offered.
November	11	Armistice.
December	4	Wilson sails for Europe to begin the peace negotiations.
1919		
February	24	Wilson returns to the United States to discuss his proposal for a League of Nations with members of Congress.
March	13	Wilson returns to Europe to negotiate peace.
April	21	Victory Loan offered.
May	7	Treaty of Versailles is presented to Germany.
June	28	Treaty of Versailles is signed by Germany.
August	12	National War Labor Board abolished.
September	25	Wilson collapses while on a nationwide speaking campaign for the treaty and the League.
1920		
March	1	Railroads returned to private ownership.
	19	Congress refuses to ratify the Treaty of Versailles.
1921		
July	2	Congress declares the war with Germany and Austria-Hungary over.
October	18	Congress ratifies separate treaties with Germany, Austria, and Hungary.

Sources: Linton (1975), Schlesinger and Bowman (1993), Morris and Morris (1996), other chronologies of American history, the *New York Times*, and the *Wall Street Journal*.

World War I would require the largest mobilization of resources in the United States since the Civil War. Although America's losses would be small compared with those of the European nations, they would nonetheless be traumatic for the United States. About 53,000 Americans died in battle, and another 63,000 from injury and disease, many from the influenza epidemic that ravaged the American forces alongside everyone else at the end of the war. About 204,000 suffered non-mortal wounds.

The origins of the war and American involvement

On June 28, 1914 in Sarajevo, Bosnia, Gavrilo Princip, a young Serbian revolutionary, shot and killed Austrian Archduke Franz Ferdinand and his wife, Sophie. This set off a deadly chain reaction that produced an explosion of astonishing violence. First, the Austro-Hungarian empire, perhaps motivated in part by a desire to annex Serbia, presented that country with a list of demands. When Serbia failed to meet them, the empire attacked it. Russia mobilized. Germany entered on the side of Austria-Hungary. France entered on the side of Russia. And Great Britain entered on the side of France. Two bullets fired by a single revolutionary had launched what was to become, up to that time, the bloodiest war in human history.

As Niall Ferguson (2003) has argued, it is far from clear that the war was an inevitable result of fundamental forces; it may have been an avoidable, if tragic, accident. Still, it is clear that the world had become a dangerous place. But why? Many factors, political, social, and economic, were at work. Europe's long and bloody history, despite the peaceful interlude between the Franco-Prussian War (1870–1) and World War I (1914–18), showed the capacity of the continent for organized violence and left a residue of resentment beneath the surface. Ethnic tensions created numerous grievances within the Austro-Hungarian empire. Bitter rivalries among the European powers for territory produced increased tensions and an unprecedented arms race. Austria-Hungary wanted to add Serbia to its empire; France wanted to recover Alsace-Lorraine, the region lost to Germany in the Franco-Prussian War.

One economic factor that has often been singled out is the scramble among the Great Powers at the end of the nineteenth century for colonies in Africa, Asia, and other parts of the world.[1] This scramble,

[1] The literature on the economics of imperialism is enormous. The remarks in the next few paragraphs are intended merely to provide an overview. Eckstein (1991) is a thoughtful summary of an important segment of the literature.

it is said, intensified tensions among the European powers and contributed to the arms race, particularly the naval arms race. John A. Hobson (1900, 1902) argued that the scramble for colonies was produced by the machinations of financiers, rather than any broad economic interest. Imperialism in his view was not in the interest of the capitalist class as a whole, let alone of the public as a whole – traders, manufacturers, farmers, and workers gained nothing. Rather, imperialism was the result of foreign investors asking the government for help to make their investments pay.[2] Vladimir Lenin (1939 [1916]), in his famous monograph, *Imperialism, the Highest Stage of Capitalism*, developed similar themes, so the idea is often termed the Hobson–Lenin thesis. In the hands of some historians the argument became linked with a problem of inadequate macroeconomic demand. There was, in this view, a glut of savings in the late nineteenth century that had to be relieved by foreign investments. The European imperialists, in other words, needed large export surpluses in order to maintain aggregate demand, and full employment. Fearful of the unrest caused by high unemployment, the imperialists competed desperately for the investment outlets and markets provided by colonies.

Recently, however, trends in macroeconomics have weakened the foundations of the argument that imperialism was a product of the goal of maintaining full employment. Traditionally, Keynesian economists emphasized the tendency of market economies to fall below full employment and the need for government policies, such as deficit spending on public works, to maintain aggregate demand and full employment. In this sort of model, a policy of imperialism to expand export markets made sense. It may have been a second-best solution compared with using deficit spending to build hospitals and universities – but it made economic sense. In recent years, however, first monetarist models and then real business-cycle models, which emphasize the tendency of economies to recover from shocks and return to full employment, have displaced the Keynesian model. In the newer models the logic of imperialism as a means of generating aggregate demand is questionable.

[2] This statement greatly simplifies Hobson's argument – he saw many factors, economic and non-economic, at work – but it does speak to the heart of his argument.

Economic historians, moreover, by uncovering additional data and exploiting new types of data have challenged other parts of the "it was all about economics" interpretation of the war. Davis, Huttenbach, and Davis (1986) found that the British investment in its empire was unprofitable. Some research has challenged parts of the Davis–Huttenbach–Davis thesis. And it is possible that Britain's rivals overestimated the value of its empire. But it is hard to maintain the view that the war could have been justified as a purely economic calculation. Whatever Germany and the Austro-Hungarian empire may have suffered because they lacked a large colonial empire, moreover, it is clear that they experienced rapid growth and prosperity in the years leading up to World War I. Indeed, World War I came to a prosperous part of the world after a long period of economic growth that lifted the standard of living of the bulk of the population. Whatever the war shows, it does not provide evidence for the idea that wars are produced by growing misery.

It may be that the race for distant colonies was as much a product of the arms race, including the naval building race, as a cause. During peacetime nations can buy resources – coal, iron ore, petroleum, or whatever one deems crucial – on the open market. They can lodge their ships and refuel at ports around the world. There was always a fear, however, a fear frequently reiterated by the military, that access to these resources might be cut during a war. The military logic then was to secure political control over the areas that produce crucial raw materials, and over points where those resources could be transferred to the navy. The arms race, moreover, tended to push countries toward war, encouraging dreams of victory and fears of defeat. Each nation was engaged in a complex game with other nations. If the coalition to which one belonged fell behind in spending, the fear that war and defeat lay ahead would spur additional spending. Jari Eloranta (2007) documents the arms race in detail. In his view, the failure of the United States to establish a military position consistent with its economic power was the destabilizing factor. True, the United States was spending more after the Spanish–American and Philippine–American wars than it had before. But American military spending was still small compared with that of the major industrial powers in Europe.

If one looked only at the resources of the two sides one might be tempted to assume that a war, at least between the alliances that actually emerged, would be impossible because the Entente Powers

(Britain, France, Russia, Italy, and their allies), as Niall Ferguson (2001, 401) noted, had a population that was 4.5 times as large as the population of the Central Powers (Germany and Austria-Hungary) and enjoyed an advantage over the Central Powers in GNP of 60 percent. But victory does not always go to the economically superior power: witness the United States in Korea, or Vietnam, or for that matter Britain in the American Revolutionary War. Superior organization, superior resolve, superior access to new technologies, and the ability to fight within compact lines, may tip the balance in favor of the economically weaker side. War is often the result of mistaken evaluations of these offsetting factors.

Despite the dangers entailed by the arms race, especially the naval race, and despite the prescience of certain jeremiahs who predicted the conflict, the evidence is that on the eve of the war Europeans in general had little or no inkling of the catastrophe that was about to unfold. Niall Ferguson (2006) has made this point by examining financial markets, a source of information that historians traditionally neglected, but which economic historians are now turning to frequently. Not everyone owned stocks and bonds, but a large part of the European elite did, so the prices paid for stocks and bonds should provide some insight into how seriously the most influential classes of Europeans took the prospects of war. Figure 5.1 shows some data of the sort Ferguson examined: the yields on the long-term government bonds issued by Britain, France, and Germany. While there is some increase in yields after 1910, the rates were fairly stable in the eighteen months leading up to the war. There is little evidence here that a great cataclysm was expected, one in which bond markets would be closed – in Britain for several months, and in Germany for the duration, the source of the gaps in the curves in Figure 5.1 – and in which inflation would skyrocket (in all of the belligerents), undermining the value of these long-term bonds.

Although it is likely that investors who anticipated the war would sell their long-term government bonds, there were considerations that would make them hesitate. After all, where else could they put their money? Cash? But cash itself was subject to many of the same problems as bonds: it would lose value from wartime inflation. Investors who had chosen the stability of income and principal provided by long-term government bonds, moreover, might be reluctant to move to the private bond market or the private stock market, with its

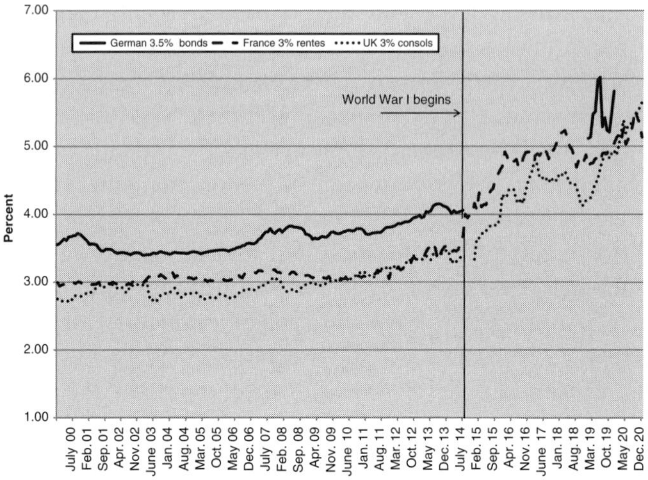

Figure 5.1 Yields on long-term government bonds issued by Britain, France, and Germany, 1900–15. Investors reading the bond market tea leaves in 1914 would not have expected the catastrophe that was about to unfold.
Source: www.nber.org; NBER Macrohistory Database; series m13041c, m11020, and m11021.

reputation for violent fluctuation. Stocks of private firms, moreover, while they might profit from higher wartime prices, and might therefore be a hedge against inflation, might be affected by disruptions in the supply of raw materials and by heavy taxation. It is therefore worth looking at how the stock market, which might reflect the views of a different class of investors, moved in the period leading up to the war. Figure 5.2 shows the prices of shares on the London stock exchange from 1910 to 1920. It shows separate indexes for all British security prices and prices for coal, iron, and steel shares, since the latter were likely to profit from an industrial war. Here there is even less evidence before the war that British investors were worried about a great cataclysm. Indeed, it took a few months after the start of the war for British investors to realize that coal, iron, and steel was a particularly good sector in which to invest.

What about the United States? Figure 5.3 shows the average for all stocks, for United States Steel, and for chemical stocks. The latter two series show the prices of companies likely to earn high profits during a war. The chemical index, for example, was heavily influenced by the shares of DuPont, which became the major supplier of gunpowder to

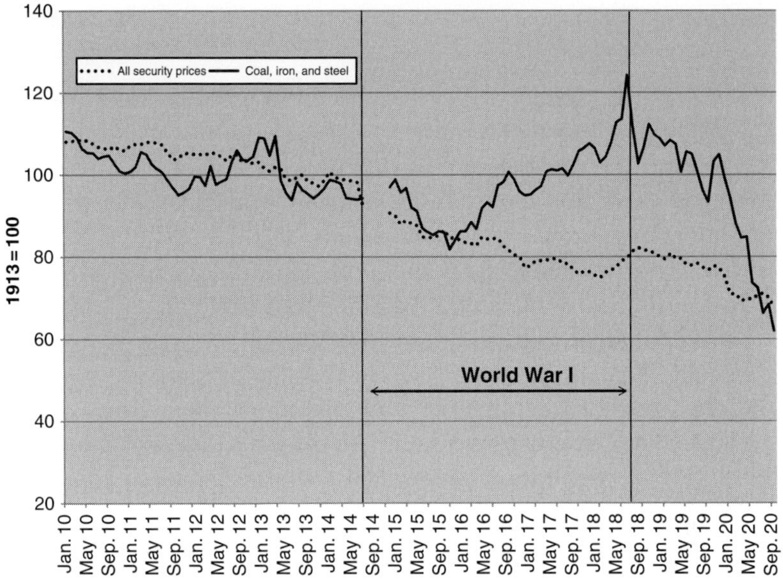

Figure 5.2 British share prices, 1910–20. British stock market investors did not anticipate World War I. Prices for coal, iron, and steel stocks did rise, but not until the war was underway.
Source: www.nber.org; NBER Macrohistory Database; series m11022 and m11013.

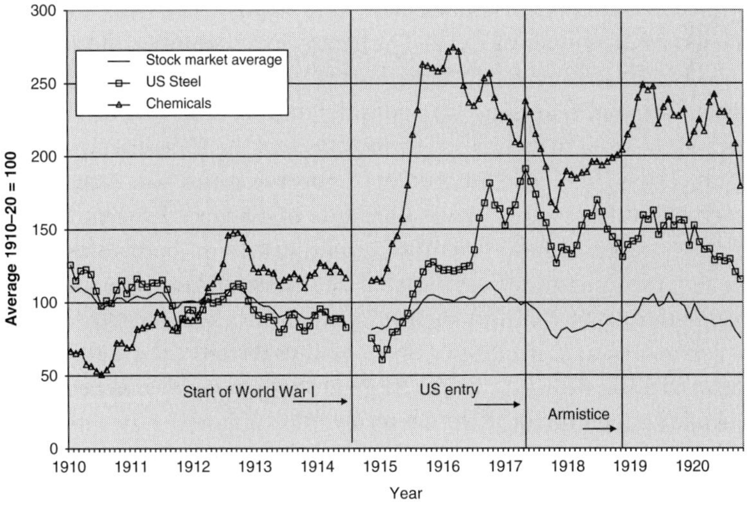

Figure 5.3 The US stock market, 1910–20. Prices for shares of steel and chemical companies rose dramatically during the period of US neutrality.
Source: Cowles Commission (1939) (S&P, S&P Steel, S&P Chemicals).

the Allies. The average for each index from 1910 to 1929 was set equal to 100 for ease in comparing values. Evidently investors in the American market had no inkling that the outbreak of the war would soon make steel and chemical stocks highly valuable. Either they did not know the European war was coming or if they did, they did not realize that it would be highly profitable for these US firms.

In fact, the entry of the United States brought a downturn in the stock market in general, and, surprisingly, in the war-related stocks in particular. Perhaps investors believed that the disruptions caused by the war would offset the demands placed on these firms by the mobilization. Or perhaps the threat of taxation, especially an increase in the excess profits tax, outweighed the expectation of additional spending on war matériel. The Wilson administration had included an excess profits tax in its 1917 emergency revenue bill (*New York Times*, February 12, 1917, 14) and there was every reason to think that the administration would rely even more heavily on taxes of this sort when the high expenditures of preparedness became the massive expenditures of war.

While the Europeans may have been naïve in 1914 about the destructive forces they were unleashing, there could have been no such naïveté when the United States declared war in April 1917. By then the awful destructiveness of the war was abundantly clear. Why then did the United States enter the war? The causes were complex. One factor, surely, was that Britain and France were reeling under the weight of German attacks, and there was considerable sentiment in the United States for coming to their aid. The insistence of the United States on its trading rights was also important. Soon after the war began the Entente Powers set up a naval blockade of Europe. Even food was considered contraband. The Wilson administration complained bitterly that the Entente actions violated international law. US firms took to using European neutrals, such as Sweden, as intermediaries. Surely, the Americans argued, international law protected the right of one neutral to trade with another. The Entente responded by extending the blockade to include the Baltic neutrals. The situation was similar to the difficulties the United States experienced during the Napoleonic Wars, which drove it almost to war against France, and actually to war against Britain.

Ultimately it was not the Entente's use of conventional surface vessels to enforce its blockade that enraged American opinion, but rather the German use of submarines. To be sure, the British blockade created substantial opposition in the United States. In 1914 and 1915 the British embargo of shipments of cotton to Germany and Austria created a wave of opposition in the South that threatened to undermine Southern support for Wilson's preparedness policies. The crisis was resolved when the British agreed to buy the cotton that would have been sold in Germany and Austria (Gaughan 1999, 775–7).[3] But the British were practicing an old, and in the view of many Americans a civilized, form of warfare. When the British (who provided most of the blockading ships) intercepted an American ship, the ship was escorted into a British port, the crew was treated well, and there was a chance of damages if it turned out that the interception was a mistake. The situation was very different when the Germans turned to submarine warfare. Submarines attacked without warning, and civilians had little chance to save themselves. The Germans felt they had little choice about adopting submarine warfare because their surface fleet was too small to establish a blockade. But submarine warfare risked bringing in the Americans. The first attack by a submarine to inflame American opinion was the sinking of the *Lusitania* in May 1915. The liner had left New York with a cargo of passengers and freight, including war goods. It was sunk as it approached British waters and more than 1,150 passengers were lost including 115 Americans. To many Americans this form of attack was an uncivilized violation of the laws of war.

In the months that followed further sinkings brought more angry warnings from President Wilson. For a time, the Germans gave way and agreed to give warnings before attacks and to save passengers. In February 1917, however, the Germans renewed unrestricted submarine warfare in an attempt to starve Britain into submission. The loss of several ships led President Wilson to break diplomatic relations with Germany in February 1917 and to ask for a declaration of war in April. There were other issues, such as the "Zimmermann note," in which Germany offered to support Mexico if it undertook military actions against the United States, and conceivably, other concerns may have been at work below the surface, but Wilson's war message focused almost exclusively on Germany's resumption of unrestricted submarine warfare.

[3] Once the USA entered the war the price of cotton rose. Southerners now began to associate war with prosperity.

From a dollar and cents point of view it is hard to justify the war based on the trade lost to the United States because of the German blockade. US exports to Europe rose from $1.479 billion in 1913 to $4.062 billion in 1917. Exports hit a peak of $5.188 billion in 1919. To be sure, some of this increase was the result of inflation. Over the period 1913–17 the unit value of exports rose from 100 to 177. Nevertheless, it is clear that exports to Europe rose substantially in real terms. If we use the unit value of exports as a deflator the increase was from $1.479 billion in 1913 to $2.295 billion in 1917 at 1913 values. Suppose the United States had stayed out of the war, and that as a result all trade with Europe was cut off. Suppose further, that the resources that would have been used to produce exports for Europe were able to produce only half as much value when reallocated to other purposes such as producing goods for the domestic market or exports for non-European countries, surely an extreme assumption. Then the loss of output at 1917 prices would have been $2.031 billion. How large an amount was this? It was about 3.7 percent of GDP in 1917, and about 6.25 percent of the total US cost of the war.[4] In other words, giving up exports to Europe, even for a long period of years, would have been less expensive for the United States than going to war. But of course, it wasn't the profit from trade for which the United States fought, but rather the idea of free trade: not the principal, but the principle.

The first decision that the United States had to make upon entering the war was about the size of the army. In 1917 the US army stood at approximately 200,000, hardly enough to have a significant impact in Europe where giant armies numbering in the millions were slugging it out. But a draft was imposed and the numbers were rapidly increased. Overall some 4,791,172 men would serve in the US military in World War I. Some 2,084,000 would reach France, and 1,390,000 would see active combat. This was a remarkable achievement given that the United States was only involved in active fighting for a year and a half.

The arrival of this army rapidly changed the course of the war. On March 21, 1918 the Germans, with a temporary superiority of numbers on the western front, had launched a massive offensive on the

[4] US exports to Europe are from US Bureau of the Census (1975, series U324). The unit values of exports are series U226 and U238. GDP is from Johnston and Williamson (2004).

Somme battlefield and were successful in pushing back the British and French. In May and early June they followed up with fresh attacks that brought them within fifty miles of Paris. Although some Americans fought in these battles it was mainly the old war: the Germans against the British and the French. The Battle of Belleau Wood fought from June 6 to July 1, 1918 was the first in which significant numbers of Americans fought. And it was a victory for the Allies. The turning point was the Second Battle of the Marne fought between July 18 and August 6. Here the Allies, bolstered by American forces, halted a German offensive.

The initiative now passed to the Allies. The Germans were driven back in a series of attacks in which American troops played an important role. The first distinctively American offensive was the Battle of the St. Mihiel Salient fought from September 12 to 16, 1918 in which more than half a million US troops participated. The last major offensive of the war, the Meuse–Argonne Offensive, was launched on September 26, with British, French, and American forces pushing back the Germans on a broad front. The Germans now realized that their military situation was deteriorating rapidly and that they would have to agree to an end to the fighting. The Armistice was reached on November 11, 1918 – at the eleventh hour of the eleventh day of the eleventh month.[5]

Financing the war

The problem faced by the US Treasury during the war is illustrated in Figure 5.4 which shows monthly federal receipts and expenditures from 1914 to 1921. Prior to the war federal receipts and expenditures were roughly balanced at a level well below $100 million. The tariff was the main source of revenue, although there were various other sources including sales of certain services and minor receipts from the new income tax passed in 1913. Once the war began, expenditures soared. Within months they had reached a level five times the prewar level and by the end of the year a level twelve times the prewar level. Receipts did rise because of a booming economy and higher taxes, but the deficit (the difference between the expenditure line and the receipts line) skyrocketed.

[5] If the warring sides had agreed to end the fighting at, say, 9:30 that morning, the alliteration would have been lost – and many lives would have been saved.

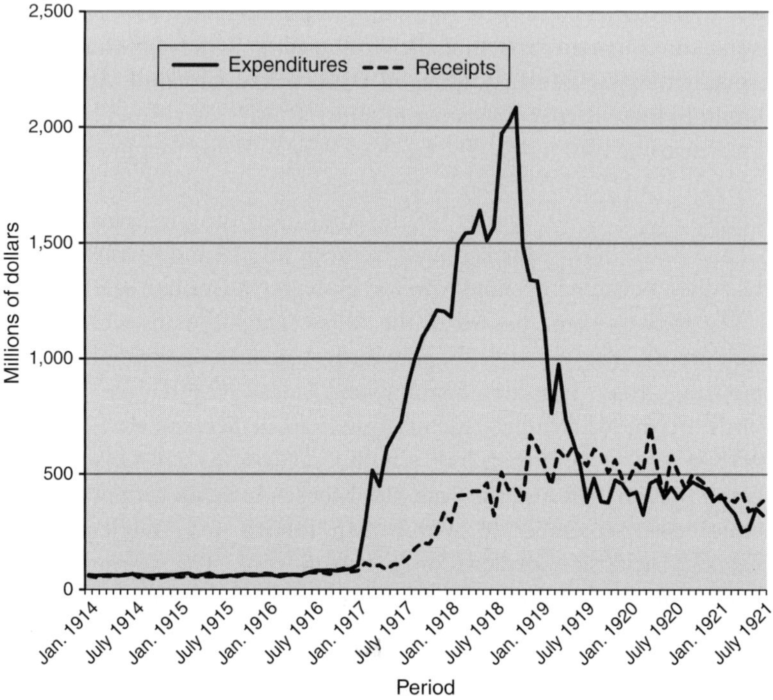

Figure 5.4 Federal receipts and expenditures, 1914–21. Government receipts rose during World War I, but expenditures rose much faster. Balance was restored after the war.
Source: Firestone (1960, Table A3, seasonally corrected data).

The United States was again faced with the classic problem of war finance: taxes, borrowing, or simply printing money? On the eve of America's entry into the war, Oliver M. W. Sprague – a professor at Harvard and one of America's leading monetary economists – was given the task of discussing the optimal means of financing a major war at the annual meetings of the American Economic Association. Sprague, in line with the classical tradition, made a strong case for taxation. Borrowing, according to Sprague, was unjust.

The injustice of treating those who furnish the funds for war more generously than those who risk life itself will not be questioned. Consider for a moment the contrast under the borrowing method of war finance of a soldier in receipt of an income of $2,500 before a war and his neighbor who remains at home in continued receipt of a similar amount. The civilian reduces his expenditures in every possible way and subscribes a total of $4,000 to war loans. He is rewarded with a high rate of interest to which his soldier neighbor must contribute his quota in higher taxes if he is fortunate enough to return from the front. (Sprague 1917, 204)

Would high taxes reduce output?

Taxation on this onerous scale [sufficient to finance a major war] would virtually eliminate the ordinary economic motives for effort and sacrifice. What would be the effect on production? There is no experience whatsoever on which to base a judgment. I venture to think, however, that no serious difficulties would be encountered when millions of men were fighting in the trenches in a great war in which a people believed that its vital interests were at stake. (Sprague 1917, 208)

In other words, Sprague recognized that high taxes might discourage effort, but thought that this effect could be offset during a war by patriotism. Four leading economists commented on Sprague's paper, (Miller, Lutz, Lincoln, Urdahl, and Sprague 1917). In general Sprague's discussants agreed that tax finance was best. Miller alone worried that relying entirely on taxes would weaken the "motive to industry."[6]

At a conference held a few months later (after the declaration of war and the passage of the War Revenue Act), one can find more acceptance of the need to borrow. Edwin R. A. Seligman (1918) thought that taxes should be raised, but that possible adverse effects on consumption and investment should be kept in mind. For Seligman financing 25 or 35 percent through taxes was about right. Even Sprague (1918) recognized that the war was going to be financed mainly (perhaps 75 percent) by debt whatever he or other economists might say. But he still believed that it would have been better to finance it 75 percent by taxes. Greater reliance on taxes, he added, would have reduced consumption and speeded conversion.[7]

The debates among the economists were echoed by the debates among the public. The socialists thought that all of the war could be

[6] Henry C. Adams (1918) agreed that a balance had to be struck between taxation and borrowing, a position based on a much earlier study of the War of 1812 and the Civil War (Adams 1886).

[7] As noted in Chapter 2, in recent years the classical fear of debt finance has eroded further. Following the lead of Robert J. Barro (1987, 1989) economists tend to emphasize the advantages of smoothing taxes over time through the use of debt.

financed by the appropriation of all incomes over $10,000 per year. The *Wall Street Journal*, as might be expected, advocated reducing the income tax exemption from $4,000 to $1,000. The *Journal*, moreover, thought that considerable reliance should be placed on bonds. It was a matter of equity: "It is not right that the present generation should bear the whole burden of a conflict fought for the freedom of our children's children."[8]

Secretary of the Treasury William Gibbs McAdoo rejected the view that the war should be financed entirely by taxes. He saw a partly political tradeoff between taxes and bonds: excessive reliance on taxation would frighten the wealthy and reduce support for the war; excessive reliance on bonds would be inflationary.[9] Given this trade-off, the practical matter became one of naming the optimal percentage to be financed by each. McAdoo, according to his memoirs, initially thought that a fifty–fifty split was about right. J. P. Morgan, America's leading investment banker, when questioned by McAdoo, advised financing 20 percent through taxes. Later McAdoo thought that financing 33 percent through taxes would do. Davis Rich Dewey (1931, 506–7) summed up the outcome of the debate this way:

> Some indeed advocated a policy of "pay as you go" [financing 100 percent with taxes] and even proposed a conscription of wealth, if necessary to meet the war costs. Others favored a more equal division between taxes and loans. These views, however, did not prevail. There was fear of "frightening capital" and arousing popular discontent which would retard the progress of military and naval plans. Although no exact ratio was formally adopted, there slowly developed an accepted conviction that taxation should provide at least one-third of the costs of the war.

When it came to practical details about what the types of instruments to market and how to market them, and what rate of interest to pay, the economists were less helpful, although they did offer some advice. Arthur Cecil Pigou was the leading British economist of the day and after the war he offered what he considered to be three decisive objections to allowing interest rates to increase in wartime (Pigou 1941 [1921], 92–4).

[8] This paragraph including the quotation from the *Journal* is based on Kennedy (1980, 16–17).

[9] A monetarist might argue that debt became inflationary only when monetized by the Federal Reserve. But McAdoo seems to have believed that issuing debt would be inflationary in any case.

(1) Higher rates, in particular rates that rise above rates in enemy countries, might be seen as a sign of weakness. (2) Higher rates might not stimulate much in the way of additional savings, and in any case would store up problems for future finance ministers. (3) Higher rates, like loans themselves, may be viewed as inequitable, as allowing the rich to "make a good thing out of war." It seems likely that concerns such as these, although not necessarily derived from economists, explain the determined effort made in the United States and in Britain to keep rates down during the war and to disguise rate increases.

Irving Fisher was perhaps the leading American economist of the day, certainly the one that we know best today. He accepted the need for issuing bonds, and made three points about how patriotic citizens should respond (Fisher 1918). (1) People should buy them by reducing their own consumption, not by borrowing from banks. (2) People should hold them, and not resell them unless the need was strong. (3) It was important that poor people invest in bonds so that after the war the government wouldn't be in the position of taxing the poor in order to pay the interest and principal on bonds owned by the rich. All of these points were stressed in the campaigns to sell what would be called the Liberty bonds.

Support for higher taxes, to sum up, was widespread, including among economists and, to an extent, business leaders, as well as the general public. The debate in Congress over how to raise taxes was divisive, but on October 3, about four months after the declaration of war, Congress passed the War Revenue Act. This Act introduced a sharply progressive surtax to the income tax, a graduated excess profits tax on corporations and individuals, higher postal rates, and higher taxes on alcohol, tobacco, assorted luxuries, and other items. The tax on alcohol, tobacco, and other luxuries was an old story. These taxes had been used during the Civil War and the Spanish–American War. The income tax was a less familiar resource. True, there had been personal and business income taxes during the Civil War. But a Supreme Court decision had taken them off the table, and as we have seen, they were not used during the Spanish–American War. But the sixteenth amendment to the Constitution, ratified in 1913, had created a legal basis for an income tax. The income tax amendment, although a cherished goal of populists and progressives, owed its final adoption, as shown by Baack and Ray (1985), to the need for additional revenues for the military, especially to the attractiveness for certain states of naval construction. In the October 3 legislation existing rates were raised sharply by adding a wartime surtax. The term "surtax" was used to suggest an additional tax made necessary by the war and therefore one that would be temporary.

One potential source of revenue that had broad public support was an excess profits tax simply because abhorrence of wartime profiteering was widespread. Something resembling an excess profits tax had been imposed in the South during the Civil War, but not (as far as I am aware) in the more business-oriented and Republican North (Shultz and Caine 1937, 275; Bank, Stark, and Thorndike 2008, 31–2). There were also no excess profits taxes during the Spanish–American or Philippine–American wars, perhaps because they were small wars, or perhaps because the McKinley and Roosevelt administrations and their Republican Congressional allies were unwilling to impose a tax on business profits and set a precedent for peacetime levies.

The Wilson administration, a progressive Democratic administration, found an excess profits tax more congenial. The Revenue Act of 1916, passed during the period of US neutrality, included a tax on munitions manufacturers (Shultz and Caine 1937, 520; Bank, Stark, and Thorndike 2008, 55). The United States, moreover, was not alone: there was a widespread movement in Europe and the British empire to impose excess profits taxes (Stamp 1917), so US legislators had many examples to draw upon. For the most part debate over the excess profits tax focused on the distinction between a "high profits tax" and an "excess profits tax" (Lent 1951). A high profits tax was levied on profits that exceeded the amount that would yield a "reasonable" rate of return. To take a simple example, suppose that a firm's prewar capital was $1,000 and that a "normal" rate of profit was 8 percent. Then profits that exceeded $80 per year ($1,000 × .08) would be subject to additional taxation. On the other hand, an excess profits tax was levied on profits that exceeded prewar profits. For example, if a firm's profits had been $70, $80, and $90, an average of $80, in the three years before the war, then again wartime profits exceeding $80 would be subject to additional taxation.

Liberal legislators favored the high profits tax because it reflected their belief that even in peacetime profits beyond some maximum were objectionable and that as a practical matter continuing a high profits tax after the war would be straightforward. A high profits tax, moreover, was already implicit in some legislation regulating public utility rates. The high profits approach, however, suffered from some practical deficiencies. Capital was hard to measure. A firm with low measured capital because it had remained in the same hands for many years could end up paying more in taxes than a similar firm whose measured capital had been augmented in frequent mergers and acquisitions. Conservative legislators favored the excess profits tax because it was tied more closely to the war and less likely to survive it. But the excess profits tax also had practical problems. Firms that had made large prewar profits during a prewar arms buildup would pay less tax during the war than a comparable firm that had not joined in the prewar "profiteering." Moreover, how would one tax firms that had not existed, and therefore earned no profits before the war? Both the excess profits tax and the high profits tax reduced the incentive to convert to war work.

The "Special Preparedness" Tax of March 3, 1917 included a high profits tax (Shultz and Caine 1937, 521; Bank, Stark, and Thorndike 2008, 55–7). This tax was modified during the war to include features of both the high profits tax and the excess profits tax based on prewar profits, but it remained largely a high profits tax (Shultz and Caine 1937, 528, 532; Lent 1951; Bank, Stark, and Thorndike 2008, 64–5). The World War I excess profits tax was repealed in 1921 as part of Secretary of the Treasury Andrew Mellon's tax reductions. The excess profits tax was renewed during the 1930s as part of Roosevelt's New Deal.

Although the presence of the excess profits tax during the war has been noted frequently, its importance in financing the war has not been appreciated. Part of the reason is that it is hard to reconcile various Treasury figures on an annual basis. This is not as surprising as it sounds. Taxes, for example, can be listed according to the time when the income that is subject to taxation is accrued, the time when the taxes are paid to Treasury agents, or the time when the officials who keep the accounts at the Treasury are notified of the payment, and taxes can be listed gross or net of refunds. If one aggregates over the whole course of the war, however (as in Appendix 4, which shows the sources of federal tax revenues in World War I, World War II, and the Korean War), these problems tend to net out, and the importance of the excess profits tax becomes clear. If we simply add all dollars together without paying attention to the price level we can see that the excess profits tax was the most important source of taxes during World War I, producing about 30 percent of all tax revenue; more than the individual income tax. If we adjust for inflation and make an allowance for prewar receipts to identify the tax revenues available to finance the extra spending occasioned by the war, then the contribution of the excess profits tax to total taxes approaches 40 percent, substantially more than any other form of taxation.

Relying on the excess profits tax helped maximize political support for the war. The average voter was not paying; "they" were – that is, the "war profiteers." And it may very well be true that the excess profits tax was paid by the shareholders of firms paying that tax. A strong economic case could be made against an excess profits tax on economic grounds: the tax discouraged the transfer of resources into areas of the economy where they were most needed. Why stop producing civilian good X and start producing military good Y, if the profit would be no higher in Y than in X? Moreover, as economists stress, the burden of taxation can (sometimes) be shifted to others, and it can be extremely difficult to figure out who actually pays. The classic case of shifting the burden is a tax on a single commodity paid by the producer. Producers write the checks, so from a legal point of view producers are paying, but if the price of the product rises, part of the burden falls on consumers of the product. Something like that may have happened in this case, but it is hard to know whether shifting actually occurred. Producers tried to game the system. Money spent on advertising raised costs and reduced excess profits, but might result in higher profits after the war. Money paid to executives during the war reduced excess profits, and might reduce the size of postwar salary increases (Bank, Stark, and Thorndike 2008, 67). The possibilities were endless, but it is hard to know how important they were. In any event, the political case for financing part of the war with an excess profits tax – a tax that appears to protect the average citizen, rather than take money out of their pockets – was overwhelming.

Taxes were an important source of finance for the war, but they were not sufficient. The government would have to turn to the bond market. Secretary McAdoo studied the record of Salmon Chase, his Civil War predecessor, and concluded that while Chase had done a good job, especially in hiring investment banker Jay Cooke to sell bonds to middle-class investors, his policy could have been pushed much further. Britain and Germany had already undertaken noisy "drives" aimed at selling bonds, especially to middle- and working-class investors

(Noyes 1926, 181–2), and McAdoo enthusiastically adopted the same strategy. He crisscrossed the country on an exhausting speaking tour, urging the public to express its support for the war by buying bonds, and he arranged rallies at which movie stars such as Douglas Fairbanks, Mary Pickford, and Charlie Chaplin exhorted the crowd to buy bonds (Kennedy 1980, 105). In the closing week of the campaign for the Fourth Liberty Loan $4.8 million was raised from an audience at Carnegie Hall who heard Enrico Caruso and other stars perform (Noyes 1926, 185). But it wasn't just stars. Everyone who could was asked to sell bonds. The Boy Scouts were enlisted under the slogan "Every Scout to Save a Soldier." Even the names of the bonds reflected the emphasis on patriotism. While one of the most popular Civil War issues was known prosaically as the 5–20 (callable after five years, redeemed at twenty), the World War I debt consisted of "Liberty loans," and a final "Victory loan" to celebrate winning the war. McAdoo's policy, as he put it, was to "capitalize patriotism."

There were, as shown in Table 5.1, four issues of Liberty bonds during the war, and one issue of Victory bonds afterwards. McAdoo could have chosen to sell bonds continuously. In other words, he could have opened the bond-selling window of the Treasury and urged the public to buy bonds. This was the practice followed during the war for short-term instruments in the United States, and for longer-term instruments in France. McAdoo, however, chose to offer the bonds in separate blocks. The Treasury announced in advance the amount to be offered. Then on a particular day the subscription books were opened and offers for the bonds were accepted or rejected. This system allowed the Treasury to create public drives for the bonds that used patriotism to whip up enthusiasm. Would the American people show their support for the war by buying all of the bonds offered? Each region of the country, moreover, was given a quota, creating a basis for regional competition: which region of the country would be the most patriotic and exceed its quota by the widest margin? As shown in Table 5.1, the campaigns were, in this sense, a great success. All of them were oversubscribed: the public offered to buy more than the government put on sale.

The most controversial feature of the bonds was their exemption from taxes. The first issue was exempt from normal (peacetime) income taxes and from the wartime surtax which would be, it was hoped, temporary. The exemption drew considerable criticism: the

Table 5.1 *The properties of the Liberty bonds and the results of the campaigns to sell them*

	First Liberty Loan	Second Liberty Loan	Third Liberty Loan	Fourth Liberty Loan	Fifth Liberty (Victory) Loan	
					Fully taxable	Partially tax-exempt
Dated	June 15, 1917	November 15, 1917	May 9, 1918	October 24, 1918	April–May	1919
Coupon (percent)	3.50	4.00	4.25	4.25	4.75	3.75
Callable in (years)	15	10	...	15	3	3
Maturity (years)	30	25	10	20	4	4
Interest exempt from "normal" income tax	Yes	Yes	Yes	Yes	No	Yes
Interest exempt from the surtax	Yes	Yes (limited to the income on $5,000 face value of the bonds)	Yes (limited to the income on $5,000 face value of the bonds)	Yes (limited to the income on $30,000 face value until two years after the war)	Yes	Yes
Offered on	May 14, 1917	October 1, 1917	April 6, 1918	September 28, 1917	April 21, 1919	

Amount offered (billion $)	2.000	3.000	3.000	6.000	4.500
Amount subscribed (billion $)	3.035	4.618	4.177	6.959	5.250
Rate of over-subscription (percent)	52	54	39	16	16.66
Subscriptions accepted (billion $)	2.000	3.809	4.177	6.959	4.500
Number of subscribers (millions)	4.000	9.400	18.377	22.778	11.803
Average subscription ($)	759	491	227	306	445
Share of the issue in denominations of less than $10,000 (percent)	42	40	66	52	60

Source: Kang and Rockoff (2006).

Wilson administration, nominally a progressive Democratic administration, was raising taxes on the wealthy with one hand, and then creating a huge loophole for them with the other. The surtax exemption for the second and third bonds was therefore limited to the interest on the first $5,000 worth of bonds at face value. When it came to planning the fourth issue, however, concerns about finding a market led to backtracking. The limit to the exemption from the surtax was raised to $30,000, and provision was made to extend the surtax exemption to interest on the second and third issues, provided specified amounts of the fourth issue were purchased. The history of the surtax exemption is telling: evidently, prosaic tax considerations could not be swept aside, even while calling on the powerful force of patriotism to help market the bonds. A study of the yields on the bonds also suggests that the ability of McAdoo to increase the demand for bonds through the bond campaigns was limited (Kang and Rockoff 2006). The most important contribution of the campaigns, therefore, may have been psychological. Buying bonds provided a way for people who were frustrated because they weren't participating directly in the war effort to feel that they were making a contribution. The fears of children could be assuaged by involving them in the bond campaigns. And perhaps the campaigns also served to increase political support for the war, and signal such support to the enemy.[10]

During the period of US neutrality (June 1914 to March 1917) foreign demand for American products increased dramatically. Partly this was the result of trade diversion. Goods that Britain and France had formerly bought from Germany and its allies now had to be purchased in the United States. More importantly it was the result of the heavy demand for goods with which to fight: steel, gunpowder (a DuPont specialty), and so on. Britain, France, and their allies paid for these goods in a number of ways: by shipping gold, borrowing from the United States, and selling private securities commandeered by their governments.

This last source of finance was particularly troubling for the British (Burk 1979). The individual security holders were compensated by the British government which exchanged its own bonds for the foreign securities. The British then used Morgan Grenfell, an investment

[10] Further information on the Liberty bonds, including their distribution across income groups and the role of the Federal Reserve in financing their purchase, can be found in Kang and Rockoff (2006).

bank in London, to sell the commandeered securities to J. P. Morgan in New York, meanwhile maintaining an official fixed exchange rate of dollars to pounds for these transactions. However, from the point of view of Britain as a whole, the loss of the foreign securities was a major blow.[11] As the first industrial nation Britain had enjoyed a long lead in per capita income and savings over its rivals. A substantial part of those savings had been invested overseas, especially in Argentina, Canada, the United States, and Australia. Even as other nations caught up with Britain industrially, Britain could hope to maintain a relatively high standard of living based partly on its savings, much like a retiree who had prudently saved for his or her old age. But World War I and World War II upended those plans. Britain would not be able to maintain a higher standard of living than its rivals based on the savings made during its glorious industrial past.

Fears about the potential effects of a selloff of foreign-owned securities in New York (by private or government owners), and the resulting withdrawals of deposits from American banks as funds in the form of gold were repatriated, had created a small financial panic at the outset of the war, a crisis that the newly established Federal Reserve was not well prepared to meet head on. Fortunately, the crisis was contained by the issue of an emergency currency, the so-called Aldrich–Vreeland currency, and the temporary closing (by the federal government) of the New York stock exchange (Silber 2007). It soon became clear, however, that the long-run problem would not be the loss of gold to Europe, but rather the inflow from Europe as a result of US exports of war matériel. Ultimately, the gold that flowed into the United States produced a substantial increase in the money supply and a substantial inflation.

Had the Federal Reserve been a well-established institution with a large portfolio of domestic securities it could have "sterilized" the gold inflow. That is, it could have sold securities equal to the gold inflow, thus offsetting the effect of the inflow on bank reserves and the money supply. However, the Federal Reserve, which had only recently gone into operation, was not ready either in terms of its balance sheet or in terms of its understanding of monetary policy to attempt to offset the gold flow.

[11] In other words, any compensation paid to holders of British securities meant higher taxes for other British citizens.

Once the United States entered the war, this state of affairs changed. The US government now made loans to its allies, relieving them of the immediate constraints on arms buying, although laying the groundwork for future conflicts over repayment of the loans. The Federal Reserve, moreover, was now prepared to play a major role. It still might have based its policy on constraining the growth of the stock of money and prices, but instead it made every effort to help the Treasury sell its bonds without producing a substantial increase in interest rates. As we have seen, an increase in rates over prewar levels was seen as a very bad thing, in part because it might be taken as a signal of a weak economy or a lack of support for the war. Hence the Federal Reserve used its discount rate and its open market operations to support the bond market. Despite increased taxes, sales of bonds to the American capital market, and the broadening of that market through appeals to patriotism, the Federal Reserve directly or indirectly monetized a substantial portion of the new wartime debt. Milton Friedman and Anna J. Schwartz (1963, 216) put it this way:

> The Federal Reserve became to all intents and purposes the bond-selling window of the Treasury, using its monetary powers almost exclusively to that end. Although no "greenbacks" were printed, the same result was achieved by more indirect methods using Federal Reserve notes and Federal Reserve deposits.

How much was involved? Between June 1916 and June 1919, the federal debt increased by $24.3 billion (from $1.2 billion to $25.5 billion). High-powered money (which includes mainly Federal Reserve notes and deposits) increased by $2.1 billion, according to Friedman and Schwartz (1963, 801–2). So the increase in high-powered money could have purchased only about 10 percent of the increase in the federal debt. But commercial banks also contributed to the monetization of the debt. They did so by purchasing bonds for their own portfolios and by lending money that borrowers then used to purchase bonds. Generally the banks lent at the coupon rate or at a slight advance over the coupon rate. Obviously, these were relatively secure loans because the Liberty bonds were the collateral for the loan.

Since the amount of bonds purchased with newly created money was not matched one for one by bonds held by banks, we cannot form an accurate estimate of how much of the debt was monetized by examining the balance sheets of the banks. We can get an upper

Table 5.2 *Financing World War I*

	Amount (billion dollars)	Percentage of expenditures[a]
Total federal expenditures during the years of wartime deficits, 1917–19	33.1	100.0
Tax and other revenues	16.9	29.8
Borrowing from the public	115.8	39.9
Direct money creation	1.4	7.2
Indirect money creation	4.9	23.0

[a] The sum of the percentages in the subcategories does not equal 100 because of rounding.

Sources: Expenditures and revenues: Carter *et al.* (2006, series Ea636 and Ea588). Direct money creation: Friedman and Schwartz (1963, Table B-3, High-powered money, 801). Indirect money creation: Friedman and Schwartz (1970, Table 1, M2, 15–17). Borrowing from the public was computed as a residual.

bound, however, by looking at the increase in the total stock of money and assuming that all of the money that was created was backed directly or indirectly by government bonds. I follow this procedure in Table 5.2 which breaks the finance of the war into its three classic components. The story told by the table is clear. Taxes were raised: as we have seen a surtax was added to the newly established income tax, and businesses were subjected to a surprisingly effective excess profits tax. But the bulk of the finance was produced in ways that hid the cost of the war from the public: borrowing and printing money.

Mobilization

Once the United States entered the war it was clear that it would have to field a massive army and mobilize the economy on a huge scale. The European powers already had huge armies in the field and the United States, if it was to change the course of the war, would have to do likewise. Congress had already taken some actions toward mobilizing the economy before the US declaration of war. On August 29, 1916, a Council of National Defense, an advisory commission charged with coordinating industry, was established, and on September 7 the US Shipping Board was established, with the power to build or lease ships through an Emergency Fleet Corporation capitalized at $50 million.

After the declaration of war Congress went into high gear. On April 14, 1917 it established the Committee on Public Information to create propaganda for the war. On April 24 it passed the Liberty Loan Act authorizing the issue of debt. On May 18 the Selective Service Act creating a draft was passed and on June 15 the Espionage Act to suppress seditious or treasonable activities. On July 28 the War Industries Board replaced the Council of National Defense, and was given the task of coordinating and increasing production. On August 10 Congress passed the Lever Food and Fuel Act to control food and fuel prices and maintain supplies. Herbert Hoover, the future President, became the food administrator, and Harry Garfield, the son of President James A. Garfield, became the fuel administrator.

Taxes proved to be one of the most contentious issues, but as I discussed above, on October 3 Congress passed the War Revenue Act. This Act introduced a sharply progressive surtax to the income tax, a graduated excess profits tax on corporations and individuals, higher postal rates, and higher taxes on alcohol, tobacco, assorted luxuries, and other items. Overall it was an impressive performance, at least in terms of sheer activity. The United States would not see a similar flurry of legislation until Franklin Roosevelt's "100 days."

Where did all these ideas come from? How did a country that had not fought a major war for more than fifty years take action so quickly? Some ideas, as we have seen, came from looking back at US experience. Treasury Secretary McAdoo, for example, reexamined the policies followed in the Civil War. But the examples of Britain and Germany were also very important. Presumably they had learned something. Following suit, moreover, made sense strategically. The United States had a larger population and economy than Germany. If it organized the economy in the same way as the Germans, then superior US resources would tell, and it would win. If it organized differently, there was always the chance, however remote, that the country would use its greater resources less efficiently, and lose. Following suit was the course of prudence.

Although the basic structure of the war economy was in place by the end of October, several important pieces of legislation followed. On December 18, 1917 Congress passed the Prohibition Amendment to the Constitution which, when ratified, outlawed the production and sale of alcoholic beverages. Prohibition had been gaining in strength for some time: by 1917 nineteen states had banned the sale of alcoholic beverages. The war strengthened the "dries" and weakened the "wets." How could America allow drunken workers in war factories making arms for its boys at the front? How could it allow grain, desperately needed as food for its allies, to be made into alcohol? On December 26, in the midst of a national coal crisis – caused by a hard winter and the disruption of rail schedules by the war – Wilson placed the railroads under government control. His Secretary of the Treasury, William Gibbs McAdoo, was placed in charge.[12] Congress later passed legislation providing for compensation for the railroads, and creating the US Railroad Administration to run them. On April 5, 1918, Congress created the War Finance Corporation, capitalized at $500 million (and with permission to borrow $3 billion more), to help finance the war industries. The last major piece of economic legislation was the creation, on April 8, 1918, of the National War Labor Board to adjudicate labor disputes.

Did this flurry of activity leave a permanent imprint on the institutional structure of the economy? Were institutions created during the war that lived on after their original *raison d'être* had disappeared? It is sometimes claimed that once institutions are created for any reason, even a war emergency, they create a constituency – customers, suppliers, workers, politicians – who work to keep them going indefinitely at the taxpayer's expense. For the most part, however, the institutions created during World War I were unwound afterwards. Partly this was the result of changing political tides: conservative Republican administrations in the 1920s were keen to scale back wartime expansions in the role of government.

The railroads were typical. They and other carriers that had been seized by the government were returned to private ownership on March 1, 1920. The Railroad Administration itself survived somewhat longer, but only for the purpose of winding up all of the accounts. The War Finance Corporation, however, lasted much longer. It was used to aid agriculture during the 1920–1 contraction, and this function was moved in 1923 to the new system of Federal Intermediate Credit Banks. The affairs of the War Finance Corporation were not finally wound up until 1929. Its director, Eugene Meyer, would serve

[12] The energetic McAdoo, who became Wilson's son-in-law in 1914, would play a role in the establishment of the Federal Reserve, run for the Democratic nomination for President, and serve as a senator from California.

as the chair of the Federal Reserve Board during the fateful period 1930–3. In 1932 he, and men who had served under him at the War Finance Corporation, were instrumental in pushing for the establishment of the Reconstruction Finance Corporation to meet the challenge of the Depression. The Reconstruction Finance Corporation in turn was used to help finance industrial expansion in World War II. The Small Defense Plants Administration created in 1951 was assigned to the Reconstruction Finance Corporation, and its activities in turn were continued in the Small Business Administration created in 1953. So, in a sense, the Small Business Administration, still active today, is a descendant of the War Finance Corporation.

How many men were required in the military? This was the first key question, and the one from which all else flowed. The decision ultimately belonged to the man Wilson picked to head the American Expeditionary Force, General John J. Pershing. Pershing, who had served, as I noted, in the Philippines, and was just back from chasing Pancho Villa in Mexico, quickly came to some basic conclusions.[13] First, America's soldiers should not be used to simply fill the depleted ranks of the British and French armies. America, in other words, should have its own army. Second, America's troops should not be kept in the trenches and used to help Britain win a long war of attrition. They should be used, in other words, in aggressive attacks designed to break through and destroy the German army. And, third, the United States would need to supply a large number of troops in order to obtain a decisive numerical superiority over the Germans.

The troops came in record time, and American war planners were justifiably proud of what they accomplished. In January 1918 Secretary of War Newton Baker reported on the rapid increase in the size of the armed forces.[14] In April 1917 the United States had 211,834 men under arms, consisting of 9,324 officers and 202,510 enlisted men. At the end of December 1917 the United States had 1,539,485 under arms, consisting of 110,835 officers and 1,428,650 enlisted men. General Pershing was already in France planning for a force of 2 million. Although the army was the big show, the air force was expanded as well. Only fourteen years had passed since the Wright

[13] Our discussion of Pershing is based on Kennedy (1980, 169–77).
[14] *New York Times* (January 11, 1918, 3). Ironically, Baker was chosen for the post partly because of his well-known pacifist leanings.

Brothers had first flown at Kitty Hawk. In April 1917 the Aviation Division of the Signal Corps consisted of 65 officers and 1,120 men; at the beginning of 1918 it consisted of about 3,000 officers and 82,120 men.[15]

This force had to be fed, clothed, housed, armed, trained, and transported to the front. Accordingly, contracts for food, clothing, housing, munitions, and transport flowed from the army, the navy, and the Emergency Fleet Corporation. The army, for example, purchased 19 million blankets, 21 million pairs of woolen gloves, and 10 million pairs of shoes. While these are large numbers, one must keep in mind that the United States had a large economy. In 1914 it had produced 98 million pairs of men's shoes and 80.9 million pairs of women's shoes (US Bureau of the Census 1975, 693) The army, in other words, was contracting for about 10 percent of the output of male shoes; a significant share, but one that it was possible to meet, especially since there would be some diminution in civilian demand as a result of the draft.

In response to these contracts the flow of materials began to mount. Table 5.3 shows the figures for some key munitions.[16] Altogether, the United States produced about 3,550,000 rifles, 226,557 machine guns, and 10,817 tons of toxic gas (column 1). In some cases production was accelerating when the war came to an end. This can be seen in column 2, which shows the peak monthly production, which generally occurred in the month before the Armistice, and column 3, which shows the peak monthly production as an annual rate. While 10,817 tons of toxic gas were produced during the war, to take one example, the peak annual rate was 32,712; while 3,227 de Havilland-4 bombers were produced (although only 1,885 shipped), the peak annual rate was 13,200. In World War II President Roosevelt was considered audacious when he called for 50,000 planes. However, as you can see in Table 5.3, peak production of Liberty airplane engines reached 46,200 per year.

Inevitably, there were complaints that the production program was moving too slowly and was mired in confusion and corruption. The aircraft program was a prominent example. In 1903 the United States

[15] A number of estimates are available, and I have not succeeded in reconciling them, but all agree on a massive increase.

[16] This table appeared originally in Rockoff (2005).

Table 5.3 *Production of selected munitions in World War I*

Munition	Total production to the end of the war[a]	Peak monthly rate of production[b]	Production in the peak month at an annual rate
Rifles	3,550,000	271,000	3,252,000
Machine guns	226,557	35,000	420,000
Artillery units	3,077	410	4,920
Smokeless powder (pounds)	632,504,000	na	na
High explosives (pounds)	375,566,000	na	na
Rounds of artillery ammunition	20,326,000	3,072,000	31,104,000
Toxic gas (tons)	10,817	2,726	32,712
Tanks	799	na	na
Training planes	9,503	na	na
Training engines	17,073	na	na
De Havilland-4 bombers (shipped)	3,227 (1,885)	1,100	13,200
Liberty airplane engines (shipped)	13,574 (4,435)	3,850	46,200

[a] Typically, this is the period from April 1917 to March or April 1919. Production after the Armistice was usually limited, reflecting the completion of units in the pipeline.
[b] Typically, October 1919.
Source: Ayres (1919 *passim*).

had been the first in flight, but by 1917 it lagged far behind the Europeans in military aircraft. Once the war began, however, the push was on. The Aircraft Production Board was established in May 1917, with Edward A. Deeds, a prominent industrialist, in charge. Preliminary investigations suggested that the United States should not attempt to build its own fighter planes because it lagged so far behind the Europeans. Instead, it should focus on supplying raw materials – such as the fast-growth clear spruce that was ideal for building airframes – to the Europeans and on mass-producing an airplane engine that would allow the Allies to dominate the skies in the years to come. European aircraft engines such as the Rolls-Royce and the Hispano-Suiza were very good, but they were essentially handcrafted. The American experts were convinced they could mass-produce aircraft engines even though the precision required was much greater than for the automobile engines with which they were familiar. Deeds, now Colonel Deeds as the result of a military commission, soon developed plans for mass-producing a powerful new engine, the Liberty engine.

The initial reaction to the Liberty engine program was favorable. The economist John Maurice Clark responded to a September 1917 newspaper story about the program by declaring that it proved that "there are great unused possibilities for immediate advancement in private industries" (Clark 1917, 779). The production of the Liberty engine would reveal the latent potential of socialism. By the beginning of 1918, however, enthusiasm had waned. Where were the planes? The Liberty engine was in production but fitting it to an aircraft was proving difficult. The engine was too powerful for the British Bristol fighter. Eventually, it was successfully fitted to an American version of the de Havilland DH-4 bomber. But the de Havilland had many critics; it was nicknamed, perhaps unfairly, "the flying coffin." Stuart Brandes (1997, 163), after totaling the pluses and minuses of the aircraft, concludes that it is best described as a "contemporary but not advanced design." In the end few de Havillands reached France before the Armistice.

The aircraft program had, critics charged, not only been a failure in terms of output, but it had also been corrupt. Several years before the war, while at National Cash Register, Deeds had been convicted of violating anti-trust laws, although the conviction was overturned. More to the point, his claim that turning over his stock holdings to his wife during the war had constituted a divestiture was thin, to say the least. The critics also charged that Deeds had steered contracts to his friends in Dayton, Ohio. The de Havillands, for example, were built by Delco, a Dayton company he had helped to organize; some were tested on Deeds's private airstrip. There were a number of investigations. Perhaps the most important was a Justice Department investigation headed by Charles Evans Hughes that recommended prosecution. Deeds, however, survived the criticisms and investigations. He had vociferous critics, but also staunch defenders. Isaac F. Marcosson's admiring biography, *Colonel Deeds: Industrial Builder*

(1948), takes on the critics point by point. Yes, Deeds did steer some contracts to friends in Dayton, to take Marcosson's strongest point, but the "cronies," to use the modern term, included outstanding men such as Charles F. Kettering, who had developed the self-starter for the automobile among many other inventions, and Orville Wright who had developed the airplane itself.

If we take a step back from the personalities, we see two problems that in some measure afflicted all of the procurement programs. First was the lack of prewar planning and development. When it entered the war the United States simply did not have the military and industrial infrastructure to support, or the plans to guide, a major mobilization. The Aircraft Production Board, like other government procurement agencies, started from scratch. Second was the assumption that the war would last for several years after American entry. The Americans who developed the Liberty engine knew that it would take time to develop an engine that could be mass-produced. They assumed that the Liberty engine would help the Allies dominate the skies as the war dragged on into 1919 or even 1920. When the war ended quickly and unexpectedly the investment in mass-production had no time to pay off. Had they known that the war would end as soon as it did, they might have concentrated to a greater extent on simply producing European-designed engines.[17] The decision to go for mass-production would arise again in the early days of World War II. The British pressed for the conversion of existing factories, which would ensure that some production would come quickly, while the American planners wanted new factories, which would assure maximum production. In World War II, however, the war lasted long enough for the early decision to go for mass-production to repay the initial investment.[18]

Given these constraints, how well did the Aircraft Production Board do? The problem encountered in trying to answer this question is that there is little basis for comparison. The Europeans came to the war with different military and industrial histories; the United States had not been in a war calling for a major mobilization for fifty years. While it is easy for critics to point to mistakes that could have been avoided by an omnipotent planner – for example, the failed attempt to

[17] It was hard to follow European blueprints in American factories. Some translation and adaptation was necessary.

[18] This is not to say that a greater emphasis on current production in the early days of World War II would not have been worthwhile.

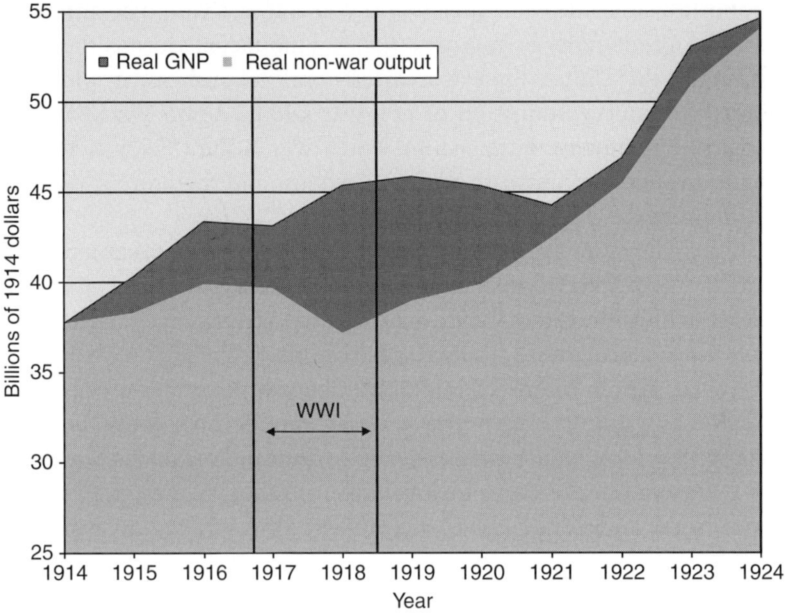

Figure 5.5 War and non-war production, 1914–24. Total output increased during the period of active US involvement; but non-war production still had to be cut to make room for war production.
Sources: Romer (1989); Kendrick (1961). This figure uses Romer's estimates of total real GNP, and estimates based on Kendrick of the breakdown between war-related and non-war-related government spending. Figure 5.6 presents an alternative set of estimates.

adapt the Bristol fighter to the Liberty engine – it is harder to point to real people or plausible institutions that would have done a better job. If not Deeds, Kettering, Wright, and Henry Ford, then who? If not the Aircraft Production Board, then what?

Although stories about individual programs and industries may give us a sense of what was going on, they may also mislead us about the overall picture. Figure 5.5 shows non-war production (baseballs, flowers, haircuts, college educations, the services provided by police officers, and so on) as the lower area and war production (planes, ships, tanks, the services of soldiers, and so on) as the upper area. Two important conclusions follow. (1) The United States, which had been devoting a small proportion of its resources to the production of war goods before 1914, returned to a small, although somewhat larger, proportion after the war. After World War II things would be different. (2) The production of non-war goods plummeted during the war. Although the United States increased total production, it was also forced to reduce production of non-war goods. Again World War II would be somewhat different. In World War II the USA was able to expand total production to a greater extent, and therefore it did not need to reduce civilian production as much.[19]

Although Figure 5.5 gives a reasonable answer to the question of how military spending affected the economy, it is worth noting that the numbers underlying the picture are subject to several uncertainties. The first concerns the price index used to deflate total spending on war goods. The upper area in Figure 5.5 is total spending on war goods divided by a price index that in principle represents the value of those goods. In other words, in principle the amount of money spent on war goods is divided by the average price (weighted average) of tanks, planes, battleships, soldiers, etc. In practice, however, an index of this sort was not available for the WWI era. There were prices, to be sure, in the government contracts for these items, but they were hard to locate, and, as I have noted previously, in truth they represented only part of the true cost: the government also helped to finance the factories where the weapons were built, helped to supply the factories with labor, and so on.

There is a still more fundamental question: should we include war output in GNP at all? Simon Kuznets wrestled with this question in *National Product in Wartime* (1945). It remains one of the best efforts to provide a broad statistical portrait of the war. Kuznets was the second American to win the Nobel Prize in Economic Science, which he won for his pioneering work in national income accounting. In World War II he served on the War Production Board. *National Product in Wartime* is his attempt to think through the meaning of national income in wartime, to compare wartime and peacetime measures of national income, and to compare World War I and World War II. Kuznets believed that GNP should exclude most war output in peacetime on the grounds that war output was an intermediate product. We would not include in GNP both the amount of automobiles produced and the salaries of the men and women hired as night watchmen at the

[19] Earlier estimates by Kuznets (1945) show all of the increase in war production coming at the expense of non-war production. Estimates by Balke and Gordon (1989) show a larger increase in total production during the war, but the decline in non-war production is still present.

factories that made automobiles. To include their salaries and the value of the automobiles would be double counting. If vandalism increased, the automobile company might withdraw workers from the assembly lines to serve as night watchmen. The production of automobiles would go down, and GNP would go down, as it should, to show that consumers were worse off than before.[20] Kuznets thought of government military spending as analogous to the spending on night watchmen. The military provided the security and protection that allowed the automobile company to produce the automobile that provided the ultimate satisfaction to the consumer. To include both the military spending and the automobile was double counting. If the world became less safe and the United States had to spend more on national security, then, other things equal, Kuznets's measure of GNP would decline to show that consumers were worse off than before.

Kuznets argued, however, that in a total war, such as World War I or World War II, society had changed. Producing consumer goods was no longer the be all and end all of economic activity. There were now two end goals of economic activity: producing war goods and producing civilian goods. Consequently in an all-out war both war goods and non-war goods should be included in national product. Most economists, however, have not been willing to follow Kuznets's lead and exclude war goods from peacetime GNP. The official statistics that we rely on include government spending on war goods as part of GNP. Ultimately, how we treat war goods depends to some extent on the question we are trying to answer. If our focus is on the amount of demand for workers, a GNP estimate that includes war goods would be best; if our focus is on the satisfaction of consumer wants, a GNP estimate that excludes war goods would be best.

Is it right to describe World War I as an era of prosperity? After all, the figures show that the flow of goods that could produce human satisfaction declined in the war, declined in fact more than in 1920–1, the first and rather severe postwar recession. But prosperity is not simply a function of the flow of goods and services. The security of full employment, and the understanding that one's employment is contributing to an important national effort, may also contribute to the sense that the nation is prosperous.

[20] We do, however, include the amount paid to private detectives in GNP because there is no alternative measure of the services they produce.

The cost of the war

Students of World War I are fortunate: the Carnegie Endowment for International Peace financed numerous scholarly studies of the war undertaken when memories were fresh and documents readily available. The task of estimating the costs of the war to the United States fell to John Maurice Clark, one of America's leading economists. The result, *The Costs of the World War to the American People* (1931), is a classic. The heart of Clark's study was his estimate of what he referred to as the "social outlays" for the war: expenditures that corresponded to real resources devoted to the war, resources that could have been devoted to producing civilian goods and services. A more common term today would be the "opportunity cost" of the resources devoted to the war. He began with an estimate of federal expenditures made by the US Treasury. This estimate included military spending (the increase over the prewar base) and the expenditures of other agencies doing war work such as the War Trade Board, the War Industries Board, the Alien Property Custodian, and so on. For the period of active involvement, fiscal 1917–21, the Treasury's estimate came to about $27 billion.

Clark then made a series of adjustments to bring the total closer to the opportunity cost of the war. The bulk of the changes came from five sources.

1 Clark subtracted interest on the increase in the federal debt from the Treasury estimate because the interest was simply a transfer from taxpayers to bond holders that did not add or subtract from the resources available to the economy either during or after the war.
2 Clark also subtracted part of the deficit of the Railroad Administration. The railroads, as we noted, were nationalized during the war and operated at a loss which was made up by the federal government. This payment represented real resources – the labor, capital, and fuel used to run the railroads – but only part of it represented the cost of the war. Some of the government subsidy went for resources that were carrying civilian products, and this portion, Clark argued, should be deducted from the Treasury's estimate of the cost of the war.
3 Clark added an estimate of the difference between what soldiers drafted for the war could have earned in the private sector and what they actually were paid. The former is clearly a better estimate of the opportunity cost of the draftees.

4 The Treasury's estimates only covered expenditures made by the federal government. These constituted the overwhelming bulk of war costs. But state and local governments and private organizations such as the Red Cross, YMCA, and so on also made expenditures that contributed to the war effort. Clark estimated the total from these sources at $800–900 million, the latter something over 3 percent of the costs borne by the federal government.
5 Clark's largest addition to the Treasury's estimate was the value of US loans to its allies. The expenditures made as a result of these loans diverted resources from the production of civilian goods to the production of war goods just as did expenditures by the US government. But what about the interest and principal repayments made after the war? If these repayments were made as scheduled they could be deducted from other ongoing costs of the war. It was possible that the present value of the future interest and principal payments would equal the wartime value of the loans. But these obligations had been scaled back substantially in the 1920s. Under the Young Plan (1929–30) the United States' allies agreed to a reduction of reparation payments from Germany in exchange for a reduction in their debt to the US. And as Clark was writing, the Hoover plan for a temporary moratorium on international reparation and interest payments was under consideration. Clark strongly supported the Hoover moratorium and thought that a permanent moratorium would be correct.

> And the whole situation increases the uncertainty as to whether it will prove practicable for us to collect the full amount of payments due us under the terms of the Young Plan. There can be no question that full collection would be an evil for the civilization of which our country forms a part. (Clark 1931, 280)

Clark went on, incidentally, to make an additional proto-Keynesian argument against deducting interest and principal repayments from the cost of the war. Suppose the Allies shipped goods or services to make their payments. This might simply displace domestic production in the United States (Clark 1931, 280). The net gain would be zero. In any case, as Clark foresaw, the present value of the interest and principal payments actually made was a small fraction of the initial value of the war loans. In considering the repayment of the war loans,

Table 5.4 *J. M. Clark's estimate of the cost of World War I, fiscal 1917–21*

Category	Amount (billions of current dollars)	Amount (billions of 2008 dollars)	Share of war costs (%)	Share of average real GDP (%)
War Department	14.85	145.21	46.4	19.8
Navy Department	3.40	33.25	10.6	4.5
Other federal agencies and corporations	5.22	51.04	16.3	7.0
Loans to Allies	7.47	73.05	23.3	10.0
Additional cost of the draft	0.23	2.25	0.7	0.7
Expenditures by state and local governments and private organizations	0.85	8.31	2.7	2.7
Subtotal	32.02	313.11	50.6	42.7
Veterans' benefits	96.20	305.70	49.40	41.7
Total	128.20	618.10	100.00	84.4

Sources: War costs: Clark (1931, 112, 120–1, 291–7). Veterans' benefits: Edwards (2010, Table 2, 36). Veterans' benefits were discounted to the midpoint of the war years at 4.00 percent. GDP and GDP deflator: Johnston and Williamson (2010).

as a potential reduction in the costs of the war, we are looking at things, it should be noted, from the point of view of the United States. From the point of view of the world economy, the loans are rightfully considered part of the opportunity cost of the war, and the subsequent interest and principal payments are transfers from taxpayers in Europe to Americans that don't in the first instance alter the total of resources available to the world economy. The addition of the war loans added nearly 28 percent to the Treasury's estimate of the costs of the war.

Altogether, Clark estimated the cost of the war, as shown in Table 5.4, at $32 billion in current dollars, about $313 billion in 2008 dollars. The largest cost was expenditures of the War Department (army and army air force). No surprise there. Next in importance, however, were

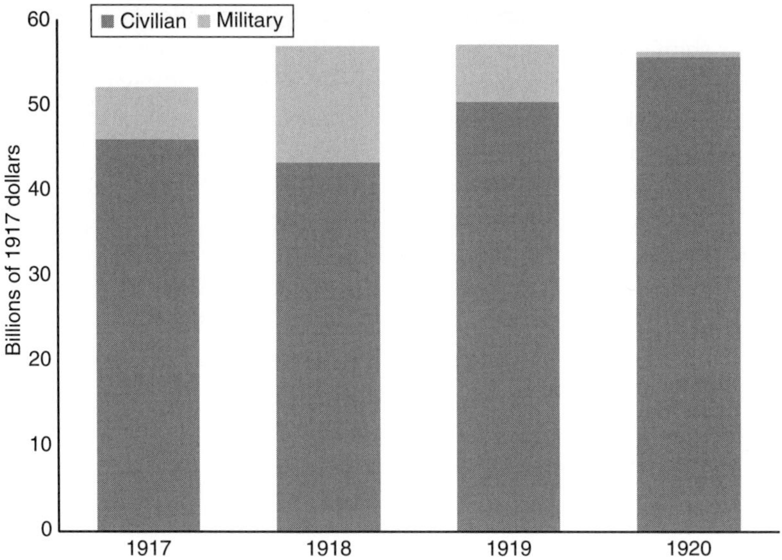

Figure 5.6 Clark's estimates of the costs of the war and the civilian component of GDP, 1917–19. The big push in 1918 was accomplished by increasing total production and diverting resources from the civilian to the military sector. *Sources:* Cost of the war: Clark (1932, 121). GDP: Carter *et al.* (2006, series Ca10).

expenditures for loans to the Allies and then, expenditures by federal emergency agencies and corporations. Expenditures by the navy came fourth. The contribution of state and local governments and private organizations, although important, added only marginal amounts to the total cost of the war. All of these numbers were first computed in nominal terms. Prices, it is true, were rising rapidly during the war and in the early postwar years, so a computation in constant dollars would produce a somewhat different total. But since much of the inflation came in 1919 and 1920 when expenditures were being cut back, the effect is not as great as one might imagine. In constant 1917 dollars the cost of the war would have been about $27 billion, rather than the $32 billion shown in Table 5.4.

Figure 5.6 shows Clark's annual estimates of war-related spending (in constant 1917 dollars) compared with civilian spending (also in constant 1917 dollars).[21] Clark's estimates, broadly

[21] Clark did not present estimates by category (war, loans to Allies, etc.) in constant 1917 dollars.

speaking, confirm more recent estimates that focus on long-term data shown in Figure 5.5. Evidently, the mobilization reached its peak in 1918 when about 24 percent of the economy was devoted to the war effort. The push from 1917 to 1918 was impressive. The increase in military production was accomplished partly by pushing up total production by 9 percent, but it was still necessary to reduce production for the civilian sector by about 6 percent. This mobilization, like the mobilization in World War II, would be accomplished partly by pushing the production possibilities frontier outward, and partly by moving along it. Although the economy reached full employment, Americans may have felt the disruptions caused by the war – railroad congestion, problems in the distribution of coal for the winter months, and so on – more than they would in World War II.

Legacies: a new role for the USA in the world economy

Americans would have liked their involvement with Europe to have ended when the war ended, but the peace treaty, the Treaty of Versailles, and the problem of German reparations that it created – and the problem of the debts owed to the United States by its wartime Allies which was entangled with the problem of reparations – would continue to vex them for a generation. These problems were closely tied to profound changes in the international financial system.

The Treaty of Versailles

President Wilson sailed for Paris on December 4, 1918 to take part in the negotiations that would decide the fate of Germany. Ultimately, the decisions would be made by the "Big Four": Wilson, Georges Clemenceau (France), David Lloyd George (Great Britain), and Vittorio Orlando (Italy). The basic economic issues were straightforward: Britain (and the other members of the British empire), France, and Italy wanted cash, land, and other resources from Germany.[22] Wilson's goals were, it is usually said, more idealistic: an end to the

[22] Other nations had claims on Germany. Japan, for example, wanted territorial concessions in Asia.

secret treaties that had accelerated the march to war, independence for the ethnic minorities of central and eastern Europe, and a "League of Nations" that could prevent future conflicts. Punishing and taking resources from Germany were not his top priorities.[23] Perhaps one can see in Wilson's attitude toward Germany his view of the American Civil War. Wilson was a historian and a Southerner and believed that the harsh treatment of the South after the Civil War was a mistake that had fueled bitter resentment. In World War II we will see Roosevelt invoking a Northern view of the Civil War toward Germany: the right policy is the policy Lincoln had intended to follow with the South, to seek unconditional surrender and follow it with political reconstruction that produces a robust democracy.

For economists, thinking about the Treaty of Versailles begins with John Maynard Keynes. Keynes had served as an advisor to the British Treasury during the war and to the British delegation to the Paris peace conference. But he returned to England before the end of the conference to write *The Economic Consequences of the Peace* (1920 [1919]), a brilliant criticism of the forthcoming treaty, which he denounced for imposing a vindictive peace, a "Carthaginian Peace," that would produce further turmoil in Europe. Keynes's book is a classic. His descriptions of Lloyd George, Wilson, and other participants are masterful, and his economic analysis acute.

Keynes's criticisms of the treaty covered a broad front, but there were two main points. First, the bill for reparations that the Allies were presenting to the Germans was simply too large. A major part of the bill was for separation payments for military personnel, pensions for veterans, and compensation and pensions for veterans and their families. Germany had agreed to the Armistice based on Wilson's promise that it would be required to pay for damages to civilians but not for military expenditures by the Allies or for punitive damages. As Keynes himself pointed out, a woman who loses her soldier-husband suffers just as much as a neighbor who loses her factory-worker husband. But Keynes argued that separation payments, pensions, and widows' compensation had been excluded by prior commitments to the Germans. The damage to the civilian economies where the war

[23] But Trachtenberg (1982) criticizes the conventional view that Wilson single-mindedly favored a conciliatory policy and stresses the punitive aspects of Wilson's approach to the treaty.

was actually fought, Keynes agreed, was horrendous. But the damage he argued, was confined to a surprisingly thin and stable band where trenches were dug and artillery fire exchanged. On either side of that band farmland and industrial capacity remained intact.

In practice it was impossible to persuade the Allies that Germany should not pay for veterans' benefits (mustering out pay, compensation, and pensions), which it was easy to see would be the largest source of postwar expenditures by governments resulting from the war. According to Niall Ferguson (2004, 264) the most important voice demanding that Germans pay veterans belonged to "Australian Prime Minister William M. Hughes, who discerned that his country would gain nothing from the Treaty if a narrow definition of reparations were adopted." Hughes's concern was understandable because Australia had made a major contribution to the Allied war effort. About 62,000 Australians died, 53,993 in battle, and about 137,000 were wounded.[24] The battle losses were similar to those of the United States.

The second point was that Germany, according to Keynes, lacked the capacity to pay the reparations that were to be set by a separate commission. The final figure was about $56 billion in gold, about $550 billion at today's (2010) prices, a substantial sum for a country devastated by war. There was, to be more precise, an insurmountable problem that Keynes later referred to as the "transfer problem," a term that became standard among economists. In order to pay $56 billion in gold Germany would either have to sell assets or run a large balance of payments surplus. The treaty, however, stripped Germany of most of the assets, such as the merchant marine, that could be easily carried away. And sustaining a large balance of payments surplus over many years would be an impossible task. Policies would have to be put in place that significantly reduced imports or raised exports. But import reduction simply wasn't possible: a prostrated Germany would need to maintain or even increase imports of fertilizer, railroad rolling stock, and other forms of capital just to get back on its feet. There was a greater possibility of expanding exports. But it would not be easy, Keynes thought, to reorganize German industry to focus all its energies on export markets. And would producers in other countries allow themselves to be drowned by a flood of cheap German exports of steel, chemicals, and electrical products,

[24] Australian War Museum: www.awm.gov.au/index.asp.

or instead would they insist on tariff barriers that kept the flow of German goods to a trickle? Would newly empowered working classes stand idly by while jobs were lost to Germany, the deadly enemy of a few years past? In short it was simply not possible for Germany to make the transfers it was being called upon to make. Forcing Germany to pay would result in privation, and possibly in open debt repudiation and Bolshevism.

Keynes was later criticized for being excessively pessimistic about Germany's capacity to pay the reparations. The most famous criticism was Étienne Mantoux's *The Carthaginian Peace; or The Economic Consequences of Mr. Keynes* (1952 [1946]). Mantoux, a brilliant young Frenchman, wrote the book during World War II and, a flyer, he was killed in action in April 1945. Mantoux argued that Germany did in fact have the capacity to pay reparations; it simply lacked the will to do so.[25] The rapid recovery of the German economy after the war shown in statistics on coal production, exports, national income, and so on proved, as far as Mantoux was concerned, that Keynes's depiction of Germany as a nation that could never recover sufficiently to meet the terms of the treaty was simply wrong. The passionate feelings that drove Mantoux are revealed in the use he makes of Hitler's military buildup and attack on France. Keynes had suggested, as I noted above, that it would be difficult for Germany to reorganize its economy to focus on exports. Here is Mantoux's (1952 [1946], 123) impassioned answer:

> The huge transformation involved in the building up of the German war machine did not only mean "a radical change in the kind of work performed" [a quote from Keynes,] the goods thus produced were very literally and very materially "transferred" and "exported" abroad. Is it to be seriously maintained that even the vast increase of production of exportable peacetime goods implied by the Reparation scheme would have met with *greater* [Mantoux's italics] difficulties?

A long technical debate over the transfer problem followed which eventually generated contributions from many of the leading macro and international trade theorists of that generation including Paul Samuelson, Harry Johnson, Lloyd Metzler, Fritz Maclup, Bertil Ohlin, and many others. To go into the details of this debate would take us

[25] Also see White (2001) who shows that the French did pay the Napoleonic reparations, which were of a similar magnitude.

beyond the scope of the current discussion. Here we can note that Keynes's book also helped produce a belief in the United States that the treaty was too harsh and that the solution to European problems involved a reduction in the excessive claims of the victors.

In *The Economic Consequences of the Peace* (1920 [1919], chapter 7) and subsequently in *A Revision of the Treaty* (1922), Keynes had argued for a loan from the United States to Europe to help get Europe back on its feet, and an all-around cancellation of Allied war debts (the United States had lent mainly to Britain, France, and Italy). The idea of a loan, despite Keynes's eloquent appeal, was initially a non-starter in the United States. Lending money to America's allies to help them defeat the enemy seemed a good investment. It was similar to building tanks and planes or hiring mercenaries: a way of minimizing American casualties. Lending money to former enemies to turn them into economic competitors was something else altogether. Forgiving wartime debts from the Allies also seemed like bad business during the prosperous 1920s.

But the depiction of the United States as unsympathetic to claims for relief, and blind to the consequences of debt and reparation payments for the international economic and political system, is overdrawn. President Coolidge is alleged to have said, "They hired the money didn't they?" But no one knows for sure that he did, and in fact the Americans made important efforts to deal with the problem of Allied war debts (Rhodes 1969), and the closely associated problem of German reparations. In 1922 Congress created the World War Foreign Debt Commission which concluded agreements with America's debtors reducing the principal and interest on their debts in line with their ability to pay. In 1923 Germany defaulted on its obligations, and in retaliation French and Belgian troops occupied the Ruhr Valley in Germany. This impasse was resolved by the Dawes Plan of 1924 which provided for the removal of the French and Belgians, stretched out the reparations payments, and provided for loans from the United States to Germany to make possible the resumption of payments. Charles G. Dawes, an American, was awarded the Nobel Peace Prize for 1925 for his work on the plan. The Dawes Plan, however, did not solve the German reparation problem. Germany found it hard to pay even the smaller annual amounts due under the plan and opposition to the treaty in Germany grew. In 1929 a second plan – named the Young Plan, after the American in charge, Owen D. Young, a Wall Street financier – further reduced and extended Germany's reparation obligations. To administer the reparations payments this plan also created the Bank for International Settlements, which still survives and plays a role in international bank supervision. But the assumptions that underpinned the Young Plan were dashed by the stock market crash and the onset of the Great Depression.

Once the Depression started President Hoover proposed a moratorium on all payments on Allied debts and on German reparations. It is unlikely that the moratorium had a major impact on the Allies, but it may have made a more expansionary policy possible in Germany, suggesting that had the reparation payments been cancelled earlier, the Depression in Germany would not have been as severe as it was (Fleisig 1972). In the end, a decade of negotiations, refusals to pay, and scaling down and canceling of debt had produced more or less what Keynes had called for in 1919: a reduction in German reparations and the cancellation of inter-Allied debts. Although some payments on the Allied debt were made, Clark's decision to include loans to Allies as part of the "cost of the war to the American people" was correct. Whatever was received was surely offset by the anti-Americanism set in motion by the US attempt to see the loans as anything other than payments for services rendered – for a time the United States became "Uncle Shylock" and Americans became "USorors." In World War II the United States would turn to "Lend-Lease," a policy essentially of giving weapons to its allies, rather than indebting them in some way, in part to avoid a repetition of the problems encountered in World War I.

The international gold standard

The international gold standard reached the high tide of its prestige in the years before World War I. All of the major industrial countries – Britain, the United States, France, and Germany – and many other nations were on the gold standard, meaning that their currencies could be converted into fixed physical quantities of gold. The US dollar, for example, was the equivalent of about 0.05 ounces of gold (0.0484 to be more exact). The British pound, however, was heavier, about 0.25 ounces of gold (0.2353). Therefore the exchange rate stayed in the neighborhood of $4.86 to the pound. The great advantage of the gold standard was that it insured that exchange rates among nations on the standard would be fixed within narrow limits. Fixed exchange rates simplified and facilitated international trade. One could buy raw materials in one part of the world, process them in another, and sell the final product in a third, without worrying that a sudden change in exchange rates would undo all the careful calculations on which the ultimate profit was based. Long-term investment was facilitated by the fixed exchange rates of the gold standard, and by the ideology of the gold standard which held that nations had to be prepared to defend their exchange rates even when the costs of doing so were extremely high. Under the "rules of the gold standard game," as John Maynard Keynes styled it, with some irony, a nation that was running a balance of payments deficit, and hence was losing gold, was supposed to raise its domestic interest rate, tightening money and credit, and thus reversing the flow of gold. Investors in capital-rich Britain could buy stocks and bonds or make direct investments in the United States without having to worry that the value of interest payments or profits brought home in later years would be adversely affected by changes in exchange rates. Indeed, London became the center of a worldwide capital market that sent capital out in all directions to build railroads, dig mines, create telephone networks, and so on. Rapidly developing, relatively high-income nations such as Canada, the United States, and Australia were the major recipients, but the flow of capital reached less developed nations in Europe, Africa, Latin America, and Asia.

The gold standard provided another important dimension of economic stability: price stability. Under the gold standard increasing the money supply required an increase in the amount of gold backing the money supply. Normally, that meant mining gold domestically or acquiring gold from abroad by running a balance of payments deficit. Some monetary gold could be had by diverting gold from artistic or industrial uses, but that was a costly process. A money supply tied down by a "golden anchor" simply could not grow as fast as a pure fiat (paper) money system. Indeed, in the 1880s and early 1890s, the gold standard had produced deflation. The demand for monetary gold rose with the growth of economic activity, and as more and more countries adopted the gold standard. The demand for monetary gold exceeded the supply and as a result the real value of monetary gold – the nominal value divided by the price level – rose. Deflation did not stop economic growth in the United States or other countries on the gold standard: real GDP per capita continued to rise. But deflation produced considerable political tension. Farmers felt particularly aggrieved. Typically, farmers are debtors and debtors tend to suffer during deflations. Interest rates may adjust (fall) to reflect deflation, but the adjustment may be slow, and does nothing for those who entered into contracts before the deflation became evident. In the United States western farmers were especially upset, because many of them had purchased farms on the frontier based on optimistic projections of crops and prices. They were the heart of the populist movement that roiled American politics at the end of the nineteenth century.

After 1896, however, prices in countries tied to gold turned up. The reason was an increase in the supply of gold. New discoveries in the Klondike, Western Australia, and most importantly, South Africa (where the new cyanide process for extracting gold from gold ore could be used) added to the flow of gold and turned a mild deflation into a mild inflation. The change in the trend of prices quieted opposition to the gold standard. The years leading up to World War I were the golden years of the classical gold standard. In *The Economic Consequences of the Peace*, Keynes memorably described the functioning of the prewar gold standard.

> The inhabitant of London could order by telephone, sipping his morning tea in bed, the various products of the whole earth, in such quantity as he might see fit, and reasonably expect their early delivery upon his doorstep; he could at the same moment and by the same means adventure his wealth in the natural resources and new enterprises of any quarter of the world, and share, without exertion or even trouble, in their prospective fruits and advantages; or he could decide to couple the security of his fortunes with the good faith of the townspeople of any substantial municipality in any continent that fancy or information might recommend. He could secure forthwith, if he wished it, cheap and comfortable means of transit to any country or climate without passport or other formality, could despatch his servant to the neighboring office of a bank for such supply of the precious metals as might seem convenient, and could then proceed abroad to foreign quarters, without knowledge of their religion, language, or customs, bearing coined wealth upon his person, and would consider himself greatly aggrieved and much surprised at the least interference. (Keynes 1920 [1919], 11–12)

All that changed with the outbreak of World War I. All of the belligerents faced enormous costs. The printing press was an obvious source of funds, one that could not be ignored. And all of the nations at war turned in some degree to the printing press to finance the conflict. In Britain, the heart of the prewar international gold standard, the gold standard was abandoned, the money supply was expanded, and prices (measured by the GDP deflator) rose by a factor of 2.7 between 1914 and 1920, the postwar peak. In the United States, although President Wilson banned exports of gold in 1917, the internal connection to gold was maintained, and gold remained in domestic circulation. America as a safe haven for financial assets was a recipient of gold, and America's resources were immense. Hence, the inflation was less in the United States than in Britain or the other major powers – prices rose by a factor of 1.9 in the United States. Even in America, however, the commitment to the gold standard was probably saved by the abrupt end of the war. Altogether, the United States was actively engaged only for about eighteen months, from April 1917 to October 1918. Had the war gone on for several more years the United States would have followed the other belligerents off the gold standard.

After the war there was, naturally, considerable sentiment for reconstructing the gold standard, a system that had worked well in many ways before the war. But there were several obstacles. The main problem was the inflation. At higher price levels the world needed larger money supplies to finance transactions. Larger money supplies meant, under the gold standard, more gold to back the money supply, but the physical quantity of gold had not expanded in nearly the same proportion as the world money supply. Currencies would have to be devalued, that is made equivalent to smaller quantities of gold, or prices would have to be reduced through restrictive monetary policies, generally a painful process involving temporary periods of high unemployment. A uniform international devaluation would have been possible if prices had risen at the same rates in different countries. But they had not: traditional trading partners had often experienced very different rates of inflation during the war. If every country went back to gold at the prewar exchange rates, but at some common devaluation in terms of gold, some countries would find themselves with overvalued currencies and balance of payments deficits. Each country separately then had to decide the exchange rate at which it would return to the prewar gold standard.

The decisions to be made about the return to the gold standard, moreover, were compounded by the rise of political parties representing the working class. Under the gold standard maintenance of fixed exchange rates and stable prices had taken precedence over the use of monetary policy to stimulate economies in recession. Note that the famous description of the system by Keynes, quoted above, describes the world from the point of view of a middle-class Englishman. Keynes described the condition of the working class before the war in these terms: "The greater part of the population, it is true, worked hard and lived at a low standard of comfort, yet were, to all appearances, reasonably contented with this lot" (Keynes 1920 [1919], 11). The rise of the left meant that politicians and monetary authorities could no longer adhere to the traditional ideology of the gold standard with the same absence of criticism as they had before the war. More weight had to be given to reducing unemployment when that emerged as a major problem, even if it meant endangering or abandoning the commitment to gold. The rise of the left was a long-term trend, but World War I greatly accelerated it. The triumph of Bolshevism in Russia, and the need to secure the cooperation of labor in the war effort in the other belligerents, strengthened the left, and undermined political support for the gold standard.

Nevertheless, attempts were made to reestablish ties to gold during the 1920s. France went back to gold at an undervalued rate (a rate that made it attractive to holders of other currencies) and as a result enjoyed a balance of payments surplus during the 1920s. Indeed, France accumulated a substantial fraction of the world's monetary gold. Some observers at the time, and some subsequent scholars, have blamed France for accumulating so much gold that other countries were forced into restrictive monetary policies that contributed to the onset of the Great Depression (Irwin 2010). There were many reasons for France's commitment to accumulating gold. But the notion that a large reserve of gold would be a useful war chest may have played a role.

Britain, however, followed another course, and decided to return to the gold standard at the prewar par with the dollar. In 1924 economist John Maynard Keynes warned Winston Churchill, then Chancellor of the Exchequer, that going back to gold at the prewar par would impose unnecessary costs on the British economy. It would price British goods out of world markets, and inhibit employment growth. Better, Keynes thought, to devalue in line with the changes in American and British prices. Churchill, however, rejected that advice. Devaluation, he thought, would be inflationary (Wolcott 1990), and he was under pressure from the City (the financial district of London) to maintain the prewar parity. The City believed that its preeminent position in world finance before the war had rested in part on the reputation of the pound as a currency of unchanging value. After all, the gold content of the pound had not been changed between the Napoleonic Wars and World War I. There is some evidence, however, that Britain's economic stagnation and high unemployment in the late 1920s were aggravated by its decision to return to par at the prewar exchange rates. These problems might have been alleviated if the countries accumulating gold, the United States and France, had allowed the gold inflows to increase their stocks of money and produce inflation. Higher prices in those markets would have made British exports more attractive. But, instead, the United States and France "sterilized" the gold inflows, as it was said, that is they prevented the gold flows from increasing the money supply.

However, it seems unlikely there was any policy that Britain could have followed after the war that would have altered the fate of the pound, which had to surrender its top position as an international reserve currency to the US dollar (Eichengreen 2011). The United States had been overtaking Britain and its European rivals for many years. Total real GDP in the United States had passed that of Britain in the 1880s, and its real per capita income had drawn close to Britain's as a result of the war. Before the war a central banker might be indifferent between holding gold and pounds, given the unchanging gold content of the latter since the early nineteenth century. After WWI, however, it made more sense to hold at least part of one's reserves in US dollars, a currency that had remained on the gold standard and the medium of exchange in the world's largest economy.

New York, moreover, supplanted London as the world's most important capital market. The United States had gone from being a debtor nation, the normal condition for a developing nation, to being a creditor nation, the normal condition for a mature economy. British citizens had surrendered a part of their overseas holdings of securities. Developing nations trying to raise capital had to go where the money was, and that was Wall Street. London did not, of course, disappear as a financial center. And there is no reason why it should have. After all, there are many examples, such as Switzerland, of small nations that have been successful in nurturing financial centers. Nevertheless, World War I had produced a shift in financial power from an exhausted Britain to the United States. The benefits of providing the world's reserve currency and housing its most important financial center were benefits to the United States and costs to Britain, not necessarily benefits to the world as a whole. The international financial system had been well served by Britain before the war, and US financial houses would make mistakes in the process of learning how to make international investments.

The veterans

Veterans' benefits proved to be the largest long-term cost of the war and the source of the biggest political headaches. When the United States entered World War I the idea of a general pension for veterans was in bad repute because of the excesses (or so they were perceived) produced by the Civil War pension system. William Glasson and David Kinley's *Federal Military Pensions* (1918) is a superb work of careful scholarship written for the Carnegie Endowment for International Peace, based on earlier studies by Glasson. It is not, however, a neutral summary of the facts. Corruption of the pension system is, to a surprising extent, one of the central themes, perhaps it would be fair to say *the* central theme. The implication is that in the future veterans' benefit systems should be tightly controlled. The "Editor's Preface" written by David Kinley, a distinguished economist who had served as president of the American Economic Association in 1913, is even more pointed in describing what Kinley saw as the downward moral spiral of the Civil War pension. The reader of Glasson's account, according to Kinley (Glasson and Kinley 1918, vii), will "be depressed by the account of moral degeneration and political corruption that gradually crept into the administration and operation of our old pension system." One response to the warnings and criticism was to change the language describing the benefits to be provided to veterans. Instead of using the traditional term, the veterans' "gratuity," the legislation and government documents now talked about "compensation." The new term acknowledged an obligation to veterans – veterans had suffered wounds, faced dangers, missed out on experience and training in the civilian workforce, and therefore deserved compensation – but the new term also suggested limits. Once the veteran had been compensated, he was not entitled to more.

In line with the idea of compensating the veteran for losses, and perhaps with the idea of avoiding the corruption inherent in cash payments, the legislation emphasized several in-kind benefits: (1) government-subsidized life insurance (or as it was more accurately termed "death compensation"), (2) vocational education, and (3) free medical and hospital care. The actual cash compensation for total disability, $360 per year, was, as a later President's Commission noted, "a low rate of compensation" (US President's Commission on Veterans' Pensions 1956, 28). Stanley Lebergott's estimate of annual earnings of all employees (US Bureau of the Census 1975, series D723) is $748 for 1917, making the replacement rate for veterans unable to work 48 percent. Possibly the legislators were not taking the inflation into account: based on 1914 earnings, the replacement rate was 65 percent.

Shortly after World War I ended, veterans led by the American Legion, which had been formed in Paris after the end of the war, began campaigning for a cash bonus.[26] Part of the argument for the bonus was simply to express the gratitude of the nation for what the soldiers had done. However, there was also a new economic argument based on the idea of compensation. The veterans had been receiving $30 per month in the army while their friends who stayed home were making considerably more. Thus, veterans were entitled to "adjusted compensation" (Bodenger 1971, 199–201). As proposed by the American Legion the veterans were to receive $1.25 for each day of active overseas service and $1.00 for each day of active home service. The maximum was to be $625 for overseas service and $500 for home service. The postwar recession with its intensive deflation added to the case for "adjusted compensation:" those who stayed at home saw their wages rise during the war, and the dollars they saved, the Legion argued, were now worth more as prices fell, a sophisticated economic argument.

The plan was popular, but it ran into trouble when the costs came into view: more than 3 million men would be eligible. In 1921 a bill for immediate payment of a bonus passed the House by a large

[26] Veterans' organizations, and their ability to lobby for pensions, were nothing new. The Grand Army of the Republic, a veterans' organization for Union veterans of the Civil War, had been instrumental in pushing for an enlargement of the Civil War pension. The Veterans of Foreign Wars had worked hard on behalf of the veterans of the Spanish–American War and the other conflicts of that era. The veterans of World War I, of course, were well aware of these precedents.

majority. Before his election President Harding had said that he supported such a bill. However, once in office he was swayed by Secretary of the Treasury Mellon's argument that a bonus would damage the economy by undermining Mellon's policy of tax cutting and retrenchment. First Harding moved to the position that a bonus would be proper if there were new taxes, for example a national sales tax, to finance it. Eventually, he vetoed the bonus. Harding's policy was followed by his successors. In 1924 Coolidge vetoed another bill that would have paid an immediate bonus to the veterans. However, legislation was passed and signed that would pay a bonus, but not until 1945.[27] The latter bill, moreover, created some mechanisms by which veterans could gain immediate access to some of their funds. This was adequate in the 1920s, but not in the 1930s. In 1932, with the Depression at full throttle, a "bonus army" of veterans and their families gathered in Washington to press for an immediate payment. In June 1932 the House passed a bill that would pay the bonus, but it failed in the Senate. The bonus army remained in Washington and tensions ran high. In the fall, on President Hoover's order, the bonus army was driven out, by the regular army at bayonet point. The army, incidentally, was led by General Douglas MacArthur. In 1933 a new bonus army descended on Washington. These veterans were met warmly by President Roosevelt, and various promises of aid were made, but there was no promise of an immediate payment of the bonus.

Indeed, early New Deal legislation went against the veterans. The little-known Economy Act of 1933, one of the many pieces of legislation passed during Roosevelt's first hundred days, repealed all laws providing benefits for veterans of the Spanish–American War and World War I, and gave the President, within broad limits, the power to set new entitlements, more or less generous, as he chose. The reason for this extraordinary grant of power is understandable. In 1932 the federal budget was deeply in the red: the deficit was close to 60 percent of expenditures. To be sure, the gain from cutting veterans' benefits was likely to be small. The benefits (excluding the amounts spent on education and training) amounted to only 5 percent of total

[27] In 1930, however, needy disabled veterans of World War I were pensioned, even if their disability was not service connected (US President's Commission on Veterans' Pensions 1956, Staff Report No. I, 35).

spending. Still, the pull of the idea that "everything should be on the table" was powerful, and the President's initial executive orders, made possible by the Economy Act, cut benefits significantly. The American Legion and other representatives of the veterans then went to work to restore the benefits. Many were reinstated, but not the pure service pensions; benefits were restored only for needy, disabled veterans. These actions may seem at odds with an image of Roosevelt as a President with broad social sympathies. But, influenced by the belief that rewarding veterans would weaken support for broader reforms, and perhaps influenced as well by the reputation of the Civil War pension, Roosevelt was not willing to meet the demands of veterans for increased relief. Social security, for example, would provide relief for all elderly Americans, veterans and non-veterans. However, political pressure to do something for the veterans with respect to their bonus remained strong. In 1936 legislation was finally passed over Roosevelt's veto that led to payment of the bonus to more than 3 million veterans, ending the long and sometimes demoralizing history of the bonus. The additional purchasing power created by the bonus appears to have been spent rapidly, providing a temporary Keynesian stimulus for the economy (Telser 2003).

6 *World War II*

We must be the great arsenal of democracy. For us this is an emergency as serious as war itself. We must apply ourselves to our task with the same resolution, the same sense of urgency, the same spirit of patriotism and sacrifice as we would show were we at war.

President Franklin Roosevelt, radio address (fireside chat), December 29, 1940

A chronology of World War II

1939		
August	2	President Roosevelt receives a letter signed by Albert Einstein advocating that the United States build a nuclear bomb.
	9	The War Resources Board is established.
September	1	Germany invades Poland.
	3	Prime Minister Neville Chamberlain announces to the British people that a state of war exists with Germany.
1940		
January	3	Roosevelt's budget message calls for more defense spending and a production program of 50,000 planes per year.
April 9–June 11		Germany invades and conquers Norway.
May 10–June 4		Germany invades and conquers Belgium, Luxembourg, and the Netherlands.
May	29	Roosevelt establishes the National Defense Advisory Commission.

May 28–June 4		British and French troops evacuated from Dunkirk.
June 5–July 10		Germany invades and conquers France.
June	25	First War Revenue Act decreases personal income tax exemptions about 20 percent and raises rates about 10 percent.
August 8–October 31		"Battle of Britain." Germany attacks Britain by air and is defeated.
September	27	Selective Service Act creating a draft for military service is signed.
December	20	Office of Production Management established, William S. Knudsen director.
	29	In a fireside chat Roosevelt calls for the United States to become "the great arsenal of democracy."

1941

March	11	The Lend-Lease Act, which provides credits for Allies to purchase munitions, is signed.
April	11	Office of Price Administration and Civilian Supply created.
May	7	British cabinet agrees to a plan to destroy fifty-eight of Germany's largest towns and cities by air.
	10	British Prime Minister Winston Churchill writes Roosevelt asking for obsolete destroyers to use against German submarines in the "Battle of the Atlantic."
June	22	Germany invades Russia.
July	26	The USA freezes Japanese credits in the United States, ending most trade with Japan.
August	28	Roosevelt creates the Office of Price Administration and Civilian Supply, and the Supply Priorities Allocation Board.

October	31	First US–Soviet Protocol providing Lend-Lease aid is signed.
December	7	Japan attacks Pearl Harbor.
	8	The United States declares war on Japan.
	11	The United States recognizes a state of war exists with Germany and Italy after they declare war on the United States.
	19	Congress extends conscription to men aged twenty to forty-four.
	21	The first US rationing program: automobile tires.
1942		
January	2	Japan captures Manila.
	13	Donald M. Nelson is appointed chair of the War Production Board, the agency that succeeds the Office of Production Management.
April	9	US forces on Bataan in the Philippines surrender unconditionally to the Japanese.
May 30–August	19	The Allies carry out major bombing campaigns including 1,000-bomber attacks on Cologne and Essen.
June 4–5		The United States wins an important naval victory over Japan at Midway in the Pacific.
September	10	The Baruch Committee issues its report on synthetic rubber.
	17	General Leslie Groves is appointed the military leader of the Manhattan (atomic bomb) Project.
October	15	J. Robert Oppenheimer is appointed the scientific leader of the Manhattan Project.
November	8	Allied forces land in North Africa.

1943		
January	14–24	At a conference at Casablanca the Allies agree that their goal is the unconditional surrender of Germany, Italy, and Japan.
January	18	The Soviets break the siege at Leningrad.
February	2	German forces at Stalingrad surrender.
July	10	Allied forces invade Sicily.
August 17–October	15	US Eighth Air Force bombs ball-bearing factories at Schweinfurt and Regensburg.
September	3	Having secured Sicily, Allied forces land at Salerno on the Italian mainland.
1944		
January	22	Allied forces make an amphibious landing at Anzio, south of Rome.
March	6	The United States bombs Berlin.
June	4	Allied forces liberate Rome.
	6	D Day: Allied forces land in France.
July	1–22	The structure of the postwar international financial system is hammered out in a conference at Bretton Woods, New Hampshire.
October	20	American ground forces under General Douglas MacArthur return to the Philippines.
October	23–25	Japanese naval forces suffer heavy losses in the Battle of Leyte Gulf.
November	3	The Strategic Bombing Survey is established.
December	16–26	Battle of the Bulge: German forces launch a surprise attack on Allied forces in the Ardennes, which is halted after heavy losses.
1945		
March	7	Cologne and Düsseldorf fall to the Allies.
April 1–June 21		American forces capture Okinawa after heavy fighting.

April	24	Soviet forces enter Berlin.
May	8	V-E Day: Victory in Europe, Germany surrenders to the Allies.
June	11	The Franck Report: a group of scientists working on the Manhattan Project argue that the bomb should be detonated in an unpopulated area to demonstrate its destructive power.
	16	An atomic bomb is successfully tested in the United States.
August	6	The United States uses an atomic bomb to destroy Hiroshima.
	9	The United States uses an atomic bomb to destroy Nagasaki.
	14	Japan surrenders.
	15	V-J Day: Victory over Japan. Japan surrenders unconditionally.
August 27–September 9		The United States occupies Japan.
September	2	Japan surrenders in a formal ceremony held aboard ship in Tokyo Bay.
1946		
November	26	President Truman establishes the Atomic Bomb Casualty Commission.
1947		
June	5	Secretary of State George C. Marshall speaks at the Harvard commencement where he makes the case for aid to promote Europe's recovery from the war.
1948		
April	2	Congress passes the European Recovery Program, popularly known as the Marshall Plan.
June	19	A new currency, the Deutschmark, is introduced in West Germany, and controls on prices and wages are lifted.

1949		
May	23	Occupation of Germany by the Western Allies ends with the creation of the Federal Republic of Germany.
1951		
December	31	The Marshall Plan ends.
1952		
April	28	Occupation of Japan ends.

Sources: Linton (1975), Schlesinger and Bowman (1993), Morris and Morris (1996), other chronologies of American history, the *New York Times*; and the *Wall Street Journal.*

Fighting World War II would require the largest mobilization of resources in the history of the United States. The Civil War required a massive mobilization of the labor force – and in the end would leave more men dead (North and South together) – but World War II would require the mobilization of industry on an unprecedented scale. Although America's losses would be small compared with those of many other nations, they would nonetheless be traumatic for the United States. About 292,000 Americans died in battle or from wounds suffered in battle, and another 114,000 died from disease and injury, a total of 406,000; and about 672,000 suffered non-mortal wounds (see Appendix 2). Since the population of the United States has more than doubled since 1945, an equivalent loss today might, in a sense, be the equivalent of more than 800,000 deaths and 1.4 million non-mortal wounds. It was, clearly, a staggering price to pay for victory.

The origins of the war

World War II was a product of the imperial ambitions of Germany, Japan, and Italy. In all three countries militarists believed that first power status ought to be the overriding national objective and could be achieved only by building an empire. Hitler wanted to restore Germany to its central role in Europe by reuniting the German people, reverse what he saw as the humiliations of November 1918 and

Versailles by defeating France, and provide the German people with room to expand by conquering the Soviet Union and destroying Communism. Japanese militarists, such as Hideki Tojo who would serve as Prime Minister during the war, wanted to achieve first power status by carving out an empire in Asia. Mussolini also had imperial ambitions, but they were limited initially to winning an empire in Africa by defeating less technologically advanced nations. For some people in these countries territorial expansion and first power status was an end in itself. For them it was worth making material sacrifices to bask in the reflected glory of a powerful and respected nation. For some government officials it meant new worlds to rule. The capture of territory, however, also promised material benefits for the average citizen, or so it was said. Hitler promised that by conquering territory in the east and driving off or killing its inhabitants he would win *Lebensraum* (living space) for the German people. Conquering territory, to put it simply, would make Germans – especially the German farmers who would replace the peasants of eastern Europe – richer. War, in short, promised empire, and empire promised glory and material gain.

There was an economics that underlay this worldview, but it was not the classical liberal economics of Adam Smith, John Stuart Mill, and Alfred Marshall that had long dominated the economics profession, but rather the older economics of the mercantilists. Classical liberals identified the maximization of consumer utility as the ultimate goal of economic activity and argued that free trade was the best means of achieving that end. An interventionist state, in their view, could do little to raise incomes, and much to lower them. Mercantilism, on the other hand, emphasized the important role the state could play in economic activity and the importance of military power.[1]

Military power required a secure supply of raw materials. A peaceful state might rely on international markets to supply raw materials that it did not produce domestically. A militaristic state, however, could not rely on the market because the supply might be cut in time of war. A successful militaristic state, therefore, required an empire, an empire big enough to contain within it all the raw materials crucial to the military forces: iron, coal, oil, and so on. To be sure, there were actions

[1] The Austrian school attributes considerable influence to the change in economics. Friedrich A. von Hayek (1976 [1944]) blamed the rise of totalitarianism on the decline of laissez faire. And Ludwig von Mises (1949) traced the rise of total war partly to the welfare state.

that a state could undertake to protect its supply of raw war materials short of absorbing their sources within an empire: inventories could be accumulated, sources of foreign supplies could be purchased, and internal supplies, possibly synthetic supplies, could be developed.

In the 1930s Germany developed a number of these sources.[2] Spanish sources of raw materials were secured by purchasing controlling interests in suppliers and reinforcing the close ties with Spain's Fascist dictator, Francisco Franco, that had been forged during the Spanish Civil War. And German sources of synthetic rubber, synthetic oil, and other "ersatz" materials were developed. Germany, in short, was better prepared on the eve of World War II for a British naval blockade than it had been on the eve of World War I. But synthetic materials, such as synthetic oil and rubber, were generally costly to produce, and Germany would still suffer serious shortages in World War II (Tooze 2007, chapter 7, and *passim*). The Japanese story was similar. As Japan industrialized after the Meiji restoration it became a net importer of raw materials, but for many years the rapid growth of Japanese exports meant that Japan never encountered difficulties providing itself with raw materials. However, during the 1930s Japan's wars in China increased demands for raw materials and so created a problem that had not existed previously (Yasuba 1996).

Financing the war

"World War II ended the Great Depression." There is a good deal of truth in that commonplace, but it sometimes leads to the mistaken conclusion that Pearl Harbor was the beginning of the end of the Depression. But the recovery that began in June 1938 (according to the NBER chronology), long before Pearl Harbor, was what lifted the United States out of the Depression. Unemployment fell steadily, especially in 1940 and 1941. By the time the Japanese attacked Pearl Harbor on December 7, 1941, the US economy was close to full employment. There were still discouraged workers and pockets of unemployment, so the United States was able to increase employment still further during the war, but the idea that the Depression lasted unabated until Pearl Harbor is a mistake. For many American industries, including the auto industry and other makers of

[2] This paragraph is based on Klein (1948), Yasuba (1996), Caruana and Rockoff (2003, 2007), and Tooze (2007).

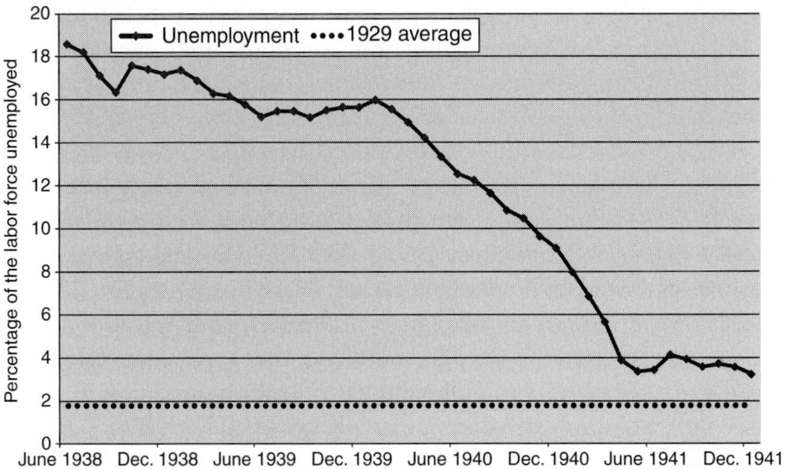

Figure 6.1 The rate of unemployment, June 1938–December 1941. Unemployment remained stubbornly high throughout the 1930s, but then fell rapidly and steadily after the outbreak of the war in Europe. The economy was close to full employment when the United States entered the war.
Source: National Industrial Conference Board, National Bureau of Economic Research Historical Series M08292a, www.nber.org.

consumer durables, 1941 was a banner year. Figure 6.1 shows the monthly unemployment rate and, for comparison, the 1929 average rate. The rates shown in Figure 6.1 are not strictly comparable to the rates reported today; the methodologies for measuring unemployment were very different. And there are more recent annual estimates that are more comparable to modern rates. But the monthly rates shown in the figure are useful for gaining a broad-brush picture of the course of events. It is clear that the unemployment rate, which had remained stubbornly high throughout the 1930s, dropped very quickly after the German invasion of Poland and British declaration of war with Germany in September 1939. By June 1941 the unemployment rate was close to the pre-Depression level.

The outbreak of the war in Europe set in motion three forces that ended the Depression. First, there were increases in US military spending, especially for the navy, after the war began in Europe. The public was uncertain about a large ground force, but it was willing to build ships to protect its shores and merchant fleet. Second, there were vastly improved profit expectations that encouraged private investment. The period of US neutrality in World War I had proved extraordinarily profitable and many corporate executives assumed that it would work the same way in World War II. Now was the time to invest in the plant and equipment that would make it possible to take advantage of a new set of opportunities. It is possible from these simple facts to compute an old-fashioned Keynesian multiplier. During the period of US neutrality, real GDP rose by \$338.5 billion in 1996 dollars, government spending rose by \$138.4 billion, and investment rose by \$73.5 billion. This gives a crude estimate of the multiplier of about $1.5 = [338.5/(138.4 + 73.5)]$. In other words, every additional dollar of private investment spending (often driven by expectations of war contracts) and government spending produced about \$1.5 in additional GDP. Finally, monetary policy was also very expansionary during the period of US neutrality. Many Europeans were looking for a safe haven for their assets. The result was a substantial flow of gold into the United States. The Federal Reserve could have sterilized this flow by selling bonds from its portfolio for gold, but it chose not to do so. The stock of money rose at an annual rate of about 11 percent per year between the outbreak of the war in Europe in September 1939 and Pearl Harbor in December 1941.[3]

The entry of the United States created an enormous fiscal challenge that was met in part by raising personal income taxes repeatedly. Figure 6.2 plots marginal tax rates for families earning \$50,000 or \$100,000 in 2009 dollars.[4] At best Figure 6.2 provides only a general idea about the taxes imposed on middle-class families. Today a family pays many taxes besides income taxes – social security and state and local taxes – so the figure does not show the full burden of taxation over time. Nevertheless, it tells a striking tale. Evidently, income taxes for middle-class families in the twentieth century were raised mainly during World

[3] How much of the improvement in the economy should be attributed to monetary policy and how much to fiscal policy has been a matter of dispute. Important contributions include De Long and Summers (1988), Romer (1992), Vernon (1994), and Gordon and Krenn (2010).

[4] The marginal tax rate is the rate that a taxpayer pays on additional income. The average rate might be lower. Typically, economists stress marginal rates because they influence the incentives taxpayers face when making decisions about how much to work. Nominal incomes were adjusted by the consumer price index so they would represent the same purchasing power as \$50,000 or \$100,000 in 2009. In 1920, for example, an income of \$9,341 had about the same purchasing power (according to the consumer price index) as \$100,000 in 2009, and a married couple filing a joint return faced a marginal tax rate of 11 percent on an income of \$9,341.

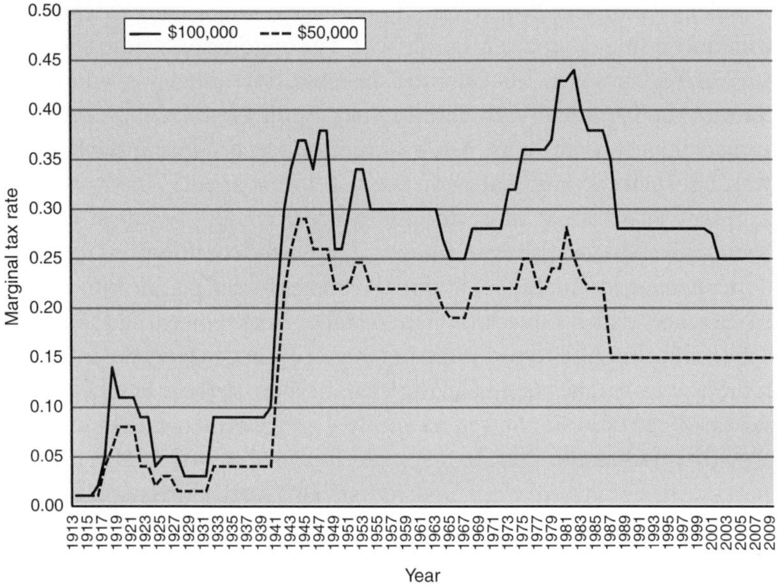

Figure 6.2 Marginal federal income tax rate for married couples filing jointly, 1913–2009. The solid line shows the marginal tax rate applicable to an income of $100,000 in 2009 dollars; the dashed line shows the marginal tax rate applicable to an income of $50,000 in 2009 dollars. Nominal incomes in earlier years were computed by deflating by the consumer price index. Middle-class federal income tax rates today are mostly the result of increases in World War II.
Sources: Income tax rates: Tax Foundation, www.taxfoundation.org (accessed December 2010); consumer price index: Measuringworth.com, www.measuringworth.com (accessed December 2010).

War II. For a family earning the equivalent of $50,000 in 2010 dollars, for example, the marginal rate went from 0.04 in 1939 to 0.29 in 1944. Everything else in the twentieth century was second order by comparison.

The smaller movements, however, are worth noting because they were the objects of intense political controversy. Rates increased in World War I, and were cut back in the 1920s, the famous cuts pushed through by Secretary of the Treasury Andrew Mellon. However, they were not cut back to the pre-WWI level because some costs of the war, mainly interest payments on the debt and veterans' benefits, were ongoing. Rates were also raised in the early years of the Depression, reflecting fears about the growth of the federal debt, a fear shared by Republicans and many Democrats, including, at least initially,

President Roosevelt. World War II produced a major increase in rates, with only a small cutback after the war. The ongoing expenditures – for interest on the debt, for veterans' benefits, for military spending to counter the Communist threat, and to pay for New Deal programs – argued against major cuts. Rates were raised again during the Korean War, but then cut afterwards. In the late 1960s and 1970s there were increases in marginal rates due to "bracket creep." Inflation caused nominal incomes to rise even when real (adjusted for inflation) incomes were unchanged. But higher nominal incomes forced people into higher tax brackets which subjected them to higher rates: you earned the same real income but had to pay more in taxes. To some extent, the inflation in these years can be blamed on the Vietnam War, so these bracket-creep increases can also be viewed as partly a product of war. Rates were brought down under President Ronald Reagan, as part of his effort to increase incentives to work and invest, and further cuts were made under President George W. Bush. For families earning $50,000 in 2010 dollars the marginal rate was somewhat lower than it had been at the end of World War II, but for families earning $100,000 there was little change from the rates reached in the wake of the war.

As in World War I the case for an excess profits tax was, first of all, a moral one. In a fireside chat delivered on May 26, 1940 President Roosevelt spelled out his loathing for wartime profits.

> Our present emergency and a common sense of decency make it imperative that no new group of war millionaires shall come into being in this nation as a result of the struggles abroad. The American people will not relish the idea of any American citizen growing rich and fat in an emergency of blood and slaughter and human suffering.[5]

Just as in World War I, business was more inclined to debate the details – whether the excess profits tax should be based on a profit rate standard (for example, no more than 8 percent) or on a firm's prewar earnings, whether it should apply to all businesses or just corporations, and so on – than to oppose an excess profits tax altogether. At one point the National Association of Manufacturers even endorsed a flat 90 percent tax rate on excess profits (Bank, Stark, and Thorndike 2008, 67). After all, an excess profits tax had the merits, compared with

[5] Woolley and Peters (2008), available at www.presidency.ucsb.edu/ws/?pid=15959.

increases in corporate tax rates, that charges of profiteering were disposed of at once, and that the tax might be repealed after the war, at least if the Republicans returned to power, as had the excess profits tax enacted in World War I. Also as in World War I, the excess profits tax played a larger role in financing the war than has usually been recognized. As shown in Appendix 4, which compares federal tax revenues in World War I, World War II, and the Korean War, the excess profits tax was second after the income tax as a generator of revenue in World War II, and brought in far more than customs, alcohol and tobacco taxes, and estate and gift taxes. If we adjust for inflation and make an allowance for "normal" revenues (based on what was taken in during 1940), then the contribution of the excess profits tax approaches one-quarter of all tax revenues, an impressive showing.

Despite an impressive willingness to increase taxes, a substantial gap quickly opened up between federal government spending and revenues, as shown in Figure 6.3. The budget, as can be seen in the figure, was already in deficit when the war began: a small (in comparison with what was to follow) and stable gap existed between expenditures and receipts throughout 1939 and 1940. That gap was the subject of much handwringing. Republicans regularly assailed the wild spending of the Roosevelt administration. Politics, of course, was the main consideration, but the fear that an unconscionable burden was being placed on the current generation's grandchildren was genuine and widespread. The Roosevelt administration scrambled for an answer: the idea that the debt was not a burden because "we owe it to ourselves" had an element of truth, but satisfied mostly those who already supported the administration. Once the United States entered the war, however, concerns about the deficit disappeared; a debt of any size was preferable to losing the war. The Treasury issued a variety of securities to tap as many sources of funds as possible. About 50 percent of the new debt was made up of traditional long-term bonds and about 30 percent was made up of short-term securities – treasury bills and notes. And an important share, about 20 percent, was made up of US savings bonds. These were small-denomination securities intended for the average American.

As in World War I, the government and private sector engaged in a vigorous campaign to encourage the public to buy bonds (Samuel 1997). Billboards and milk cartons carried advertisements for savings bonds. A billboard sponsored by the brewer Anheuser-Busch sent a clear message: "Buy War Bonds Today, For Better Living Tomorrow" (Samuel

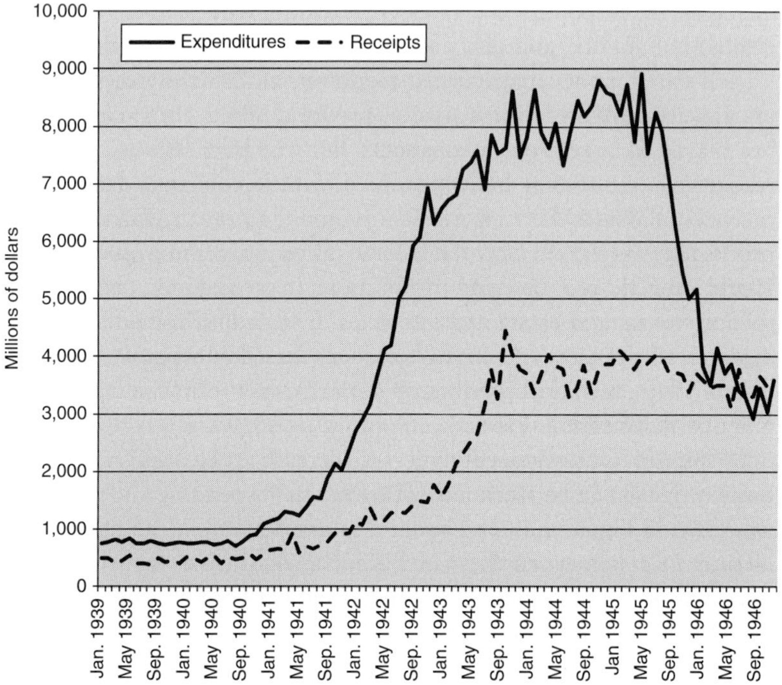

Figure 6.3 Federal expenditures and receipts, monthly, January 1939–December 1946. Government receipts rose during World War II, but expenditures rose much faster.
Source: Firestone (1960, Table A3, seasonally corrected data).

1997, 53). The Boy and Girl Scouts and Hollywood stars got involved. A Hollywood movie, *All Star Bond Rally*, featured crooner Bing Crosby singing "Buy a Bond" and actress Betty Grable – "the number-one pin-up girl of World War II" – and her "bondbardiers." The campaign served many purposes. For many adults and for their children participating in a bond drive helped to ease fears of powerlessness in the face of wartime dangers. Corporations that participated created goodwill and minimized the danger of being accused of profiteering. But the drive also served a more narrowly economic purpose. Bond sales reduced inflationary pressures by taking purchasing power out of the marketplace, but did so in a way that maintained the incentive to work: the bonds could be cashed in after the war was over. Taking the same amount of purchasing power out of the marketplace by raising taxes would have decreased the incentive to work. Moving to a war production center and working long hours still paid large dividends, even if they would not be realized until the war was over.

To some extent the issue of bonds, as we have emphasized, also served to hide the full cost of the war. The individual buying bonds probably had a clear idea of the uses to which they would be put after the war. Taxpayers, on the other hand, may not have fully absorbed the fact that they would be paying higher taxes after the war simply to pay interest and principal on a larger national debt. John Maynard Keynes's proposal for war finance, in his famous tract *How to Pay for the War* (1940), had a similar goal, but would have achieved it through different means. Part of wages would have been "taxed" and paid into blocked accounts in savings banks. There they could be released en masse by the government in the event of an economic downturn, or could have been accessed by individuals in personal emergencies. Wartime and postwar inflation reduced the value of the bonds. But they still helped finance the postwar boom and ease the transition to a peacetime economy. The postwar economy thrived on sales of consumer durables and houses financed by assets accumulated during the war, partly in the form of war savings bonds.

In the end, however, the government was unwilling or unable to raise all of the funds needed for the war effort by raising taxes and borrowing from the public. As in the great wars that preceded it – the Revolution, the Civil War, and World War I – the government turned to the printing press. In the Revolutionary War and the Civil War, the term "printing press" was more than a useful metaphor; it was an accurate description of how it was done. The government hired companies that printed notes – the continental dollar and the greenback – that could circulate from hand to hand. These notes were used to pay the expenses of the government including the wages owed to soldiers. In World War I the process was more complex, although the metaphor was still meaningful. The Federal Reserve lent newly created reserves to banks. The banks then made loans to private individuals who used the loans to buy Liberty bonds. In World War II the Federal Reserve went into the bond market directly and purchased government debt. You and I cannot write checks upon ourselves and expect the world to take them, but the Federal Reserve can and did.

There was never any doubt that the Federal Reserve would use its power to create money to stabilize the government bond market. On the Monday following the Sunday attack on Pearl Harbor the Board of Governors of the Federal Reserve released a statement which made clear the System's commitment to the war effort:

> The System is prepared to use its powers to assure that an ample supply of funds is available at all times for financing the war effort and to exert its influence toward maintaining conditions in the United States Government security market that are satisfactory from the standpoint of the Government's requirements. (Chandler 1949, 407)

A few weeks later Mariner Eccles, the chairman of the Federal Reserve Board, explained what this had meant in practice. Immediately after Pearl Harbor, Eccles told Congress, "The market was very weak, very jittery, and we purchased in the market that Monday and a few days after about $100,000,000 of securities, giving stability and support" (*New York Times*, February 5, 1942, 10).[6]

Although the question of *whether* to stabilize the bond market was not contentious, the question of *at what price* was extremely contentious. It could be expected in the near future that all the pressure in the bond market would be toward lower bond prices – the government would be issuing immense amounts of debt to finance the war. So, in practice, stabilizing the market meant setting a floor under the price of bonds. The question, to put it simply, was at what price would the Federal Reserve jump in and buy bonds to keep their prices from falling further? Here the Treasury and the Federal Reserve were at odds. The Treasury, under Henry Morgenthau Jr., wanted the Federal Reserve to freeze existing bond prices. These prices were a remnant from the Depression when prices of government bonds were extraordinarily high because government bonds were islands of safety. The Treasury saw the continuation of high bond prices as a policy that would ease its day-to-day work by eliminating price fluctuations and insure the lowest nominal cost of financing the war: high bond prices, in other words, meant that future interest payments by the Treasury would be low. But the Federal Reserve was worried that maintaining high bond prices would mean that the Federal Reserve would be pumping more new money into the economy and stoking inflation (Hyman 1976, 293–5). The resolution came soon enough. In March 1942 the Federal Open Market Committee (the body within the Federal Reserve which is directly responsible for determining the pace and price of bond purchases) agreed that the market "should be maintained on about the then existing curve of rates"

[6] The Federal Reserve had previously attempted to stabilize the market after the outbreak of the war in Europe. On that occasion it had bought $500 million in bonds (Chandler 1949, 406).

Table 6.1 *Financing of the US federal government during World War II (figures for January 1939–December 1946)*

	Expenditures (billion dollars)	%
Total federal expenditures	413.7	100.0
Total tax revenues	202.9	49.0
Borrowing from the public	115.8	28.0
Direct money creation	22.3	5.4
Indirect money creation	72.7	17.6

Sources: Total federal expenditures and total tax revenues: Firestone (1960, Table A3). Direct money creation: Friedman and Schwartz (1963, Table B-3, High-powered money, 801). Indirect money creation: Friedman and Schwartz (1970, Table 1, M2, 15–17). Borrowing from the public was computed as a residual.

(Chandler 1949, 408). This pattern would be maintained throughout the war and the early postwar period. The commitment of Treasury Secretary Morgenthau, who was a close confidant of the President, to a low interest rate policy, and the simple argument that nothing should get in the way of winning the war, had proved overwhelming. The policy of maintaining fixed rates at a low level was finally ended during the early days of the Korean War, when the Federal Reserve could argue effectively that without the freedom to allow rates to rise, the Federal Reserve would be forced to monetize a high proportion of the debt, as it had in World War II, and that the result would be inflation, as it had been during that war.

Table 6.1 shows the relative contributions of taxes, borrowing from the public, and creating new money to the finance of the war during the years of active engagement.[7] Evidently, war finance was "good" (at least from the viewpoint of the classical economists) in the sense that taxes were the most important source of finance, supplying 49 percent of the cost of the war. This was a better showing than in World War I when taxes had financed only 30 percent. Borrowing from the public in World War II financed 28 percent, lower than in World War I. Direct money creation, mainly the result of Federal Reserve purchases of government debt, accounted for 5 percent of war finance, compared with 7 percent in World War I. And what we have called indirect money creation,

[7] In other words, it does not provide estimates of how future war costs, such as veterans' benefits, were financed.

following Friedman and Schwartz, accounted for 18 percent of war finance in World War II compared with 23 percent in World War I.

To explain the latter figures, let me recall, if I may, the reason for distinguishing two types of money creation. When the Federal Reserve acquired and held government bonds (direct money creation) few would disagree with the conclusion that the money that ends up in the Federal Treasury came from the printing press and not from private savings. But this is only part of the story. When the recipients of government spending deposited their payments, the banks found themselves with more reserves. The increase in reserves in turn produced a multiple increase in bank lending. Suppose that the borrowers used the proceeds of the loans to purchase government bonds for their portfolios. In that case we can again see that the money that ends up in the US Treasury was really created by the banks – really came from the printing press. To estimate the amount of this sort of finance, however, is difficult. The assumption in Table 6.1 is that all new money backed the purchase of bonds in one way or another. This assumption may produce an overestimate of the amount financed by money creation because some of the new loans produced by the banking system went for other purposes. On the other hand, the definition of money used to create the table was M2. If a larger monetary aggregate had been used, the estimate of the amount of total spending financed by money creation would have been somewhat larger.[8]

What explains the "full-boil" economy of the war years, an economy where everyone who wanted to could find a well-paid job and the main problem was inflation? Was it the large deficit? Was it the rapid increase in the money supply? Table 6.2 provides some relevant data. In 1929 the economy was close to full employment (until the stock market crash). The federal budget was in surplus and the stock of money stood at $47 billion. By 1933 the economy had fallen into a deep depression. Unemployment stood at 21 percent. The federal budget was now in deficit, although this was more the result of falling tax revenues than rising expenditures. The stock of money had fallen to $32 billion, a decline of more than 30 percent. This was due to the widespread banking crisis. Monetarists blame the Federal Reserve for allowing this decline to occur, and consider it a prime cause of the Great Depression.

[8] Turvey (1961) examines the effects of inflation, whether resulting from monetary expansion or not, on the value of the government's nominal liabilities, a related problem.

Table 6.2 *Deficit spending, money, and unemployment, selected years*

Year	Unemployment (% of the labor force)	GNP (billions of dollars)	Federal budget deficit (billions of dollars)	Federal budget deficit (% of GNP)	Stock of money (billions of dollars)
1929	3.2	103.9	0.7	0.67	46.6
1933	20.6	56.0	−2.6	−4.64	32.2
1939	11.3	91.3	−2.8	−3.07	49.2
1944	1.2	211.4	−47.6	−22.52	106.8

Source: Walton and Rockoff (2010, 470).

Things did recover to an extent, but by the end of the decade, the economy, as Table 6.2 shows, was still in the doldrums. Unemployment remained stubbornly high at 11.3 percent. There was a budget deficit, about 3 percent of GNP. As we noted above, some critics of the Roosevelt administration pointed to the deficit as an example of reckless spending that would burden future generations. Others pointed out that high unemployment persisted despite large deficits, thus showing that fiscal policy didn't work. The stock of money had increased slightly from the 1929 level. But the annual rate of increase between 1929 and 1939 was only about 0.5 percent per year, not enough to provide for growing demand due to growth in real income.

But things changed dramatically when the USA entered the war. The public no longer paid attention to either the deficit, a major political issue in the 1930s, or monetary policy. The deficit soared to 23 percent of GNP, the stock of money more than doubled, and unemployment, already close at the time of Pearl Harbor to peacetime norms, fell to 1.2 percent in 1944, the lowest rate on record. So which factor propelled the United States out of the Depression and produced the super low rates of unemployment during the war itself: large deficits or a big increase in the stock of money? The wartime experience can't answer the question. Both occurred. Indeed, the usual distinction between fiscal policy and monetary policy is problematic in a war economy in which one branch of the federal government, the US Treasury, is making large expenditures and financing them by selling government bonds at a fixed price to another branch of the government, the Federal Reserve.

Although the combined force of fiscal policy and monetary policy during the war was unprecedented, it is not sufficient to provide a complete explanation of the supercharged wartime economy.[9] As Mulligan (1998) showed, conventional explanations of labor markets based on the behavior of real wages and real interest rates cannot explain the extraordinary increase in the supply of labor during the war. Clearly, there were a number of unique forces at work, although no one has succeeded in separating them and assigning exact roles. For one thing young men, the class of workers who normally have the highest rates of unemployment, were drafted into the armed forces. The unemployment rate that prevailed during the war is evidently not comparable to unemployment rates in peacetime when these men are still in the labor force. There was, moreover, a unique set of expectations that prevailed during the war. Many workers must have expected a return to the Great Depression after the war. World War II was a unique opportunity to learn new skills and save money that would be valuable after the war, savings that would rise in real terms if there was another run of deflation. Discrimination against women and minorities also decreased during the war (Goldin 1991; Collins 2001). And finally, old-fashioned patriotism undoubtedly played a role. Patriotism, it is true, created social pressures to work that may have been the real motivator for some workers. But surely some people chose to work and work hard because they wanted to help the United States win the war.

Wage, price, and production controls

Given the enormous inflationary pressures created by expansionary monetary and fiscal policies it is no surprise that prices began to rise even before Pearl Harbor. The United States then turned to wage, price, and production controls to restrain price increases and to allocate resources. Controls had been used, as we have seen, in World War I and were being used in the countries already at war. Controls, moreover, had gained considerable intellectual stature. Some of the glory of the US victory in World War I had rubbed off on controls, as on most policies adopted during the war. Indeed, a number of people involved in World War I controls, such as the economist Frank W. Taussig (1919), who had served on the Price Fixing Committee of the War Industries

[9] I use the term "supercharged" to distinguish the period 1941–5 from the return to nearly full employment in 1939–41. Monetary and fiscal policy can go much further in explaining what was happening in the latter period.

Board, and the financier Bernard Baruch (1936), who had headed the War Industries Board, became fans. Baruch's determined advocacy of wartime price and ration controls during the 1920s and 1930s was especially important in paving the way for their adoption in World War II. Enthusiasm for free markets and the price system, moreover, had fallen to a low ebb during the Great Depression. And it was widely believed, although mistakenly, that Germany and Japan had ruthlessly planned and controlled economies. If the USA adopted the same system, then it would achieve about the same level of efficiency and its superior resources would eventually lead to victory. But if it adopted a different system for managing the economy, there was a chance that it would be more efficient, but also a chance, however remote, that by choosing a different form of mobilization it would be less efficient and undermine the advantage of greater resources. Prudence demanded that the United States copy its foes.

The public did not see wage, price, and production controls as part of the system for financing the war – but they were. To the extent that resources could be redirected from the civilian sector to the military sector at fixed prices through a system of priorities, rationing, and controls, there was less need to spend money to bid them away. In part the system of controls merely postponed inflation: the price peak associated with World War II inflation came more than a year after the war began. But delayed inflation was also a part of the financing of the war. Rather than levy an explicit inflation tax during the war, the government was able (through controls) to levy an inflation tax on the holders of money and bonds after the war. Postponed inflation better hid the cost of the conflict. If few people associated the wartime inflation with the way the war was financed, fewer still associated postwar inflation with the way it was financed.

Price controls moved through a series of phases during World War II. These phases and the associated rates of inflation are shown in Table 6.3. During the first phase, which I have labeled "exhortation," the government relied mainly on persuasion: appeals to patriotism and promises of rewards for cooperation or penalties for non-cooperation. Consumer prices were only increasing at an annual rate of 2.1 percent per year during this period, but wholesale prices, which reflected the tightness in resource markets produced by domestic and foreign military demands, were rising at close to a 6 percent annual rate. Beginning in April 1941, still well before Pearl Harbor, the system

Table 6.3 *Phases of price control in World War II*

	Type of control	Explanation	Annual rate of inflation (consumer price index) (%)	Annual rate of inflation (wholesale price index) (%)
May 1940–April 1941	Exhortation	Government urges firms to maintain stable prices	2.1	5.9
April 1941–April 1942	Selective	Controls are placed on "strategic" prices	11.9	16.9
April 1942–April 1943	GMPR	The General Maximum Price Regulation: firms set their own prices based on rules set by the Office of Price Administration	7.8	5.1
April 1943–February 1946	Hold the line	The Office of Price Administration sets specific maximum prices	1.4	1.3
February 1946–June 1946	Adjustable	The Office of Price Administration grants increases, especially when such increases settle strikes	9.8	13.9
June 1946–January 1948	End of controls	Price controls are removed	15.0	22.4

Sources: The second and third columns are based on Rockoff (1984, *passim*). The fourth and fifth columns show the annualized percentage increase in the consumer price index and wholesale price index from the start of one phase to the start of the next; consumer price index for all urban consumers, all items: US Department of Labor, Bureau of Labor Statistics; wholesale price index: US Index of Wholesale Prices, Bureau of Labor Statistics, NBER Macrohistory Database, series m04048c; www.nber.org/databases/macrohistory/contents/chapter04.html.

was strengthened and violators were subject to penalties. Price controls, however, were not placed on all products. The hope was that by formally controlling strategic prices – items that were key ingredients in a wide range of products; steel, rubber, and so on – the entire price structure could be kept under control. But as Table 6.3 shows, this approach failed to stop inflation. Consumer prices surged at an annual rate of nearly 12 percent per year, and wholesale prices at nearly 17 percent. Selective controls, moreover, raised some troubling questions. If prices were held down in one sector, what was to prevent demand from shifting to the uncontrolled sector? And if prices in the uncontrolled sector rose faster than prices in the controlled sector, wouldn't that send exactly the wrong signal? Wouldn't it encourage entrepreneurs to move resources from the production of goods in the controlled sector, goods which had been selected for control because of their importance to the economy and to the war effort, to the production of goods in the uncontrolled sector, goods which had been left uncontrolled because they were unimportant?

A consensus quickly formed among the administrators of controls that across-the-board controls were needed. The General Maximum Price Regulation – affectionately known as General Max – attempted just that. Firms were ordered to set the price of each item they sold based on the price of that item in a base period with an allowance for subsequent cost increases. The rate of inflation subsided somewhat during the General Max period, but new problems emerged. Labor was now subject to wage control, and workers felt that the rates of inflation that prevailed under General Max were reducing their standard of living. And the decision to leave the computation of prices in the hands of private firms opened the door to some "creative accounting." For example, if a firm had not sold an item during the base period, it was instructed to use the price at which the item had been sold by a competitor. The temptation was to choose the highest price at which the good had been sold by any firm. A clothing store selling a particular shirt on Main Street could look to the price at which the shirt had been sold in the base period on New York's Fifth Avenue.

In April 1943, then, a new system was introduced. Now most prices and wages would be frozen, and the prices would be set by the Office of Price Administration. It was called "dollar and cents" pricing. The Office of Price Administration would simply set the price of shirts and ties, hammers and nails, tomato soup, and other items affecting the cost of living, and it was up to the sellers to obey or face the penalties. President Roosevelt called his executive order a "hold-the-line order:"

> To hold the line we cannot tolerate further increases in prices affecting the cost of living or further increases in general wage or salary rates except where clearly necessary to correct substandard living conditions. The only way to hold the line is to stop trying to find justifications for not holding it here or not holding it there. (*New York Times*, April 10, 1943, 16)

Under the hold-the-line order the price indexes, as shown in Table 6.3, remained remarkably stable given the inflationary pressures that continued unabated. The consumer price index rose only 1.4 percent per year during the hold-the-line phase, and the wholesale price index rose only 1.3 percent per year.

Measured unemployment, moreover, averaged 1.8 percent during this phase (NBER Macrohistory Database, series 08922).[10] Inflation at 1.4 percent and unemployment at 1.8 percent = Utopia! In the postwar era attention was often drawn to the "misery index" – the sum of the rate of inflation and the rate of unemployment. President Jimmy Carter famously criticized the administration of Gerald Ford and Richard Nixon for its high misery index when first running for president, only to be faced with a higher misery index when running for reelection. No postwar era could come close to a misery index of 3.2. Indeed, some economists, notably John Kenneth Galbraith, would look back fondly on the hold-the-line era when a combination of expansionary monetary and fiscal policies and price controls had produced outstanding results (Galbraith 1981, 170–5). Galbraith attributed the success of controls to the willingness of technocrats in large firms to work with the price controllers, rather than see them as adversaries (Galbraith 1952).

There were, however, some features of the wartime utopia that might give one pause when thinking about adopting it as a permanent model for a peacetime economy. For one thing, there was the possible, although hard to measure, role of patriotism. Some people probably complied with price and ration controls because they thought it was their patriotic duty to do so. Is this what motivated the technocrats at the large corporations, who Galbraith thought had complied so readily with wartime controls? And there were several problems in civilian

[10] www.nber.org/databases/macrohistory/contents/chapter08.html (accessed May 8, 2011).

markets that make the comparison of prices in controlled markets with prices in free markets problematic.[11] One problem was rationing. Meat, coffee, and gasoline were among the products that were rationed. Consumers needed ration tickets to buy them, and the amount of tickets was limited. New automobiles were simply not available. Normally, if we want to buy 10 pounds of meat at the market price, we can do so. What if rationing limits us to 8 pounds? An index that says that the price has remained constant fails to convey that decline in the consumer's well-being. Second, the quality of some products deteriorated. Clothing had fewer buttons, candy bars shrank and were made of fewer ingredients. A third problem was the black markets. Substantial amounts of meat, for example, moved through clandestine slaughterhouses to restaurants where it could be purchased at premium prices or to "meateasies" (following the "speakeasies" where bootleg whiskey had been sold during Prohibition) where it could be purchased at black market prices without ration tickets. Surprisingly, however, the most important problem turned out to be something different: "forced uptrading." Typically, manufacturers produced several lines of merchandise: low-price, low-quality lines and high-price, high-quality lines. The low-priced lines were sold in high volumes at low unit profits, while the high-priced lines were intended for smaller, harder-to-please markets; the volumes were smaller, but the profit margins were higher. This was true over a surprisingly wide range of markets from underwear to steel. Given strong wartime demand combined with price controls, manufacturers found it in their interest to discontinue their lower-priced lines, "forcing buyers up" to the high-priced lines with the high profit margins. Producers might be able to say, honestly, that they hadn't raised any prices, but the effect was to make the consumer worse off, and to raise the profits of manufacturers. The Office of Price Administration was aware of the problem, and introduced a number of plans to keep low-priced lines in production, but forced uptrading remained a major headache.

How much these problems would have grown had controls been continued into the postwar period is hard to know because once the war ended, controls unraveled. The main problem was strikes. There had been few strikes during the war: labor had agreed to a no-strike pledge and employers had agreed to no lockouts. Although there were

[11] I discuss these problems in more detail in Rockoff (1981a, 1984, 127–76).

a few strikes in the coalfields, for the most part these pledges were adhered to, a good example of how patriotism had encouraged compliance with controls. But as a practical matter these pledges were "for the duration." Once the war was over many union leaders felt that their workers deserved wage increases, in part because the hidden price increases discussed above had depressed real wages. There was a wave of strikes, and now a peculiar dynamic took hold. Employers were in a position to say "we are willing to grant the union a wage increase that will meet their demands and end the strike, but of course, the Office of Price Administration must grant us a commensurate price increase." The Office of Price Administration did not want to make these exceptions to the overall price freeze. But when the public saw the supply of goods interrupted by strikes that the Office of Price Administration could end, the pressure to make exceptions became overwhelming. In effect strikes that on the surface appeared to be classic confrontations between labor and capital had in fact become collaborations between labor and capital working against the government agencies controlling wages and prices. As more and more exceptions were made, the system became untenable.

Once controls were removed, there was a burst of inflation. As shown in Table 6.3 consumer prices rose at an annual rate of 15 percent between June 1946 and January 1948, and wholesale prices rose 22 percent. To some extent this burst of inflation was offset by the elimination of hidden price increases (quality deterioration, forced uptrading, and so on), but part of the increase was a genuine decline in purchasing power. People who had saved in the form of cash or government bonds during the war, perhaps expecting these savings to be worth more after the war as prices declined, were sadly disappointed. Government finances, on the other hand, benefited: the real value of the wartime debt was reduced between the end of the war and the postwar price peak. The postwar inflation, in other words, was an unveiling of costs of the war that had been hidden by controls.

Mobilization

The Phony War ended in May and June 1940 with the successful German attack on Belgium and France. The Roosevelt administration then began to gear up for the war by creating a plethora of new federal agencies to control the war economy. The models were the New Deal and World War I. In this case, unlike in World War I, the United States would not wait until war was declared to take action. On April 11, 1940, even before the German advance on France and Belgium, Roosevelt created the Office of Price Administration and Civilian Supply to limit inflation and regulate civilian supplies. On May 25, he created the Office of Emergency Management to provide him with information and advice. On May 28 he created the Petroleum Coordinator for National Defense to oversee the production and distribution of petroleum. On June 28 he created the Rubber Reserve Company to buy natural, synthetic, and scrap rubber, and the Metals Reserve Company to buy metals and subsidize their production. On August 29 he created the Defense Plant Corporation to finance war industries, and on September 16 he created the Selective Service System to draft men for military service. More agencies were created in 1941. Most importantly, on August 28, 1941 Roosevelt reorganized the basic control apparatus by creating two agencies: the Office of Price Administration to set prices and the Supply Priorities and Allocation Board to determine production priorities.

All this was before Pearl Harbor. After Pearl Harbor the system was reorganized. On January 12, 1942 Roosevelt created the National War Labor Board to oversee wage rates and labor supply, and on January 16 he replaced the Supply Priorities and Allocation Board with the War Production Board which would be the primary agency overseeing munitions procurement and production during the remainder of the war. Table 6.4 shows year by year how many civilian war agencies were created and how many survived into the postwar era. Counting agencies can be a daunting and subjective task. In some cases old agencies were continued, but given new names. Sometimes the change was merely cosmetic, but sometimes it reflected an increase in power and responsibility. Similar interpretive problems arise when several agencies were merged. Table 6.4, then, is subject to a margin of error, but I believe it provides a broad-brush picture of the size of the bureaucracy created during the war and the long-term changes that resulted. All in all, more than a hundred agencies were created. Rubber, petroleum, housing, shipping, food, information, and most other sectors of the economy had agencies overseeing them. Evidently, most war agencies were terminated when the war ended. But about 15 percent were continued as separate agencies or as parts of other agencies. In the case

Table 6.4 *Federal civilian agencies created during World War II*

Year	New agencies	Agencies that survived into the postwar era
1939	4	1
1940	20	4
1941	33	3
1942	29	6
1943	15	2
1944	7	1
1945	1	0
1946	3	0
Total	112	17

Notes: In most cases when an agency was terminated, some residual activities and personnel were transferred to other agencies. For that reason, the decision on whether an agency survived often involved a judgment call. In 1941, twenty-eight agencies were created prior to Pearl Harbor.
Sources: The main sources are the US Bureau of the Budget (1972 [1946], Appendix I) and the National Archives Guide to Federal Records (www.archives.gov/research/guide-fed-records/index.html).

of the Selective Service and the Mexican Farm Labor (Bracero) Program, wartime programs were continued for some years before they were discontinued. Existing agencies that can trace some of their roots to war emergency agencies include the Civil Air Patrol, Voice of America, the US Information Agency, and the Southwestern Power Authority.

This stream of new agencies, many of them created before Pearl Harbor, must have struck many observers, including those in Germany and Japan, as preparation for war. The institution of a military draft in September 1940 was a clear signal. I have excluded from the table many joint domestic and international committees, but the formation of these committees must also have added to the expectation that the United States was going to war. On June 17, 1941, for example, the United States and Canada (which had already entered the war) formed a joint economic committee to, in the words of the US Bureau of the Budget's *The United States at War* (1972 [1946], 526), "assist in the collaboration of the two countries in the utilization of their combined resources for the requirements of the war."

Between the world wars, Bernard Baruch, who enjoyed immense prestige based on his leadership of the War Industries Board in World War I, had argued for a command system for organizing a war economy (*New York Times*, May 4, 1924, XX4; Baruch 1936). In his view, the price system should be jettisoned during wartime as a mechanism for allocating resources (prices should be frozen), and decisions about how resources are allocated should be made by a single all-powerful government bureau on the basis of priorities set by that bureau. The bureau should be headed by one masterful executive (Baruch?!) who should be granted whatever power it took to get the job done. Baruch saw this theory about mobilization as the unarguable lesson of his experience in World War I. But Baruch was not alone. New Dealers saw it as the logical implication of the failure of capitalism revealed by the Depression, and it struck a responsive chord in the media and in the general public who felt that if there was an important job to be done, someone should be "in charge." But until there was a declaration of war, Roosevelt could take only slow and halting steps.

An important first step toward a system of control was taken in August 1939 when Roosevelt created the War Resources Board to survey the available resources and to suggest a plan for mobilizing them in the event of war. Edward Stettinius Jr. from United States Steel headed the Board, which was composed entirely of businessmen. The Board immediately and predictably drew the fire of liberals, agriculture, and labor, all of whom wanted to be represented. The initial composition presaged Roosevelt's heavy reliance on businessmen during the war. Dr. "New Deal" was becoming Dr. "Win the War." The Board wrote a report, for Roosevelt's eyes only, that maintained that America already had abundant capacity to meet the needs of any conflict; expansion of capacities in steel and aluminum, for example, were not needed. It also recommended that in the event of US involvement, mobilization be entrusted to an all-powerful bureaucracy along the lines suggested by Baruch. In November 1939, the Board was dissolved, its members were thanked, and its *Report* was filed, to be made public after the war.

In May 1940 Roosevelt established the National Defense Advisory Commission. More representative of the economy, it included William S. Knudsen, President of General Motors, Sidney Hillman, of the United Ladies Garment Workers, and representatives of other interest groups. Its purpose was to expedite the awarding of contracts for munitions and to plan future policies. The members of the Commission, although nominally advisors, quickly built up staffs that became the nuclei of succeeding agencies. The deteriorating situation in Europe increased the pressure on Roosevelt to create a more powerful agency. In November 1940 he created the Office of Production Management, which began operations in January 1941, taking over the functions and personnel of the National Defense Advisory Committee. Roosevelt stoutly resisted pressures to appoint a single executive to head the agency, insisting that there was no need for a "Poobah, Czar, or Akoond of Swat." Instead he appointed Knudsen as Director-General and Hillman as Associate Director-General – insisting that the question of who was the head man was irrelevant. Putting someone from either the management side or the labor side in a position to become the boss of the war economy would have created political headaches.

The most important problem that the new agency faced was the priority system (Koistinen 2004, 175–90, 204–6, 314–17). In theory the system long advocated by Baruch was very simple. A government agency – the most important being the Army–Navy Munitions Board – would rate contracts according to their importance for the war effort. Manufacturers were required to complete higher-rated contracts first: tanks before jukeboxes. But the system was soon clogged with high-priority contracts, the beginning of "priorities inflation," a problem that would dog the priority system for the remainder of the time it was used (US Bureau of the Budget 1972 [1946], 114–18). What was "priorities inflation"? Initially, priority ratings consisted of three letters, A, B, and C, each divided into ten numerical bands – A-1, A-2 … A-10, and so on. In theory each contract was assigned a priority corresponding to its importance to the war effort. The natural tendency, however, was for a bureaucrat to award an A-1 priority to all of the contracts coming across his or her desk, thus avoiding blame if a project was not completed on time – like an untenured professor giving all the students As to avoid a bad review. Prime contractors, moreover, were responsible for rating subcontracts. In theory the rating on the subcontract was supposed to reflect the rating on the prime contract. But again, the smart thing to do was to place an A-1 rating on every subcontract. Thus, the A-1 rating quickly became merely a "hunting license" for materials. In November 1941 the A-1 rating was broken into A-1-a through A-1-j. Later, still higher ratings were added. Eventually, the system stabilized with ratings of AAA and A-1 … A-4. The stabilization of the ratings, however, did not reflect some kind of perfection of the system, but rather the abundance of raw materials during most of the time when the final set of priorities was used. In August 1941, in the midst of the priorities crisis, Roosevelt created the Supply Priorities and Allocation Board to address the problem. This Board brought together representatives of the various agencies issuing priorities, including the Army–Navy Munitions Board and the Office of Production Management, to set, hopefully, an overall policy. Donald Nelson, a Sears executive (from purchasing) who was working for the Office of Production Management, was made executive director. The administrative structure of the agency was heavily criticized at the time: Knudsen was a member of the Supply Priorities Allocation Board and in that capacity superior to Nelson whose job was to implement the Board's decisions; but Nelson as executive director of the Supply Priorities and Allocation Board then gave orders to the Office of Production Management, making him, in that capacity, superior to Knudsen!

Pearl Harbor (and the continuing problem of priorities inflation) led to the establishment of the War Production Board in January 1942 with Nelson becoming the sole director. The press greeted the new organization enthusiastically: at last someone was "in charge." In the next few months Nelson reached "concordats" with the army and navy that ceded to them the right to place orders for munitions without prior approval by the War Production Board. There may well have been little else he could do. The War Production Board did not have the personnel to evaluate the enormous number of contracts that was flowing from the military. But the crucial tool for controlling production thus passed from Nelson's hands, to be regained only partially and with difficulty. Nelson's honeymoon with the press was short lived. Munitions production was below expectations (although no one had a clear idea of how fast munitions could be produced), small business was angry about a system that seemed to be giving all the contracts to big business, and the priorities mess was growing worse. By the spring of 1942 it was clear that the priorities system was broken and needed to be replaced.

The first attempt was the Production Requirements Plan (US Bureau of the Budget 1972 [1946], 119–20). Under this plan manufacturers would file detailed reports with the War Production Board showing their contracts (including preference ratings), and their inventories of raw materials. Then the Board would decide on the amount of raw materials the manufacturer was allowed to buy, and the preferences ratings that it could assign to those purchase contracts. The Production Requirements Plan still made use of priorities, but it promised improvement along two lines. First, it took the power to issue priorities for raw materials away from prime contractors (a source of priorities inflation) and secondly, it created a flow of information from which the War Production Board could compute aggregate supplies and demands. Despite high hopes for it, however, the Production Requirements Plan turned out to be a disappointment. Novick, Anshen, and Truppner (1949, 19–135) attribute the difficulties to the inadequacy of the bureaucracy set up to administer the plan – the bureaucracy wasn't big enough and wasn't given enough time to get organized – and to opposition to the Production Requirements Plan from elements within the War Production Board.

In 1942 Ferdinand Eberstadt, an investment banker during peacetime with considerable experience in government, was brought to the War Production Board from the Army–Navy Munitions Board. He immediately went to work on what would become the final plan for allocating scarce resources: the Controlled Materials Plan (CMP). I will discuss the CMP in detail below, but first I should note that as a result of its apparent success Eberstadt emerged as a hero of the mobilization. In most retellings of the war mobilization he was the man who saved the day by installing a system of central planning, but did not get the promotion to head of the War Production Board that he deserved because of the conniving of Nelson. This narrative is similar in some respects to the standard narrative of German war production. Mobilization went slowly at the start of the war under armaments minister Fritz Todt. But when Todt died in a plane crash in February 1942 and was replaced by Albert Speer things turned around. Speer centralized authority over production and achieved miracles; under Speer production of munitions continued to rise despite massive bombing. The "great man" theory of mobilization can also be seen in the story of Max Aitken, Lord Beaverbrook, who has been credited with accelerating aircraft production in Britain. In the Soviet Union the successful evacuation of industry from the front after the German attack has been attributed to the formation of powerful government agencies: the State Defense Committee under Stalin, and the Council for Evacuation, initially under Lagar Kaganovich (Lieberman 1983). For Japan, however, the story is somewhat different. Hideki Tojo and his deputy Nobusuke Kishi were placed in charge of a newly created Ministry of Munitions in November 1943. But apparently severe differences among private firms, the government civilian bureaucracy, and the military prevented coordination and an acceleration of production (Rice 1979).

While Eberstadt is the hero in most narratives of the mobilization, Robert R. Nathan, an economist who served as chair of the War Production Board's planning committee, garnered praise for his supporting role. He is said to have pressed for an early end to the production of consumer durables, especially refrigerators. More generally he is credited with cutting through red tape and constantly pushing subordinates at the War Production Board to maximize production. A colorful man, it is said that he liked to drive around Washington on Sundays in a red Pontiac convertible and heckle slow-moving trucks, presumably to speed up the war effort (obituary, *New York Times*, September 10, 2001).

The Controlled Materials Plan, although complicated in detail, was essentially a system for rationing three important raw materials: steel, copper, and aluminum. The system, although modified over time, went ahead for the most part according to an outline issued in November 1942 when the plan was announced (US War Production Board 1942). The idea was relatively straightforward, at least in comparison with earlier plans. (1) Each "claimant agency" was to submit estimates of its requirements for controlled materials to the War Production Board. Initially, there were seven claimant agencies: the War Department, Navy, Maritime Commission, Aircraft Scheduling Unit, Office of Lend-Lease Administration, Board of Economic Warfare, and the Office of Civilian Supplies. (2) The Board would then evaluate these estimates in the light of its estimates of existing supplies. (3) The Requirements Committee of the Board would then decide on monthly allotments of controlled materials for each of the claimant agencies. (4) The claimant agencies would then be notified of their allotments, to which they would have to adjust their programs. (5) Each claimant agency would then divide its allotments among its major contractors. Each sub-allotment would be accompanied by an allotment number, in effect a ration ticket, showing the program and month. (6) These allotment numbers would then move from contractors to subcontractors, accompanying orders for raw materials, eventually reaching the mills where they would be honored. (7) The mills would then report their shipments to the Board. (8) Cheaters were guilty of a criminal act, and subject to a $10,000 fine, a year in prison, or both. All of this applied to "A" products, those manufactured by major government contractors and their subcontractors who were typically closely tied to one claimant agency. It was recognized that some manufacturers sold products, sometimes in small quantities, to a wide range of firms on the open market. Producers of these "B" products could obtain their allotments directly from the Board. A substantial period was allowed for the Board, the other agencies involved, and for industry to prepare for the expected volume of paperwork. The plan went into operation on a trial basis in April 1943 and on a compulsory basis in July. Why was so much time allowed to set the plan in motion? The files labeled "Controlled Materials Plan" in the Eberstadt papers (Princeton University) may contain a clue: they deal almost exclusively with staffing. It was evidently extremely hard to find men experienced with materials control who were willing to go to Washington on a full-time basis. Reading these files, one can see how difficult it was to put together the team that would actually administer the CMP.

The plan was, as the preceding history should make clear, a retreat from the attempts at micromanaging production that preceded it. This plan was restricted to three materials, steel, copper, and aluminum; the Production Requirements Plan, by way of contrast, tried to control a much longer list of materials, including a wide range of chemicals. The Controlled Materials Plan left decisions about how much major contractors would get to the claimant agencies, and how much subcontractors would get to the major contractors; the Production Requirements Plan centralized these decisions in the War Production Board. In principle, moreover, the Controlled Materials Plan specifically excluded attempts to expedite the supply of controlled materials to individual projects (Novick, Anshen, and Truppner 1949, 170). The Controlled Materials Plan, in other words, was not the final stage in a process of ever more detailed central planning; it was just the opposite: an acknowledgement that detailed planning was unworkable.

A basic problem in the mobilization – the cause of unfinished projects, hoarding, bribing of suppliers, and so on – was believed to be the excessive demands placed on the economy by the huge number of contracts being issued by the military. This is what was known as the "feasibility problem." It may have been first identified in a March 1942 memo written by Simon Kuznets (Edelstein 2001). The

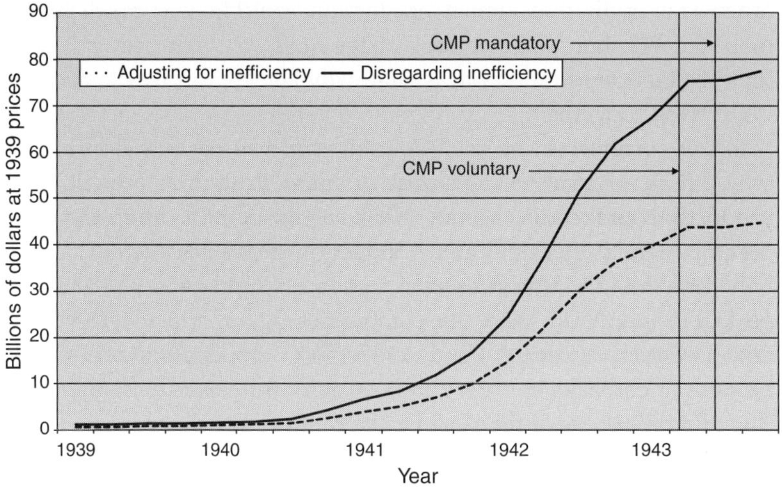

Figure 6.4 Net war output and the Controlled Materials Plan, showing that war output was leveling off by the time the CMP went into effect.
Source: Kuznets (1949, 90).

Controlled Materials Plan would attack the feasibility problem because demands would be scaled back to match the available raw materials. Even demand for uncontrolled materials and labor would be scaled back when claimant agencies cut programs to make them consistent with allocations of controlled materials.

Many historians have sung the praises of the Controlled Materials Plan. Perhaps the most influential was Eliot Janeway whose *The Struggle for Survival* (1951, 316) identified it as the masterstroke that won the war:

It [the Controlled Materials Plan] quickly balanced the input of economy energy and the output of fire power. In 1942 the war economy produced something over $30 billions of finished munitions. In 1943, at virtually the same price level, munitions production fell just short of $60 billion ... CMP flooded the fighting fronts with firepower.

Janeway's enthusiasm carried along generations of historians. But his "proof" that the plan produced a jump in munitions production is flawed. Figure 6.4 plots two of Simon Kuznets's estimates of munitions production: his unadjusted estimates and his estimates which incorporate his maximum adjustment for possible inefficiencies in munitions production; his other estimates fall between these two.

Janeway is right that annual production in 1943 was much higher than in 1942, but when we look at the quarterly estimates it is clear that production of munitions was already leveling off by the time the CMP went into effect.

Indeed, production of raw materials was also peaking by the time the CMP was put in place because of cutbacks in procurement. Steel production peaked in March 1944, eight months after the plan became mandatory; aluminum production peaked in October 1943, only three months after it became mandatory; and copper production peaked in June 1943, while the plan was being put in place (Dewhurst and Twentieth Century Fund 1947, 778). Production fell simply because of cutbacks in orders; mill capacity was more than adequate. The official history of the Steel Division of the War Production Board notes that mill capacity for ferroalloy steel exceeded orders placed throughout the CMP period (Hunter and Hogan 1950, 78). In other words, the main problem the CMP was created to deal with – excess demands for several crucial raw materials – had largely been resolved by the time the plan went into operation.

During the time that the Controlled Materials Plan was being put in place, tensions between Nelson and Eberstadt, and more fundamentally between Nelson and the military, had been growing (Koistinen 2004, 334). According to Nelson the differences were technical: Eberstadt wanted the War Production Board to focus on materials allocation; Nelson wanted it to focus on the scheduling of production, a job for which Nelson brought in Charles Wilson of General Electric. Nelson may also have felt that Eberstadt was a potential rival. By February 1943, after the announcement of the Controlled Materials Plan but before it went into effect, criticism of Nelson reached a crescendo. Roosevelt finally decided to resolve the controversy by replacing Nelson with Baruch. But Nelson got wind of the threat, and (by one account, hours before Roosevelt was set to offer the job to Baruch) he fired Eberstadt and announced it to the press. Roosevelt, unwilling to appear to side with Baruch and the military (recall that Eberstadt had started with the military), kept Nelson on at the War Production Board. Thus, Eberstadt was fired before the plan which made him famous went into effect. Many historians have assumed that Nelson was concerned solely with defending his turf and have given short shrift to his criticism of the CMP. The assumption concerning Nelson's motives may be correct, but that doesn't automatically invalidate his criticism. In fact, what he has to say about the plan (Nelson 1946, 383–4) is as consistent with the evidence as Janeway's enthusiastic endorsement: "by the time requests came in for materials under the Controlled Materials Plan the contracts had been let and the manufacturers were in the market actively seeking supplies. Control simply could not be exercised at the Controlled Materials Plan level."

The gold rush of 1942

If the activities of the War Production Board (in particular the often-heralded Controlled Materials Plan) and other government agencies do not explain the success of the mobilization, what does? I would suggest that historians have been using the wrong metaphor. They have viewed the war economy as an example of central planning. William H. McNeill is typical. After taking note of the early "quarrels over the allocation of scarce resources and raw materials" (McNeill 1982, 355), he reports that the "end result was a spectacular increase in American output of war materiel, and of the other goods needed to supplement British, Russian, and other Allied economies as well." His explanation: "The kind of scheduling required to keep a complicated assembly line running smoothly in a great factory was, in effect, applied to the entire national economy of the United States." I would suggest, however, that a better understanding comes from a different metaphor: it was the gold rush of 1942.[12] When gold was discovered in California in 1848 the favorable relationship between the price the government would pay for gold and the cost of producing it was recognized immediately. Men and women stopped plowing, unhitched their horses, and headed for California. There were shortages and overcrowding, and many people who hoped to get rich did not; many died trying. But in a few years a flood of gold was flowing from the stream beds and mines of California and changing economic conditions throughout the world. Something similar was true in 1942. Once the favorable relationship between the prices the government

[12] Although economists have shied away from the gold-rush analogy, others have embraced it. The novelist and journalist John Dos Passos (1968) wrote during the war about the "Gold Rush Down South," and Johnson's (1993) social history of Oakland, California and the East Bay during the war is entitled *The Second Gold Rush*.

would pay for munitions, or for the factories to produce munitions, and the cost of producing them was recognized the rush was on. Corporate profits after taxes, including wartime excess profits taxes, rose about 40 percent between 1939 and 1942. Alcoa, for example, was criticized for not expanding capacity fast enough in the later 1930s through 1941. But when the Defense Plant Corporation contracts were made available that provided substantial profits at little risk, Alcoa went to work building new plants. Production tripled between 1941 and 1943.

Labor responded enthusiastically to the availability of high wage jobs. Here is Janeway (1951, 172) on one episode:

> At Charleston in Southern Indiana, DuPont went to work on a major powder project. Attracted by the atmosphere of boom, swarms of unskilled labor swelled the population from 800 to 5,000, to 15,000, to a mass of unabsorbed and unhoused workers spread over all the neighboring towns.

Bret Harte, who won fame for his stories about the gold rush ("The Luck of Roaring Camp"), would have recognized the scene. Although established firms had obvious advantages, it was often outsiders who were the first to take advantage of new opportunities. Richard C. Reynolds, for example, used his political connections to secure a Reconstruction Finance Corporation loan and enter aluminum refining (Smith 1988, 217). The most spectacular success was Henry Kaiser who used the war to enter shipbuilding, and magnesium, steel, and aircraft production (Adams 1997). There were, it is true, important differences between the California gold rush and the war mobilization. For one thing, there were more centers of production during the war, although California was a magnet for labor and capital in 1942 as it had been in 1849 (Rhode 2004). The main difference for our purposes was that in 1942 an important segment of the public believed that the mobilization ought to be centrally controlled both to assure speed and efficiency, and to ameliorate unwanted effects on the distribution of income. For that reason the government became far more involved in the gold rush of 1942 than it had in the gold rush of 1849.

In 1849 the government's policy of a fixed price for gold created and sustained the boom; in 1942 it was the government's willingness to purchase munitions production that created and sustained the boom. There was even a parallel in the way the gold rush of 1849 and that of 1942 were financed. Gold production was financed ultimately by increases in the demand for money and by a tax on cash balances as inflation eroded the real value of existing money holdings. Similarly, munitions production was financed partly by selling bonds to the Federal Reserve, creating new money that satisfied increased demands for money at current prices and produced inflation. A gold rush was not the only way of producing gold in California in 1849. One can imagine, for the sake of argument, gold being produced by federal employees in nationalized mines, or by tightly regulated and coordinated private firms. And one can imagine munitions being produced in 1942 in nationalized arsenals or by tightly regulated and coordinated private firms. But this was not the way it was done in 1849 – or in 1942. Although the actions of the War Production Board, the Office of Price Administration, and many other government agencies did not cause or determine the shape of the boom in munitions production, they did help solve problems, and may have made a positive overall contribution. People picked up and moved to war production centers during the war because there was money to be made – in this respect the war boom was like a nineteenth-century gold rush. In the nineteenth century the gold miners were on their own, but during the war there were various agencies working on labor problems and at least some of their programs made positive contributions. George Q. Flynn (1979, 69), for example, argued persuasively that the War Manpower Commission's "West Coast Plan" eased labor recruitment at key plants.

The course of the war

The best way to obtain a broad-brush picture of the way economic forces influenced the war is through the statistics on annual war production. Table 6.5 shows annual production of aircraft by country from 1939 to 1945, and Table 6.6 shows annual expenditures (cumulative for 1933–9) for all munitions valued at 1944 US prices. Several conclusions follow.

First, both Germany and Japan spent more on arms during the second half of the 1930s than did the United States. Military leaders in Germany and Japan realized that if they hoped to alter the world's international political order by force they had to win quick victories based on surprise, careful planning, and a cache of arms built up before the war. Germany and Japan could not win a war of attrition

Table 6.5 *Annual production of military aircraft by country, 1939–45*

	USA	USSR	UK	Germany	Italy	Japan	Hungary
1939	5,856	10,382	7,940	8,295	1,692	4,467	0
1940	12,804	10,565	15,049	10,826	2,142	4,768	0
1941	26,277	15,735	20,094	11,776	3,503	5,088	0
1942	47,836	25,436	23,672	15,556	2,818	8,861	6
1943	85,898	34,845	26,263	25,527	967	16,693	267
1944	96,318	40,246	26,461	39,807	0	28,180	773
1945	49,761	20,052	12,070	7,544	0	8,263	0

Source: Ellis (1993, 278).

Table 6.6 *Combat munitions produced by the major belligerents in World War II (billions of dollars, 1944 US munitions prices)*

Country	1935–9	1940	1941	1942	1943	1944
USA	1.5	1.5	4.5	20	38.0	42.0
Canada	0.0	0.0	0.5	1.0	1.5	1.5
Great Britain	2.5	3.5	6.5	9.0	11.0	11.0
USSR	8.0	5.0	8.5	11.5	14.0	16.0
Germany	12.0	6.0	6.0	8.5	13.5	17.0
Japan	2.0	1.0	2.0	3.0	4.5	6.0

Source: Goldsmith (1946, 75). The figures are shown to the nearest half billion to avoid, as Goldsmith noted, a spurious appearance of accuracy. The figures are imprecise, but are useful as indicators of broad trends. Also see Harrison (1998, 1–42).

against an alliance that included the United States; their economies were simply too small. Creating a temporary superiority in munitions was a plausible strategy because opposition to military spending in the United States, Britain, and France was strong. Many Americans believed that their country's policy of remaining aloof from European wars had served it well in the nineteenth century – the Atlantic had provided nearly free security – and that the decision to become involved in World War I had cost America dearly. In Britain the threat of German expansionism was seen more clearly than in the United States, but in that country as well as in the United States, opposition to military spending prevented it from keeping pace with the Germans.

Second, the Soviet Union, although it had not stockpiled as many munitions in the 1930s as Germany, had nonetheless been far more active than the United States or Britain. In 1939 the Soviet Union produced more military aircraft than Germany; in 1940, nearly as many; and in 1941, substantially more. The total expenditure figures tell a similar story. In 1941 through 1943, production of war goods in the Soviet Union, despite the German attack, exceeded production in Germany. To be sure, there are many uncertainties in these statistics, but the overall success of the Soviet munitions program cannot be doubted. This is well known now, but because of the secrecy of Stalin's regime, the Germans underestimated the quantity of munitions possessed by the Soviets. The difficult time that the Soviet Union had in its war with Finland (1939–40), and perhaps a poor opinion of the competence of a Slavic and socialist regime, appears to have led the Germans to underestimate the quality and quantity of Soviet arms and their capacity to produce more.

Third, in the long run the German and Japanese gambles failed. German forces overwhelmed France in a *blitzkrieg* (lightning war) and drove British forces off the continent. In June 1941 Germany launched a massive attack on the Soviet Union. Initially, the Germans experienced the same sort of success that they had enjoyed against France, but their attack stalled before Moscow. Japan too enjoyed a series of initial successes. Pearl Harbor was successfully attacked in December 1941; Manila, the most important urban area in the Philippines, was captured in January 1942; and the last remaining forces in the Philippines, on the Bataan peninsula, surrendered in April. But in June 1942 the Japanese navy suffered a major defeat at Midway. Blitzkrieg victories by the Axis had given way to a war of attrition.

Tables 6.5 and 6.6 show how little time Germany and Japan had to make their blitzkrieg strategies work. In 1939 Germany produced more aircraft than the United States, and Japan about three-quarters as many. But in 1940, with the United States getting its war production in gear, both fell far behind. In 1942, the first year of US involvement in the war, the United States produced more military aircraft than Germany, Italy, and Japan combined. The more comprehensive spending figures in Table 6.6 tell a similar story. In 1942 the United States spent more on munitions than Germany and Japan combined: \$20 billion versus \$11.5 billion. And, of course, the United States was not alone: Great Britain and the USSR each spent more on arms than Germany. The Allied advantage continued unabated into 1943 and 1944. Indeed by 1944 the Americans were beginning to talk about cutbacks in spending and the problem of disposing of surpluses. Winning the war still required fighting and dying, and it was always possible that the Allies might decide that the price of victory was too high and give up the fight, but it was clear that in the end they could win the war of attrition with the Axis.

Fourth, despite an unrelenting air bombardment and a fearsome naval blockade, Germany and Japan managed to increase production until very near the end of the war. Military aircraft (Table 6.5) and total munitions production (Table 6.6) reached all-time records in both countries in 1944.

3. An index number problem

Table 6.6 uses US munitions prices (as of 1944) to evaluate production in all countries. Obviously, different prices and dates could be used. How does using 1944 US prices affect the results? In general, using US prices produces *underestimates* of the difference between the US level of production and the levels in other countries. This is the classic *index number problem*: we obtain different estimates depending on which set of prices we use. Nations tend to produce more of what is relatively cheap for them to produce. The Soviet Union, for example, would be likely to produce more tanks and fewer aircraft carriers than the USA, even leaving to one side the difference in their military circumstances, simply because the relative price of tanks was lower in the Soviet Union. Valuing Soviet output at US prices, where, tanks are relatively more expensive, means valuing the items that the Soviet Union focused on because they were relatively inexpensive at relatively high prices. So these estimates are biased against finding large percentage differences in favor of the United States.

The war in the Pacific

The Pacific War was the first, and perhaps the last, in which the aircraft carrier reigned supreme. Figure 6.5, which plots the number of carrier-based aircraft of the United States and Japan, shows Japan's dilemma. By 1941 it had come close to matching the United States in carrier-based planes, thanks to a major building program. By one count the United States had a fleet of 640 carrier-based planes

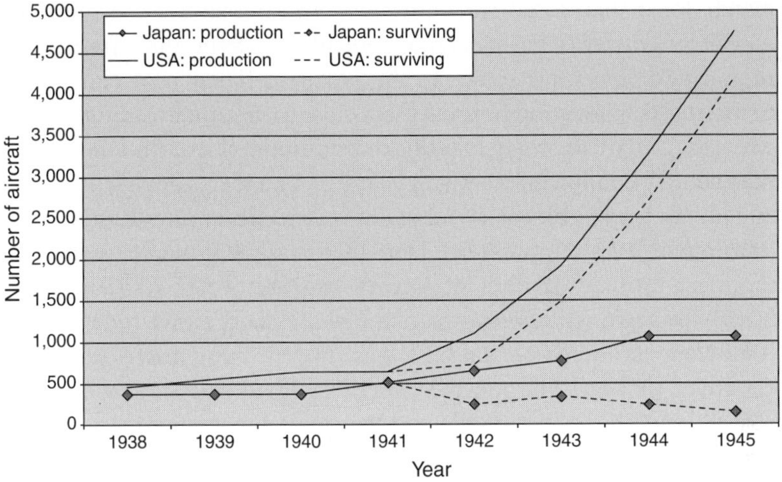

Figure 6.5 Carrier-based aircraft, United States and Japan, 1938–45. Ellis (1993) provides only the launch date for the first ship in a particular class. Therefore, I made some arbitrary assumptions about when other ships in a class were launched in order to complete the figure. I doubt, however, that using the exact launch dates would change the broad-brush conclusions drawn in the text. In 1941 Japan had nearly as many carrier-based planes as the United States, but after Pearl Harbor it quickly fell far behind. Even if Japan had never lost a single carrier, it would have fallen far behind the United States.
Source: Ellis (1993, 293–4).

compared with 516 for Japan.[13] But it was clear that this was as close as Japan was going to get: the Americans had more carriers under construction than the Japanese.

To be sure, carrier-based planes were not the whole story. There were also conventional naval vessels to consider: battleships, cruisers, destroyers, submarines, and so on. Here, however, the US advantage was even greater. Japan's naval construction had been limited by the naval agreements of the 1920s. Indeed, this was one source of humiliation for the Japanese that could be reversed with victories over Britain and the United States. It is doubtful, however, that even in the absence of the treaties the United States would have allowed Japan to get very close in conventional naval strength. Money would have been found to

[13] See the source for Figure 6.6. Some of the American planes were based on smaller escort carriers whose mission was somewhat different from that of the larger attack carriers.

match Japan battleship for battleship. The possibility that aircraft, especially carrier-based aircraft, were more potent than traditional ships could give some solace to the Japanese. Their near equality in carrier-based planes might bring them close to the Americans in overall strength, despite their gap in terms of traditional ships. And the carrier fleet could be supplemented with island airbases. Occupying an island and building an airbase was like building (at relatively low cost) a giant (but immobile) aircraft carrier. Here then was what would seem to be the most rational account of Japan's strategy (Toland 1970; Overy 2010). To begin with, strike the first blow, a major blow, reducing the American advantage on the high seas. If even two carriers had been destroyed at Pearl Harbor, the American advantage in carrier-based planes would have been eliminated. Fortunately for the Americans the carriers were at sea, and the Japanese could only destroy traditional surface ships. Second, use the breathing space to occupy and construct airbases on a series of islands around Japan. This would create an air fortress that the American navy could not penetrate or could penetrate only at great cost. Eventually the Americans would be forced to consent to a Japanese empire in Asia. But this was not to be. As Figure 6.5 shows, the Japanese carrier-based fleet declined dramatically in 1942 while the American fleet held steady (compare the dotted lines). The Battle of Midway in June 1942 was especially important. The Japanese lost four carriers with a total of 327 planes while destroying one American carrier with 100 planes (Ellis 1993, 293–4).

Although the Japanese continued to launch new carriers, they were not able to make up for battle losses, let alone keep pace with the Americans who were offsetting losses and then adding to their fleet. Indeed, as Figure 6.5 shows, the American production advantage was so great that its fleet would have grown relative to the Japanese fleet even if the Japanese had avoided losing even one of their own carriers while continuing to inflict the same damage on the Americans as they actually did. In other words, the Japanese could have won every battle in 1942 and 1943 and still faced an expanded American carrier fleet. (Compare the American fleet net of losses, the higher dotted line, with Japanese production gross of losses, the lower solid line.) America's astonishingly rapid economic and military responses, its early victories, and its strategy of island hopping, in other words, meant that Japan was never able to construct the impenetrable ring of island fortresses that might have justified its decision to go to war.

The economics of strategic bombing

To its defenders strategic bombing was an unfortunate but necessary measure needed to defeat Hitler and Tojo; to its critics strategic bombing was a barbarism, ineffective and immoral. The ethical debate centered on *strategic* rather than *tactical* bombing. Tactical bombing targets the enemy on the battlefield. The airplane is used as a form of artillery, throwing heavy shells and explosives at the enemy; or as a form of cavalry moving rapidly behind enemy lines, observing the disposition of enemy forces and attacking targets of opportunity. Strategic bombing, on the other hand, targets the enemy's economy. The purpose is to destroy the enemy's ability and will to fight by destroying factories, farms, railroads, oil refineries, and so on – and perhaps the people who work in them. The idea of destroying the enemy's economy and will to fight has been a part of warfare since ancient times. William Tecumseh Sherman's march to the sea was a classic American example as were many campaigns waged against Native Americans in which villages and crops were burned. Naval blockades often served a similar purpose. The airplane simply offered a new means for carrying out a time-honored strategy.

When the war began, the case for strategic bombing was largely theoretical. To many military observers it was self-evident that "the bombers would always get through" and that the destruction they would bring would devastate the enemy both materially and spiritually. General Giulio Douhet, an Italian air power theorist, is often cited as the author of this view and the father of strategic bombing (Brodie 1955). There had been some bombing during World War I, but the equipment was too rudimentary and the campaigns too short to provide hard evidence on the costs and benefits. Advocates of strategic bombing, however, could instead reason by analogy. The British naval blockade of the continent in World War I was widely credited with undermining the German economy and civilian morale (Davis and Engerman 2006, chapter 5, 159–238). A shortage of fertilizer reduced crop yields and led to starvation in central Europe, thereby contributing to the Allied victory. Aircraft, with their ability to penetrate into the farthest reaches of the enemy, one might think, would be even more effective.

The Spanish Civil War (1936–9) provided the best evidence about the potential effect of bombing. It was a large-scale conflict and the first in which aircraft played a major role. Both sides enlisted outside support.

Stalin supplied the leftist government, whose supporters were known as the Loyalists, with air power, while Hitler and Mussolini supplied the insurgents under Francisco Franco, known as the Nationalists. Strategic bombing, it must be said, did not win a great reputation in Spain. Picasso's masterpiece *Guernica*, which depicts the bombing of the Basque city of that name by the Germans on April 26, 1937, illustrates the ultimate horror of a modern air war. But there is little evidence that this or other examples of the bombing of cities in Spain destroyed production or morale as the advocates of strategic bombing had predicted. The bombing of Barcelona in March 1938, ordered by Mussolini on the theory that it would undermine civilian morale, was, according to Corum (1998, 329), "the heaviest bombing of a major city that had been seen in warfare up to that time." Nevertheless, far from undermining morale, it strengthened Catalonia's will to fight.

For the Germans, Italians, and Soviets, and to some degree the French, the lesson learned in the Spanish Civil War was that strategic bombing was ineffective – the damage done to productive facilities was limited and civilian resolve might actually be strengthened – but that tactical bombing, based on close coordination of the air forces with ground forces, paid huge dividends. The Germans tried out the Junkers Ju-87 dive bomber – the brainchild of Colonel Ernst Udet who had been an airplane stunt rider in the 1920s – and found it to be a devastating weapon, at least in Udet's estimation (Overy 1996, 104). The Soviets, as a result of their experience in Spain, developed the IL-2 Sturmovik ground-attack plane that would prove highly effective in World War II (Corum 1998, 330). Although some American and British observers absorbed the lessons of Spain, the molders of opinion about air power in both countries maintained their faith in strategic bombing. One line of argument was that despite a few examples, strategic bombing had not really been tried in Spain. Since the Spanish Nationalists were trying to capture the cities, and since they represented the people who owned the property in the cities, they would not engage in the kind of strategic bombing that would have worked. Brigadier General Henry H. "Hap" Arnold, who would command the American army air force in World War II, later endorsed this argument, claiming that strategic bombing was not employed in Spain because it was a civil war (Corum 1998, 318).

The United States and Britain allocated considerable resources to strategic bombing. According to Overy (1996, 128) more than

140,000 British and American airmen were lost and 21,000 bombers. Separate figures on expenditures for the US air force are not readily available for World War II because it was still part of the army – it did not become a separate service until 1947 – but Werrell (1986, 707) estimates that 25 percent of the US war effort went into aviation. During the Korean War, conducted after it had become a separate service, the air force absorbed about 20 percent of all military spending, so Werrell's figure seems reasonable. Of course, only part of the expenditure by the air force during World War II was for strategic bombing: the US air forces also engaged in tactical bombing, reconnaissance, transport, and so on. Overy (1996, 128) says that only 7 percent of the British war effort went into strategic bombing. Again, we should remember that such figures are only approximate. In both the United States and Britain, aircraft production benefited from having the highest priority throughout the production process.

The initial idea when considering how to conduct strategic bombing was to aim at "sensitive points" in the German and Japanese economies. If one could find a material that was a crucial input in a wide range of industrial processes, but produced in few places, one could cripple the enemy's war machine by concentrated bombing of those points. The Allied air attacks on the German ball-bearing industry at Schweinfurt and Regensburg in the late summer and fall of 1943 are a good example of this idea in operation. Relying on attacks against sensitive points, however, proved difficult, especially for the British. The Germans protected such sensitive points with fighters and rings of anti-aircraft artillery, and exacted heavy tolls on the British, who began the war with slow-moving bombers and without fighters that could protect them all the way to their targets. The Germans, moreover, dispersed munitions factories, built them out of the range of Allied bombers and fighters, and constructed them underground. For the British, the realization that striking at sensitive points was too costly came early. The only feasible way to use their air force, it seemed, was to bomb at night and to use area bombing. On May 7, 1941 the British cabinet formally agreed to a plan to destroy fifty-eight of Germany's largest towns and cities (Tooze 2007, 510). It was, as it came to be called, a policy of "dehousing" the German workforce, of "city busting." The Americans, whose planes could fly higher and faster and were well armed (although they carried smaller bomb loads), and who were confident that their Norden bombsight made it possible to hit enemy targets precisely, continued daylight bombing and the attempt to strike at sensitive points. It was a pragmatic decision, not an ethical one. The Americans saw daylight bombing as the best way to use their bombers. And they understood and approved of the idea of a one–two punch: Americans bombing by day and the British bombing by night.

4. Strategic bombing and the Cobb–Douglas production function

Behind the philosophy of seeking sensitive points was the idea that resources must be combined in fixed proportions. It assumed, to use the economic term, a fixed-coefficient production function. In fact, however, the Germans found numerous ways to substitute for materials affected by bombing. The formula for making hardened steel, for example, was changed to economize on alloys in short supply, such as tungsten, and the technique of quenching hot steel to make it harder was used.

When substitutions are possible, a better model of the economy is a production function that allows for substitution among forms of capital and among forms of labor, and for substitutions between capital and labor. This sort of aggregate production has become standard for economists studying peacetime economies, but the implications for strategic bombing are sobering. Suppose the aggregate production function for Germany was Cobb–Douglas: $Q = AK^{(1-\alpha)} L^{\alpha}$, where Q is total output, A is an index of total productivity, K is total capital (including land), α is the share of labor income in total income output, and L is total labor. Then, to reduce aggregate German output by 10 percent, the Allies would have to destroy 10 percent of the German capital stock and 10 percent of the labor force. Since the Germans could maintain production by shifting capital and labor from the production of civilian goods to the production of war goods and by exploiting capital, labor and raw materials from conquered territories, the Allies would have to destroy far more than 10 percent of the total capital and labor in Germany to reduce output of German munitions by 10 percent. Strategic bombing, in other words, would have to be horrific to achieve its ends.

How effective was strategic bombing in World War II? Was it worth the cost in men and machines? As the war was coming to an end, President Roosevelt established the United States Strategic Bombing

Survey to investigate the effects of the bombing.[14] It was a remarkable enterprise. The survey employed hundreds of soldiers and civilian personnel who visited targets in Europe and Japan and interviewed government bureaucrats, factory managers, and workers, in some cases only days after Allied forces had secured an area. The survey drew mixed conclusions about the effectiveness of strategic bombing. Some targets that American planners had thought were utterly destroyed had, it turned out, been put back into operation quickly. A factory building might be completely destroyed, leading US aircrews, and bureaucrats relying on their reports, to conclude that the factory had been destroyed, while the equipment housed inside had survived with repairable damage. But the survey concluded that some attacks had been effective. Attacks on oil refineries toward the end of the war produced a severe fuel shortage that hampered German military operations.

John Kenneth Galbraith, who would emerge as one of the most prominent American economists of the postwar era and win public recognition as part of President Kennedy's "brain trust," was one of the civilian directors of the Bombing Survey. He arrived at this position by a circuitous route. At the start of the war he was recruited from Harvard to the Office of Price Administration, where he served as deputy director. He was forced to resign when Republicans pushed through legislation requiring price controllers to have five years of experience in business. He then moved to *Fortune* magazine and from there to the Bombing Survey. To Galbraith, the ultimate lesson of the Strategic Bombing Survey was that strategic bombing did not work; it was barbarism to no purpose. Bombing, Galbraith maintained, had failed to reduce German munitions production or German morale. Indeed, production had increased well into 1944.

The Allied attack in July 1943 on Hamburg, Germany's second city, a port and manufacturing center, was a classic lesson in the problematic value of strategic bombing. Bombing created a firestorm, a tornado of super-heated air, which multiplied the destruction. The tornado, it was said, literally sucked its victims from the streets of Hamburg. It is estimated that 45,000 people died, 37,000 were

[14] US Strategic Bombing Survey (1945, 1946b) are the summary reports on the European and Pacific campaigns. The Bombing Survey also published many specialized studies. MacIsaac (1976) provides the historical background.

injured, and 1 million were made homeless (Lowe 2007, 294). Despite the unprecedented (at that time) loss of civilian lives, war planners in the USA and Britain considered the attack a great success. But the Bombing Survey found that production setbacks were only temporary. The main industrial centers and the harbor area had been missed. The Blohm and Voss shipyards, which produced U-boats, were soon back in business, and by the end of 1943 total shipbuilding output in Hamburg was higher than it had been before the July attack (Lowe 2007, 295). German confidence in the war effort was shaken by the attack, but it also increased the resolve of the Luftwaffe to protect Germany, unified its leadership, and inspired important changes in tactics and the methods for producing aircraft that frustrated the Allies for months to come.

The Allies followed up the success, as they saw it, of the attack on Hamburg with attacks on other cities with the intention of creating firestorms by using incendiary bombs. Particularly devastating were the attacks on Dresden in Germany and on Tokyo and many other cities in Japan. The attacks on Dresden in February 1945 left perhaps 135,000 dead (Hewitt 1983). Kurt Vonnegut, who witnessed the bombing of Dresden as an American prisoner of war, described it in his acclaimed anti-war novel *Slaughterhouse-Five* (1991 [1968]). Japanese cities consisting of densely packed wooden structures were extremely vulnerable to firebombing. In a single raid on Tokyo on March 10, 1945 fires made refugees of a million people and left an estimated 100,000 dead.[15] Further attacks, including more on Tokyo, destroyed most of Japan's major cities before atomic bombs were dropped on Hiroshima and Nagasaki, discussed in more detail below.

Bombing of rail lines and synthetic oil plants in Europe had been somewhat effective, Galbraith and the Bombing Survey conceded, but had come rather late in the day. For the most part, bombing had been a costly failure. Table 6.7 illustrates the heart of Galbraith's case. In 1944 the Allies dropped more than a million tons of explosives on Germany, an increase by a factor of five over the amount dropped in 1943. But it was also the peak year for German production of tanks and self-propelled guns, aircraft, and many other munitions.

[15] The Center of the Tokyo Raid and War Damages: www.tokyo-sensai.net/english_page/index.html (accessed October 15, 2010).

Table 6.7 ***Strategic bombing and German munitions production***

	Bombs dropped by Britain in Europe (tons)	Bombs dropped by the USA in Europe (tons)	German production of tanks and self-propelled guns (units)	German production of aircraft (units)	German production of oil from all sources (tons)
1941	31,704	0	3,790	11,776	8,485
1942	45,561	1,411	6,180	15,556	8,965
1943	157,367	57,329	12,063	25,527	10,497
1944	525,518	629,379	19,002	39,807	6,504
1945	181,740[a]	279,472[a]	3,932	7,544	NA

Notes:
[a] January through May.
Bombs dropped by the United States include small amounts dropped by Balkan allies.
Sources: Ellis (1993): bombs, pp. 233–5; tanks and self-propelled guns, p. 277; aircraft, p. 278; oil, p. 275.

Production of tanks and self-propelled guns increased from 12,063 to 19,002 in these years, and aircraft production increased from 25,527 to 39,807. Oil production, however, did fall. To be sure, one could argue that production of munitions would have been still higher in the absence of the bombing campaign. But the postwar revelation of German production achievements in the face of Allied bombing came as a shock to many Americans. My former colleague Sidney Ratner, an economic historian who had been involved in target selection during the war, told me that he cried when he read the report of the Strategic Bombing Survey. He knew, of course, that many American flyers had died on missions that he had supported – casualty rates among the bombing crews were extraordinarily high – but he thought that they had died bringing German production to a standstill. Learning that production had been increasing despite the bombing was devastating.

Figure 6.6, which plots monthly indexes of German aircraft production, total German munitions production, and the amount of bombs dropped on Germany from January 1942 through January 1945 (1944 = 100 in each case) illustrates additional parts of the debate over strategic bombing. Galbraith's interpretation is straightforward. Production (both total munitions and aircraft taken separately) reached its monthly peak in July 1944 despite more than a year of ferocious bombing that had leveled cities and killed hundreds of thousands of civilians. But the

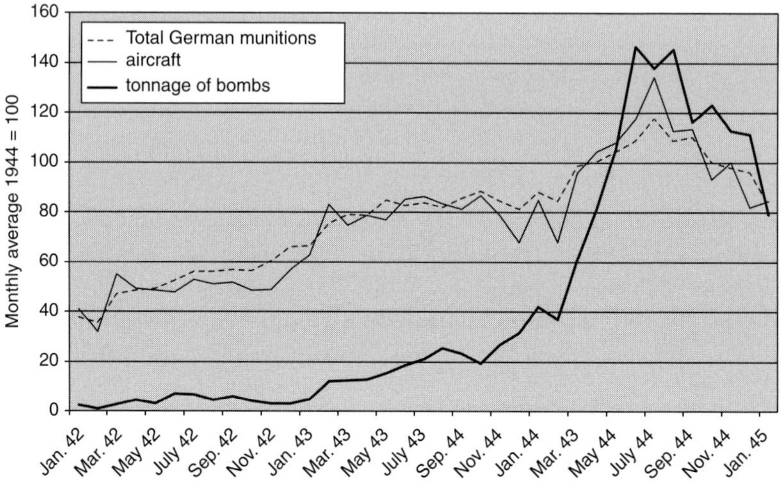

Figure 6.6 Strategic bombing and German munitions production, 1942–5. German munitions production rose in the first half of 1944 despite intense bombing.

Sources: Tonnage of bombs: Ellis (1993, 233–5); German munitions production: Tooze (2007, 687–8).

path of production was not smoothly upward. German munitions production evidently leveled off in the first quarter of 1943 at the same time as the bombing, measured by tons of bombs dropped, increased. Tooze (2007, 597–600) traces this to the bombing of the Ruhr, which reduced German coal production, a raw material crucial for making steel and armaments. The Allies, in other words, had found a sensitive point in the German economy.

However, this pause was followed by an extraordinary increase in munitions production in the first half of 1944. From January to June of that year aircraft production increased by a factor of nearly 1.4, even though the weight of bombs dropped on Germany each month increased by a factor of nearly 3.5. It was this surge in munitions production that endowed Albert Speer, Germany's munitions minister, with the reputation of miracle worker. Although the German success in increasing production in 1944 has been ascribed to Speer's rationalization and management of the German war economy – this was Speer's own claim in his fascinating memoir, *Inside the Third Reich* (1970 [1952]) – and while there is undoubtedly some truth in his claim to have reorganized production for greater efficiency, Speer's methods are somewhat misrepresented by the term "management" with its connotation of MBAs applying the latest academic theories. The Germans were desperate, and we now know they were willing to use any means, however horrific, to increase production. Slave laborers, including inmates from Auschwitz, were worked to death to maximize production in Germany's final, futile push (Tooze 2007, 630–1).

One early and important challenge to Galbraith's view that strategic bombing had been ineffective came from Walt W. Rostow. Like Galbraith, Rostow could claim to be an expert on strategic bombing: in World War II he had served in the Enemies Objectives Unit of the Office of Strategic Services, the forerunner of the Central Intelligence Agency.[16] The unit's purpose was to choose targets for strategic bombing. Military personnel are, presumably, the best judges of military targets, but if the goal is to destroy the enemy's economy, then, presumably, economists are the experts. Like Galbraith, Rostow would emerge as a prominent economist during the postwar era and like Galbraith would be a member of President Kennedy's brain trust. But these two great economists differed profoundly on strategic bombing. Rostow claimed that the Allied attacks on German aircraft factories in the latter part of 1943 were a crucial blow. Those attacks, Rostow claimed, paved the way for attacks on German fuel production and engagements with the German air force (the Luftwaffe) that produced heavy losses of German aircraft and pilots. Losses of fuel, aircraft, and pilots in turn had given American and Soviet pilots control of the air, a crucial ingredient in the ultimate victory of the Allied armies. Rostow never surrendered this interpretation (2003, 39–41). Galbraith's conclusion that bombing had been ineffective during World War II informed his steadfast opposition to bombing during the Vietnam War (*New York Times*, April 27, 1965, 36; November 12, 1967, 236). Rostow, on the other hand, would be one of the most persistent advocates of bombing in Vietnam, and as President Johnson's national security advisor he would be one of the most influential (Milne 2007). Indeed, Rostow's faith in air power remained undiminished long after American public opinion had begun to doubt that the Vietnam War was winnable. His reputation, especially on the left, would suffer irreparable damage. Once hailed as part of the flow of brilliant liberal intellectuals from Cambridge to Washington during the Kennedy

[16] Technically the Enemies Objectives Unit was attached to the US embassy.

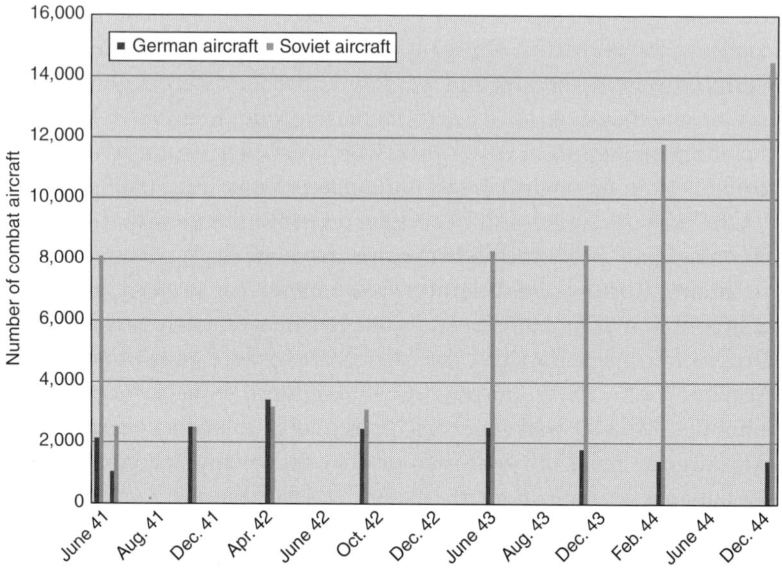

Figure 6.7 Combat aircraft on the eastern front, selected dates. Although the Germans increased production of aircraft, they lost air superiority on the eastern front.
Source: Ellis (1993, 233).

administration, he ended his career reviled in many quarters as Walt "Bomber" Rostow. Rostow and Galbraith had what was obviously a deeply felt exchange in 1971 over the effectiveness of the WWII bombing campaign (*New York Times*, April 4, 1971, BR20), debating as it were the ongoing bombing in Vietnam while debating the effects of bombing in World War II.

Although it may not have been relevant to the Vietnam War, at least one part of Rostow's argument, that strategic bombing worked by forcing German planes into the air where they were destroyed, thus giving the Allies air superiority and making possible the advance of Allied armies, has won support from subsequent students of the war (Overy 1980, 1996; Tooze 2007, 627). Although figures on aircraft available for combat are only approximate, the available data tell a clear story unlikely to be changed significantly when more accurate counts are available. Figure 6.7 shows the eastern front. Here the Germans, although starting behind, were able to achieve a temporary superiority in the air during their initial blitzkrieg attack on the Soviet

Union. But the picture soon changed. Despite ramping up their production of aircraft, the Germans were unable to increase the size of their air force on the eastern front, while the Soviet air force kept expanding. The Luftwaffe was fighting on too many fronts and losing too many planes and pilots. By July 1943, when the great Battle of Kursk began, the Soviets enjoyed a marked numerical air superiority.

Even though the Allied bombing policy had, in Rostow's view, been successful in World War II, he maintained that the Allies had made mistakes. In the months before D Day they had stressed attacks on railroad marshalling yards. Rostow believed that if more attacks had been carried out against bridges and oil refineries, as he and some of his colleagues had recommended, the war could have been shortened (Rostow 2003, 45–50). Eisenhower, in whose hands the final decision had lain, chose to reject the advice of Rostow and his colleagues for political reasons. The implication of this mistake for the future, one might infer, was that the military should defer to the civilian experts (as in Vietnam?). To be sure, the policy of camouflaging and dispersing aircraft factories, and moving them into underground facilities, made it possible for Germany to increase production after Albert Speer took charge of German aircraft production in 1944. But by then, according to Rostow, it was too late: attacks on oil and the loss of pilots doomed the German air force. Speer's contribution, moreover, in Rostow's view, was overrated: the dispersal program was underway before Speer took over and the Allies had decided to move on to other targets. John Kenneth Galbraith would have none of this. In his view the declines in German aircraft production were simply due to mismanagement of the production program, mismanagement that Speer corrected. Bombing had nothing to do with it.

George Santayana was right to claim that "those who cannot remember the past are condemned to repeat it." But the lessons of history are seldom clear. For Galbraith, who opposed the bombing campaigns undertaken by the United States in the Vietnam War, the important points to remember about strategic bombing in World War II were that bombing had failed to prevent the Germans from significantly increasing arms production and it had failed to undermine the support of German civilians for the war effort. For Rostow, an architect of the bombing campaigns in Vietnam, the important points to remember were that bombing had helped to win the war, and that it would have won the war sooner if only Eisenhower had listened to the advice from the academics – including, of course, Rostow.

Strategic bombing, perhaps more than any other aspect of the war, raises troubling moral issues. If the attacks on German production facilities were ineffective in reducing German munitions production, and reducing munitions production was the whole point, then the huge loss of civilian life that occurred as a result of strategic bombing – 600,000 people died and 800,000 suffered non-mortal wounds (Hewitt 1983, 263; Werrell 1986, 709) – was at best a tragic mistake. In Britain Sir Arthur Harris was a hero during the war for successfully energizing and leading the bombing campaign; he is now regarded in some circles as a war criminal. But if attacking German cities was necessary to draw the Luftwaffe into the air where it could be engaged and destroyed, and to prevent it from adding its weight to German forces on the fighting fronts, most importantly the eastern front, then the devastation of German cities, it could be argued, was a necessary cost of victory over the Axis. The issue is unlikely to ever be resolved. We cannot rerun history and see how the war would have gone had the resources devoted to the bombing campaign been devoted to other ends.

In some ways the change in attitudes toward strategic bombing is understandable. We can look back and see that hatred toward Germany and Japan was deliberately fostered. We can see that the advocates of strategic bombing claimed major successes without sound evidence. What seemed obvious at the time, that bombing would destroy the ability and will of Germany to fight, turned out to be wrong. But we can also question how large the opposition to bombing would have been if more accurate estimates of its effectiveness had been available at the time. History shows that when people feel fundamentally threatened, they fight murderously. It is possible that even if the lightness of the destruction of industrial damage and the heaviness of the loss of civilian casualties had been known, the public would have overwhelmingly supported strategic bombing. The fate of civilians in times of war was an old story even in Adam Smith's day. Recall his description of how civilians are treated in wartime in his *Theory of Moral Sentiments* (Smith 1976 [1759], part III, chapter 1):

> the goods of the peaceable citizens are seized both at land and at sea; their lands are laid waste, their houses are burnt, and they themselves, if they presume to make any resistance, are murdered or led into captivity; and all this in the most perfect conformity to what are called the laws of nations.

The morality of bombing becomes even more problematic when we turn to the ultimate form of strategic bombing: the atomic bomb.

The atomic bomb

By the late 1930s a number of scientists had concluded that an atomic bomb could be built and that a nation that possessed the bomb would have an enormous military and diplomatic advantage over any nation that did not.[17] On August 2, 1939, Albert Einstein, perhaps the world's most famous scientist, and a beloved celebrity in the United States, wrote to President Roosevelt explaining that a bomb of massive power could be created from uranium, and asking the federal government to establish a relationship with and to finance the scientists who were working on nuclear fission. This letter – which was probably drafted by the Hungarian-born physicist Leo Szilard, who had been working on nuclear fission with Enrico Fermi – was the beginning of the American effort to build a nuclear weapon.[18] It was in some ways a familiar academic exercise, a grant proposal, but the stakes were enormous. Roosevelt responded by establishing a board to work with the atomic scientists, but it would take Pearl Harbor, and further evidence of the feasibility of the project, for the government to launch an all-out effort. By mid-1942, however, the administration was willing to allocate sufficient resources to build a bomb. Things began to move quickly in September when General Leslie Groves was appointed to head the project. Groves had recently finished directing the construction of the Pentagon, the world's largest office building, and had a reputation for getting things done fast; the bomb project would add to that reputation. Groves then appointed the physicist J. Robert Oppenheimer to head the scientific side of the project. Theirs would be a productive but fraught relationship. Together they would successfully build an atomic bomb in a short period of time. But Oppenheimer's many personal connections on the left led to ongoing difficulties with the government based on questions about whether he was a security risk. Groves designated the bomb project the

[17] Rhodes (1986) is a well-regarded general history of the Manhattan Project; Rhodes (1995) covers the hydrogen bomb.

[18] Einstein's letter, Roosevelt's reply, and related documents can be found on the website of the Franklin D. Roosevelt library, http://docs.fdrlibrary.marist.edu/psf/box5/folo64.html (accessed July 15, 2010).

"Manhattan Project" after the location of some of the early work, but eventually the project required the construction of many large-scale secret facilities. They were located in various parts of the country based on the availability of existing plant and resources, and the possibility of carrying out the work in secret. One of the largest facilities was at Oak Ridge, Tennessee, a location chosen in part because of the large amounts of electricity that could be supplied by dams built by the Tennessee Valley Authority in the 1930s.

The total cost of building the atomic bomb is not known with a high degree of accuracy. Robert J. Gordon (1969) put the value of plant and equipment built for the project during 1940–5 for private operators and used by private operators after the war at $1.322 billion. A frequently cited number for the project as a whole, and probably the best estimate we are likely to get, is $1.89 billion (Brookings 2002). Costs are hard to estimate for a secret project undertaken during a major war, but it is likely that this estimate understates the true cost of the project. For one thing, orders for materials placed by the Manhattan Project received the highest priorities from the War Production Board. That meant that that these orders were rushed through ahead of others. In a peacetime economy one has to pay a price for rushed delivery. In principle one could place a shadow price on the short delivery time for orders rushed through for the Manhattan Project, but it is not likely that this sort of economic accounting could actually be undertaken. Another example of how hard it is to measure the costs of the project is the time of the "dollar-a-year" men involved in it. These executives were seconded to the government by private firms for the token amount of one dollar. The firms, of course, received compensation in the form of contracts from the Manhattan Project and from other government projects. In principle we should evaluate their time at the market wage rate, but it is likely that in practice no record was kept or adjustment made. Despite these difficulties, it is clear that, as path-breaking as it was historically, and as large as the project seems in terms of facilities created, the Manhattan Project required a small part of the resources that the United States devoted to the war effort: only 0.59 percent of total defense spending from 1941 to 1945. That the United States could achieve such an amazing breakthrough in such a short period of time – it was two years and nine months from the time Leslie Groves was appointed to head the Project to the time when a weapon was tested successfully – while utilizing such a small share of its resources, illustrates the advantage the United States had in terms of the size and sophistication of its economy. Britain, the Soviet Union, Germany, and Japan all had nuclear programs, but were unable to devote sufficient resources to them to push them through to completion during the war.[19]

An atomic bomb was first successfully tested on June 16, 1945. Germany had surrendered, but the war against Japan raged on. On August 6, the city of Hiroshima in Japan was destroyed by an atom bomb.[20] On August 9, the city of Nagasaki was destroyed, and on August 14, Japan surrendered unconditionally to the United States. World War II was over. The destruction produced in Hiroshima and Nagasaki was horrific.[21] Exact estimates are not possible, but it is believed that between 90,000 and 166,000 people, mostly civilians, died in Hiroshima and between 60,000 and 80,000 in Nagasaki.[22] It is possible, then, to take the upper-bound estimates, that a quarter of a million people died in the two blasts. There were, in addition, many non-fatal casualties. A new illness, unanticipated by many of the scientists and engineers building the bomb, affected many of the survivors: radiation poisoning. And the health effects lingered: rates of death from cancers such as leukemia and rates of birth defects were higher for people exposed to radiation in the atomic bomb attacks.[23]

[19] The United States enjoyed other advantages: it was not under direct attack, it had combined its research efforts with those of the United Kingdom, and it was able to draw on many scientists and engineers who had been forced to leave central Europe.

[20] The description of the devastation by journalist John Hersey (1946), one of the first non-Japanese to enter the city after the blast, is now a classic.

[21] Museums in Hiroshima and Nagasaki tell the story of the nuclear attacks, and make a powerful case against nuclear weapons. The website for the Hiroshima museum is www.pcf.city.hiroshima.jp/top_e.html; for the Nagasaki museum, www1.city.nagasaki.nagasaki.jp/peace/index_e.html. Visiting is a powerful emotional experience.

[22] Radiation Research Foundation, at http://www.rerf.or.jp/general/qa_e/qa2.html (accessed July 15, 2010). The Radiation Research Foundation is descended from the Atomic Bomb Casualty Commission established by President Truman in November 1946 to study the health effects from the atomic bombs. In 1975 the Commission's work was continued by the Radiation Research Foundation which is jointly funded by the United States and Japan, with the hope that the interests of both nations would be taken into account. It is still one of the best sources of data on the medical effects of the bombings.

[23] The Hiroshima Peace Memorial Park contains a moving memorial to Sadako Sasaki, a young girl who contracted a fatal case of leukemia. She responded by folding hundreds of paper cranes, based on an old Japanese story about

The bombs forced Japan to surrender. But were there alternatives to imposing such enormous costs on the Japanese people? This question has gnawed at Americans ever since, and has produced a bitter and ongoing debate. One alternative was to give up the idea of an unconditional surrender and negotiate a peace agreement. Japan might well have agreed to give up its overseas empire in exchange for an armistice if its government and emperor were allowed to remain in authority on Japan's home islands. J. William Fulbright, the American senator and expert on foreign affairs, later argued (during the Vietnam War) that the policy of unconditional surrender was a mistake that had prolonged the war, and forced the United States into an immoral choice between nuclear bombing of civilians and an invasion with, possibly, hundreds of thousands of American casualties. A few years after World War II we were treating Germany and Japan as valued allies. That could have been achieved, Fulbright implicitly argued, without imposing enormous costs on the German or Japanese people through bombing if the constraint of unconditional surrender had been jettisoned (Fulbright 1966, 253).

The commitment to unconditional surrender, however, was an unchallenged goal of Allied war policy. It was first stated at the Casablanca Conference – Roosevelt, Churchill, Stalin, and the Free French leaders Generals de Gaulle and Giraud were present – in June 1943. Unconditional surrender appears to have originated with Roosevelt and was connected in his mind to the Civil War policy of Grant and Lincoln. After the conference some of Roosevelt's advisors opposed unconditional surrender because they believed it would prolong Axis resistance, but Roosevelt was firmly committed to the policy (Chase 1955).

Another alternative was to explode a nuclear bomb over some lightly inhabited area to demonstrate its power. Once the Japanese understood the devastating weapon now in the hands of the Allies they would probably surrender. If they didn't there would still be an opportunity to use the weapon later against civilian targets. Alternatively, the first bomb could have been used against Hiroshima alone. If enough time had been allowed for the Japanese to understand what they faced – a weapon of unparalleled power that the Americans were

wishes being granted when a thousand paper cranes are folded. Children around the world still fold paper cranes and send them to Hiroshima in her memory.

prepared to use against civilians – they would surely have surrendered. At least the horror of Nagasaki might have been avoided.

But these alternatives were rejected. The reason for doing so has been the subject of bitter controversies among historians. Some maintain that the decision to use the atomic bomb against civilians was mainly the product of momentum (Baldwin 1950). Once the project to build an atomic bomb had been launched it was inevitable that the people in charge would want to carry the job to completion. Using the atomic bombs, moreover, was simply a way of continuing the policy of destroying Japanese cities from the air, but at a lower cost in the lives of American airmen. Other historians maintain that the Japanese were near surrender, that this was known in the United States, and that the bombs were used mainly to intimidate the Soviet Union and end the war before the Soviets could invade Japan and lay claim to part or all of the Japanese home islands (Alperovitz 1995). Still others maintain that President Truman and his advisors were convinced that the bomb was a legitimate weapon of war and that its use would save the lives of young American fighters. The Battle of Okinawa finally ended less than a week after the first successful test of the atomic bomb. It was the bloodiest battle of the Pacific War. The United States lost 12,520 fighters, about 5,000 from the navy. In addition there were 36,631 fighters who suffered non-mortal wounds.[24] The assumption that the losses would be far higher in an attack on the main Japanese islands was natural. The administration was prepared to kill many Japanese civilians to save the life of an American soldier, and the decision to use the bomb, if it would do so, according to some historians, was never an issue (Bernstein 1975, 1998).

The cost of the war

The human costs of the war to the American people, as I have already noted, were heavy, second only to the Civil War: 406,000 deaths and 672,000 non-mortal wounds. The financial costs were also staggering. The largest component was the money spent by the federal government on the armed forces. In 1938 defense spending was only 1.4 percent of GDP, a level typical of the 1930s. But that would change.

[24] US Army Center of Military History, "Okinawa: the Last Battle," at www.history.army.mil (accessed July 20, 2010).

In 1940 spending was 1.6 percent of GDP, and in 1941, 5.1 percent. The latter was a record for the United States in peacetime (although it would be typical of the troubled post-World War II years). But then in 1942 military spending reached 16 percent of GDP and during the period 1943–5 it averaged more than one-third of GDP. The peak year was 1945 when spending on the armed forces was 37 percent of GDP. Altogether, as shown in Table 6.8, the United States committed about 1.7 years' worth of GDP to direct military spending.[25] The second row of Table 6.8 adds $120 billion (2008 dollars) of increased spending on international affairs, a substantial amount compared with prewar spending in this category, but a small amount compared with direct spending on the armed forces. There was more spending by civilian agencies such as the Maritime Commission, the Rubber Reserves Corporation, and so on. The third row of Table 6.8 adds an estimate, $42 billion (2008 dollars), of these additional spending streams. Lend-Lease, civilian ship construction by the Maritime Commission, and similar programs were vital to the war effort, but the big money, clearly, went to the American military machine.

As in World War I, the draftees were "taxed": the difference between what they could have earned in the private sector and what they earned in the military. Some personnel served voluntarily, and in those cases the difference between what the individual earned in the military and what they could have earned in the private sector can be viewed as a voluntary contribution to the war effort rather than a tax. A crude estimate of the amount of these taxes and contributions hidden in the draft is reported in the fourth row of Table 6.8.

State and local governments, private firms and charitable organizations, and individuals, also made contributions to the war effort, although their contributions were less important relative to those of the federal government in World War II than in World War I. The New Deal had greatly strengthened the role of the central government and prepared it to take control of the war economy. Spending money and creating agencies – the main efforts required of the federal government

[25] The results are similar if we use the Kendrick–Kuznets estimates of National Security Expenditures (Kendrick 1961, 290–1) and adopt the modern definition of Gross National Product which treats military spending as final product.

Table 6.8 *The costs of World War II (in billions of 2008 dollars)*

Category	Amount	As a share of average GDP during the war (%)
Armed forces[a]	3,023	170.1
International affairs[b]	120	6.8
Other war-related federal expenditures[c]	42	2.4
Additional cost of the draft[d]	63	3.6
Expenditures by state and local governments and private organizations[e]	43	2.4
Subtotal	3,291	185.3
Historical and projected veterans' benefits[f]	1,373	77.3
Total	4,664	262.5

Notes:

[a] The sum from 1939 through 1947 of defense spending in each year less defense spending in 1938. These are the years in which defense spending seems to have been elevated by the coming of the war, the war itself, or the postwar costs of maintaining order in the conquered areas. Figures are from Carter *et al.* (2006), series Ea638 plus Ea639 for 1938–9 and Ea705 for 1940–7. All figures have been deflated by the GDP deflator.

[b] The sum from 1939 through 1947 of spending on international affairs in each year less spending on international affairs in 1938. Figures from Carter *et al.* (2006), Ea646 for 1938–9 and Ea706 for 1940–7.

[c] The sum from 1939 through 1947 of spending by other federal agencies in each year less spending by other federal agencies in 1938. Figures from Carter *et al.* (2006), Ea649 in 1938–9 and Ea704 less the sum of Ea705, Ea706, Ea715, Ea716, Ea717, and Ea724 for 1940–7.

[d] Total personnel years in World War II were estimated by multiplying the total military personnel in World War II (Ed82) by the average years served: Carter *et al.* (2006), series Ed96. This total was then multiplied by the difference between the average annual wages of full-time workers for the years 1942–5 (Ba4419) and the annual pay and allowances of all military personnel (Ed117) to get the costs of the draft.

[e] Assumed to equal 1.3 percent of total war costs, one-half the ratio in World War I.

[f] Figures from Edwards (2010, Table 2, 36). GDP and GDP deflator: Johnston and Williamson (2010).

in World War II – were things with which the Roosevelt administration had plenty of experience. Indeed, it appears that spending at the state and local level fell in real terms during the war. Real spending by state governments on highways – one of the few time series on state and local spending available for both World War I and World War II – rose to a limited extent during World War I, but fell dramatically during World War II (Carter *et al.* 2006, series Df251). These cutbacks at the state and local level helped with war finance. Had state and local governments attempted to maintain their real levels of spending, they would have had to raise taxes, or borrow additional amounts in capital markets, making it more difficult for the federal government to do so. Nevertheless, I have also included, for completeness, an arbitrary estimate of spending by state and local governments and private organizations equal to 1.3 percent of total war costs, about one-half of the World War I contribution.

Veterans' benefits were the most important continuing cost of the war: $1.4 trillion in 2008 dollars, more than three-quarters of a year's average GDP during the war. In the years after the Civil War veterans' benefits were one of the largest and most controversial items in the federal budget. Veterans' benefits were not, as we will see below, without a measure of controversy after World War II, but overwhelming support for the war in all regions, the halo of victory, and the USA being now a richer nation, meant that there was far less controversy.

Altogether, as shown in the totals in Table 6.8, the United States devoted more than two and a half years' worth of GDP to the war effort.[26] This was an unprecedented amount. Never before or since has the United States devoted such a large percentage of its economy to war. At the start of World War II the United States was an industrial nation, close to its peak in terms of the share of resources that it devoted to manufacturing. It is doubtful that the more agricultural economies of the nineteenth century, or the more service-oriented economies of the late twentieth and early twenty-first century could usefully employ such a large proportion of their resources in a war effort. The United States was the premier industrial nation, and this was the premier industrial war.

[26] Estimates in today's money of the amount of spending in the 1940s for the war will vary depending on the price index that is used to inflate wartime spending. The GDP deflator rose by a factor of 9.8 between 1945 and 2008, while the consumer price index rose by a factor of 12.0. For wartime spending I use the GDP deflator because much of the spending went for munitions which required a wide range of material inputs along with labor and capital. For veterans' benefits, however, I follow Edwards (2010) who uses the consumer price index because one of the central purposes of these benefits was to provide funds for consumption.

Looking back, most Americans would agree that the war was worth it. Allowing the Fascist powers to have control over great swaths of the earth, a likely possibility had the United States remained neutral, would have been a catastrophe. Had the threat of war not arisen, the United States might well have continued on the path it was on, gradually recovering from the Depression. But we can at least imagine another possibility. The United States might have administered a powerful dose of monetary and fiscal stimulus, but one focused on domestic spending, which restored full employment in the same way that the war did. In that alternative world the resources used to build the war machine would have been used to build highways and hospitals, lighthouses and airports, and a thousand private investments, making the United States a far richer economy in 1945 than it actually was. In other words, there is an important sense in which the United States paid a high economic cost for the war, even though it emerged more prosperous at the end than it was at the beginning.

The legacies of World War II

The list of economic advances that have been attributed to World War II is impressive: higher labor force participation of women based on a wider array of opportunities in the labor market, major breakthroughs in race relations, major technological advances, greater equality in wage rates, increased capital formation, and increased financial stability. The reasons for attributing so much to the war are clear. The war was a dramatic event that profoundly altered the lives of millions of Americans. Economic conditions during the war years and the years that followed, moreover, represented a stark contrast with the depressed conditions of the 1930s. Finally, there was an ideological dimension: it is natural for liberals to attribute positive postwar developments to the enlarged role undertaken by the federal government during the war. Whatever the motive, the tendency to attribute postwar advances to the war itself also tends to lower estimates of the cost of war, and to some extent to lower our expectation of the costs of future wars. There is hardly sufficient room here for a discussion of all of these conjectures. Here I will briefly discuss three: (1) the new international financial order in which the United States would play a key role, (2) the transformation of the role of women in the American economy, and (3) the synthetic rubber program. As you will see, in some cases the war did indeed produce important changes. In others, the changes attributed to the war were more heavily influenced by long-run trends.

A new international economic order

Perhaps the most important legacy of World War II was the new international economic and political order in which Germany, Japan, and Italy would play positive roles. All three would recover rapidly and become major economic powers. During the war few Americans could have anticipated that the "reconstruction" of these nations would follow with such speed and success; few Americans of the war generation could have believed that their children would be driving Volkswagens and Hondas. Indeed, when the Allies adopted their policy of "unconditional surrender," the future of the Axis looked bleak – a future of total destruction and poverty. Nevertheless, Roosevelt's policy of unconditional surrender laid the basis for the reconstruction of the economies and polities of Germany and Japan. Shortly after surrendering, Germany was divided into four zones controlled, respectively, by the United States, the Soviet Union, Britain, and France. The Soviets, of course, imposed a Communist system on their zone. In the Allied zones, however, a capitalist course was followed which led eventually to Germany returning as a powerhouse on the world's economic stage. Initially, some thought was given to forcing Germany to give up its strong industrial sector and to rely primarily on agriculture: without an industrial base Germany could not rearm and threaten the world again. This idea had been pushed, notably, by Roosevelt's Secretary of the Treasury, Henry Morgenthau. But this idea was inconsistent with the view that unconditional surrender should be followed by a magnanimous peace, Lincoln's intention in the Civil War. It soon became clear, moreover, that a reinvigorated Germany could be a valuable ally in the fight to contain Communism, so the Morgenthau plan was shunted aside (Gareau 1961; Kimball 1976; Morgenthau *et al.* 1995).

The political reconstruction of Germany began in November 1945 with the Nuremberg trials of leading Nazis. A dozen Nazi leaders received the death penalty and several others were imprisoned. But three were acquitted. One of these last was Hjalmar Horace Greeley Schacht. Schacht had been a supporter of the Nazi regime in the 1930s, when he had served as Minister of Public Works and as head of the Reichsbank, the German central bank. As head of the Reichsbank Schacht had developed the system of exchange controls that the Nazis used effectively in their preparation of the German economy for the war (Ellis 1940). Schacht, however, did not play an important role during the war years, and actually spent the last months of the war as a prisoner of the Nazis. The Nuremberg trials focused on major figures, but attempts were made, most strongly in the Soviet zone, but in the other zones as well, to purge lower-level Nazis from public life.

Rapid economic recovery of Germany was promoted by the European Recovery Program, popularly known as the Marshall Plan. It was first proposed by General George C. Marshall, the American Secretary of State, in a commencement address delivered at Harvard University on June 5, 1947. The essence of the plan was financial aid to help get Europe back on its feet (Milward 1984; Dornbusch, Nölling, and Layard 1993; DeLong and Eichengreen 1993; Eichengreen 1995). The amount delivered was about $13 billion, approximately $100 billion in 2009 dollars.[27] The amount, if thought of simply as a way of buying or repairing capital, was not sufficient to account for more than a small part of the recovery of Europe. But the Marshall Plan also played an important role in strengthening the hand of politicians who wanted to introduce free market economic reforms and draw Germany and other war-torn economies into the American orbit, and those policies paid large dividends.

Shortly after the US Congress voted to fund the Marshall Plan the German Economics Minister, Ludwig Erhard, introduced a new currency, the Deutschmark, and removed wage and price controls. Erhard's reforms addressed West Germany's currency "overhang" head on. During the war the inflationary pressures generated by heavy reliance on the printing press had been held in check by wage and price controls; if controls were lifted without addressing the currency overhang, a substantial inflation would result. Erhard also lifted many controls on foreign trade. His bold moves have been widely credited with setting Germany upon a path of rapid recovery. By the 1950s, the level of per capita income in West Germany was such that observers were talking about the "German economic miracle" (Wallich 1955).

The American occupation authorities also attempted to remake the economic and political systems of Japan, initially with the goal of

[27] Overall, the United States spent about $31 billion on international affairs from 1947 to 1954, the period of postwar reconstruction.

preventing a resurgence of Japanese imperialism, and later with the goal of creating a bulwark against Communism. At the start of the occupation the Americans targeted the "*zaibatsu*." These were large, tight-knit conglomerates, basically family-owned holding companies, combining finance, mining, and manufacturing. Partly, the *zaibatsu* were targeted simply because they represented concentrated economic power which the New Dealers thought exploited consumers and workers. True, in the first part of the New Deal there was some sympathy for monopolies and oligopolies because they seemed to bring stability (Hawley 1966). Indeed, there was some hope that the bureaucracies that ran big corporations could be harnessed to the purposes of the New Deal. But by the end of the 1930s, the New Dealers had come to oppose monopoly. The shift toward "trust busting" reflected the influence of Thurman Arnold, a flamboyant and increasingly influential assistant attorney general during the latter part of the New Deal, although his star waned during the war when the organizational ability of large corporations once more came to the fore. So it was natural for the New Dealers to favor breaking up the *zaibatsu* to create a fairer, more competitive economy. But there was another, political, reason for breaking up the *zaibatsu*: it was thought that they had promoted Japanese militarism. Some early successes were achieved, but over time, enthusiasm for breaking them up waned, and they made something of a comeback in post-occupation Japan (Rotwein 1964). The comparison may be somewhat strained, but to follow our previous observation that Americans understood unconditional surrender and reconstruction in terms of the American Civil War, we can note that the New Dealers failed to break up the *zaibatsu*, which they saw as the backbone of Japanese militarism, much as the Radical Republicans had failed to break up the large plantations, which they saw as the backbone of secession. Japan, like Germany, made rapid economic strides after the war, and soon Americans were talking about a "Japanese economic miracle" to go with the German economic miracle. Indeed, by the 1960s Germany and Japan had become feared industrial competitors of the United States. Many working in the US automobile and automobile parts industries were far from sure that facilitating the reemergence of Germany and Japan had been the right decision. To judge from their strong support for free trade in the postwar era, however, one can guess that few economists would disagree with the conclusion that the policy of "reconstructing" Germany and Japan was a good investment for the United States as a whole.

The war led to a thoroughgoing restructuring of the world monetary system. During World War I, as we noted in the previous chapter, most of the warring nations except the United States were forced off gold. Government demands for revenue were enormous and heavy reliance was placed on the printing press. Using the printing press to finance wars was not consistent with the gold standard's basic requirement that each unit of paper money be backed by a fixed quantity of gold. Attempts were made after World War I to return to the gold standard. In 1925 Britain returned to gold at the prewar par, a rate that may have overvalued the pound. The 1925 British pound contained the same amount of gold as the prewar pound and exchanged at the same rate for the US dollar (which had not been forced off gold during the war). But the British price level had risen more than the US price level, so the old exchange rate made British exports relatively more expensive. In 1926 France returned to the gold standard at a rate that undervalued the French currency. Despite these strains, it could be said that the gold standard was in the process of being rebuilt in the 1920s, but the efforts to rebuild it collapsed in the Great Depression. Nations were determined to stimulate exports by devaluing their currencies, even if this meant abandoning traditional commitments to gold.

Finance in the United States during World War II, and in the other belligerents, was similar to World War I: huge demands by governments for revenues financed in part by printing money. Inflation and exchange controls were the order of the day. But during the war sentiment grew among policymakers for constructing a new international monetary system for the postwar world. The hope was that the new system could preserve the fixed exchange rates of the gold standard, which had encouraged international trade and investment, without the rigidities and lack of control by governments that had frustrated the attempts to reconstruct the gold standard during the interwar years. An international conference to establish the postwar system was held at Bretton Woods, New Hampshire from July 1 to 22, 1944.[28] The British delegation included the economist John Maynard Keynes, the author of *The General Theory of Employment, Interest*

[28] Bordo and Eichengreen (1993), the result of a conference held at Bretton Woods to commemorate the agreement, has papers by a number of economists that together cover most aspects of the origins and effects of the Bretton Woods system, and is the main source of the following paragraphs.

and Money (1936), who by then was widely considered the world's leading economist. The American delegation was led by an economist from the Treasury Department, Harry Dexter White. White was less well known than Keynes by a wide margin, but nonetheless was a forceful and determined advocate of American views.

The most important issue to be determined at Bretton Woods was the role to be played by the dollar in the postwar international financial system. Keynes proposed the formation of a new international currency, the "bancor," to be issued by a world central bank. The bancor would not circulate from hand to hand, but would be used to settle accounts among central banks. It would play much the same role that gold had played before the war, but it would cost nothing to create – it would be a "paper gold" – and its growth rate could be monitored and controlled. The seigniorage from creating the bancor would be available for use by international financial institutions. This imaginative proposal was not adopted owing to American opposition, but was frequently referred to in subsequent years as a possible path for international monetary reform.

The Americans proposed, and won acceptance for, a more US-centric system. Since the United States, unique among the major industrial nations, would emerge from the war with an enhanced industrial system, and would be called upon to finance reconstruction, it was almost inevitable that the American proposals would win acceptance. Exchange rates would be fixed in terms of dollars. Gold would still play a role, although an attenuated one, because the dollar would still be fixed in terms of gold. Instead of Keynes's world central bank, two international agencies would also be created. The International Bank for Reconstruction and Development, usually known as the World Bank, would make longer-term investments. The International Monetary Fund would monitor the system of exchange rates and the balance of payments, and would make loans to countries running temporary deficits. Permanent deficits would, however, require adjustment of exchange rates. Under the gold standard as it had been reconstructed after World War I deficit countries were forced to contract their money supplies (as they lost gold) and surplus countries might choose to sterilize the inflows. Even under the classical gold standard, the effects appeared to be asymmetric: the contractions forced on the deficit countries caused more pain in the form of high unemployment than the expansions forced on the surplus countries caused in the form of inflation. The plan was for the International Monetary Fund to oversee a more balanced approach to adjustment.

Both international banks were to be financed, initially, mainly by the United States. The substantial investments that the United States made in the International Monetary Fund and the World Bank were properly part of the cost of the war to the American people. But the United States also received a hidden benefit. The Bretton Woods system, as it came to be called, strengthened the role of the US dollar as a reserve currency. The United States was able to run larger international deficits than would have been possible under a gold or bancor system because foreigners were more willing to hold dollars or dollar-denominated assets such as Treasury bills as reserves. In effect, the world had asked the United States to make an investment: money now in the form of direct aid and endowments for international financial agencies in exchange for seigniorage to be earned later by issuing dollars for use in international trade. The Bretton Woods system survived from the end of World War II until the late 1960s. In the end, it was brought down by persistent US inflation and balance of trade deficits, which, in turn, were partly the result of the war in Vietnam.

The role of women in the economy

Although women had always participated in America's wars, in World War II women entered the military services on an unprecedented scale. In all, about 200,000 served. The largest number served in the Women's Army Corps (WAC) and the Women Accepted for Volunteer Emergency Services (WAVES), with smaller numbers in the Marine Corps, Coast Guard, and the Women's Auxiliary Ferrying Service. They also entered the civilian labor force in large numbers to take advantage of high wages and job opportunities, and to help win the war. Many women served in clerical positions – the typewriter had become an important weapon of war – but it was those who were doing factory jobs traditionally done by men who made the most indelible impression. Propaganda encouraging women to aid the war effort was churned out by both the government and the private sector (Rupp 1978). The most memorable figure, undoubtedly, was "Rosie the Riveter," Norman Rockwell's memorable cover for the *Saturday Evening Post*.

What happened to Rosie the Riveter after the war? The simplest answer goes like this. During World War II women rolled up their sleeves and went to work in the nation's factories, turning out the guns and ammunition, the ships and planes, needed to win the war. After the war, they did not go back willingly to unpaid household labor. Some, it is true, quit their jobs or were forced to leave; others, however, stayed. Some employers, moreover, learned an important lesson: women could be as productive as men. The result was a revolution: more women went to work in the paid labor force.

Although there is some truth to this story, the reality was more complicated. Many women did join the paid labor force during the war, and attitudes about women, especially about married women working in the paid labor force, did change.[29] But when we look at longer-term trends the wartime period looks less important than this story suggests. As shown in Figure 6.8, which is based on information collected by the census, the labor force participation of married white women (a larger proportion of unmarried women were already in the labor force) did not suddenly ratchet upward. The ratio had been rising before the war, and it continued to rise long afterwards. The story for non-white married women, shown in Figure 6.9, was somewhat different. Here we do see an upward ratchet, but it comes between 1950 and 1960, rather than between 1940 and 1950 when we would expect it if the wartime experience was crucial.

Work by Claudia Goldin (1991) has helped to clarify what was happening. She examined several surveys of married women conducted during the war and subsequently. She found that about half of the married women who were working in 1950 had been at work in 1940, and that among those who had entered the labor force after 1940, the rate of entry was about the same during the war years as in the peacetime years that followed. She concludes that while the war did play a role by changing the attitudes of employers and workers, it was long-term trends – the rise of the clerical sector, the increase in education levels, a diminished supply of younger unmarried women,

[29] A smaller number of women left the labor force during the war. There were many reasons: the improved employment and wages of spouses, the need to move so that a spouse could take advantage of improvements in the labor market, the increased difficulty of finding domestic help, the increased childcare duties when spouses were in the military, and so on.

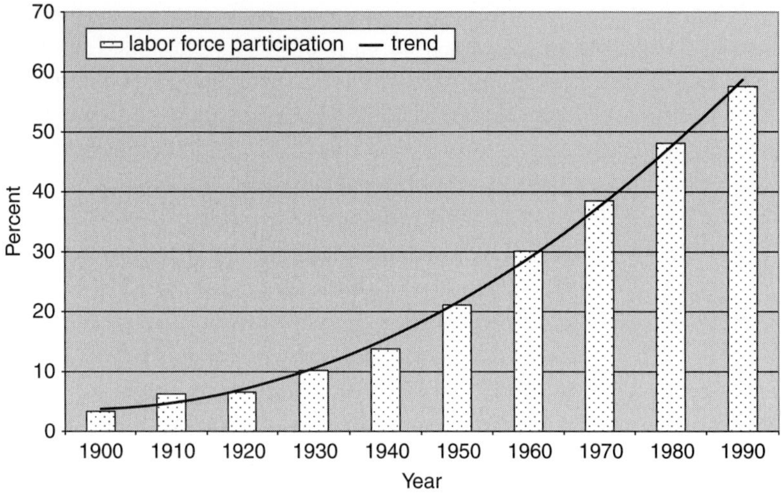

Figure 6.8 Labor force participation of married white women, 1900–90. The estimate for 1930 is simply the average of the 1940 and 1920 estimates because the census did not ask the appropriate question. This imparts some additional smoothness to the series. The trend is exponential. The labor force participation of married white women does not exhibit a strong upward wartime ratchet.
Source: Carter *et al.* (2006, series Ba429).

and so on – that had the biggest impact on the labor force participation of married women in the long run.

We cannot leave the discussion of the role of women without addressing the so-called "baby boom." The story that dominates the public imagination is the stuff from which movies are made. A man and a woman have been separated through the long and dangerous years of the war. The husband returns, triumphant but conscious of the costs of war; the job has been done. They embrace; at last they can begin their life together.[30] The real story, however, is more complicated. Birth rates surged in the late 1940s but did not peak until the late 1950s, long after the reunification of couples separated by war could account for the phenomenon. Indeed, many of the women having children at the peak

[30] The best of the movies about returning veterans, I believe, is *The Best Years of our Lives*, starring Myrna Loy and Fredric March, released in 1946. It tells a much more complicated and challenging story about the struggles of three returning servicemen to adjust to civilian life.

Figure 6.9 Labor force participation of married non-white women, 1900–90. The estimate for 1930 is simply the average of the 1940 and 1920 estimates because the census did not ask the appropriate question. The estimate for 1910 is also an average because the question asked in that census evidently produced an overestimate of women in the paid labor force. These interpolations impart some additional smoothness to the curve. The trend is a 2-period moving average. There is an upward ratchet in the labor force participation of non-white married women, but it occurs between 1950 and 1960 rather than during World War II. *Source:* Carter *et al.* (2006, series Ba432).

of the baby boom were too young to have had their child-bearing years disrupted by the war. One explanation that at least fits the timing of the baby boom somewhat better attributes it to a burst of technological advances that eased the burden in the household in terms of hours of work spent on feeding, clothing, transporting, and entertaining children at home: electric washers, driers, refrigerators, freezers, automobiles, and radio and television (Greenwood, Seshadri, and Vandenbroucke 2005). Rather than the generals, perhaps the men behind the baby boom were those like William Durant of General Motors, who led the way in mass-producing refrigerators, and Clarence Birdseye, the frozen food pioneer. The extraordinary sense of economic stability and optimism about future economic growth that prevailed during these years must also have played a role.

Synthetic rubber

There is a popular notion, one that is occasionally reiterated by knowledgeable historians, that WWII produced a large cluster of crucial technological advances: computers, jet engines, atomic energy, radar, and synthetic rubber are the most prominent. It would seem to follow that the war produced major improvements in the standard of living by creating new technologies – another example, some might claim, of how World War II proved to be a net economic benefit rather than a cost. In most of these cases, however, the war did not produce new technologies; it merely accelerated the deployment of existing technologies because they were useful given the changed economic conditions created by the war.

Synthetic rubber is the most compelling example of what seems like a technology brought into being by the war because mass production of synthetic rubber for civilian uses was solely a result of the wartime program. The synthetic rubber program is also of interest because it could be viewed as a successful precedent for a massive government investment in some sort of green technology. Before the war the United States consumed only tiny amounts of synthetic rubber in specialty uses; after the war synthetic rubber supplied a large share of America's rubber needs. Before the war, to be more specific, the United States relied on rubber produced from trees on plantations in Southeast Asia. When the war began, the supply was cut, and the United States began a frantic effort to find substitutes.[31] There were a number of possibilities. One was to recycle existing supplies. Large scrap drives were launched, with considerable fanfare, and brought in substantial amounts of rubber. As shown in Table 6.9, in 1943, the peak year for production of reclaimed rubber, scrap supplied more than 50 percent of the rubber produced in the United States. But there was a limit to how far this source could be pushed. For one thing, the amount of rubber that could be recovered from scrap declined each time rubber went through the reclaiming process. A second possibility was to produce rubber in other parts of the world, such as the Amazon (where the rubber boom had started at the end of the nineteenth century), Sri Lanka (then Ceylon), and Liberia. There was also a hope

[31] The supplies of several other raw materials were also cut. The most important of these was silk. It was replaced by nylon, a DuPont product.

Table 6.9 *Rubber production and consumption in World War II (long tons)*

		1941	1942	1943	1944	1945
Natural rubber[a]	New supply	1,029,007	282,653	55,329	107,834	137,237
	Consumption	775,000	376,791	317,634	144,113	105,429
	Exports	5,376	10,856	20,815	9,665	6,743
	Year-end stocks	533,344	422,714	139,594	93,650	118,715
Synthetics[b]	New supply	8,383	22,434	231,722	773,673	830,780
	Consumption	6,259	17,651	170,891	566,670	693,580
	Exports	672	1,419	23,875	105,644	76,673
	Year-end stocks	1,702	4,612	41,568	142,927	203,454
Reclaimed	New supply	274,202	286,007	310,429	260,514	238,772
	Consumption	251,231	254,820	291,082	251,083	241,036
	Exports	13,851	30,405	15,678	11,800	13,413
	Year-end stocks	41,750	42,532	46,201	43,832	28,155
Total	New supply	1,311,592	591,094	597,480	1,142,021	1,206,789
	Consumption	1,032,490	649,262	779,607	961,866	1,040,045
	Exports	19,899	42,680	60,368	127,109	96,829
	Year-end stocks	576,796	469,858	227,363	280,409	350,324

Notes:
[a] Including latex.
[b] Including rubber produced in privately owned plants, but excluding Thiokol.
Source: Herbert and Bisio (1985, 127).

that rubber could be extracted from guayule, a desert shrub that yielded substantial amounts of latex, which could be grown in the American Southwest. None of these alternatives, however, proved to be practical; they were, at best, a long-run solution. The real substitute for plantation rubber from Southeast Asia would be synthetic rubber.

As shown in Table 6.9, only small amounts of synthetic rubber were produced in the United States before the war. In 1941 only 8,000 tons of synthetics were produced, less than 1 percent of total US production. Synthetic rubber simply cost too much to compete with natural rubber except in a few niche markets where its physical properties justified the higher price. When the war began, however, the United States launched a crash program to build new synthetic rubber plants. It was financed entirely by the Reconstruction Finance Corporation. The program got off to a rocky start: there were time-consuming debates about which synthetic rubber should be the mainstay of the program, about how the feed stocks should be produced, and about how rights to existing patents should be treated. But despite delays the synthetic rubber program was a resounding success. In 1945 the United States produced 831,000 tons of synthetic rubber, an amount that made up close to 70 percent of total production and exceeded total production in most prewar years.

It would be a mistake, however, to jump to the conclusion that the war led to the *discovery* of synthetic rubber. The molecules that could be used to replace natural rubber had been discovered in the 1920s and 1930s. What the war did was create the economic conditions when it made sense to produce these molecules on a commercial scale. There were several candidates for mass production. One, neoprene, was an American creation. The earliest version was discovered by Father Julius Nieuwland of Notre Dame. With further refinements by Wallace Carothers and Elmer Bolton at DuPont, a commercially viable product was introduced in 1931. The slump in the market for tires and in the price of natural rubber caused by the Depression, however, scotched efforts to market it as a general purpose rubber. Neoprene was economically viable only in a small specialty market based on uses for which its physical properties made it especially useful. The possibility of a shortage of natural rubber, perhaps as the result of another war, was, however, on people's minds. In 1934, to fulfill an army request to build tires entirely out of materials produced in the United States, tires were successfully made from neoprene by the

Dayton Rubber Manufacturing Company (*New York Times*, June 23, 1934, p. 1). Neoprene made good tires, but required large amounts of electricity to produce it (Wolf 1952).[32] What would become the main form of synthetic rubber in the United States in World War II had German origins.

Work on so-called methyl rubber had been undertaken by chemists in a number of countries before World War I. But the increasing supply of natural rubber from plantations in Southeast Asia, and the resulting decrease in its price, diminished interest. For Germany, however, World War I changed everything. Britain controlled the sea lanes, and Germany was soon desperately short of rubber. Renewed research led to the production of a series of methyl isoprene rubbers, including one that could be used to make (not very satisfactory) automobile tires. By the end of the war the Germans were making about 150 tons of synthetic rubber per month, and plants for making more were under construction (Wolf 1948).

After World War I work on synthetic rubber continued, especially in Germany and the Soviet Union, because of the fear that a future war could lead to a cutoff of supplies of the natural product. During the 1920s chemists at Germany's I.G. Farben developed a number of synthetic rubbers, including one designated Buna S, which was an acceptable substitute for natural rubber in tires, and another, Buna N, which was an acceptable substitute when oil resistance was important.[33] Beginning in the late 1920s I.G. Farben and Standard Oil of New Jersey began cooperating in research and development, especially in synthetic oil and rubber. In 1930 they formed a joint company (the Joint American Study Company) for sharing patents and developing and marketing chemicals including synthetic rubber. Later critics of Standard Oil would condemn it for its association with I.G. Farben. But from a business point of view, it was a natural partnership. I.G. Farben had developed the molecules in its laboratories and Standard Oil had extraordinary expertise in scaling up laboratory processes for mass production. Standard Oil, moreover, had

[32] My father, who was the research director at Dayton Rubber at the time, told me that the test results were so good that for a while the Germans considered changing their commitment to other synthetics. But I don't have any other evidence for his claim, and he was prone to exaggerate!

[33] The name was derived from Bu for butadiene and Na for natrium, the Latin name for sodium and origin of its chemical symbol.

expertise in marketing products in the American automobile tire market, the world's largest market for rubber (Howard 1947).

Meanwhile, in Germany political pressure and subsidies set I.G. Farben on the road of production of Buna rubbers (Tooze 2007, 227–9). In September 1935 at the seventh Nazi Party Congress at Nuremberg, Hitler announced that the problem of producing synthetic rubber had been "definitely solved" and that the erection of the first factory would be "started at once" (Herbert and Bisio 1985, 35). I.G. Farben complied immediately. Continued expansion followed, and by 1943 German production reached a peak of 109,173 tons. Even with a head start (the United States didn't get going until 1941), German production in 1943 was only about 65 percent of American production, an indication of the difference in the size of the industrial sectors in the two economies. In 1944 and 1945 German production declined as a result of strategic bombing while American production soared.

In September 1939, as a result of the outbreak of the war in Europe, Standard Oil bought I.G. Farben's interest in their joint company for the development of Buna S in North America. Along with other firms, business leaders, and government officials, it then began a campaign to win government funding for experimental factories to produce Buna S. However, it was not easy going: there were many voices that cautioned against going too fast. The United States was not at war, and the war that was going on was in Europe, not the Far East, the USA's source of rubber. The United States, moreover, was building up a reserve of natural rubber that might see it through a future shortage. Then, too, synthetic rubber was a new, expensive product, and the government might end up financing a white elephant. Eventually, the Reconstruction Finance Corporation took responsibility for financing a small synthetic rubber program. By mid-January 1941 Standard Oil, DuPont, and the major tire-makers had submitted bids to build plants producing 40,000 tons. Bending to pressures to go slowly, however, the Reconstruction Finance Corporation came up with a new, smaller 10,000 ton plan. This decision was reversed in May 1941 and the 40,000 ton program was reinstated. In retrospect, of course, the long period of debate and delay was a mistake. Once the war began, the synthetic rubber program was rapidly expanded, from 40,000 tons per years to 120,000, to 400,000, and after the fall of Singapore on February 15, 1942 to 600,000, and finally to 800,000. There was also a plant in Canada (Bellamy 2005). Although speed was of the essence, the program was beset in the early months of the war by a number of controversies and delays. One involved Standard Oil's patents. Buna S, it was decided, was going to be the main form of synthetic rubber produced in the United States. How would Standard Oil's patents on Buna S be treated during the war when other firms were building Buna S factories and the Reconstruction Finance Corporation, that is the federal government, was paying for them? Eventually, a deal was worked out in late October 1941 under which the Reconstruction Finance Corporation would pay royalties starting in the second year of the program. A modified agreement was reached on December 19, 1941 that revised the royalty payments and provided for cross-licensing with the other participants and exchanges of technical information.

These agreements, however, were voided in March 1941 when Roosevelt's famous trust-buster, assistant attorney general Thurman Arnold, who had charged Standard Oil with violating the anti-trust laws, obtained a decree forcing the company to give up its royalties and control of its patents for the duration of the war (*New York Times*, March 26, 1942, 1). Standard Oil consented, but claimed that it was doing so only in order to allocate all its resources to the war effort, and maintained that its actions prior to the war had furthered American preparedness. In particular, it argued that the patents it had obtained from I.G. Farben had contributed to the American war effort by making it possible to produce 100 octane aviation fuel, large amounts of TNT, and Buna S. The next day Arnold testified before the Truman Committee, arguing that the attempt by Standard Oil and I.G. Farben to monopolize the world market for synthetic rubber was the main reason for the current shortage in the United States. After Arnold's testimony, Senator Truman told reporters that Standard Oil's actions "constituted treason" (*New York Times*, March 27, 1942, 1). The issue continued to simmer – there was, for example, a civil suit against Standard Oil – but with the eventual success of the synthetic rubber program, the case against the company faded from the headlines. The charges must have hurt deeply. Extremist language, including charges of treason, is frequently a cost of the march to war, and World War II was no exception. Frank A. Howard, a vice president of Standard Oil and the president of its research and development corporation, was named as a defendant in the criminal portion of

Arnold's suit. After the war he wrote *Buna Rubber, the Birth of an Industry* (1947), a detailed account and defense of his and Standard Oil's roles in the synthetic rubber program. Whatever one's view of Howard, the book is of considerable value to historians.

At the time that Standard Oil was under attack for its relationship with I.G. Farben, the rubber program was also being attacked from other directions. A politically important debate concerned how to produce butadiene, one of the key ingredients of Buna S. Butadiene could be made from oil and this is what the chemical engineers who had first laid out the plan for the synthetic rubber program planned to use. However, it could also be made from alcohol, and alcohol soon had strong support in the farm states. If oil was needed to fuel planes, ships, and tanks, why not use the abundant products of American agriculture to produce alcohol and from alcohol, butadiene? This pressure produced a bill to create a new agency dedicated to producing synthetic rubber from butadiene made from alcohol. Roosevelt vetoed the bill, and on August 6, 1942 appointed a committee consisting of Bernard Baruch, who headed the War Industries Board in World War I, Dr. James B. Conant, President of Harvard University, and Dr. Karl T. Compton, President of the Massachusetts Institute of Technology, to look at the rubber situation. Baruch would be the chair. In what must be something of a record, the Baruch Committee issued its report on September 10, 1942.

The committee's report (US Special Committee to Survey the Rubber Situation 1942) made a number of recommendations. First, the most important recommendation, at least from the public's point of view, was nationwide gasoline rationing. The recommendation was not made, as the committee emphasized, to conserve gasoline, which was not in short supply except in certain areas, but rather to conserve tires. Second, it recommended a 35 mile per hour speed limit for the same reason. Third, when it came to the technical choices the committee endorsed the existing program. Indeed, the committee argued that it would be a mistake to try to introduce new and untested synthetic rubbers. Major reliance would be on Buna S. Neoprene, it noted, was the best substitute for natural rubber in heavy-duty and combat tires. However, it was simply too costly to produce for use in general tires, in part because its production required large amounts of electricity. Fourth, the committee made a gesture to the advocates of alcohol. There should be a new 30,000 ton Buna S plant in the grain-producing area, and a 100,000 ton alcohol plant, also located in the grain-producing area. However, with this, and a few other minor exceptions, the committee essentially endorsed what was already being done. Somewhat surprisingly, the alcohol-to-butadiene plants were finished quickly and produced above their rated tonnages. Converting distilleries from production of spirits to production of industrial alcohol for butadiene quickly provided an adequate supply of alcohol. Throughout 1943 and through the first three quarters of 1944 this was the major source of butadiene (Howard 1947, 298). Although motivated, in part, by parochial concerns about farm surpluses, the farm state legislators had been right. The alcohol-to-butadiene plants were closed after the war, however, because of high operating costs. Finally, the Baruch Committee recommended the appointment of a strong administrator with (one can hear Baruch's voice here) the authority and the will to "bull" the program through. Roosevelt soon followed through on most of the committee's recommendations. William Jeffers, President of the Union Pacific Railroad, was appointed the rubber "czar."

Although it seemed to Americans at the time that progress on synthetic rubber was agonizingly slow, in retrospect the industry was created with amazing speed. The first plant went online in April 1942. By the second quarter of 1944 the industry was producing at an annual rate of more than 800,000 tons per year: the rubber shortage had been solved.

The synthetic rubber program is a good example of what can be accomplished when government is able to funnel large amounts of resources into a clear, technologically feasible, goal. In other words, it shows what can be accomplished by gold rush economics. As Vernon Herbert and Attilio Bisio (1985, 215) concluded, a task had been completed in two years "that in more normal times might have taken at least ten years to achieve." The benefits for the economy were substantial. Some of the plants created during the war, such as the alcohol-to-butadiene plants, were not profitable in the postwar world, but the basic Buna S plants were, even though natural rubber production and distribution resumed after the war. However, it is also important to keep in mind that the war did not create a new technology; it created conditions in the marketplace that justified the use of an existing technology. Indeed, Alexander Field (2008) has looked at the broader question of whether the war decade was a period of unusually rapid growth in total factor productivity and has found that it was not.

The veterans

The United States decided to provide more help for the veterans of World War II than it had for the veterans of World War I. The most important factor behind this generosity was simply that the entire nation had been united behind the war, and the armed forces had achieved a clear-cut victory. They were conquering heroes. There were, moreover, a great many veterans. More than 16 million men and women had served in the armed forces, about 11 percent of the 1946 population, and thanks partly to the draft, the veterans had been drawn from every part of the country and from every rank of society. No politician could ignore the veterans.

Providing generous benefits for such a large number of veterans raised the specter of higher taxes or a larger deficit. The federal budget had been in deficit since 1930, and the deficit at the end of the war was huge even by the standards of the 1930s. The threat to the federal budget had been a major obstacle for veterans' benefits after World War I. In the 1920s, as I noted in Chapter 5, Treasury Secretary Andrew Mellon opposed immediate payment of the WWI veterans' bonus mainly because economic prudence, as he saw it, demanded low taxes and a balanced budget. Ideas about spending and deficits, however, had changed. Now the Keynesian idea that large government expenditures and, under some circumstances, large budget deficits were good things had replaced the balanced-budget orthodoxy of Mellon's day. Full employment during the war had, seemingly, confirmed Keynesian ideas, as least as far as many top economists were concerned. Many people, of course, clung to the old orthodoxy, but for many others veterans' benefits were no longer a fiscal negative, a charge on the taxpayer; they were now a fiscal positive, a path to full employment.

A report published in 1950 by a committee of the American Economic Association that included future Nobel Prize winners Milton Friedman and Paul Samuelson among its authors documents the new consensus. Government expenditures including veterans' benefits, "taken by themselves," tend to increase employment or raise prices (Despres *et al.* 1950, 519). Thus, an increase in spending unmatched by taxes might be appropriate depending on the state of the economy. Generous benefits were seen not as something like unemployment benefits that would be in place permanently to act as an "automatic stabilizer" – after all, the number of veterans would gradually diminish – but rather as a good way to protect the economy from the depression that was expected to return after the war was over.[34] With wartime spending being cut, it was widely assumed that unemployment would rise. The educational provisions of the GI Bill (the legislation laying out the benefits for World War II veterans), which would keep returning veterans out of the job market during the postwar depression, made good Keynesian sense.

The perception that the United States had failed the veterans of World War I was another factor behind the support for generous benefits for the veterans of World War II. As Democratic Senator Ernest McFarland put it:

> We cannot afford to have our boys wandering over the country as they did after the last war. We must meet this problem now and prevent a recurrence of that unfortunate situation. The stark tragedy of Anacostia Flats [where the bonus army was encamped in the Depression] must not be reenacted. We must and are facing this problem today in this GI bill of rights.
>
> (quoted in US President's Commission 1956, Part 1, 54)[35]

When veterans' groups, in particular the Veterans of Foreign Wars and the American Legion, began approaching Congress with proposals for generous veterans' benefits, they were met with an enthusiastic reception. The Servicemen's Readjustment Act, known popularly as the GI Bill of Rights, or simply the GI Bill, was passed in 1944. Its purpose was to help veterans readjust to civilian life by providing four types of assistance: (1) education and training; (2) guarantees for loans

[34] There was, however, an attempt to use the loan program (intended mainly for housing) in the GI Bill as a stabilizer. The loan provision required a down payment by the veteran. When the Korean War began in 1950 the down payment was raised to offset expected inflationary pressures; when a recession developed in 1954 the down payment was reduced; and in 1955 when a building boom loomed, the down payment was raised again (US President's Commission 1956, Part 1, 59).

[35] McFarland seems to be arguing that the high unemployment experienced by veterans in the 1930s was the result of a lack of sufficient help with readjustment after the war rather than an independent result of the Depression. Unemployment rates in general were fairly low during the 1920s. I am not aware of a study of the postwar employment patterns of World War I veterans.

for the purchase of homes, businesses, or farms; (3) unemployment compensation; and (4) job counseling and employment services. The most famous provisions were for education and training. Any veteran who had served ninety days and had received a discharge other than dishonorable was eligible for one year of training. Service beyond ninety days entitled the veteran to additional education up to three years. This remained the basic structure of the law in future years, although a number of changes were made in response to perceived abuses. Requirements were added, for example, that the school where the training took place was in existence one year before the war (to prevent the money being used in fly-by-night schools set up simply to take money from veterans) and that schooling not be used for avocational courses.

The lending provision initially guaranteed a loan to a veteran of up to $2,000 at a maximum interest rate of 4 percent. This provision was gradually liberalized in the early postwar years. The maximum amount of the loan, for example, was raised to $4,000 in 1945 and to $7,500 ($60,000 in 2010 dollars) in 1950. The maximum interest rates were also raised in response to market conditions. The other provisions were less controversial. The law provided fifty-two weeks of unemployment compensation for veterans who could not find work, and it set up a veterans' employment service to provide job counseling. The veterans were also entitled to certain benefits that derived from other legislation. Mustering-out pay of $100 per month up to $300 depending on rank was provided under a separate act, and veterans were entitled under certain circumstances to return to their old jobs. Reemployment rights, as they were known, were a new element in veterans' benefits.

The GI Bill has been widely praised by economists and historians of all political persuasions. To liberals it is an example of how government can do good by redistributing income. Millions of young people, liberals like to point out, were able to attend college who would have been unable to do so without the GI Bill, and went on to highly successful lives. Staid east coast universities, it is said, were democratized as they adjusted to an influx of mature students from lower income backgrounds. To conservatives, such as Milton Friedman, the great thing about the GI Bill was that it was a voucher system. The money went first to the veteran. The veteran could then choose the institution he wished to attend and pay the voucher to it.

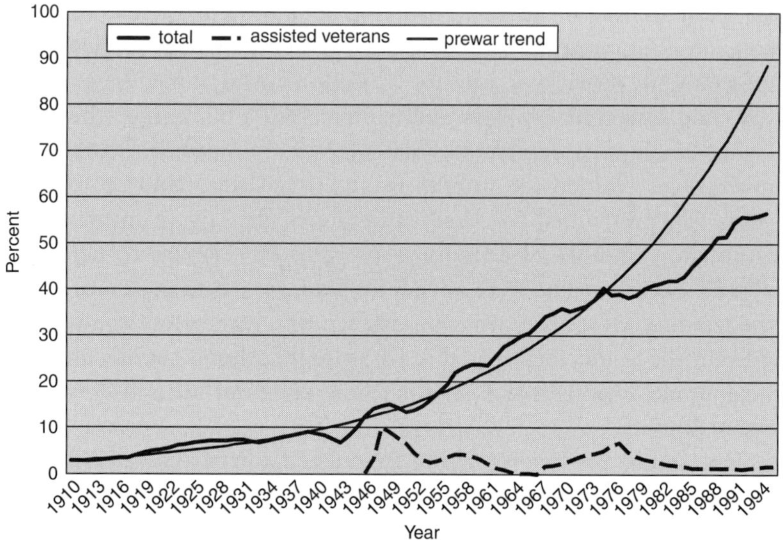

Figure 6.10 Enrollment in higher education as a percentage of the population aged 18 to 24, 1910–95. The GI Bill was important in the late 1940s, but more fundamental forces account for the continued rise in the proportion of the population enrolled in higher education.
Source: Carter *et al.* (2006, series Bc523–4, Ed468, Ed 472, Ed476, Ed480, and Ed 481–2).

Figure 6.10 shows the percentage of all young Americans attending colleges and universities, the percentage attending on the GI Bill of World War II and subsequent GI Bills, and what the total would have been had it grown in the postwar era at the rate given by the prewar (1910–38) trend.[36] Evidently, the upward long-run trend in college attendance began before World War II and continued long after the GIs of that war had finished their education. The claim that the GI Bill explains all or even most of the long-run increase in college attendance appears unlikely. But the GI Bill probably had some impact. A recent study by Marcus Stanley (2003) found that the WWII and Korean War GI bills increased the total amount of schooling attained by men born between 1921 and 1933 by between 15 and 20 percent. We can also

[36] The prewar trend eventually exceeds the percentage attending because there is a limit to the percentage of the population that can benefit from higher education.

suggest some historical reasons why the GI bills may have accelerated the long trend, even after the GIs had completed their education. The success of the programs may have demonstrated the benefits of attaining a college degree to families that in the past might not have considered college educations for their children. Also the wave of more mature students from lower-income families may have shaken up staid educational institutions and demonstrated to skeptical college faculties and administrations the benefits of making higher education widely available. I should note, however, that the halo of success surrounding the World War II GI Bill has tended to glow brighter over time. When I explore the shaping of the Korean War GI Bill in the next chapter, some of the criticisms of the veterans that were made when the WWII program was in full swing will come to the fore.

7 *The Korean War*

I recalled some earlier instances: Manchuria, Ethiopia, Austria. I remembered how each time that the democracies failed to act it had encouraged the aggressors to keep going ahead. Communism was acting in Korea just as Hitler, Mussolini, and the Japanese had acted ten, fifteen, and twenty years earlier. I felt certain that if South Korea was allowed to fall Communist leaders would be emboldened to override nations closer to our own shores.

Harry S. Truman, *Memoirs* (1955, volume II, 333)

A chronology of the Korean War

1948		
March	1	A constitution, said to apply to all Korea, is adopted by Communist North Korea.
May	10	Elections are held in US-occupied South Korea.
August	15	Republic of Korea proclaimed at Seoul with Syngman Rhee as President.
1949		
June	29	USA completes withdrawal of forces from South Korea, leaving only a small contingent of advisors.
September	24	Russia explodes its first atomic bomb.
1950		
June	25	North Korea invades South Korea.
	27	UN Security Council orders North Korea to withdraw and calls on member states to assist South Korea. President Truman orders US armed forces to Korea.
	28	Seoul falls to North Korea.

July	7	It is announced that the draft will be used to enlarge the army.
	8	US General Douglas MacArthur appointed to command UN forces.
	20	Truman calls for a $10 billion rearmament program.
August 6–September 15		Battle of Pusan Beachhead. North Korean forces fail to destroy UN forces.
September	8	Defense Production Act gives the President broad economic powers including stabilization of wages and prices.
	15	UN forces under General Douglas MacArthur land at Inchon on the western coast of South Korea and launch a counterattack.
	22	The House votes overwhelmingly to increase personal income taxes, corporate taxes, and excise taxes to finance the war.
	26	General MacArthur announces the recapture of Seoul.
October	11	The Chinese Communists denounce the crossing of the 38th parallel and threaten intervention.
	20	UN forces capture Pyongyang, capital of Communist North Korea.
	26	Chinese forces cross the Yalu River and join the war.
November	26	Chinese forces launch a massive attack in the Yalu Valley.
December	15	Truman declares a national emergency.

1951

January	3	Truman signs the excess profits tax law.
	4	Seoul is captured by Chinese and North Korean forces.
	26	The Economic Stabilization Administration freezes most wages and prices.

February	5	UN forces attack the North Koreans and Chinese in "Operation Roundup."
March	4	The Treasury–Federal Reserve "Accord" relieves the Federal Reserve of the obligation to maintain a floor under the price of government bonds.
	9	William McChesney Martin is appointed chair of the Federal Reserve, replacing Thomas McCabe.
	14	UN forces recapture Seoul.
April	11	General MacArthur is replaced by General Matthew B. Ridgway after MacArthur threatens China with naval and air attacks.
July	10	Negotiations to end the war begin at Kaesong.
October	20	President Truman signs the Revenue Act of 1951, which raises personal and corporate income tax rates and excise taxes.
	25	Peace negotiation renewed at Panmunjom.
1952		
March	27	The Office of Price Stabilization orders restaurants to display maximum prices.
April	8	Truman seizes the steel mills to prevent a strike.
June	2	The Supreme Court rules Truman's seizure of the steel mills unconstitutional and returns them to private ownership.
July	16	Truman signs the Veterans' Readjustment Assistance Act, popularly known as the Korean War GI Bill.
December	3–5	Carrying out a campaign pledge, newly elected President Dwight D. Eisenhower visits Korea.
1953		
February	6–25	Controls on wages and many consumer goods are lifted. Remaining controls are lifted on March 12.

June	17–18	South Korean guards allow 25,000 anti-Communist prisoners to escape.
	26	An armistice is signed and hostilities halted.

Sources: Linton (1975), Schlesinger and Bowman (1993), Morris and Morris (1996), other chronologies of American history, the *New York Times*, and the *Wall Street Journal.*

When World War II ended, Americans breathed a collective sigh of relief: the war was over – the job was done. Five years later, however, they found themselves at war again. It began as a war against a second-tier power, like the Spanish–American War. But in the background was the potential that it would become a war against one of the major Communist powers, a fear that was realized, and the potential even for it to become World War III.

The origins of the war

The Korean War erupted with unexpected fury in the summer of 1950: Communist North Korea invaded non-Communist South Korea on June 25, 1950, capturing Seoul, the capital and most important urban area, three days later. There was a history behind this attack: North Korea and South Korea had long been on a collision course. In 1948 the Communists in North Korea adopted a constitution which they claimed applied to all of Korea, while elections were held in US-controlled South Korea. The following year, the United States, convinced that the situation in Korea had stabilized, withdrew most of its troops. Just why North Koreans felt emboldened to start a war that risked a counterattack from the United States remains unclear, although it is possible that the successful explosion of an atomic bomb by the Soviet Union in September of 1949 persuaded them that the United States would not go to war in Asia without nuclear superiority. In any case, the Western reaction was immediate. Just days after the attack the United Nations Security Council ordered North Korea to withdraw and President Harry S. Truman ordered US troops to South Korea.

The war developed in three distinct phases. (1) The initial thrust went well for the North Koreans. After capturing Seoul, they pushed the South Koreans and their allies south. At the Battle of the Pusan Beachhead in August and September 1950, however, the North Koreans failed to drive the South Korean and UN forces into the sea. (2) On September 15, UN forces landed at Inchon, behind the Communists, forcing them to retreat. The Inchon Landing was a triumph for its commander, Douglas MacArthur, the hero of America's World War II campaigns in the Philippines. On September 26, 1950 UN forces recaptured Seoul, and on October 20 they captured Pyongyang, the capital of Communist North Korea. In four months of war there had been a complete reversal of fortune. (3) The Chinese warned that by crossing the 38th parallel the UN forces had gone too far, but in the headiness of the initial UN triumphs these warnings were ignored. In October Chinese forces crossed the Yalu River and engaged UN forces, and in November they launched a massive attack in the Yalu Valley. Now it was UN forces that were forced to retreat. In April 1951 Truman replaced General MacArthur with General Matthew B. Ridgway, after MacArthur publicly called for attacks on China and communicated these views to Congress, in defiance of orders from Truman. In the summer of 1951 UN forces were able to stabilize their lines, and the war headed into a stalemate. Peace negotiations, which would drag on for years, began at Kaesong in July 1951. An armistice was signed on June 26, 1953.

Financing the war

The financing of the Korean War was unique in American experience in the twentieth century. Taxes were raised substantially while the Federal Reserve followed an anti-inflationary policy. There was an initial surge in prices, and price controls were imposed, but by the end of the war prices were stable.

Fiscal policy

President Truman favored pay-as-you-go taxation. He acknowledged that there could be "emergency conditions" that would make a deficit necessary, including "maintaining the economy on a high level," but he concluded that "there is nothing sacred about the pay-as-you-go idea so far as I am concerned, except that it represents the soundest principle of financing that I know" (Truman 1955, volume II, 40). When the Korean War erupted Truman was adamant that as large a share as possible of the war should be financed by taxation (*New York Times*, July 20, 1950, 14), and Congress supported him. On September 22,

1950 the House voted 328 to 7, a remarkable majority, to raise personal income taxes, corporate income taxes, and excise taxes (*New York Times*, September 23, 1950, 1). It was a substantial increase in taxes and would go a long way toward financing the war on a pay-as-you-go basis. There were several reasons for this remarkable consensus. The most important, most likely, as Bank, Stark, and Thorndike (2008, 115–16) suggest, was the "rally round the flag" effect. Congress wanted to show its support for the war. It didn't hurt that at that moment the war was going well: UN forces under General Douglas MacArthur had landed at Inchon on September 15, the start of a massive counterstrike against the North Koreans. But there were domestic considerations as well. Large deficits, financed in part by money creation, had created substantial inflationary pressures in World War II. To some extent, and for a time, they had been held in check by a growing network of wage and price controls. Controls, however, had been irksome, and so pay-as-you-go tax policies that would obviate the need for controls seemed a good idea. This train of thought resonated particularly with Republicans and especially with their leader, Senator Robert A. Taft of Ohio, "Mr. Republican."

The personal and corporate income taxes were expected to be the major revenue generators. But sin and luxury taxes were also utilized, in an echo of the Spanish–American and earlier wars. The excises on furs, jewelry, and coin-operated gambling machines were increased, and new levies were imposed on televisions and household freezers. The latter, in addition to being luxuries, represented goods that used materials and manufacturing facilities that might be important to the war effort. There was also an excess profits tax during the Korean War, as there had been in World War I and World War II, but it was not a major source of revenue. In World War II the excess profits tax produced about one-quarter of all tax revenues (after adjusting for prices and prewar taxes); in the Korean War it produced, by the same measure, less than 5 percent (Appendix 4). The small impact of the excess profits tax was partly a matter of timing. The first tax bill that Truman sent to Congress did not include an excess profits tax, presumably because he was concerned that debate over the excess tax provision would slow passage of the bill. When Congressional liberals tried to add an excess profits tax, the Speaker of the House, the legendary Sam Rayburn, told them flatly that they could not have it in the emergency tax bill (Bank, Stark, and Thorndike 2008, 115). The excess profits tax was left for a lame duck

Congress. There, however, it did receive widespread support, perhaps because the deterioration in the military situation in Korea had underscored the need for additional revenues (Bank, Stark, and Thorndike 2008, 120). The excess profits tax in a form similar to what had been proposed earlier became law on January 3, 1951.

The excess profits tax was justified first of all on moral grounds: it was wrong to make extraordinary profits from the war; fairness required that the fat cats, who were staying at home while young men were drafted and sent to Korea to fight, pay a heavy price. There were also economic justifications for the tax. An excess profits tax, like other taxes, would remove purchasing power from the marketplace and reduce inflationary pressures. There was, however, another macroeconomic justification, although one that appealed more to the public than to economists: the excess profits tax would fight inflation by taxing it. After all, this line of thought went, if inflation was caused by war profiteers raising prices, taxing the profiteers would reduce the incentive to raise prices. That ideas such as this were in the wind was the reason that during the war Milton Friedman (1951, 191) was moved to quote John Maynard Keynes (1923) on post-World War I European inflations: "A host of popular remedies vainly attempted to cure the evils of the day; which remedies themselves – subsidies, price and rent fixing, profiteer hunting, and excess profits duties – eventually became not the least part of the evils." Avoiding a broad-based increase in taxes by relying on the printing press, and supplementing it with politically popular taxes, may be bad economics: the government may set in motion forces that may produce even greater damage to the economy. But it may be good politics: it may hide the cost of a controversial war. However, this was not the policy followed in the Korean War; the United States did not follow the path to the conditions that Keynes described as prevailing in post-World War I Europe and that Friedman warned against.

There would be further tax increases under the Revenue Act of 1951. The Revenue Acts of the Korean War were not sufficient to prevent a deficit in the federal budget, but they did a good job. As shown in Figure 7.1, the budget was in surplus from the outbreak of the war until mid-1951. It remained in the red for the remainder of the war, but a substantial gap did not open up until the second half of 1952. The deficits were manageable, averaging about 6.5 percent of revenues on a monthly basis during the course of the war. As a quick, broad-brush summary, the claim in the literature (based on annual

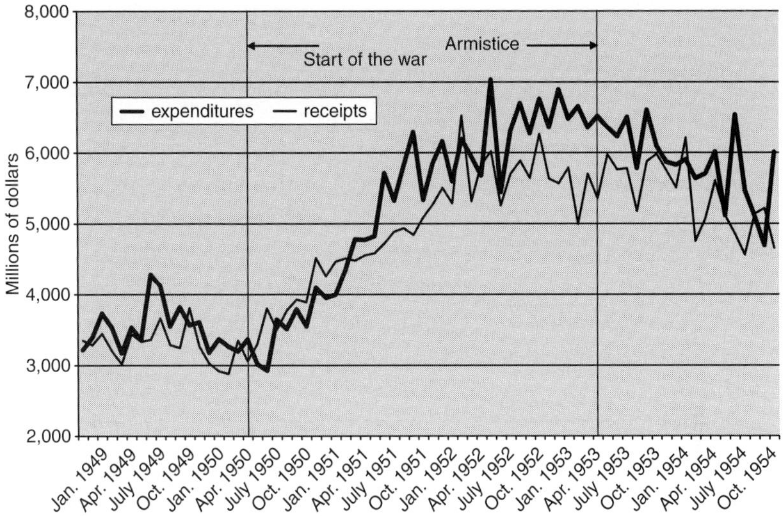

Figure 7.1 Federal receipts and expenditures, 1949–54. Rising receipts covered most of the increase in federal spending during the Korean War, although a small gap between expenditures and receipts opened up in the second half of 1951.
Source: Firestone (1960, Table A3, seasonally corrected data).

data) that the Korean War was financed 100 percent by taxation (Ohanian 1997, 24; based on Goldin 1980, 938–40) is correct.

Monetary policy

The most important issue for the Federal Reserve during the Korean War was whether it should simply continue its prewar policy of setting a floor under the prices of government bonds – pegging the price of government bonds, as it was known – a policy that dated to the early days of World War II, or whether it should allow bond prices to fall, in order to restrict the growth of money and credit, and thus restrain inflation. President Truman and his Treasury Secretary, John W. Snyder, strongly favored pegging. Truman remembered having bought Liberty bonds during World War I only to see their price sag in the postwar period because the Federal Reserve had failed to maintain it. He considered pegging to be a policy that helped the little guy, and he felt that given the challenge of Communism it was crucial to maintain the credit of the government (Stein 1996, 272). Snyder

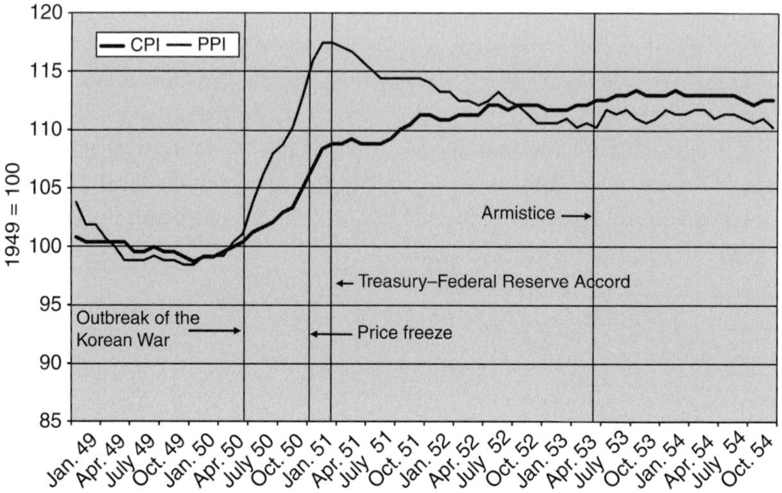

Figure 7.2 The consumer and producer price indexes during the Korean War. Prices surged when the Korean War began, but then leveled off when price controls and restrictive monetary and fiscal policies were put in place.
Source: US Department of Labor, Bureau of Labor Statistics.

also believed that the job of the Federal Reserve was first and foremost to support the Treasury by pegging government bond prices and he was confident of Truman's support; he was a close personal friend of the President, a fellow Missourian, and had served with him in World War I. The Federal Reserve, however, saw things differently. It had a duty, as it saw it, to promote macroeconomic stability, and in the current environment that meant fighting inflation. As shown in Figure 7.2, the price level surged upward after the outbreak of the Korean War. The monthly increase in the consumer price index reached nearly 20 percent on an annual basis by February of 1951. As the Federal Reserve saw it, the nation was in the midst of an inflationary crisis, and the Federal Reserve was duty bound to do something about it, even if that meant an increase in the interest rate on government bonds.

The fight between the Federal Reserve and the Treasury over which philosophy of war finance should prevail, or to put it more crudely, but perhaps just as accurately, over who should be the boss of monetary policy, was a classic case of bureaucratic infighting. Herbert Stein (1996, 272) describes a crucial meeting at the White House as "a masterpiece of deliberate misunderstanding." The President tried to pin the Federal Reserve to the Treasury view by releasing a letter that interpreted the meeting as one in which the Federal Reserve had agreed to continue pegging. The Federal Reserve, however, resisted this tactic, and in the end was able to assert its independence from the Treasury. On March 4, the famous Treasury–Federal Reserve "Accord" was reached. The announcement to the public was brief and to some degree cryptic.

The Treasury and the Federal Reserve System have reached full accord with respect to debt-management and monetary policies to be pursued in furthering their common purpose to assure the successful financing of the Government's requirements and, at the same time, to minimize monetization of the public debt.

The last phrase was critical. To place a floor under the price of public debt the Federal Reserve had to be ready to purchase all of the excess supply of debt, even if that meant creating new money to do it; that is, it had to be ready to monetize the debt. The Accord, in other words, recognized the right of the Federal Reserve to stop purchasing government debt. The Federal Reserve had reasserted its independence after nearly a decade of subservience to the Treasury.

Viewed in a long historical perspective, the ability of the Federal Reserve to stand up to the President in wartime was remarkable. When the Second Bank of the United States had "gone to war" with President Andrew Jackson in the 1830s it had lost badly.[1] The office of the President had become far more powerful in the intervening years, and the country was now at war, something that always strengthened the President's hand. But the circumstances in the early months of the Korean War were unique. Inflation, as we have noted, had reached the frightening rate of nearly 20 percent per year. This may have been a temporary surge rather than a rate that was likely to be sustained for a long period of time. It may have been, to put it somewhat differently, a price panic caused by the outbreak of the war and memories of inflation in World War II and earlier wars, a panic that might subside in its own in time. But it was understandable that policymakers inside and outside the Federal Reserve would be demanding that the Federal Reserve do

[1] The issue in the 1830s was similar. Jackson didn't like the bank's interest rate policy.

something about the inflation. This concern naturally influenced the Congress. The Democrats had only a thin majority, and some of them supported the Federal Reserve. The latter group included Senator Paul Douglas of Illinois, who had been a distinguished economist at the University of Chicago, and was now a leader on economic affairs. President Truman's public approval rating at this point, moreover, was extremely low. The reason had little to do with the intricacies of monetary policy, and more to do with the fact that the war was going badly for the United States. Chinese forces had entered the war in November, with North Korean forces they had captured Seoul on January 4, and American casualties were heavy.

Price controls

The outbreak of the war produced a wave of buying of items that had been in short supply during World War II.[2] Consumers rushed to buy automobile tires, sugar, nylons, and so on. Manufacturers increased their purchases of raw materials in response to the rise in consumer purchases and in anticipation of war orders (Hickman 1955, 10–21). All of this speculative buying contributed to the surge in prices, which began to rise rapidly after the outbreak of the war, with producer (wholesale) prices, as shown in Figure 7.2, leading consumer prices. But if the surge was produced by the outbreak of the war, what brought it to a halt in early 1951? Undoubtedly, the fiscal (the tax increase in September 1950) and monetary policies (the Accord reached in March 1951) discussed above helped. The public could see that the government was getting its house in order by raising taxes. And the financial community could see that the Federal Reserve was going to follow a low-inflation policy. We also cannot rule out a role for the change in military fortunes. After the Chinese attacks along the Yalu, UN forces retreated southward – it was one of the longest retreats in US military history – but by the beginning of 1951 they had managed to stabilize their lines, and in February they launched a counterattack. In March UN forces recaptured Seoul. It was soon clear that the UN forces would be able to maintain their position, but it was also clear that they were not going to attempt to liberate all of North Korea. The war would end in a stalemate rather

[2] This section is based mainly on Rockoff (1984, 177–99).

than World War III. Once this was clear the speculative pressure on prices, especially raw material prices, would naturally abate.

Another reason for the moderation in the rate of inflation was the price freeze introduced on January 26, 1951. An across-the-board freeze was adopted because the World War II policy of gradually tightening controls over a long period had done more harm than good. Michael V. DiSalle, the director of Price Stabilization, told Senator Taft that it was better to cut off all of the cat's tail at once. If you do it an inch at a time, "you always have a sore tail – and a mad cat" (*New York Times*, January 2, 1951, 15).

From the outbreak of the war to the start of the price freeze, prices rose at an annual rate of 11.1 percent; but from the price freeze to the termination of controls prices rose at an annual rate of only 2.1 percent. There was some evasion of price controls during the Korean War, although not on the scale seen during World War II. The market for steel was especially problematic. Demand was strong, and steel was rationed, but some was diverted into so-called gray markets. (Presumably, the participants believed, or hoped, that although they were evading price controls and rationing, their actions were not illegal.) Large steel producers engaged in a game of chicken with the government, refusing to grant increases in wages unless the government granted increases in the price of steel, the tactic which had undermined controls after the end of World War II. President Truman became so incensed that he seized the steel mills in April 1952. This action was blocked by the courts, and led to a long strike that was eventually ended with a concession on wages by the steel producers and a concession on prices by the Office of Price Stabilization. Smaller producers evaded controls by selling steel through long "daisy chains" of intermediaries.

Thus some of the price stability observed after the price freeze (and the tax increases and the Treasury–Federal Reserve Accord) may be misleading: a failure of the price indexes to accurately reflect the true level of prices. There can be little doubt, however, that the general impression conveyed by Figure 7.2, a surge in prices led by producer's prices followed by stability, is broadly correct. Indeed, the use of price controls during the Korean War may be close to an optimal use of this tool. After the outbreak of the war, consumers and producers were caught up in something that might be called a price panic. After all, this might have been the start of World War III. Price controls were put in place to calm things down, but at the same time the government adopted restrictive fiscal and monetary policies that would stabilize demand. There was no outburst of suppressed inflation after the Korean War. Prices rose at a rate of a mere 2.6 percent per year in the eight months after controls were lifted.

Price controls and rationing did not significantly alter the cost of the war in the sense that they did not in the first instance reduce the amount of resources that had to be shifted from the private sector to the public sector, but they did alter the way those costs were perceived. Consider the steel situation. The government could simply have allowed steel prices to rise freely and then have purchased as much steel as it required on the open market, raising taxes as needed. Such a policy would have succeeded in acquiring the requisite amount of steel. But the cost of the war would have been transparent to taxpayers. Price controls and rationing limited the financial cost of acquiring steel for the war, and the need to raise taxes, but created other difficulties such as the three-way tug-of-war among labor, management, and the government described above. This tug of war and its outcome, the seizure of the steel mills by the President and the constitutional crisis that ensued, were costs of the war. But it seems unlikely that costs that have been transformed from simple increases in taxes to complicated questions about compliance with regulations can be part of a rational calculation in which a citizen tries to decide whether a war is "worth it."

The cost of the war

About 34,000 Americans were killed in action, and about 2,800 died from disease and injury during the Korean War. Total US casualties (dead, wounded, missing in action) amounted to 139,860 (Appendix 2). South Korean casualties have been estimated at 320,000 and those of other US allies at 14,000. The combined casualties for the North Koreans and Chinese are estimated to have been as many as 1.5 million. The number of civilian deaths caused by the war has "been put as high as 1 million" (Koh 1971, 478, n. 9). There was also great damage to physical capital – factories, farms, homes, schools, and hospitals were all destroyed in great numbers – as the war swept back and forth across the peninsula. For the Korean peninsula this was devastation on the scale of World War II.

When the Korean War began military spending in the United States was already elevated because of the ongoing tensions with the Soviet

Union, but it was pushed even higher by the war. If we project real defense spending forward from 1950 to 1955 at a constant rate, and then subtract these projections from actual military spending, we obtain estimates of the marginal costs of the Korean War. They sum to $415 billion in 2008 dollars, about 17 percent of average real GDP during the war. This calculation is relevant when we consider the point of view of a policymaker deciding whether the Korean War was a "worthwhile" investment given the high level of spending dictated by the ongoing commitment to contain Communism. If we look at the war as part of the process of maintaining this commitment we should include some part of the cost of maintaining Cold War levels of military spending. In other words, we would want to include some part of the fixed costs. An alternative calculation that includes all military spending during the war in excess of the post-Cold War norm would be $1,119 billion in 2008 dollars, about 47 percent of average real GDP during the war. If we add veterans' benefits, the total cost of the war increases to $1,186 billion in 2008 dollars, 48.2 percent of average real GDP at the time.

These estimates exclude some smaller costs: costs of civilian war agencies, the cost of the draft to the men who were drafted, the long-run costs of stationing forces in South Korea, and so on. It does not appear that the addition of these costs would change the overall picture sufficiently to justify the time needed for these refinements, but it is clear that $1,335 billion in 2008 dollars is a lower bound.

The estimate of half a year's GDP is less than the equivalent estimate for the two world wars, but more than for the Spanish–American and Philippine–American wars. Was it worth it? Unfortunately, economic accounting cannot furnish a persuasive answer. While economists can measure the costs, the benefits – preventing the expansion of the territory controlled by the Communist powers, maintaining international law, and so on – lie on other dimensions. We can say, however, that the American people soon became discouraged with the war. In August 1950, shortly after the Inchon landing, a Gallup poll asked Americans the following: do you think the United States made a mistake going into the war in Korea, or not? At that time total battle deaths stood at 4,631 and 66 percent of the respondents answered no. But this consensus was quickly eroded. Mounting casualties, lack of progress on the ground, and higher taxes levied under the Revenue Act of 1950 quickly took their toll on public support for the war. By December 1950 total battle deaths stood at 13,991 and only 39 percent answered no; most Americans in other words, either were not sure or thought that the war had been a mistake (Larson 1996, 109). Afterwards, support fluctuated but a majority of Americans were never again convinced that the war had been the right thing to do. Today many Americans remember Harry Truman as a great president, but at the time Truman's war was deeply unpopular.

The veterans

The "Korean War GI Bill" became law in 1952. Eventually it covered veterans serving between June 27, 1950 and February 1, 1955.[3] It included the same portfolio of benefits as the WWII GI Bill and associated legislation: mustering-out pay, financial support for education, guarantees for home and business loans, unemployment compensation, and job placement. This bill, however, was less generous in a number of ways than that for World War II. This was especially true in the provisions for education. The WWII GI Bill provided twelve months of financial support for education plus one additional day of support for each day of service in the war, with a limit of forty-eight months. The Korean War GI Bill, however, provided for education equal to one and a half times the amount of service with a limit of thirty-six months. In essence, a year of service in WWII entitled a veteran to two years of education, while a year of service in the Korean War entitled a soldier to only one and a half years of education. At two years the rewards were the same, but longer service in WWII was rewarded, while longer service in the Korean War was not. Thus, to take the iconic example, a high school graduate who served three years in WWII could complete a traditional four-year college education under the WWII GI Bill, but a high school graduate who served for three years in the Korean War would have to pay for the fourth year of college himself. To be sure, the Korean War was shorter than World War II, but it was conceivable that a veteran of the Korean War who had faced more danger in Korea than a friend who had served in World War II would receive less in educational benefits.

[3] The following discussion of the Korean War GI Bill is based mainly on US President's Commission (1956, 61).

The formula determining the amount of educational benefits paid to the veteran was also changed. Under the WWII GI Bill the government paid the tuition up to $500 directly to the school while the veteran received a monthly subsistence payment of $50 if there were no dependants, with additional amounts payable if there were dependants. Under the Korean War GI Bill, the veteran received $110 per month if there were no dependants, but the veteran was responsible for paying tuition. What did this mean? A Korean War veteran who paid $500 in tuition for nine months of schooling (the maximum tuition benefit under the WWII GI Bill) was left with only $54 per month for nine months. The Korean War veteran would be equal in nominal terms to a WWII veteran under the 1948 version of the law only if he chose a school that charged $315 for nine months of schooling. Since prices had risen about 10 percent between 1948 and 1952, the veteran attending school under the Korean War GI Bill would have to choose a school with tuition of about $250 for nine months to remain equal in after-tuition real payments to a veteran going to school under the 1948 version of the World War II GI Bill. The Korean War GI Bill, to sum up, left the Korean War veteran with less money in real terms, unless he was fortunate enough to find a school that met his needs and charged a modest tuition.

In addition, the Korean War GI Bill altered unemployment benefits in a way that hurt some veterans. The payment was raised from $20 per week under the WWII GI Bill to $26 per week under the Korean War bill, but the maximum period covered was halved from fifty-two weeks to twenty-six weeks. The Korean War bill, in other words, reduced the maximum amount from $1,040 to $676 despite the rise in prices. Figure 7.3 shows real benefits per veteran (in 1950 dollars) for veterans of WWII over the first ten years after World War II and for veterans of the Korean War for the first ten years after that war. The effects of the changes in the law are immediately evident. The veterans of WWII received significantly more real income from the government during their readjustment period than did the veterans of the Korean War. The one area in which the veterans of the later war appear to have come out ahead was in medical care: the upgrading of the medical system after WWII under the leadership of General Omar Bradley remained intact (Longo *et al.* 2005).

Several factors probably account for the change in the level of benefits between the WWII and Korean War GI Bills. One was the

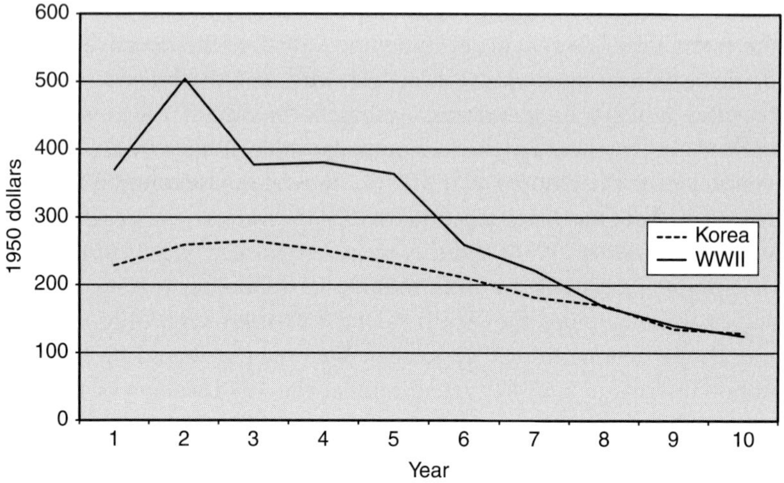

Figure 7.3 Real expenditure per veteran, WWII and Korea, the first decade after the war. Veterans' benefits were curtailed for veterans of the Korean War. *Source:* Carter *et al.* (2006, series Ed252, Ed254, Ed331, Ed332, and CC1).

perception that some veterans had abused the generosity of the WWII bill. Veterans had gone off to college, some critics charged, simply to enjoy a vacation at government expense rather than to prepare themselves for the future. Requiring the veteran to pay for a larger share of his education would save money and would be good for society and for the veteran. In addition, the macroeconomic picture had changed dramatically. When the WWII GI Bill was written it was widely assumed that the Depression would return after the war. Spending on education for GIs was a way of keeping them out of a crowded labor market, and of injecting additional purchasing power that would partly offset the decline in war spending and help prop up the economy. The feared postwar depression, however, failed to materialize. By 1952 inflation rather than unemployment had become the major concern of policymakers. As a consequence, restraining government spending, including spending on veterans' readjustment benefits, now seemed the course of fiscal prudence.

There is another possible factor, one that is not susceptible to definitive confirmation, but which is worth considering. The Korean War ended differently than World War II: in a struggle for an armistice rather than an unequivocal victory. Perhaps Americans unconsciously felt less enthusiastic about rewarding veterans because they had not "accomplished" as much; they were not conquering heroes. It would be hard for us to see ourselves in this way, and there is not enough experience to judge for certain. But there are certainly other examples, such as the War of 1812, whose veterans seem to have been less well rewarded than the more successful veterans of the Revolution and the Mexican War (Kang and Rockoff 2006).

8 *The Cold War*

From Stettin in the Baltic to Trieste in the Adriatic an iron curtain has descended across the Continent. Behind that line lie all the capitals of the ancient states of Central and Eastern Europe. Warsaw, Berlin, Prague, Vienna, Budapest, Belgrade, Bucharest and Sofia; all these famous cities and the populations around them lie in what I must call the Soviet sphere, and all are subject, in one form or another, not only to Soviet influence but to a very high and in some cases increasing measure of control from Moscow.

Winston S. Churchill, the "Iron Curtain" speech, Westminster College, Fulton, Missouri, March 5, 1946[1]

A chronology of the Cold War

1946		
February	22	George F. Kennan, a US diplomat stationed in Moscow, sends his "long telegram," "The Sources of Soviet Conduct," which warns of Communist aggression and calls for a policy of "containment."
March	5	In a speech at Westminster College in Fulton, Missouri, Winston Churchill warns that an "iron curtain" has descended over central and eastern Europe.
1947		
March	12	President Harry S. Truman asks Congress for economic and military assistance for Greece and Turkey so they can defend themselves against Communist insurgencies. The "Truman Doctrine" calls for American support for regimes that face armed minorities or outside pressures.

[1] Modern History Sourcebook, available at www.fordham.edu/halsall/mod/churchill-iron.html (accessed July 19, 2010).

1948		
June	24	Start of the Berlin blockade. The Soviet Union and East Germany blockade the city of Berlin. The Western Allies resupply Berlin by air.
1949		
May	12	End of the Berlin blockade.
August	29	The Soviet Union tests a nuclear bomb.
1950		
March	1	Klaus Fuchs, a German who had worked on nuclear weapons in Britain and the United States, is convicted of spying for the Soviet Union.
June	25	North Korea invades South Korea.
	27	The UN Security Council orders North Korea to withdraw and calls on member states to assist South Korea. President Truman orders US armed forces to Korea.
	28	Seoul falls to North Korea.
July	7	It is announced that the draft will be used to enlarge the army.
	17	Julius Rosenberg is arrested for espionage.
August	11	Ethel Rosenberg is arrested for espionage.
September	15	UN forces land at Inchon and launch a counterattack in Korea.
October	20	UN forces capture Pyongyang, capital of Communist North Korea.
November	26	Chinese forces launch a massive attack in the Yalu Valley.
1951		
January	4	Seoul is captured by Chinese and North Korean forces.
February	5	UN forces attack the North Koreans and Chinese in "Operation Roundup."
March	6	Trial of Ethel and Julius Rosenberg for espionage begins.

	14	UN forces recapture Seoul.
	29	Ethel and Julius Rosenberg are convicted and sentenced to death.
July	10	Negotiations to end the Korean War begin.
1953		
June	26	An armistice is signed ending the Korean War.
1954		
August 11–May 1955		The People's Republic of China and the Republic of China (non-Communist Taiwan) engage in air and artillery duels over the disputed islands of Quemoy and Matsu.
1956		
October	24	Soviet forces enter Budapest to quell anti-Communist unrest.
1958		
August 23–September 22		The People's Republic of China and the Republic of China (non-Communist Taiwan) again engage in air and artillery duels over the disputed islands of Quemoy and Matsu.
1959		
January	8	Cuban revolutionaries under Fidel Castro enter Havana.
February	16	Fidel Castro is sworn in as Prime Minister of Cuba.
July–September		The Castro regime nationalizes US-owned properties and establishes close economic and military ties with the Soviet Union.
July	24	US Vice President Richard Nixon debates Soviet Premier Nikita Khrushchev at an American industrial exposition in Moscow.
September	17	Fidel Castro addresses the United Nations, attacking the United States and praising the Soviet Union.
1961		
April	17	Cuban exiles, backed by the United States, land at the Bay of Pigs in an attempt to overthrow the Castro regime. They are quickly defeated.

August	16	East Germany begins constructing a wall to prevent East Germans from moving to the West.
1962		
February	7	The United States imposes an economic embargo on Cuba.
October	22	In a televised broadcast President John F. Kennedy tells the nation that the Soviet Union has installed missiles in Cuba and proclaims his intention of imposing a naval "quarantine" of the island.
	23	The naval quarantine which bars Soviet missiles from being landed in Cuba goes into effect. A confrontation between the United States and the Soviet Union leading to a nuclear war becomes possible. Intense negotiations follow.
	28	Nikita Khrushchev, the leader of the Soviet Union, announces that he has agreed to remove Soviet missiles from Cuba, ending the crisis. In return, the United States promises not to invade the island. US missiles in Turkey, another issue, are subsequently removed.
1963		
June	23	President John F. Kennedy delivers a speech in Berlin in which he says "Ich bin ein Berliner" (I am a Berliner).
1968		
August	21	Soviet troops invade Czechoslovakia, ending the "Prague Spring," a period of liberal reform.
1972		
February	21	President Nixon lands in China on a mission to improve relations.
	28	The United States and the People's Republic of China issue the Shanghai Communiqué, promising to work toward better relations.
1979		
June	16	The Soviet Union begins sending forces to Afghanistan to support its Communist regime.
December	27	The Soviet Union launches a full-scale invasion of Afghanistan.

1988		
May 15–February 15, 1989		The Soviet Union withdraws from Afghanistan.
1989		
June	4	Tanks clear protesters from Tiananmen Square in Beijing.
	4	Solidarity wins an overwhelming election victory in Poland, producing the first non-Communist government in eastern Europe.
November	9	The Berlin Wall falls.
	17	In Czechoslovakia a mass demonstration is held which begins the "Velvet Revolution" against Communist rule.
December	3	At a conference in Malta, Soviet leader Mikhail Gorbachev and US President George H.W. Bush declare an end to the Cold War.
	10	In Czechoslovakia a non-Communist government is sworn in.
1990		
March	11	Lithuania declares independence from the Soviet Union.
May	4	Latvia declares independence from the Soviet Union.
	29	Boris Yeltsin, a reformer, is elected President of Russia.
1991		
August	19	An attempt by Soviet hardliners to remove Mikhail Gorbachev from power fails.
August–September		Many member states of the Soviet Union declare independence.
December	25	Mikhail Gorbachev resigns.
	26	The Soviet Union is dissolved.

Sources: Linton (1975), Schlesinger and Bowman (1993), Morris and Morris (1996), other chronologies of American history, the *New York Times*, the *Wall Street Journal*, and other online sources.

The Cold War resembles the period of increased military spending that followed the Philippine–American War and Theodore Roosevelt's "large policy." Casualties were few during the Cold War, but it was punctuated by two hot wars, in Korea and Vietnam. However, the financial cost of the Cold War was substantial, although it often faded from view in the political arena – accepted to some degree as part of the normal background of economic and political life. Over the long run, however, the Cold War was costly, more costly in financial terms than the hot wars in Korea and Vietnam, and indeed, more costly in terms of total resources used than World War II. What might be called the War against Communism – thus encompassing Korea, Vietnam, and the Cold War – was by far the longest, and in terms of financial resources the costliest, war in American history.

The origins of the Cold War

America's opposition to Communism was long standing. International action was first taken during the Russian Revolution when Woodrow Wilson sent American forces to the Soviet Union in 1918. And it was clear as soon as World War II ended, if not earlier, that the wartime alliance between the United States and the Soviet Union had not healed the divide. In February 1946 an American diplomat stationed in Moscow, George F. Kennan, sent his famous "long telegram" about Soviet intentions. Later published in *Foreign Affairs* (1947) as "The Sources of Soviet Conduct," the telegram and article argued that the Soviet Union intended to spread Communism by every means at its disposal including military force, and that the Soviet Union could and should be stopped with a forceful policy of "containment."[2] The United States should not attempt to overthrow Communist regimes where they had become entrenched, but it should try to prevent them from gaining control over new territories. Although the long telegram was crucial for the development of American foreign policy, it was the "Iron Curtain" speech given by Winston Churchill at Westminster College in Fulton, Missouri, on March 5, 1946, and quoted in the introduction to this chapter, that caught the public's imagination.

[2] Kennan's telegram was originally published anonymously. Kennan provides the text and discusses the telegram in his *Memoirs* (1967). He was subsequently extremely dissatisfied with the lessons drawn from the original argument.

True, politically minded leftists believed that the lesson of the war was that it was important for the United States to stand against Fascism and to stand with its wartime allies, the Communists. But to most Americans the lesson of the war was that it was important to stand up to aggressive dictatorships. "Isms" were the problem, and it didn't matter whether it was a right ism or a left ism. Thus, many Americans were sympathetic to the idea of containment, even many who knew little about Communism, and who in past times would have been opposed to the taxes that would be needed to finance containment. Isolationism, with its low military burden, and "appeasement" had been discredited by World War II.

The outbreak, or more accurately a perceived renewal, of a Communist insurgency in Greece proved an important accelerant to the Cold War. The civil war in Greece had its roots in the German occupation of the country during World War II. In March 1946 elections were held which were won by the right. The Communists, who had boycotted the election and who had the support of Marshal Tito in Yugoslavia, then resumed their war against the government, which was backed by Britain and the United States. In March 1947 President Truman asked Congress for $400 million in economic and military aid for Greece and Turkey. Truman's message to Congress was straightforward. The Communists represented only a minority in Greece, but they were trying to overthrow a democratically elected government by force.

Truman put it this way:

> The Government of Greece is not perfect. Nevertheless it represents eighty-five per cent of the members of the Greek Parliament who were chosen in an election last year. Foreign observers, including 692 Americans, considered this election to be a fair expression of the views of the Greek people.[3]

"I believe that it must be the policy of the United States," Truman concluded, "to support free peoples who are resisting attempted subjugation by armed minorities or by outside pressures."

Truman presented a simple economic calculation to summarize the thinking behind his request for aid for Greece and Turkey.

> The United States contributed $341,000,000,000 toward winning World War II. This is an investment in world freedom and world peace. The assistance that

[3] Address before a Joint Session of Congress, March 12, 1947; http://avalon.law.yale.edu/20th_century/trudoc.asp.

I am recommending for Greece and Turkey amounts to little more than 1 tenth of 1 per cent of this investment. It is only common sense that we should safeguard this investment and make sure that it was not in vain.[4]

Truman's calculation, of course, doesn't anticipate the ongoing costs of containment. Aid to Greece and Turkey was, as it turned out, a small down payment on what would prove to be a huge investment. Economists, as we have noted, can usually make a good estimate of the cost of a war, but the benefits normally lie along dimensions that are impossible to quantify – in this case "world freedom and peace." The Cold War, as this quotation from Truman illustrates, was no exception.

There is no precise starting date for the Cold War. Some historians date it from Churchill's "Iron Curtain" speech, but many others date it from Truman's request for aid for Greece and Turkey. The government of the United States was now committed to, or at least one could say, was in the process of taking on the commitment of, containing Communism. From 1945 to 1949 the United States was the only nuclear power, and the possibility of threatening the Soviet Union and China with nuclear strikes encouraged American hardliners who wanted to push the Communist powers back. But the explosion of an atomic bomb by the Soviets in August 1949 meant that containment had become the only feasible policy. If a war between the Communist powers and the Western powers erupted, both sides would face mass destruction of the type visited upon Hiroshima and Nagasaki.

The explosion of an atomic bomb by the Soviet Union was a severe shock to the United States. It had assumed that it was far ahead of the Soviet Union in nuclear physics and would enjoy a nuclear monopoly for many years. A natural question was whether the Soviets had developed a nuclear bomb on their own or whether atomic secrets had been stolen. It soon emerged that the Soviet Union had penetrated the British and American nuclear research efforts. In March 1950 Klaus Fuchs, a German who had worked on nuclear research in Britain and the United States, was convicted in Britain of spying for the Soviet Union, and soon after, there was a sensational case in the

[4] Truman doesn't say how this estimate of the cost of the war was computed. I came close ($350 billion) by taking the sum of total federal spending from fiscal 1941 through fiscal 1945 and half of fiscal 1946. Simply summing all federal spending on the grounds that all of it was dedicated in some way to the war effort doesn't lead to a major error. An economist would want to adjust the sums for inflation.

United States. On July 17, 1950 Julius Rosenberg, an American, was arrested for passing atomic secrets to the Soviet Union; his wife, Ethel, was arrested in early August. The Korean War had begun only a few weeks before their arrests. Many people were convinced that Stalin had given the green light for North Korea to attack South Korea, and that he did so because he possessed the atomic bomb, making the Soviet Union and its allies safe from retaliation. The conclusion from this line of thinking was that the Rosenbergs and other nuclear spies were directly responsible for the deaths of American military personnel in Korea. This was one of the considerations cited by the judge in the Rosenberg case when, on March 29, 1951, he sentenced them to death.[5] The amount of help Julius Rosenberg and other spies provided to the Soviet Union and the impact on the Soviet nuclear program is still a matter of bitter controversy. In any case, the revelation that the British and American nuclear programs had been penetrated undoubtedly escalated tensions between the Soviet Union and the United States and intensified the Cold War.

The Cold War was punctuated by a series of confrontations, each of which had the potential to escalate into a hot war, and on two occasions, in Korea and Vietnam, did so. The Berlin blockade was the first major confrontation. Berlin, traditionally Germany's capital, lay entirely within the zone controlled by the Soviet Union. In June 1948 the Soviets blocked ground access to the city. Their goal was to force the Western Allies to recognize Soviet authority in Berlin. Accepting the newly introduced Soviet currency as the sole legal tender in Berlin was an important component of their demands. The Western Allies did not attempt to break the blockade by force, an action that might have led to a war between them and the Soviet Union. Instead, they chose to bring in needed supplies by air: the famous Berlin airlift. The airlift continued for nearly a year. Supplying a large city with food, fuel, and other supplies by air was a major challenge that had never been accomplished previously. But with the help of newly introduced large transport planes the challenge was met. The Soviets made some attempts to harass Allied flights, but did not attempt to shoot down the planes: neither side was prepared to go to war to decide the fate

[5] The literature on the Rosenberg case is enormous and contentious. Their sons, Robert and Michael Meeropol, have their say in Meeropol and Meeropol (1986). One of the most frequently cited accounts is Radosh and Milton (1997). Robert Meeropol (2003) provides a moving account of his life.

of Berlin. By the spring of 1949 the Soviets found themselves on the losing end of a propaganda war and abandoned the blockade.

A year later the "free world," led by the United States, and the Communist world were confronting each other once again. On June 25, 1950 the North Korean Communists invaded South Korea, starting the Korean War. The United States entered on the side of South Korea and in October 1950 Chinese forces crossed the Yalu River, attacking the US forces and those of its allies. Two of the world's most powerful nations, Capitalist America and Communist China, were at war. The Korean War is treated in detail in Chapter 7; here I want to note that it was part of the long series of conflicts that constituted the War against Communism. There were more confrontations with Communist China. Twice – in the summer and fall of 1954 and again in 1958 – the United States and the People's Republic of China nearly went to war over the disputed islands of Quemoy and Matsu. These are small islands that lie in the strait separating mainland China and Taiwan (a non-Communist ally of the United States). The Communist regime claimed all of China including Taiwan and on these occasions was prepared to shell the islands, which had been fortified by Chiang Kai-shek's government on Taiwan. The islands had little economic value, but both sides believed that a Communist takeover of Quemoy and Matsu would have undermined the credibility of the Taiwan regime. In the end, however, neither the United States nor China was prepared to let this conflict escalate into full-scale war.

Tensions rose once again when, in the following year, 1959, Fidel Castro took power in Cuba. After some early denials of Communist leanings, Castro moved quickly to establish a Communist economic system and to establish close relations with the Soviet Union. It was a major breakthrough for the Communist powers: a base in the new world. Both Communists and their opponents thought that the Cuban revolution might lead to revolutions throughout Latin America. In response to the revolution the United States provided military aid and support for Cuban exiles who hoped to reclaim the island by force and embargoed US trade with Cuba.[6] The policy of aiding the Cuban

[6] Often the word "sanction" is used in this context. In recent years, however, the term has most frequently been used in cases of limited restraints on trade, prohibitions on the buying and selling of certain products, for example. The term "boycott" could also be used, although it is most often used when the ban on trade is imposed by a non-governmental institution.

exiles proved unsuccessful. A force of exiles backed by the United States landed at the Bay of Pigs on April 17, 1961, but was quickly defeated. The embargo continues to this day. It has not achieved the ambitious goal of bringing down the Castro regime. The reason, first of all, is that the Soviet Union, China, and many other nations have been willing to trade with Cuba.[7] At most, the ban on trade with the island may have weakened its economy and reduced its ability to "export revolution" (Davis and Engerman 2006, 409–10).

In October 1962 the Soviet Union and the United States came very close to going to war over Cuba.[8] The Kennedy administration became alarmed when reconnaissance photos showed that the Soviet Union had been installing on the island missiles capable of hitting the United States. On October 22 Kennedy made this threat known to the public in an address broadcast by radio and television. He also announced a "quarantine" of Cuba. The term, with its medical associations, was carefully chosen. "Embargo" would have conveyed a more menacing, warlike intention. Ships bound for Cuba would be stopped and searched: missiles would be prevented from entering Cuba, but civilian goods would be allowed to continue. Nevertheless, there was a real possibility of a naval confrontation on the high seas that would escalate into a full-scale war, conceivably a nuclear war. Some historians claim, with some justification, that the world came closer to a nuclear war during October 1962 than it had before or has since. Furious negotiations followed the imposition of the quarantine, and on October 28 Nikita Khrushchev, the leader of the Soviet Union, announced that he had agreed to remove Soviet missiles from Cuba, ending the crisis. In return, the United States promised not to invade the island. US missiles in Turkey, another issue, were subsequently removed.

Two years later, the United States would become embroiled in the Vietnam War. It would occupy the United States, at a minimum, for eight and a half years – from the Gulf of Tonkin Resolution passed in August 1964 until the Paris Peace Accords were signed in January 1973. This conflict is discussed in detail in Chapter 9. The substantial costs of the Vietnam War – the loss of life, the economic costs, and the

[7] Hufbauer, Elliott, and Schott (1990) describe many historical examples of sanctions, including the US embargo of trade with Cuba, and the difficulties encountered in making such sanctions effective.

[8] Considerable material on the Cuban Missile Crisis is available on the website of the Bulletin of the Atomic Scientists: http://thebulletin.org.

social costs in the form of the polarization of political life – reduced support in the United States for the policy of containing Communism. Some successful efforts were made to reach agreements on nuclear arms, to supply the Soviet Union with wheat, and to open trade with mainland China.[9] Together, these and other attempts to improve relations with the Communist powers were known as détente, a term popularized by Richard Nixon's Secretary of State, Henry Kissinger.

The final conflict took place in Afghanistan.[10] In 1979 the Soviet Union sent its forces into that country in order to shore up a Communist regime already established there. This was a full-scale military deployment involving air and armored ground forces, perhaps 100,000 troops in all. At first the Soviets were successful when opposition forces attempted to fight conventional battles. But soon the opposition, known as the Mujahidin, developed effective guerilla tactics. The Soviets were able to assert control over major cities and roadways, and could temporarily assert control over any particular target they chose, but they could not maintain effective control over the countryside. As was often noted, the Afghan war turned out to be the Soviet Union's Vietnam: the war they could not win despite control of the air and a vast advantage in firepower on the ground. In 1989, after suffering 25,000 deaths and numerous casualties, worn out by the seemingly endless effort to prop up their Afghan allies, the Soviet Union withdrew. The United States had aided the Mujahidin directly by supplying them with arms – as had other, mainly Islamic, governments and private individuals such as Osama Bin Laden – and indirectly by imposing an embargo on the sale of wheat to the Soviet Union. The latter, although it imposed some costs on the Soviets, was more symbolic than real because the Soviets were able to turn to other suppliers.

The end of the Cold War came soon after the Soviet withdrawal from Afghanistan. Throughout the Communist world there was a rising chorus of demands for political and economic liberalization. The response differed from country to country depending on the flexibility

[9] At the time when trade with China opened, the idea that the country would become a major trading partner of the United States was widely ridiculed. China simply did not produce anything Americans wanted to buy.

[10] There is a large literature describing the Soviet invasion of Afghanistan. Three sources I found helpful are Bradsher (1999), Maley (2009), and Russia Federation *et al.* (2002).

of the Communists in power. Two iconic events occurred on June 4, 1989, in Poland Solidarity, the reform labor union and political party, won an overwhelming victory for contestable seats in the Polish parliament, the beginning of the end of Communist rule in the country, but in Tiananmen Square in Beijing, Chinese protesters were pushed out by tanks. Poland would follow the path of democratic capitalism, while in China the Communist Party would maintain political control while allowing a vigorous free market economy to emerge. On November 9, the Berlin Wall fell, marking the beginning of the end of one of the most rigid Communist regimes.[11] The Cold War was over. It was, as we will see, enormously costly. But it could have been far more costly. It could have ended in a nuclear war.

The cost of the Cold War

Figure 8.1 shows the cost of the Cold War. The continuous line without markers shows US military and international spending as a share of GDP from 1947 to 2001. I added international spending to what is normally counted as defense spending – the cost of munitions and the wages of military personnel – because the greater part of foreign aid during the Cold War was motivated by the goal of containing Communism. Some spending in this category was for other purposes, so there might be a small overestimate from this source. Spending on international affairs, however, was a small item compared with defense spending: over the whole period 1947–91 international spending averaged only about 10 percent of defense spending. If we exclude the immediate post-World War II years, when international spending was unusually high and motivated partly by a desire to aid reconstruction in America's allies in western Europe, the average was somewhat lower, about 7 percent. There were, moreover, other areas of the federal budget that contained military spending that are not included here. Some expenditures on nuclear weapons research were recorded under the Department of Energy and veterans' benefits fell under the expenditures of the Department of Health and Human Services. The expenditures of the Central Intelligence Agency

[11] The demolishing of the Berlin Wall took place over a period of time, but November 9 is usually taken as the key date, the time when the eventual removal of the wall became inevitable.

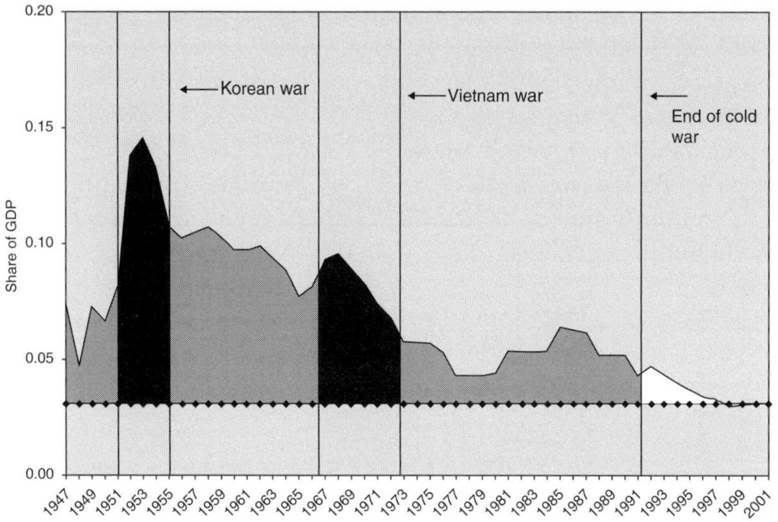

Figure 8.1 US spending on defense and international affairs, 1947–2001, as a share of GDP. Defense consumed a significant share of the United States, resources in the post-World War II era, even when the nation was at peace. *Source: Economic Report of the President* (2010, table B-80).

were hidden somewhere in the budget. There were also other Cold War-related costs, such as the implicit taxation of draftees. Nevertheless, the data plotted in Figure 8.1 probably cover most of the costs of the Cold War, and are likely, if anything, to be an underestimate by a small margin.

The line in Figure 8.1 marked with diamonds shows the average from 1997 to 2001. This is a period that begins five years after the end of the Cold War and can be taken to represent the post-Cold War equilibrium. The difference between actual expenditures and this peacetime norm can be taken to be a measure, albeit a crude measure, of the resource cost to the United States of the wars, hot and cold, against Communism. In Figure 8.1 the Korean and Vietnam wars are filled with a darker shade of gray. The remaining area, filled with a lighter shade of gray, is a measure of the cost of the Cold War. The last, unshaded part shows spending after the fall of Communism and the end of the Cold War. It includes some elevated levels of spending during the transition to the post-Communist norm, and so the lightly shaded area is a lower bound estimate of the total cost of the Cold War.

Table 8.1 *A comparative view of the cost of the Cold War*

War	Years	Cost before veterans' benefits ($ billion in 2008 dollars)	Cost before veterans' benefits as a percentage of average GDP during the war
World War II	1939–47	3,291	185.3
Korean War	1950–5	1,186	48.2
Cold War	1948–9, 1955–64, 1975–90	5,193	99.7
Vietnam War	1967–74	1,697	35.2
War against Communism	1948–90	8,076	169.9

Source: Appendix 3.

One can disagree about what proportion of war-related expenditures during the Korean and Vietnam wars should be attributed to those wars and what proportion to the ongoing costs of the Cold War. Should we include only the incremental costs of Korea and Vietnam or all military spending in these years? As indicated in previous chapters, there is no one right answer. From a short-run perspective, it makes sense to look at the incremental costs of the Korean and Vietnam wars. From a longer-run perspective, when the question is how much it costs to have a military prepared to go to war with Communist powers, including some or all of the baseline costs of the Cold War in the costs of the hot wars is more appropriate.

Even if one excludes all military spending in the hot wars from consideration and the elevated spending during the transition to the post-Cold War norm, the Cold War (the lightly shaded area) was extremely costly in terms of resources employed. In fact, as shown in Table 8.1 the total resource cost of the Cold War measured in 2008 dollars, $5,193 billion, exceeded the resource cost of World War II: the Cold War, by this measure, was the most costly war in US history. However, if we turn to a measure of effort, military spending measured as a share of GDP, we find the Cold War was not as expensive as World War II; World War II used 185.2 percent of one year's GDP, the Cold War 99.7 percent. If we look at the War against Communism, thus encompassing both the Cold War and the hot wars in Korea and Vietnam, we find that the total cost in 2008 dollars far exceeded the cost of World War II. The enormous cost of the War against Communism was also felt in the Soviet Union – which attempted to match the United States – and in some of the allies of each of these two opposing powers.

9 *The Vietnam War*

Whereas naval units of the Communist regime in Vietnam, in violation of the principles of the Charter of the United Nations and of international law, have deliberately and repeatedly attacked United States naval vessels lawfully present in international waters, ... and ...

Whereas these attacks are part of a deliberate and systematic campaign of aggression that the Communist regime in North Vietnam has been waging against its neighbors and the nations joined with them in collective defense of their freedom; and ...

Resolved by the Senate and House of Representatives of the United States of America in Congress assembled, That the Congress approves and supports the determination of the President, as Commander in Chief, to take all necessary measures to repel any armed attack against the forces of the United States and to prevent further aggression.

Excerpts from the "Gulf of Tonkin Resolution," August 10, 1964

A chronology of the Vietnam War

1945		
September	2	Ho Chi Minh declares independence for Vietnam.
1954		
March 13–May 7		The Battle of Dien Bien Phu.
May 8–July 21		The postwar fate of Vietnam is determined at a conference at Geneva: Vietnam will be temporarily divided in two parts and an election will be held to determine the final form of government.
1961		
January	20	John F. Kennedy sworn in as President of the United States.
1962		
April	10	US Steel announces a price increase of $6 per ton.

	13	The US Steel price increase is rescinded as a result of strong opposition from the Kennedy administration.
1963		
May	8	Buddhist protests in South Vietnam.
August	28	The Reverend Martin Luther King Jr. leads the "March on Washington for Jobs and Freedom."
November	2	President Ngo Dinh Diem of South Vietnam is assassinated.
	22	President John F. Kennedy is assassinated.
1964		
January	8	President Johnson declares a "War on Poverty."
February	26	Kennedy–Johnson tax cut.
August	10	Gulf of Tonkin Resolution authorizing President Johnson to use force against North Vietnam is signed by President Johnson.
1965		
July	30	Medicare is signed into law.
October	16	Anti-war rallies are held in American cities.
November	27	Thousands of anti-war protesters march in Washington, DC.
December	12	The Federal Reserve raises its discount rate to 4.50 percent.
1966		
May	11–16	University students stage "sit-ins" to protest the war and the draft.
	15	An estimated 15,000 people march in Washington to protest the war.
1967		
January	10	President Johnson calls for a 6 percent income tax surcharge in his State of the Union message.
April	15	Large anti-war marches are held in New York and San Francisco.

	28	Muhammad Ali refuses to serve in the armed forces.
May	13	A large march supporting the war is held in New York City.
August	3	President Johnson calls for a 10 percent tax surcharge.
November	30	Senator Eugene McCarthy, an anti-war Democrat, announces that he will run for President.
1968		
January	31	The Tet Offensive begins.
March	12	Senator McCarthy wins 42 percent of the vote in the New Hampshire primary to Johnson's 49 percent.
	16	Senator Robert F. Kennedy announces he will run for President as an anti-war candidate.
	16	More than three hundred civilians are slaughtered in the village of My Lai, South Vietnam.
	31	President Johnson announces that he will not run for another term.
June	5	Senator Robert F. Kennedy is assassinated after winning the Democratic Primary in California.
	28	President Johnson signs a law imposing a 10 percent tax surcharge.
November	5	Richard Nixon defeats Democrat Hubert H. Humphrey for President.
1969		
January	20	Richard Nixon is sworn in as President.
March	27	President Nixon appoints an Advisory Commission on an All-Volunteer Armed Force.
August	4	Henry Kissinger and Le Duc Tho begin secret negotiations.

November	15	The largest anti-war protest of the Vietnam era is held in Washington, DC.
December	1	The draft is altered. Young men will be assigned numbers, based on their birthdays, which will be used in a lottery to decide who is drafted.
December	30	President Nixon signs the Tax Reform Act of 1969.
December		The business cycle reaches a peak.
1970		
February	20	The President's Advisory Commission on an All-Volunteer Armed Force recommends ending the draft.
March	18	The United States begins heavy bombing of Laos and Cambodia in order to interdict the movement of men and supplies from North Korea.
April	30	President Nixon announces the invasion of Cambodia.
May	4	Four students are killed and nine wounded by the Ohio National Guard at an anti-war rally at Kent State University.
November		The business cycle reaches a trough.
1971		
August	15	President Nixon announces a ninety-day freeze on wages and prices, and declares that the dollar will no longer be convertible into gold.
December	10	A tax cut is signed into law.
1973		
January	27	The Paris Peace Accords ending the American role in Vietnam are signed.
	27	Secretary of Defense Melvin Laird announces an end to the draft.
April	21	President Nguyen Van Thieu of South Vietnam resigns.

	29	American personnel are evacuated by helicopter from Saigon.
	30	Saigon falls to North Vietnamese and the Vietcong.
2000		
July	20	Ho Chi Minh City Security Trading Center (Stock Exchange) opens.

Sources: Linton (1975), Schlesinger and Bowman (1993), Morris and Morris (1996), other chronologies of American history, the *New York Times*, and *the Wall Street Journal.*

The Vietnam War proved to be one of the most controversial in American history. The closest precedent in the twentieth century was the Philippine–American War. In both wars Americans found themselves far from home attempting to defeat an enemy that often resorted to effective guerilla tactics. In both wars a strong anti-war movement developed, based on concerns about the costs of the war to the American people in terms of lives and resources, concerns about the costs being imposed on the countries where the US was fighting, in particular the civilian populations, and in some cases sympathy for the political goals of the people whom the US was fighting.

The origins of the war

America's involvement in Vietnam had deep historical roots. Chinese rule of Vietnam began before the Christian era, but Chinese rule was always a source of resentment and sometimes of active resistance. Finally, in 1426 under the legendary emperor Le Loi, the Vietnamese won their independence, a condition they sustained under his dynastic successors for four centuries. However, while united in their opposition to the Chinese, the Vietnamese became bitterly divided between the Trinh clan that held sway in the north and the Nguyen clan that was dominant in the central and southern parts of the country. Indeed, the conflict between North Vietnam and South Vietnam in which the United States became embroiled can be seen in part as a continuation of this ancient conflict. The French began entering Vietnam in the eighteenth century as missionaries and traders. In 1802, a date that is seen as a turning point in French involvement in Vietnam, Nguyen Ahn became emperor with the aid of French military advisors and troops. This would be the beginning of a series of interventions that took place over the course of the nineteenth century. Although often thwarted for a time by local resistance movements, the French, by relying on their superior military technology, including their navy, which was effective on Vietnam's long coast, gradually established full control. American expansionists in the 1890s could point to European control of far-flung colonies, including colonies in Asia such as Vietnam, as a reason why the United States had to join the game or be left behind – a reason why the United States needed an outpost in the Philippines.

Nguyen Tat Thanh, better known by his *nom de guerre* Ho Chi Minh (sometimes translated as "bringer of light"), was born in Vietnam in 1890. In 1911 he left Vietnam for a long sojourn that took him to France, the United States, the Soviet Union, and China among other countries. In 1941, Ho, now a convinced Communist, returned to Vietnam to organize the Communist Party and lead the resistance to the Japanese who were attempting to replace the French as colonial masters. The end of World War II, perhaps inevitably, brought a period of chaos to Vietnam. The Japanese had been defeated, but who would replace them: the French or the Vietnamese nationalists? The economy, moreover, was deranged: famine was widespread. In the midst of this chaos Ho Chi Minh announced Vietnam's independence on September 2, 1945.

The French were determined to regain control of Vietnam, and a long war ensued between their forces and those led by Ho Chi Minh. The climactic battle was Dien Bien Phu which was fought from March 13 to May 7, 1954. It was a major defeat for the French: not a small-scale ambush typical of guerilla wars, but rather a full-scale battle typical of a war between well-armed nation-states. More than eleven thousand French soldiers were taken prisoner. A peace conference was arranged in Geneva, which provided for the temporary division of Vietnam until elections could be held to determine the government of the nation as a whole. The Communists under Ho Chi Minh then began consolidating power in the North, while an American-backed regime under Ngo Dinh Diem began consolidating power in the South. The election to unify Vietnam was never held; neither side was interested in an election that they might lose.

Like most US wars, the war in Vietnam began, or more accurately accelerated, with an "incident" that could be used to rally US public support for the war. On August 4, 1964 North Vietnamese gunboats, President Lyndon Johnson said, attacked American ships in the Gulf of Tonkin. Three days later Congress authorized the President to use force against North Vietnam. The Gulf of Tonkin Resolution passed unanimously in the House, and only two senators voted against it: Wayne Morse, Democrat of Oregon, and Ernest Gruening, Democrat of Alaska. Many analysts now believe that the attack, or at least some of the attacks, never happened. The American ships may have been firing at mistaken radar sightings.

Robert McNamara, who had been appointed Secretary of Defense in January 1961 by President Kennedy, was the architect of the buildup in Vietnam. When Kennedy appointed him, he was forty-four years old and the President of Ford Motor Company. He had been an analyst for the air force in World War II, but had spent his postwar years in academia (Harvard Business School) and at Ford. McNamara had a reputation for brilliance. Kennedy is said to have called him the smartest man he had ever met (McNamara obituary, *New York Times*, July 7, 2009, A20). McNamara's original mission at the Pentagon was to reduce costs. He sent teams of civilian "whiz kids" through the Defense Department bureaucracy looking for waste to cut. Inevitably, however, the war in Vietnam would bring rising expenditures.

The rapid buildup in 1965 and 1966, and the resultant costs in terms of lives and dollars, produced a vibrant anti-war movement. Led initially by students and religious leaders, most prominently Martin Luther King Jr., the movement grew with American involvement in the war. Eventually, even McNamara became convinced of the war's futility. In May 1967 he sent a long memo to Johnson urging him to negotiate an end to the war. But Johnson was determined to see the war to a successful conclusion. In November 1967 McNamara announced that he was moving on to became President of the World Bank. The anti-war movement continued to grow, spurred by the use of mass aerial bombing against North Vietnam and by the Tet Offensive, a series of attacks by Communist forces throughout South Vietnam in January and February 1968, which undermined public confidence in the US war effort. On March 12, 1968 Senator Eugene McCarthy of Minnesota, running on an anti-war platform, made an outstanding showing in the New Hampshire Democratic primary. On March 16, Robert F. Kennedy, the charismatic senator from New York, announced his candidacy for the Democratic nomination also on an anti-war platform. On March 31, Johnson announced that he would not seek reelection. His vice president, Hubert H. Humphrey, then took up the quest for the nomination, running in support of Johnson's war policy. It was a tumultuous primary campaign marked by the assassination of Senator Kennedy after his victory in the California primary, and by anti-war protests at the Democratic National Convention in Chicago. In the end, Humphrey was nominated, but narrowly defeated by Republican Richard Nixon in the general election.

The Vietnam War continued under President Nixon, as did the anti-war movement. The largest anti-war protest of the era was held on November 15, 1969 when, it is estimated, some 250,000 people descended on Washington, DC to protest the war. In March 1970 Nixon launched a campaign of intense bombing in Laos and Cambodia in order to try to stop men and supplies from North Vietnam from reaching South Vietnam. In general, Nixon followed a three-part strategy to extricate the United States without losing face, or as he put it, to achieve "peace with honor": (1) bombing, (2) Vietnamization – replacing US troops with South Vietnamese troops, and (3) negotiations with North Vietnam. Secret negotiations between Henry Kissinger for the United States and Le Duc Tho for North Vietnam began on August 4, 1969.

The agreement to end the war was finally reached on January 27, 1973, when Kissinger and Le Duc Tho signed the Paris Peace Accords. The main provision was that the United States and its allies would begin an immediate withdrawal of their troops from Vietnam. In return the North Vietnamese and Vietcong committed themselves to a reunification through peaceful elections. Once American and allied forces left, the war was renewed. The North Vietnamese and Vietcong then gradually reduced the area controlled (or partially controlled) by the South Vietnamese to Saigon and its environs. Possibly the United States would have reacted more vigorously to the North Vietnamese violations of the treaty if it had not been for the multitude of unprecedented challenges it faced in other arenas: the Yom Kippur War, ongoing negotiations with the Soviet Union, and most importantly, the final acts of the Watergate affair. But then again, the American people had grown tired of the war, and they might have permitted the fall of Saigon even without the distractions.

The end for the Saigon government came in the spring of 1975. On April 21 President Nguyen Van Thieu of South Vietnam resigned.

On April 29 American personnel were evacuated by helicopter from the roof of the American embassy in Saigon. On April 30 the city fell to the North Vietnamese and their Vietcong allies.

Financing the war

Prior to the Vietnam War, inflation had been the result of major wars: the Revolution, the War of 1812, the Civil War, World War I, and World War II. The smaller foreign wars – the Mexican War, the Spanish–American War, the Philippine–American War, and the Korean War – had not produced much inflation, and with a few exceptions, peacetime had been free of inflation.[1] But during the 1960s and 1970s the United States experienced a substantial inflation. The "Great Inflation" was not confined to the era of the Vietnam War. It lasted almost two decades. From 1962 to 1980, prices (the GDP deflator) rose about 5.11 percent per year.

The Vietnam War, clearly, was not the only cause of the Great Inflation, but it was a contributing factor, especially important for the takeoff of inflation. The path of the Great Inflation is shown in Figure 9.1 which plots the annual percentage change in the consumer price and producer price indexes. It shows that the Great Inflation occurred in three waves of growing magnitude (to judge from the consumer price index): from 1967 to 1970, from 1972 to 1974, and from 1976 to 1980. The first wave was closely tied to the Vietnam War, which influenced the direction of fiscal, monetary, and price and wage policies.

Fiscal policy

When John F. Kennedy took office in 1961 the economy, at least as far as President Kennedy and his economic advisors were concerned, was in the doldrums. A contraction had begun in April 1960 (according to the National Bureau of Economic Research chronology) and the rate

[1] There had been several mild peacetime inflations. From 1833 to 1836 prices (the GDP deflator) rose about 4.25 percent per year as a result of an influx of silver from Mexico, a period known as the "Jacksonian inflation." From 1851 to 1855 prices rose about 4.09 percent per year as a result of the discoveries of gold in California and Australia. From 1897 to 1913 prices rose about 2.15 percent per year as a result of the discoveries of gold in South Africa and other parts of the world.

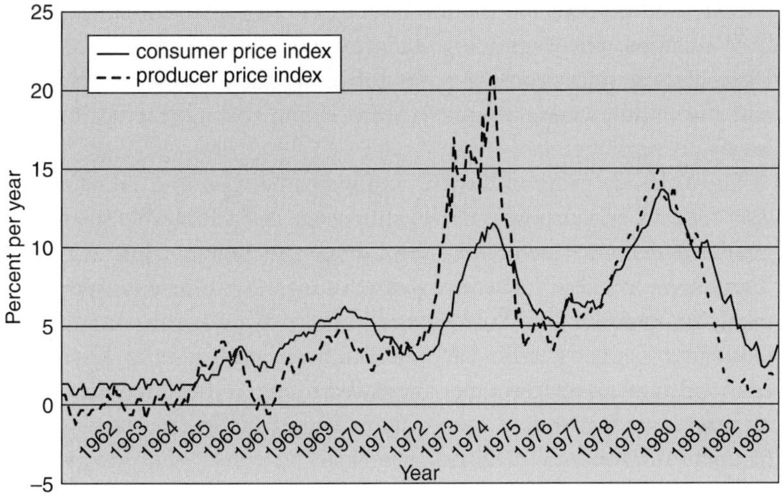

Figure 9.1 The annual percentage changes in the consumer price index and in the producer price index, monthly, January 1961–December 1983. The figure shows the change in the natural logarithm of the price index in a particular month from the same month in the previous year, expressed in percent: a fever chart of inflation. The Great Inflation began in the late 1960s and occurred in three waves of increasing magnitude.
Source: The Department of Labor, Bureau of Labor Statistics.

of unemployment stood at 6.6 percent. The right medicine, according to Kennedy's economic advisors, was a strong dose of fiscal stimulus in the form of increased spending or tax reductions and an accommodating monetary policy. This was Keynesian economics, the "New Economics" as the media was to style it (for example, *New York Times*, January 29, 1965, 28). Pushing the economy to a lower rate of unemployment might, it was true, raise the rate of inflation. But the tradeoff, known as the Phillips Curve after economist A. W. Phillips, a New Zealander, was permanent: a permanently lower rate of unemployment implied a permanently higher, but not rising, rate of inflation. And in the circumstances then prevailing the Kennedy economists were certain they knew which way the economy *should* be moved. If the rate of unemployment could be permanently lowered from 6.6 percent to, say, 4.0 percent at the cost of raising the rate of inflation, which then stood at 1.4 percent, to, say, a permanent 3 percent per year, surely that was worthwhile given the much greater social cost of high unemployment. Republicans, as the Kennedy people saw it, protected the interests of the rich and chose a point of high unemployment and low inflation on the Phillips Curve. The Democrats would choose a point reflecting the interests of the poor and the middle class, a point corresponding to higher inflation and lower unemployment.

The Kennedy program began with increased spending. Some of this was for civilian purposes. For example, the Area Redevelopment Act provided loans for economic development in regions suffering from high unemployment.[2] There was also an increase in defense spending, partly in response to a Soviet threat to turn West Berlin over to East Germany. Kennedy, who had not yet been won over to Keynesian economics, wanted to finance increased military spending with a tax increase, but was talked out of it by Walter Heller, the chair of the Council of Economic Advisors from 1961 to 1964, who thought that a tax increase would slow the recovery (Campagna 1987, 283). Eventually Kennedy was persuaded that the Keynesian diagnosis was right and he supported a major tax cut. His bill was reported out of the House in October 1963, but not passed by the Senate until February 16, 1964, after his assassination. It was the most important piece of tax legislation since World War II. Both personal and corporate income taxes were reduced. The cut in individual taxes was about 20 percent, and marginal tax rates, which had ranged from 20 percent to 91 percent, were cut in stages to a range of 14 to 70 percent (Campagna 1987, 307).

Unemployment fell over the next few years and Keynesian economists celebrated the effects of the tax cut. Heller, an academic economist from the University of Minnesota, had quickly become the leading figure among the economists advising the Kennedy and Johnson administrations. On June 8, 1962 his picture appeared on the cover of *Time* magazine (his second appearance on the cover) because of his advocacy of the tax cut. In an article published in 1965 Heller confidently summarized the Kennedy and Johnson administrations' successful management of the economy: "in the four years since 1960 we have seen . . . that with a proper mix of consumption and investment stimulus an expansionary fiscal policy can move us toward full employment and faster growth and at the same time further the ends of price stability and payments equilibrium" (Heller 1965, 235).

[2] The program was administered by the agency now known as the Economic Development Administration.

Lyndon Johnson's success in pushing the tax cut through the Senate was followed by a series of liberal spending initiatives, collectively known as the Great Society program. These included aid for Appalachia, federal education grants, and most important in terms of spending, Medicare. But just as the Keynesian economists were basking in the glow of the tax cut, and liberal politicians were basking in the glow of the Great Society, America's involvement in Vietnam escalated. The Gulf of Tonkin Resolution, authorizing President Johnson to use force, passed Congress in August 1964, just six months after the tax cut.

When the war began in earnest there were, of course, estimates of how costly it would be. Robert McNamara, the Secretary of Defense, put the cost of the war for fiscal 1967 at $10 billion, probably a deliberate underestimate designed to allay fears about the expansion of the war and discourage attempts to roll back the Great Society programs (Campagna 1987, 318; Meltzer 2009, 448–52). The Council of Economic Advisors, now chaired by Gardner Ackley from the University of Michigan, recommended a quick across-the-board tax increase to finance the war and keep inflation under control.[3] But President Johnson demurred. Across-the-board tax increases, as President Johnson knew from his long experience in politics – indeed as Adam Smith had explained in the *Wealth of Nations* – would undermine support for his war and his domestic policies. The best that could be done was a few, (hopefully) hidden tax increases: excise taxes on transportation and telephone services were restored by the Tax Adjustment Act of 1966 (Campagna 1987, 319; Meltzer 2009, 288).

As economists of every stripe quickly realized, the politics of Keynesianism was not as smoothly symmetric as its economics. Keynesian economics called for tax cuts and spending increases when the economy was in the doldrums, and for tax increases and spending cuts when the economy was overheating. The first part, the tax cuts and spending increases, were wildly popular and could sail through Congress; the tax increases and spending cuts were a hard sell.

However, continuing inflation – despite a temporary drop caused by restrictive monetary policies put into place by the Federal Reserve in 1966 (Meltzer 2009, 499–512) – persuaded Johnson to support an

[3] The popular Heller had resigned, although it is unclear whether the growing distance between the Council and President Johnson had played a role. According to his obituary in the *New York Times* (June 17, 1987) he resigned for personal financial reasons.

increase in taxes. His budget for fiscal 1968, submitted in January 1967, called for a 6 percent "surcharge" on individual and corporate income taxes. The term "surcharge" was used, as it had been in the past, to suggest that this would not be a permanent part of the tax system, but rather a temporary addition that would end with the war. But the proposal fell on deaf ears in Congress. In August 1967 Johnson renewed his call for a tax surcharge, this time calling for an additional 10 percent tax on individual and corporate incomes. Finally, in June 1968 Congress passed a tax increase. Although nominally a 10 percent tax, the rate, in fact, was lower because tax would apply to only half of the tax year 1968 and half of 1969 – it would expire on June 30, 1969. Nevertheless, it was the largest single tax increase since World War II, exceeding each of the three increases levied during the Korean War (Bank, Stark, and Thorndike 2008, 136).

Johnson might have won support for a tax increase earlier, and perhaps for a larger increase, had he promoted it simply as a "war tax." Wilbur Mills, the chair of the House Ways and Means Committee, suggested that if the surtax proposal were labeled a "war tax" it would "meet few obstacles in Congress." But Johnson was unwilling to admit that he had taken the nation into a full-scale war because it would undermine support for his Great Society programs. How could the nation be expected to increase spending on domestic programs if the nation was at war? Johnson therefore attempted to sell the tax increase as a purely economic measure, and so it took longer to get the measure through Congress, and he obtained less than he asked for. Usually, we see administrations attempting to hide the cost of war to maximize support for the war; in this case, ironically, there was support for a war tax, but the administration wanted to hide the cost of war to maintain support for domestic programs.

The surtax, at least as finally passed, was insufficient to stem the inflationary tide, which, as shown in Figure 9.1, surged upward again. In part the failure of the surtax to have a substantial effect was a result of it being explicitly a temporary increase. To be sure, economists are divided on whether a temporary increase in taxes is likely to have more or less of an impact than a permanent increase. But a majority, I believe, would be likely to agree that the explicit deadline for ending the tax reduced its effectiveness. Milton Friedman (1957), who started this debate, and whose theory still holds considerable sway among economists, argued that a temporary increase in taxes would have less effect on consumption than a permanent increase because people faced with a temporary increase would simply maintain their current consumption by reducing savings. A professor whose income falls because he has been awarded a sabbatical leave at a reduced salary is not as likely to reduce his consumption as a professor whose income falls because he retires.

Johnson, facing the uprising of anti-war sentiment in his own party described above, chose not to run for President in 1968. Richard Nixon was sworn in as President in January 1969 and in March called for an extension of the surtax to fight inflation. Congressional Democrats responded by demanding a set of tax reforms as the price for extending the surtax. Eventually, a compromise was reached. Nixon signed the Tax Reform Act of 1969 on December 31. And in a separate bill the surtax was extended for six months at 10 percent and for another six months at 5 percent – again a temporary extension unlikely to have a major effect on spending. The Tax Reform Act incorporated a number of changes in the tax code, some of which enhanced revenues, but others, such as an increase in the standard deduction, reduced revenues. There is a wide margin of error around any estimate of the effects of a complex tax measure, but the consensus is that overall the Tax Reform Act reduced taxes, a tax reduction in time of war. Much later President George W. Bush would be criticized for cutting taxes during the Iraq War. Ironically, the Tax Reform Act of 1969, a liberal Democratic initiative, was a precedent. In defense of the Tax Reform Act one could say that its purpose was fairness, even if the effect was to reduce taxes, and one could add that had the extension of the surtax been in the same act as the reforms, the net effect would have been to increase revenues (Bank, Stark, and Thorndike 2008, 140). There were no further attempts following the expiration of the surtax to renew it or to introduce other tax increases during the remainder of the Vietnam War. Indeed, in December 1971 another tax cut was put in place to stimulate the economy during a recession, even as the war in Vietnam continued.

Monetary policy

Monetary policy was considered to be of secondary importance by the New Economics: a supplement to the main instrument, fiscal policy. Basic interest rates, the Keynesian economists believed, were sticky.

In the extreme case, a "liquidity trap," monetary policy would have no effect on interest rates. Interest rate changes, moreover, could influence the economy only by influencing investment spending, and research had shown that the effect was small. Thus, monetary policy was weak medicine. Nevertheless, it was clear how monetary policy should be used during the first phase of the Kennedy–Johnson administration. Monetary policy should focus on reinforcing the tax cuts by keeping interest rates low and thus increasing investment to the limited extent possible.

In principle the Federal Reserve was independent of the executive branch, and it need not have followed the administration's lead, but as Mr. Dooley might have said, "the Federal Reserve reads the lection returns." The Federal Reserve made an effort to fall in line with the New Economics with "Operation Twist:" it would sell short-term securities and buy long-term securities. The idea was to "twist" the yield curve, the relationship between yields on bonds and their term to maturity. Higher short-term rates (the other side of lower prices for short-term securities) would encourage foreigners to hang on to their dollar accounts, while lower long-term rates would encourage US businesses to invest. Some debate occurred among economists about whether Operation Twist succeeded in influencing the term structure. But there was considerable skepticism (Ross 1966; Holland 1969), and as far as I am aware no one found very large effects. Of more importance to the Great Inflation was the steady increase in the monetary base (bank reserves and currency held by the public) that began in late 1961, which produced a steady increase in the stock of money. From that point on the monetary base would rise continuously for the remainder of the decade.

What was behind the relentless rise in the monetary base? Part of the explanation was simply the need to finance government deficits. The federal budget would be in deficit throughout much of the 1960s and the Federal Reserve was poised to purchase some of that debt. Another part of the explanation, especially relevant in the first half of the 1960s, was the consensus among policymakers inside and outside the Federal Reserve that the Federal Reserve should be helping to reduce unemployment. The Federal Reserve discount rate, the rate at which banks could borrow from the Federal Reserve, which was then considered to be a key indicator and instrument of monetary policy, was lowered from 3.50 percent to 3.00 percent in August 1960, shortly before the presidential election. It was held at that level until July of 1963 when it was raised to 3.50 percent.

Policy errors also contributed to the start of the Great Inflation (Meltzer 2003, 538–56, and *passim*). William McChesney Martin, the chairman of the Federal Reserve – his time as chair, from 1951 to 1970, would be the longest in the history of the Federal Reserve, slightly exceeding the tenure of Alan Greenspan – was not averse to fighting inflation. He famously remarked that the role of the Federal Reserve was "to take away the punch bowl just when the party was getting going." And beginning in 1963 the Federal Reserve began raising its bellwether discount rate in recognition of the threat from inflation. In December 1965 the rate was raised to 4.50 percent, a new record, and Martin was summoned to President Johnson's Texas ranch to hear Johnson's objections to higher rates. Martin emerged to say that neither man had changed his mind. The rate was lowered to 4.00 percent in March 1966, but soon it was being increased once again. So the Federal Reserve was responding to inflation, but perhaps not enough. For one thing it probably overestimated the drag on the economy from the surtax. But there were also longer-run problems in the way the Federal Reserve approached monetary policy. Today we would see an increase in the discount rate that was matched by an increase in the rate of inflation as a policy that represented little real change in the stance of monetary policy, but not so then. At that time the distinction between real and nominal interest rates was not well understood. Almost no attention was paid, moreover, to monetary aggregates such as the monetary base or the stock of money, both of which were rising rapidly. The upshot was that the increases in the discount rate being undertaken in the late 1960s were seen as more powerful anti-inflation measures than they really were.

Price and wage policy

There was a third string to the Keynesian bow: direct controls over wages and prices. Aggregate demand increases were unlikely, in the Keynesian view, to cause inflation before the economy had reached full employment. But there were other sources of inflation. Powerful unions could push up wages even in slack markets for labor, which in turn would produce higher prices (cost-push inflation), and powerful corporations could push up prices even in slack markets for final products (administered inflation). The two together, powerful unions negotiating with powerful corporations, was a formula for inflation. It was important, therefore, to take direct measures to rein in these forms of inflation, which could prevent the economy from reaching the best combination of unemployment and inflation.

Free market economists, led by Milton Friedman, argued that the idea of cost-push or administered inflation was flawed. Firms that maximized profits and unions that maximized some combination of wages and employment wouldn't choose to gradually exploit their market power, thus producing steadily rising prices. Instead they would use their market power as soon as it was won to raise their prices or wages as much as necessary to achieve their long-run goals. Continuing increases in wages and prices were produced by rising aggregate demand. But the Council of Economic Advisors under Walter Heller, and leading Keynesian economists such as Paul Samuelson, Robert Solow, and John Kenneth Galbraith, contended that federal guidelines for acceptable wage and price increases were an important supplement to the fiscal and monetary policies.[4] Galbraith, in particular, was influenced by his favorable memory of what price controls had achieved in World War II.

The Council didn't call for legally binding wage and price controls similar to those imposed during World War II and the Korean War. Perhaps the lack of consensus supporting the war made extreme measures politically untenable. Instead it suggested something much less disturbing to ordinary business practice: norms of good price and wage behavior to be enforced by the desire of business and labor leaders to be seen as good citizens. Indeed, Walter Heller told the journalist William Safire that he chose the term "guideposts" for use in the Council's reports because it sounded less constricting than guidelines (Safire 2008, 297). A guidepost is something you come across from time to time; guidelines are always with you. It was "guidelines," however, that came to be accepted by the press and the public. The Council first laid out its guidelines in its 1962 report (*Economic Report of the President* 1962, 185–90). Wage increases should be limited by the trend increase in productivity (which was

[4] A volume of essays edited by George P. Shultz and Robert Z. Aliber (1966) contains essays by Friedman, Solow, and other leading economists debating the costs and benefits of the wage–price guidelines.

then running about 3.2 percent per year). Firms in industries experiencing average labor productivity increases should keep their prices constant, but firms experiencing slower growth were entitled to raise their prices, and firms in industries experiencing above average increases in labor productivity should lower their prices. The result would be steadily rising nominal wages, steadily rising real wages, and stable prices.[5]

Despite the unthreatening discussion of the guidelines in the Council's annual reports, it was always clear that stronger measures could be used. In April 1962 President Kennedy had a brief but bitter confrontation with the steel industry. On April 10, US Steel announced an increase of $6 per ton on its basic steel. This came after the administration had been involved in labor negotiations in the industry. The administration thought that it had been promised that prices would be kept steady, and it felt betrayed. President Kennedy immediately demanded that the increase be rescinded, and on April 13 it was: Inland Steel announced its decision not to raise prices and soon the rest of the industry, including US Steel, fell in line. For the most part the President relied on the bully pulpit during the crisis – the Council said the "President expressed the country's concern over the serious threat to price stability and our balance of payments" (*Economic Report of the President* 1963, 87) – but there were also threats, the most important being prosecution under the anti-trust laws.

The next few *Economic Reports* reaffirmed the guidelines and argued that they had contributed to the strong macroeconomic performance of the economy. By 1966, however, the Council was beginning to notice exceptions to guidelines and, seemingly, endorsed more vigorous responses by the government to violations (*Economic Report of the President* 1966, 78–93). In the 1967 *Report* the Council

[5] A basic principle of economics is that the real wage should equal the marginal product of labor. And under certain assumptions, for example a Cobb–Douglas production function, that means that the real wage will be a linear function of the average productivity of labor. Let W = the wage rate, P = the price level, Q = the amount output, L = the amount of labor, and α = the share of labor in the value of output. Then the real wage $W/P = \alpha(Q/L)$. In terms of constant percentage changes, $W\% - P\% = Q\% - L\%$. For prices to remain stable, $P\% = 0$, and for equilibrium to remain in the labor market, then $W\% = Q\% - L\%$. This formula also implies, as leftist critics of the policy pointed out, that the share of labor in total income would remain constant.

acknowledged that the guidelines were being violated regularly (*Economic Report of the President* 1966, 124) and documented the steps that it had taken to enforce them. By 1968 the Council was acknowledging that its guidelines were regularly ignored (*Economic Report of the President* 1968, 125). The conversation among liberal economists was turning to mandatory forms of "incomes policies" to restrain inflation.

The "New Economics," although rooted in Keynesian economic theory, was, truth to tell, wartime economics, or more exactly, world war economics: deficit spending, cheap money, and wage and price controls to contain inflationary pressures. Of course, adaptations had to be made to peacetime. Spending would be for public works and poverty programs as well as munitions and the wages of military personnel. Price and wage guidelines based on (hoped for) voluntary compliance would be used rather than binding legal constraints. The proof that war economics worked, namely, the then recent experiences of World War II and the Korean War, appeared irrefutable to a generation of Keynesian economists.

Which contributed more to the inflation: the escalation of the war in Vietnam or the new domestic spending initiatives? The spending figures suggest that both contributed but that the war was more important. Between 1960 and 1968 total government spending increased from $92 billion to $178 billion, an increase of 66 percent. Of this increase, 42 percent was the result of civilian spending – new programs and increased spending on existing programs – and 58 percent the result of increased military and international affairs spending.

The cost of the war

Vietnam was the fourth bloodiest war in American history, after the Civil War, World War I, and World War II. Some 47,415 Americans died in battle or of wounds sustained in battle; another 10,785 died of diseases and injuries; 58,200 in all (Appendix 2). Australia, New Zealand, the Philippines, and South Korea fought as allies of the United States, and suffered losses as well; South Korea lost more than 5,000 fighters. The losses for the Vietnamese, North and South, were catastrophic. The exact numbers will never be known with certainty. In 2009 the War Remnants Museum in Ho Chi Minh City put the losses for all of Vietnam at 1 million fighters and 2 million

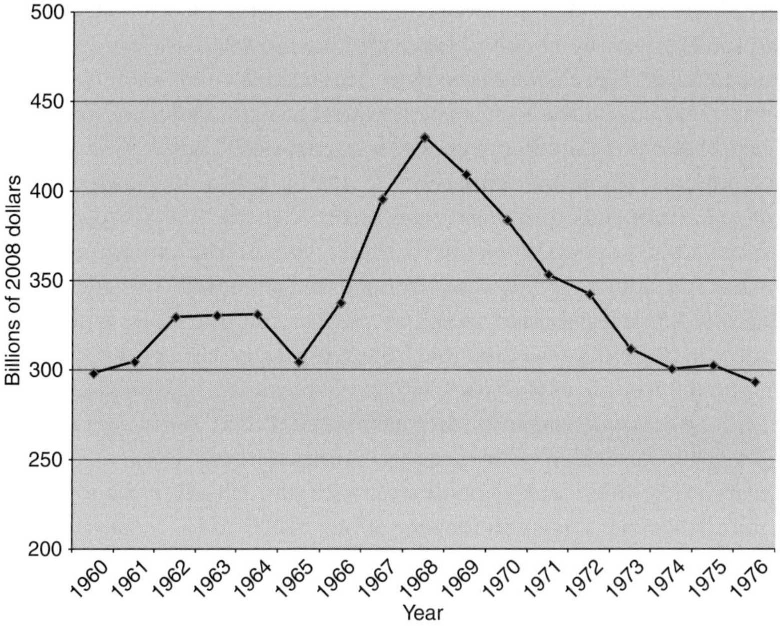

Figure 9.2 Real military expenditure, 1960–76. Military spending rose sharply in 1966 because of the Vietnam War and peaked in 1968.
Source: Economic Report of the President, 2010, Table B80.

civilians killed, 2 million fighters and civilians injured, and 300,000 missing.[6] There were more casualties in Laos and Cambodia as a result of the bombing campaigns.

What of military spending in the United States? Real military spending rose between 1966 and 1968 and then fell, returning to the 1965 level in 1974 (Figure 9.2). A good estimate of the marginal resource cost of the war would be the cumulative difference for the years 1966–73 between actual spending and baseline spending (say $302.8 billion in 2008 prices, the mean of 1965 and 1974 spending). This procedure produces an estimate of about $542 billion in year 2008 dollars, 11.6 percent of average real GDP during these years. This may not seem like a great deal; we are accustomed to think of 10 percent as the dividing line between significance and insignificance. The amount, however, is put in better perspective by comparing it with the growth of income over the period. Real GDP increased

[6] Notes taken by the author on a visit in January 2009.

by about $1,163 billion in year 2008 dollars between 1963 and 1973, so the war used up about 47 percent of the growth in the economy. As pointed out in previous cases, the marginal cost calculation is appropriate for answering some, but not all questions about the resource cost of the war. The Vietnam War was part of the larger War against Communism, and it is appropriate to attribute some of the fixed costs of military spending in those years to the Vietnam War, if we want to address the question of whether fighting wars to contain Communism made economic sense. The cumulative difference for the years 1967–74 between actual spending and baseline spending, where the latter is defined as the amount projected on the basis of the share of military spending in the post-Cold War era, was $1,697 billion in year 2008 dollars, 35 percent of average real GDP, and 165 percent of the growth in real GDP. The economy, in other words, grew during the years of the most intense fighting in Vietnam, but all of the increase, and then some, went into the war effort.

The balance of payments and the end of Bretton Woods

The Vietnam War contributed to another problem that plagued the United States during the 1960s: the deterioration in the balance of payments. Partly this was the result of the general fiscal and monetary effects of war spending described above. Rising prices in the United States, combined with a fixed exchange rate, meant that American goods and services were less attractive to foreigners, and it meant that foreign goods were increasingly attractive to American buyers. But the Vietnam War contributed in another and more direct way to the deterioration in the balance of payments: purchases had to be made abroad for transport, food, and other supplies and services that could not be brought from home. Although the balance of trade and services deteriorated during the 1960s, it was always positive. The problem was that the declining balance of trade and services was insufficient to offset the increased outflow of dollars produced by the war. According to a memo from budget director Charles Shultze to President Johnson, all of the increased outflow of dollars in 1966 and 1967 could be accounted for by spending in Southeast Asia on the war (Meltzer 2009, 700).

The classic remedy for curing a balance of payments problem is a restrictive monetary policy: higher interest rates and lower inflation would encourage foreigners to buy American goods and assets while discouraging Americans from purchasing foreign goods and assets. But the classic remedy was unavailable because American policymakers were committed to full employment. As Alan Meltzer (2009, 279) pointed out, the basic problem was that the US Congress had endorsed two policy goals – balance of payments at a fixed exchange rate and full employment – without recognizing that the two might be in conflict. As with the problem of inflation, an alternative approach to solving the balance of payments problem, as Keynesian economists saw it, lay in taxes, guidelines, and direct controls. The Kennedy and Johnson administrations adopted a number of such measures (Meltzer 2009, 418–20). For example, an "interest equalization" tax introduced in July 1963 made it more costly for Americans to invest in foreign securities. And in 1965 guidelines on direct foreign investment by American corporations were introduced. Economic historians have been doubtful about the effectiveness of these controls. Meltzer (2009, 420) concludes that "at most controls and restrictions may have given the United States more time to adopt a permanent program." A more permanent program, however, was not possible given the overriding goal of the administration of achieving full employment in the shortest time possible. Monetary and fiscal policies were not going to be diverted from the achievement of that goal in order to obtain a balance of payments at a particular exchange rate. Note that the interest equalization tax was adopted one month before Martin Luther King led the march in Washington, which was, as we sometimes forget, a march "for *Jobs* and Freedom." The trade balance would be attacked with specific trade-oriented policies, not with monetary and fiscal policies.

Other countries could have helped the United States solve its balance of payments problems, as was contemplated by the Bretton Woods agreement. One way was by allowing their price levels to rise. Higher foreign prices would increase sales of US goods, which would then be relatively cheaper compared with alternatives produced abroad, and they would also discourage Americans from purchasing goods abroad because the American-made alternative would then be relatively cheaper. Foreign governments could achieve something similar by revaluing their currencies in terms of dollars, that is, by making each unit of a foreign currency equal to more dollars (or since gold was still the intermediate good in these transactions, by raising the price of gold). Foreign central banks that were considering the conversion of some of their dollars into gold, as was their prerogative under the Bretton Woods agreement, could also decide to simply hold on to their new dollar reserves. The German and Japanese central banks were persuaded to do so, effectively ending free convertibility of dollars into gold (Meltzer 2009, 719), but other central banks were less accommodating. Part of the problem was surely the way in which policies intended to help the United States played at home in purely economic terms. Inflation and revaluation imposed costs on domestic groups who would object vehemently. But the Vietnam War also played a role. The war was highly unpopular abroad, and so was bailing out the United States as it suffered the consequences of what was widely regarded as immoral US imperialism (Meltzer 2009, 363).

Richard Nixon was inaugurated in January 1969. The balance of payments had continued to deteriorate and there was now considerable fear of a run on the dollar. The long economic expansion of the 1960s came to an end in December. The recession was brief, ending in November 1970, and partly as a result of the recession, the rate of inflation began to decline. But the decline was gradual, and an inflation that seemed to be resistant to the normal ebb and flow of business activity remained a major public concern. Things came to a head in the summer of 1971. The balance of trade moved into the red, and internationally, frustration with the United States grew exponentially. Many nations were experiencing inflation and currency problems that were universally assumed to be emanating from the United States. In October 1969 Germany floated and then revalued its currency. In May 1971 seven European nations closed their foreign exchange markets. A number of central banks, moreover, exercised their right under the Bretton Woods agreements to convert their rapidly accumulating dollar reserves into gold. France had converted nearly $200 million into gold and in July 1971 Switzerland converted $50 million. These losses were part of a long-term trend. In 1957 the US stock of monetary gold had stood at $22.9 billion, not far below the postwar peak. But then the gold stock began to erode. By the end of 1970 it had fallen to $11.1 billion (Carter *et al.* 2006, series Cj1). Bretton Woods had envisioned an adjustment process for everyone other than the United States, but had paid little attention to what would happen if the American economy became an engine of inflation.

In the summer of 1971 President Nixon, who would soon face a new election, was suffering from a low standing in the opinion polls because of both the ongoing war in Vietnam and the inflation and related problems at home. Economists had floated various proposals for dealing with the balance of payments problem and the inflation. Some thought that the balance of payments could be addressed by adopting a "crawling peg" which would produce a slow and controlled devaluation of the dollar. Others, most notably Milton Friedman, proposed a flexible exchange rate determined exclusively by market forces.[7] Some wanted to control inflation through a "tax-based incomes policy" that would impose a tax on firms that raised their prices by more than a predetermined percentage; others favored formal wage and price controls. Still others favored relying on a restrictive monetary policy.

Eventually, President Nixon, on the advice, mainly, it is said, of his Treasury Secretary, John Connally (a conservative Democrat and former governor of Texas), decided to "go big." From Nixon's point of view it made perfect sense: a bold initiative might renew the economy and his flagging political fortunes. In August 1971 Nixon introduced his "New Economic Policy." It was a four-part plan. First, he "closed the gold window." The United States would no longer convert dollars held by foreign central banks into gold on demand. Second, he placed a temporary tariff on imported goods. Third, wages and prices would be frozen for ninety days. And fourth, he announced a number of tax increases and spending cuts. The narrative supporting these actions portrayed them as temporary measures that would relieve the symptoms while more fundamental reforms were put in place that would return the United States to price stability without controls, a dollar convertible at a fixed rate into gold, and balanced international trade. The price and wage controls were eventually lifted, although only after passing through a series of phases, and after four years, not ninety days. The fixed exchange rate system that had prevailed since the end of World War II, the Bretton Woods system, would never be revived. The system, I should be clear, did not disappear instantly when Nixon adopted his new policy. A commitment to some form of fixed exchange rates survived for another year and a half. In December 1971 the so-called Smithsonian Agreement (the conference was at the Smithsonian Institution in Washington)

[7] Friedman thought that the United States should adopt a flexible rate, even if other nations continued to intervene in currency markets.

was reached that continued fixed exchange rates with the leading currencies revaluing against the dollar. This system limped along through succeeding crises until March 1973 when the attempt to maintain fixed exchange rates was finally abandoned. As the monetary historian Anna J. Schwartz put it (1987, 350): "Market forces had triumphed." For better or worse, the Bretton Woods system, which had begun with the success of American arms in World War II, was undone, at least in part, by the failure of American arms in Vietnam.

The Vietnam War would drag on, as discussed above, until a final peace treaty was signed in January 1973. But President Nixon's policy of reducing the number of Americans on the ground in Vietnam and turning over the fighting to the South Vietnamese while increasing the bombing of North Vietnam and the supply routes to the south – "Vietnamizing" the war – made possible a decrease in the amount spent on it (Figure 9.2). The final round of inflation in the 1970s, which peaked in 1979 when the consumer price index rose at an annual rate of 12 percent, cannot be blamed on the Vietnam War. There were temporary factors involved such as oil and food price increases, declining productivity growth, and continued monetary expansion on the theory that monetary policy had to be aimed first and foremost at maintaining a low rate of unemployment. One can, however, also place some of the blame on war economics: the idea based on a reading of the US experience in World War II that by combining heavy doses of monetary and fiscal stimulation with wage and price controls the economy could be permanently maintained at the nirvana reached in 1943: unemployment and inflation both below 2 percent. The 1960s and 1970s were an extended lesson in why this was not possible.

It turns out, then, that the current international financial system is a byproduct of war. Before World War I the gold standard reigned supreme. The inflations of that war led to abandonment of the gold standard during the conflict. There were fitful attempts to restore it during the 1920s but these were largely discontinued in the 1930s. The inflations of World War II led to the abandonment of what was left of the old gold standard, and the attempt to establish a new system, the Bretton Woods system, that would produce some of the benefits of the gold standard, while avoiding the costs. International cooperation through agencies such as the International Monetary Fund and the World Bank was the byword of the day. The inflations of the Vietnam era led to the discontinuance of the Bretton Woods system and the establishment of a new international financial system based on flexible exchange rates.

The all-volunteer army

The Vietnam War led to the end of conscription. This was a return to the nineteenth-century norm. The United States had drafted soldiers in major wars, but relied on volunteers to fight smaller wars or to provide a peacetime force. Soldiers were drafted during the Revolutionary War and an attempt was made to establish a draft during the War of 1812, but it failed. Volunteers made up the expeditionary force that fought the Mexican War, many of them drawn to service by substantial land grants. Both the North and the South imposed a draft to fill the ranks during the Civil War. After that conflict, however, the United States relied on volunteers to fight the wars with Native Americans, the Spanish–American War, and the Philippine–American War. It again imposed a draft during World War I, but returned to a volunteer army in the 1920s and 1930s. A draft was used again in World War II. The United States might well have returned to a volunteer army after World War II, but things were different in 1950 when the Korean War began. That war followed closely on the heels of World War II, so it was natural to utilize the system that had been in place a few years earlier. Moreover, while the war was being fought at that moment only against North Korea, there was a distinct possibility that it would escalate into a Third World War against the Soviet Union and China. After Korea, the draft remained in place as a warning to the Communist powers that the country was prepared for war. The Vietnam War, like the Korean War, was a limited war fought with drafted personnel.

The draft stirred up a hornet's nest of opposition, especially on college campuses. In May 1966 students at many colleges across the nation staged "sit-ins." They were protesting the war, and especially the role of their colleges in facilitating the draft. The draft was seen by the young protesters as a political enabler of war-making, a source of cheap "cannon fodder." Ironically, during the Afghanistan and Iraq wars the opposite argument was made: the draft increased political opposition to the war by making a wide range of young people eligible; a volunteer armed force minimized opposition to the war.

The anti-draft and anti-war movements were closely entwined and it was hard to know how much of the opposition was to the war and how much to the draft.[8] President Nixon was interested in ending the draft and made this known during his campaign for the presidency in 1968. After his election he appointed a commission, the Advisory Commission on an All-Volunteer Armed Force, popularly known as the Gates Commission after the chairman, Thomas S. Gates Jr. The well-known libertarian economists Milton Friedman and Alan Greenspan were members of the Commission. Walter Y. Oi, a distinguished University of Rochester labor economist, was one of the key directors of research. Oi had already (1967) published an important paper on the economic costs of the draft in the *American Economic Review*, the leading American journal of economics. The Gates Commission issued its report detailing the costs of the draft and recommending an all-volunteer force in February 1970 (US President's Commission on an All-Volunteer Armed Force 1970).

The draft, as the Gates Commission contended, imposed three kinds of costs on draftees. Consider, first, the case of a volunteer whose opportunity costs in the private sector are less than what he earns in the military.[9] Since he is a true volunteer, it is tempting to think that he is not hurt, not taxed, by the presence of a draft. But there is a real cost to him if he earns less than he would earn if the draft was eliminated and military salaries had to be increased to attract men in sufficient numbers to fill the ranks. To give a concrete example, say he earns \$25,000 in the military, which exceeds his opportunity cost of \$15,000. If the draft was ended, the competition for military personnel might lead to an increase of wages to \$30,000. The difference of \$5,000 is a loss to our volunteer but not a loss to society as a whole. Rather, it is a transfer from the soldier to taxpayers, a hidden tax on a member of the military. Although it does not represent a lost opportunity cost to society, it does hide the cost of the war and distort decisions about when to go to war and how long to continue the fight.

Consider next the reluctant volunteer or draftee who would not serve in the absence of a draft simply because his opportunity cost in the private sector was higher. He could earn, say, \$30,000 in the

[8] I was one of those protesting students. But even in my own case it is hard even now to say what my own motives were.

[9] In those days, only men were drafted, and most of the volunteers for military service were men. The women in the military were all true volunteers.

private sector, but earns only $25,000 in the military. If we make the usual assumption that the individual's wage equals his or her marginal product, then society is forgoing $30,000 in output, but counting only $25,000 in increased government spending. The difference of $5,000 is not a transfer; it is a true loss of output, again a cost that is hidden from the taxpayer.

Finally, consider the reluctant volunteer or draftee who has a strong distaste for the military, perhaps based on the rigors of military life, or perhaps based on moral concerns about a particular war or about war in general. This individual pays a heavy price when he is drafted because he is not being compensated for his distaste for military service. Military pay of $25,000 may represent his opportunity cost, but he would require a salary of $40,000 to compensate for his loss of income in the private sector and the "disutility" of military service. In this case the measured output of the economy is not reduced by more than $25,000, but the total "utility" produced by the nation's resources is clearly reduced.

One famous case that illustrated some of these costs was that of the champion heavyweight boxer Muhammad Ali. In 1967, then at the height of his boxing career, he was drafted, but he refused to serve on the grounds that he was a conscientious objector to the war. Ali's case threw both the economic and ethical dilemmas of the draft into sharp relief: he could earn far more as a boxer than as a soldier, and he didn't believe in the war he was being drafted to fight.

The draft was continued for two more years. In the interim, military pay was raised and aggressive television advertising to attract army recruits was begun. In January 1973 Secretary of Defense Melvin Laird announced the end of the draft.

Although the draft was ended as a result of the Vietnam War, there were still veterans who had to be rewarded for their service.[10] The Vietnam War GI Bill was passed in 1966, and in some respects its education title was less generous again than the education title in the 1952 GI Bill. One would certainly reach this conclusion if one compared education benefits with current wages. The Vietnam Bill, however, did provide benefits for those who served between the Korean and Vietnam conflicts. Initially, the number of veterans taking advantage of the Vietnam era provisions was disappointing. But within a few years,

[10] The following paragraph is based on Rockoff (2006, S-349).

partly in response to an increase in benefits, utilization of the education provisions increased so that usage was comparable to that of World War II benefits. Although educational benefits were substantial, subsequent research showed that serving in Vietnam was an economic disadvantage in the long run (Angrist 1990a, 1990b). Draftees who served in the Vietnam conflict ended up earning 15 percent less in civilian life, other things being equal, than men who did not serve. The reason may simply be that the men who served lost time in the private sector that they would have spent developing their skills and advancing their careers. Military recruiters frequently tout the benefits of military service: it builds character and teaches skills. And this may well be true for some individuals. But in many cases, it appears, the time lost from the marketplace in which the veteran intended to make his or her livelihood is of more practical importance. It may also be true that the veterans of the Vietnam War were not received as well in the marketplace as veterans of some of the earlier wars; they did not return as conquering heroes.

10 *The Persian Gulf War*

This conflict started August 2nd when the dictator of Iraq invaded a small and helpless neighbor. Kuwait – a member of the Arab League and a member of the United Nations – was crushed; its people, brutalized. Five months ago, Saddam Hussein started this cruel war against Kuwait. Tonight, the battle has been joined.

President George H. W. Bush, radio address, January 16, 1991

A chronology of the Persian Gulf War

1990		
August	2	Iraq invades Kuwait. The United Nations Security Council demands that Iraq withdraw.
	4	The European Community embargos oil shipments from Iraq.
	6	The Security Council imposes a ban on most forms of trade with Iraq, including the purchase of oil.
	9	Saddam Hussein declares Kuwait Iraq's nineteenth province and appoints his cousin Ali Hassan al-Majid (Chemical Ali) as governor.
	12	President George H. W. Bush orders a naval blockade of Iraq.
1991		
January	12	The US House by a vote of 250–183 and the US Senate by a vote of 52–47 authorize the use of force to expel Iraq from Kuwait.
	16	Aerial bombardment of Iraq begins.
February	13	The Al Firdos bunker in Baghdad is bombed with heavy loss of civilian life.

	23	The ground assault by Coalition forces begins.
	24	Coalition forces enter Iraq.
	25	Iraqi Scud missile hits a military base in Dhahran, Saudi Arabia killing twenty-eight Americans.
	26	Iraqi forces retreat from Kuwait. Many are killed by Coalition air strikes.
	28	President George H. W. Bush declares Kuwait liberated and offers a ceasefire.
March	3	Iraq accepts a ceasefire.
	10	Withdrawal of US forces from the Gulf begins.
June	8	A victory parade is held in Washington, DC.
November	6	The last oil well fire ignited by Iraq's retreating forces is extinguished.

Sources: The *New York Times*, the *Wall Street Journal*, and similar sources.

The United States and a large group of allies were at war with Iraq between January 12, 1991, when the US House and Senate authorized the use of force against Iraq, and March 3, 1991, when Iraq accepted a ceasefire. The purpose of the war was to expel Iraq from Kuwait, which the former had invaded and conquered in August 1990. In some ways the Persian Gulf War resembled the Spanish–American War, the first phase of the Philippine–American War, and the first phase of the Korean War: an aggressive and well-planned American strike overwhelmed the forces of a smaller nation trying to fight a conventional war against the United States. Approximately 2.2 million Americans served in the war, employing massive amounts of munitions.

The origins of the war

Kuwait, a small nation with immense oil reserves, lies at the end of the Persian Gulf and borders Saudi Arabia and Iraq.[1] By 1990 Iraq, and its dictator Saddam Hussein, had accumulated many grievances against

[1] This section is based mainly on contemporary reporting in the *New York Times*, *Wall Street Journal*, and similar sources.

its neighbor. The Iraqis claimed that Kuwait was historically part of their nation, and also, with some truth, that it had been created as a separate country after World War I by Great Britain to further British strategic interests. The Iraqis also claimed that Kuwait was violating the quotas on oil production authorized by the Organization of Petroleum Exporting Countries to which both Kuwait and Iraq belonged. Violation of the quota by Kuwait, Iraq alleged, had contributed to the fall in world oil prices that was hurting Iraq, whose major export was oil. Iraq, moreover, was desperately short of funds after fighting a long and destructive war with Iran. Indeed, Kuwait had lent its neighbour substantial sums during that war, and Iraq wanted the relatively rich Kuwaitis to forgive the debt. It also claimed that Kuwait had stolen oil directly from its territory by drilling wells that slanted across the border (Halliday 1991, 226–7).

Attempts to mediate a non-military resolution failed. On August 2, 1990 Iraqi forces invaded Kuwait. After several days of hard fighting they overwhelmed the Kuwaitis and took full control. Hussein then installed his first cousin, Ali Hassan al-Majid, as governor. Ali Hassan had been dubbed "Chemical Ali" by the Iraqi Kurds because he had authorized the use of chemical weapons against them. The attack on Kuwait was an act of aggression that would have angered the United States even if both Iraq and Kuwait had been resource-poor nations. But the United States had a strong economic motive for being especially concerned: Iraq was the fourth nation in proven oil reserves after Saudi Arabia, Canada, and Iran. Add the massive Kuwaiti reserves and Iraq would be second. And if it were to go on and take the Saudi oil fields that lay close to Kuwait, Iraq would emerge as an immensely powerful economic actor on the world stage, controlling about 40 percent of the world's proven oil reserves.

Immediately after the invasion the administration of George H. W. Bush began a diplomatic offensive to expel the Iraqis. On August 6, 1990 the United Nations Security Council authorized economic sanctions against the country. The sanctions banned most trade with Iraq, including in oil; only humanitarian aid was permitted. On August 12 President Bush ordered a naval blockade to enforce the sanctions, an action that met some resistance within the United States, from other countries, and from the United Nations. Since Iraq's oil reached the rest of the world by ship from ports in Iraq, Turkey, and Saudi Arabia, a naval blockade was a credible threat, although in general the historical record of blockades is mixed (Davis and Engerman 2003, 2006; Hufbauer *et al.* 1990).

In the months that followed Americans debated the effectiveness of the blockade. Supporters of continued reliance on the blockade pointed to concrete signs that it was imposing costs on the Iraqis, simple things like breadlines and the failure of elevators to work in Baghdad. But skeptics maintained that sympathetic neighbors – Jordan, Syria, and Turkey – provided a link to the outside world that was bound to grow stronger over time. Even if these countries were unwilling to trade openly with Iraq, they would provide the crucial links to the rest of the world by allowing smugglers to function unchecked. And the skeptics pointed out that because Saddam Hussein wielded dictatorial powers, he could isolate his regime and his armed forces from the pain being imposed on Iraqi society at large. Even if some Iraqis went hungry, the army would not.

President Bush, growing impatient with Iraqi intransigence and concerned about his ability to hold his military coalition together, threatened to use force to expel the Iraqis from Kuwait if they did not leave by January 15. He then sought an authorization for this from Congress. For supporters of the President the time for action had come. Former President Richard Nixon, typifying the hawkish view, argued that with the vast oil wealth of Iraq and Kuwait behind him, Hussein would go on to larger and larger wars of aggression. Fighting now would save lives in the long run (*New York Times*, January 6, 1991, E19). Opponents, many of whom were concerned about the costs of the war in life and treasure and about American relations with other countries in the Mideast, urged that more time should be allowed for economic sanctions and diplomacy to work. On January 12, 1991 the US House, by a vote of 250–183 and the US Senate by a vote of 52–47, authorized the use of force to expel Iraq from Kuwait, effectively a declaration of war. It was the narrowest margin of victory for a declaration of war since the War of 1812.

The United States, although contributing the bulk of the forces, formed a substantial Coalition. Some were America's traditional allies: Britain, which contributed some 43,000 troops, and (next in order of troops committed) France, Australia, New Zealand, the Netherlands, South Korea, and Canada. The Coalition also included a number of states from eastern Europe that could not have joined with the United States during the Cold War: Czechoslovakia, Hungary, Poland, and

Table 10.1 ***Contributions to Operations Desert Shield and Desert Storm (millions of dollars)***

	Cash	In kind	Total	%
Saudi Arabia	12,002	4,001	16,003	26.23
Kuwait	16,015	43	16,058	26.32
United Arab Emirates	3,870	218	4,088	6.70
Japan	9,437	571	10,008	16.41
Germany	5,772	683	6,455	10.58
Korea	150	101	251	0.41
Other	7	22	29	0.05
United States			8,108	13.29
Total	47,253	5,639	61,000	100.00

Notes: Cash receipts are as of March 11, 1992. In-kind receipts are as of February 29, 1992. Kuwait made additional in-kind transfers after February 29, 1992. Germany offered more than $200 million in ammunition which the United States chose not to accept due to the termination of the war.
Source: US Department of Defense, *Conduct of the Persian Gulf War: Final Report To Congress* (1992), Appendix P.

Romania. Importantly, the Coalition also included a number of Middle Eastern and North African states: Kuwait, Saudi Arabia, Oman, Egypt, Qatar, Morocco, Syria, Turkey, and the United Arab Emirates.

Financing the war

The marginal costs of the Gulf War (costs in excess of normal military expenditures) incurred during the period of active fighting were relatively low. For the most part, the United States relied on munitions accumulated over the course of the Cold War with the Soviet Union and China which was ending at the same time as it was going to war with Iraq. Total military spending was only $25 billion higher in fiscal 1992 than in fiscal 1991. The Department of Defense placed the total cost of Operations Desert Shield and Desert Storm at $61 billion (US Department of Defense 1992, 60). Much of this was offset by contributions from five allies as shown in Table 10.1. This was the first time since the American Revolution – when France, Spain, and other nations contributed to its war effort – that the United States had relied on foreign nations to finance a war. In the cases of Saudi Arabia, Kuwait, and the United Arab Emirates, there were three rich countries that benefited directly from ousting Hussein from Kuwait, but had small populations and relatively small armed forces, and so could make only limited direct military contributions.

The course of the war

Operation Desert Storm began on January 16, 1991 with a massive aerial bombardment of Iraqi forces and supporting bases in Iraq and Kuwait.[2] Thus the war opened in a way reminiscent of the Spanish–American War, with which we began our story of America's twentieth-century wars, which began with a naval attack at Guantanamo Bay. Just as the Spanish navy and naval fortresses were unable to cope with the larger, technically advanced navy of the United States, Iraq's air force and ground-based air defenses were unable to cope with the Coalition air force. The United States and its allies were able to hit the Iraqis with attack helicopters, drones, B-52 long-range bombers firing cruise missiles, naval vessels firing Tomahawk missiles, electric jamming support aircraft, and a variety of jet aircraft firing missiles and dropping laser-guided and conventional gravity bombs. The Iraqi air force could do little in reply. It tried as best it could to protect its capital by dispersing aircraft (including placing them near archaeological sites), by secreting aircraft in hardened shelters (which proved vulnerable to Coalition munitions), and eventually by flying some to safety in Iran. The only offensive operation undertaken by the Iraqis was an attempt by two Iraqi jets to (possibly) attack Coalition ships in the Persian Gulf, but they were shot down by Saudi aircraft (Keaney and Cohen 1993, 37). The United States and its allies were soon able to establish control of the air over the battlefield.

Everything, however, did not go the way they hoped. Perhaps the most frustrating part of the air war was the "great Scud chase." The Scuds were long-range missiles that the Iraqis launched from mobile platforms against Israel – hoping to draw Israel into the war and thereby

[2] The next two paragraphs are based mainly on Keaney and Cohen (1993). This is the summary volume of the *Gulf War Air Power Survey*. The survey, directed by Cohen, was similar to the Strategic Bombing Survey of World War II, although more modest in scope, in the sense that the Air Power Survey was intended to provide an evidentiary base for future histories of the conflict. The authors of the Air Power Survey were well aware of their distinguished predecessor.

put pressure on predominantly Islamic states to quit the coalition. In late February a Scud warhead hit a US barracks in Dhahran, Saudi Arabia killing twenty-eight and wounding ninety-seven. Despite a major effort by the Coalition air forces, however, the Iraqis were able to continue to launch Scuds throughout the war.

Most of the 100,000 sorties flown by US planes were against targets that most observers would probably agree were legitimate military targets (Keaney and Cohen 1993, 184). The United States conducted little strategic bombing during the war, although fuel storage and electrical generating facilities were attacked. Indeed, stringent efforts were made to avoid civilian deaths and destruction of civilian property, known to the military, and often times with irony by the news media and general public, as "collateral damage." Efforts to minimize collateral damage were increased after a strike on the Al Firdos bunker on February 13 killed several hundred Iraqi civilians and ignited a storm of protest (Keaney and Cohen 1993, 22). The destruction of the bunker was widely covered in detail by CNN and other television networks (*New York Times*, February 14, 1991, A19 and *passim*). It was evident that modern electronic communication had created an unprecedented degree of intimacy with the suffering of Iraqi civilians, a level of intimacy even higher than in the Vietnam War, that increased opposition to the war both in the United States and abroad. Opposition to war, of course, is nothing new in the United States. As we have seen, opposition to American operations in the Philippines at the turn of the century and to the Vietnam War was intense. Only when sympathy for enemy civilians is at a low ebb, as it was in World War II, can American governments and military planners ignore the costs imposed on civilians. There was considerable opposition to the Persian Gulf War, and the government did not want a mounting list of civilian casualties to increase it.

Pressure therefore mounted for an immediate ground assault. Coalition forces led by US General H. Norman Schwarzkopf launched a full-scale ground attack on February 23. Schwarzkopf sent a large Coalition force around the right side of the Iraqi lines, a powerful and decisive "left hook." The Iraqi forces were overwhelmed with a great loss of life. On February 26, they began to retreat from Kuwait City and many were killed by Coalition air strikes on what became known as the "Highway of Death." On February 28, President Bush declared Kuwait liberated. Coalition forces, of course, might have continued the attack, destroyed the remnants of Hussein's armed forces, and deposed Hussein. But the Bush administration, mindful of the opposition to the occupation of Iraq by US allies, especially its Arab allies, and of the difficulties that would ensue if Coalition forces attempted to occupy the country, instead offered a ceasefire. This was accepted on March 3, bringing a short and decisive war to a close. A victory parade was held in Washington, DC on June 8.

The cost of the war

There were only 147 battle deaths of Americans in the Persian Gulf War. The closest analogue is the war that began our story, the Spanish–American War, when the United States suffered 385 combat deaths (Appendix 2). America's allies also suffered relatively few battle deaths. The small number of casualties resulted from a number of factors: the technological superiority of American and Coalition arms and the training and skill of American and Coalition enlisted troops and officers. The clear skies and barren deserts of the Middle East, moreover, gave full scope to America's advantage in air and tank power. Unlike North Korea and North Vietnam, which had the backing of the Soviet Union and China, Iraq was going it alone. And the United States had the initiative: the ability to plan and coordinate the counterattack against the positions the Iraqis had taken after occupying Kuwait. The Persian Gulf War resembled the phase of the Korean War that followed the landing at Inchon when American forces were able to drive back the North Korean forces. Unlike North Korea, however, the Iraqis had no allies like the Chinese who would enter on their side and reverse the tide of war. Chess players strive to prepare their opening moves and surprise their opponent with a "technical novelty," a move not known to the experts that they have carefully analyzed beforehand. The Coalition was in a similar position when it launched its counterstrike against the Iraqis.

The 147 battle deaths, to be sure, were only part of the story. There were another 235 deaths from injuries and disease, and there were other deaths outside the theater of war. Some of the latter would have occurred in any case, but some, such as accidents caused by the pressure to move supplies quickly, were the result of the war. Some of the deaths due to rushing occurred outside the war zone. Coalition partners also suffered relatively small numbers of casualties by historical standards. Britain, next after the United States in terms of casualties, lost 47 soldiers. The loss of life in Iraq, however, civilian as well as military, was substantial. The exact number will probably never be known. The Iraqi administrative bureaucracies broke down during the war, and the United States, chastened by the bad publicity stemming from its emphasis on "body counts" during the Vietnam War, refused to count enemy losses. Aerial bombing, moreover, can produce large losses that are hard to measure. And the Muslim tradition which emphasizes the rapid burial of the dead may also have influenced knowledge about Iraqi losses.

The veterans

In the wake of the war there was considerable controversy about the long-term consequences for the health of the veterans.[3] After considerable research and debate it now appears clear that about one-fourth of the 697,000 US veterans of the war were afflicted with "Gulf War Illness." This is a complex condition that manifests itself in a number of symptoms that may include memory and concentration problems, persistent headaches, widespread pain, fatigue, skin rashes, and gastrointestinal problems. These symptoms, moreover, persisted for years, and no cure was found. Gulf War veterans also suffered from other medical problems such as post-traumatic stress syndrome, infectious diseases, elevated rates of amyotrophic lateral sclerosis (Lou Gehrig's disease), and brain cancer, among others. It appears, also, that spouses, children, and grandchildren of veterans of the Gulf War have also been affected by various diseases.

From the first, Persian Gulf War veterans reported that they were sick, and suspicion fell on various toxic substances to which they had been exposed, but the variety of symptoms, and the failure of initial medical and epidemiological studies to pinpoint a culprit, produced frustration and, in some quarters, skepticism about whether Gulf War Illness was a real phenomenon. Since most veterans were exposed to multiple toxins, unraveling the cause of Gulf War Illness was particularly difficult: if exposure to toxin A was highly correlated with exposure to toxin B, a study that considered only A might conclude that A was the cause, when the true cause was B. Over time, however,

[3] The following four paragraphs on the long-term health effects of the Gulf War are based on US Department of Veterans' Affairs, Research Advisory Committee on Gulf War Veterans' Illnesses (2008).

research gradually clarified the nature of the illness and the role of various potential causes. One early theory was that Gulf War Illness was a form of post-traumatic stress syndrome, variants of which have been observed after most conflicts, although the name has changed: after the Civil War there was "Da Costa's syndrome;" in World War I, shell shock; World War II, battle fatigue; and the Vietnam War, post-traumatic stress syndrome. The Persian Gulf War was no exception. Veterans suffered from post-traumatic stress syndrome, although in smaller numbers than did veterans of the Vietnam War. However, wartime stress did not turn out to be a major cause of Gulf War Illness.

Another concern was exposure to depleted uranium. This is an extremely dense and heavy metal that is used in armor plating and armor-piercing shells. Not only do shells incorporating depleted uranium penetrate armor, but they also burst into flames after contact, potentially igniting fuel and ammunition, and making shells containing depleted uranium particularly effective as an anti-tank munition. The Persian Gulf War was the first in which significant amounts of depleted uranium were used. It is not the only material useful for these purposes – ceramics can be used in armor plating and tungsten can be used in armor-piercing shells – but depleted uranium is very effective and substantial amounts are available as a byproduct of the production of nuclear weapons and fuel for nuclear reactors. The long-term problem is that depleted uranium is toxic and radioactive, although it is not as radioactive as naturally occurring uranium. In the course of the war, many soldiers on both sides were exposed to the substance, raising health concerns, for example increased rates of kidney and brain cancer. Since the depleted uranium remained on the battlefield, civilians were affected after the war. However, the evidence, so far, seems to be that exposure to depleted uranium was not the primary cause of Gulf War Illness.

As they left Kuwait, Iraqi forces allowed oil to drain into the Persian Gulf from the Sea Island Terminal near Kuwait City; they also released oil from oil tankers and ignited more than six hundred oil wells. The result was an environmental disaster. This was not the first case of environmental damage in wartime: the destruction of farms and forests in World War I, the use of atomic bombs in World War II, and the use of chemical defoliants in the Vietnam War, all produced extensive environmental damage. But growing concern about the environment focused public attention on this wanton destruction in a way that perhaps previous violations of the environment had not. Igniting the oil wells and despoiling the Gulf served little military purpose beyond reinforcing the credibility of the Hussein regime's most violent threats. It was suggested, moreover, that exposure to the smoke from burning oil wells might have been a cause of Gulf War Illness. But again, although personnel exposed to burning oil fumes suffered from long-run health effects, such as increased rates of asthma, fumes from burning oil wells did not appear to have been the major cause of Gulf War Illness.

Instead of the candidates on which attention first focused, two toxic chemicals appear to have caused Gulf War Illness: pyridostigmine bromide pills and pesticides. Pyridostigmine bromide pills were given to soldiers to protect them against nerve agents that it was thought that the Iraqis were prepared to use against Coalition troops. Soldiers deployed in Iraq regularly sprayed their uniforms with pesticides, and insect repellants such as DEET. The best evidence currently is that these two agents were the primary cause of Gulf War Illness. It also appears that there was an interaction effect: use of both pyridostigmine bromide pills and pesticides produced a larger effect than the sum of the separate effects.

As with the Spanish–American and Philippine–American wars, the incremental cost of the Persian Gulf War was small compared with the likely cost in terms of veterans' service benefits. The measure included in Appendix 3, of course, is conjectural, and the reality may be very different. But if Edwards's (2010) estimate proves accurate, the cost of veterans' benefits will turn out to be about four times as much as the initial cost of the war. This is a very high ratio, but it is not unusual. As Edwards points out, veterans' benefits often exceed the costs incurred during the war. In the Spanish–American War veterans' benefits came to about three times the immediate war costs. Indeed, the Spanish–American War, which as I have had occasion to note bears many striking similarities to the Persian Gulf War, cost in total about 5.5 percent of GDP, while the Persian Gulf War cost about 5.3 percent. The Spanish–American War, that splendid little war, was followed by the Philippine–American War, with its long and bitter campaign against guerilla forces. The Persian Gulf War was followed by the still ongoing and unresolved (as this is written) conflicts in Afghanistan, Iraq, and Libya. Those wars, like the Philippine–American War, have raised issues about how and why America fights its wars that have made us forget the preceding triumph.

11 *The American economic way of war*

There is a great deal of ruin in a nation.

Attributed to Adam Smith

War played a major role in shaping the American economy in the twentieth century.[1] In part this was because there was so much of it. If we include only the major hot wars, and use the official dates, then the United States was at war for roughly a quarter of the twentieth century. If we include the long Cold War, the figure rises to 55 percent. If we were to include the many smaller conflicts, the proportion of years in the twentieth century when American forces were fighting somewhere in the world would be still higher. To be sure, wars have produced many benefits. Few Americans would have been willing to contemplate the success of the Fascist nations, the most likely outcome had the United States remained neutral in World War II. The long war against Communism encompassing the Korean War, the Vietnam War, and the Cold War remains far more controversial. But here too, one can count benefits from the decisions to go to war. But wars have also been extremely costly, perhaps more so than is generally realized because politicians often do the best they can to hide the costs of war.

The loss of life and limb, however, cannot be hidden, and it is this cost that explains why it is so hard to persuade the American people, who ultimately hold the reins of power, to go to war. As much as a political elite might believe that going to war is in the national interest, and as much as special interests might push for it for pecuniary reasons, ultimately if there is to be a war, the American people must

[1] The phrase "American way of war" was popularized by Weigley (1973) who was concerned mainly with military strategy, and the preference of American generals for the simple strategy of grinding down their enemies with overwhelming force.

be persuaded that war, and the human costs it brings, are justified by the need to protect people who are in danger in some other part of the world or to avenge a direct attack on the United States, a *casus belli*. The explosion of the battleship *Maine* before the Spanish–American War, the sinking of American ships by German submarines before World War I, Pearl Harbor, the attack by North Korea on South Korea, the Tonkin Gulf incident, and so on were more than mere historical markers, they were crucial to enlisting public support for war. In his recent book *Empire* (2004) historian Niall Ferguson argues that the United States has replaced Britain as the world's imperialist hegemon. It is America's role, whether it wants it or not, to impose its view of the correct world order, American-style democratic capitalism, on the rest of the world: always by example, usually by trade, and occasionally by war. Ferguson sees this as a good thing. The British empire, he argues – despite slavery, the slave trade, and other brutalities visited on peoples around the world – was better than the alternative empires would have been. But Ferguson's argument is designed to persuade an elite. Persuading the American people to take on such a role will not be easy; the American public demands an honorable reason for taking up arms.

Once the decision to go to war was made, the question of how to pay for it soon followed. And wars turned out to be far costlier in economic terms than was acknowledged during the time when the decision to go to war was being debated in the lofty languages of chivalry and honor; during the period when, as it is rightly put, the nation was caught up in a "war fever." On first thought, it might seem that for a rich nation such as the United States the answer about how to finance wars would be simple: raise taxes sufficiently high to pay for the war. And taxes were raised, as shown in the preceding chapters, in most of the wars of the twentieth century, an honorable tradition. But tax increases make the cost of war painfully obvious to the general public and undermine support for it. So governments typically resorted in part to means of finance that concealed the economic cost of war from the general public. The first choice for this purpose was debt finance. Issuing debt may alarm the cognoscenti who anticipate higher future taxes and may observe changes in interest rates on different types of debt, but debt finance for a rich nation with considerable credit may not be well observed by the ordinary citizen. Adam Smith's splendid statement of how debt finance hides the cost of war from the average taxpayer, although written with Britain's eighteenth-century colonial wars in mind, is still timely:

> The ordinary expense of the greater part of modern governments in time of peace being equal or nearly equal to their ordinary revenue, when war comes they are both unwilling and unable to increase their revenue in proportion to the increase of their expense. They are unwilling for fear of offending the people, who, by so great and so sudden an increase of taxes, would soon be disgusted with the war; and they are unable from not well knowing what taxes would be sufficient to produce the revenue wanted. The facility of borrowing delivers them from the embarrassment which this fear and inability would otherwise occasion. By means of borrowing they are enabled, with a very moderate increase of taxes, to raise, from year to year, money sufficient for carrying on the war, and by the practice of perpetual funding they are enabled, with the smallest possible increase of taxes, to raise annually the largest possible sum of money. (Smith 1976 [1776], 1080)[2]

"Printing money" was a second powerful device for concealing the cost of war. During World War II, for example, the Federal Reserve purchased large volumes of US Treasury securities. The result was inflation which reduced the real value of assets fixed in nominal terms, in effect a tax on money and similar assets. But probably a minority saw the connection between Federal Reserve monetary policy and rising prices. Indeed, the policy of purchasing government debt tended to keep nominal yields on government debt low, suppressing one of the signs of debt finance, and hence one of the signs of the mounting cost of the war. During the wars of the nineteenth century the use of the printing press, and hence the connection between war finance and inflation, was more visible. The average American could see that the government had printed continental dollars or greenbacks. The founding of the Federal Reserve, however, cloaked the process of monetizing debt.

During World War I, World War II, the Korean War, and the Vietnam War the government turned to wage and price controls, rationing, and

[2] By "perpetual funding" Smith was referring to the issue of consols: bonds that did not promise redemption on a particular date but rather promised a fixed rate of interest each year. The alternative that he had in mind was a funded debt, in which the debt was due in a certain number of years, and taxes were raised sufficiently high not only to cover the interest, but also to gradually pay down the debt before the final redemption date. Conceivably, the government could have perpetually funded itself by continually "rolling over" short-term debt, but this might have risked disruptions of the capital market when debt was refunded.

production controls to suppress inflation. These devices made it easier to draw resources into the war sector. To the extent that controls were effective in suppressing inflation they served to further conceal the costs of the war. At times, controls produced the usual (and some not so usual) symptoms of suppressed inflation: quality deterioration, black markets, and forced uptrading (the elimination of low-priced, low-profit lines of merchandise). Such symptoms were a sign of the costs of the war, but they were not likely to produce a clear appreciation of the tradeoffs implicit in the decision to go to war. These developments could always be seen as the product of the poor administration of controls or a lack of patriotism, rather than as an inevitable result of the decision to allocate a substantial fraction of the nation's resources to the war effort, and to finance the transfer by borrowing from the public or creating money rather than raising taxes.

The draft, which was used during World War I, World War II, the Korean War, part of the Cold War, and the Vietnam War, also served to conceal the full cost of war. The public, it is true, saw the disruption of the lives of the young people who were drafted, but when the tax bill arrived they were unlikely to reflect that it would have been higher had they agreed to compensate the draftees at a rate equal to what they could have earned in private markets, let alone a rate that might have compensated them for the dangers they faced, or the skills that they did not develop when they were at war.

True, the tradition of rewarding veterans with compensation and pensions had been well established since colonial times and could be expected to continue. As we have seen, veterans' benefits often amounted to a substantial portion of the costs of war, sometimes more than the costs incurred during the years of conflict. But veterans' benefits were "unfunded liabilities;" no taxes were dedicated to these expenditures, and these future costs were not likely to have had much of an impact on public debates when the decision to go to war was being made.

The wars of the twentieth century trace an arc of violence.[3] The century began with small, colonial wars in Cuba and the Philippines. America's enemies had limited resources and few allies, and could be defeated by devoting a small but significant share of America's resources to fighting them. The war in Cuba produced

[3] Larry Neal made this point to me when he first suggested that I write this book.

some opposition in the United States. But it was widely viewed as just because of the sinking of the battleship *Maine* and the violence of Spanish attempts to maintain control in Cuba, and the victory was quick. The Philippine–American War, however, produced far more opposition. Its purpose was less easily defended, and the tactics employed to suppress the Philippine revolutionaries were often as brutal as those that had aroused so much opposition when employed by Spain in Cuba.

America then experienced the world wars, wars that required extensive mobilization of the economy. Both, however, garnered considerable public support. This was especially true of World War II, which was widely regarded as "the good war." Pearl Harbor provided a clear *casus belli*, and the Fascist governments were an enemy on which almost everyone could agree. After World War II America began its long war to contain Communism: the Korean War, the Cold War, and the Vietnam War, in terms of resources the most expensive in American history. Costs were heavy and outcomes unclear. Opposition to the Vietnam War was especially intense.

At the end of the century America undertook distant colonial wars that remind us of the wars that began the century. The Persian Gulf War (1991) reminds us of nothing so much as the Spanish–American War. The cause was justified by sympathy for the Kuwaitis. America's chivalrous instincts were aroused. The war was short, battle deaths and wounds were few, on the same order as those incurred in the Spanish–American War, and the outcome was a clear victory: another "splendid little war." But the wars in which the US is engaged as this is written (2011) in Afghanistan, Iraq, and Libya, bear more of the hallmarks of the Philippine–American War that followed the Spanish–American War. During this later war opposition mounted as Americans found themselves enmeshed in a long war against insurgents using guerilla tactics, and one in which American forces employed cruel tactics to extract information and bring the enemy to battle. The history of the wars in Afghanistan, Iraq, and Libya is still being written. A few years ago Joseph E. Stiglitz and Linda J. Bilmes (2008) put the costs of the Iraq War at $3 trillion. They now believe that the war is going to be even more costly (*Washington Post*, September 5, 2010, 2). Since then the USA has added a new war in Libya, and costs from the old wars have continued to mount. America now (2011) has about 150,000 fighters in Afghanistan and Iraq where it has suffered about 5,876 fatalities since the fighting began in 2001 (Gregory 2011, 5–6), a number similar to the fatalities suffered more than a century ago in the Philippine–American War. We have come full circle.

But all this talk about the costs of war raises an important question. If America's twentieth-century wars were so frequent and so costly, why, despite a slow recovery from a devastating financial crisis, and despite fighting wars in Afghanistan, Iraq, and Libya, is the United States such a rich nation? How can it be that real per capita income in the USA has risen from $5,246 (2005 dollars) in 1898 when the Spanish–American War took place to $43,397 in 2008, more than eight times? The answer, of course, is that America has grown despite devoting considerable resources to war. The accumulation of capital (physical and human) and technological progress made possible a rapid advance in the standard of living despite the resources the country devoted to wars. Perhaps Adam Smith gave the most trenchant answer. Allegedly, a young friend, Sir John Sinclair, rushed to see Smith and tell him that General Burgoyne had surrendered to the Americans at Saratoga during the American Revolution. When the young man exclaimed that the nation was ruined, Smith purportedly replied: "There is a great deal of ruin in a nation" (Rae 1895, XXII.7).

Appendices

Appendix 1 *Personnel serving, by war*

War	Start date	End date	Personnel serving (number)	Personnel serving as a percentage of the population[a] (%)
Spanish–American War	April 1898	August 1898	306,760	0.42
Philippine–American War	February 1899	July 1902[b]	126,468	0.16
World War I	April 1917	November 1918	4,734,991	4.58
World War II	December 1941	August 1945	16,112,566	11.8
Cold War	March 1947	November 1989	na	na
Korean War	June 1950	July 1953	5,720,000	3.77
Vietnam War	August 1964	January 1973	8,744,000	4.56
Persian Gulf War	January 1991	March 1991	2,225,000	0.89

Notes:
[a] The number serving as a percentage of the average US population during the war years.
[b] After July 4, 1902, when officially the war was declared over, the main island of Luzon was largely pacified, but fighting continued in some outlying areas for many years.
Sources: Philippine–American War: Clodfelter (2001, 272). All other wars and population: Carter *et al.* (2006, series Ed1 and Aa93).

Appendix 2 *Deaths and non-mortal wounds, by war*

War	Service	Killed in battle	Died of wounds	Total	Died of disease	Died of injury	Total disease and injury	Total all deaths	Wounds (not mortal)
Mexican War	Army	(1,049)	(508)	1,721 (1,557)	(10,982)	(395)	(11,377)	(12,934) 13,271	4,102
	Navy	na	na	1	na	na	na	1	3
	Marines	na	na	11	na	na	na	11	47
	Total	na	na	1,733	na	na	na	13,283	4,152
Civil War (North)	Army	(69,982)	(44,775)	138,154 (114,757)	(233,789)	(10,982)	221,374 (244,771)	359, 528 (359,528)	280,040
	Navy	na	na	2,112	na	na	2,411	4,523	1,710
	Marines	na	na	148	na	na	312	460	131
	Total	na	na	140,414	na	na	224,097	364,511	281,881
Civil War (South)	Army	na	na	na	na	na	na	na	na
	Navy	na	na	na	na	na	na	na	na
	Marines	na	na	na	na	na	na	na	na
	Total	na	na	(95,000) [94,000]	na	na	(165,000) [164,000]	184,000–250,000 (260,000) [258,000]	na
Spanish–American War	Army	(272)	(107)	369 (379)	(4,795)	(288)	2,061 (5,083) [5,043]	2,430 (5,462)	1,594
	Navy	(17)	(1)	10 (18)	0	0	0 (74)	10 (92)	47
	Marines	na	na	6	0	0	0	6	21
	Total	na	na	385 (397)	na	na	2,061	2,446	1,662

Appendix 2 (*cont.*)

War	Service	Killed in battle	Died of wounds	Total	Died of disease	Died of injury	Total disease and injury	Total all deaths	Wounds (not mortal)
Philippine–American War	Army	(823)	(241)	(1,064) [1,073]	(4,874) [2,572]	(1,063) [589]	(5,937) [3,161]	(7,001) [4,234]	na
	Navy	na	na	(9)	na	na	na	na	na
	Marines	na	na	(7)	na	na	na	na	na
	Total	na	na	(1,080)	na	na	(5,937)	na	[2,911]
World War I	Army	(37,568)	(13,691)	50,510 (51,259)	(51,447)	(4,421)	55,868 (55,868)	106,378 (107,127)	193,663
	Navy	na	na	431	na	na	6,856	7,287	819
	Marines	na	na	2,461	na	na	390	2,851	9,520
	Total	na	na	53,402	na	na	63,114	116,516	204,002
World War II	Army	(210,343)	(26,706)	234,874 (237,049)	(14,243)	(50,976)	83,400 (65,219)	318,274 (302,268)	565,861
	Navy	na	na	36,950	na	na	25,664	62,614	37,778
	Marines	na	na	19,733	na	na	4,778	24,511	68,207
	Total	na	na	291,557	na	na	113,842	405,399	671,846
Cold War	Total	na	na	[384]	na	[235]	na	[619]	na
Korean War	Army	na	na	27,731	na	na	2,125	29,856	77,596
	Navy	na	na	506	na	na	154	660	1,576
	Marines	na	na	4,266	na	na	242	4,508	23,744
	Air force	na	na	1,238	na	na	314	1,552	368
	Total	na	na	33,741	na	na	2,835	36,576	103,284

Vietnam War	Army	na	na	30,952	na	na	7,261	38,213	96,802
	Navy	na	na	1,628	na	na	934	2,562	4,178
	Marines	na	na	13,091	na	na	1,749	14,840	51,392
	Air force	na	na	1,744	na	na	841	2,585	931
	Total	na	na	47,415	na	na	10,785	58,200	153,303
Persian Gulf War	Army	96	2	98	na	na	126	224	354
	Navy	5	0	5	na	na	50	55	12
	Marines	22	2	24	na	na	44	68	92
	Air force	20	0	20	na	na	15	35	9
	Total	143	4	147	na	na	235	382	467

Sources and notes: The basic source is Carter *et al.* (2006, Table Ed1–5). Figures from this source are shown without parentheses or brackets. Also shown without parentheses or brackets are estimates from: "US Navy and Marine Corps Personnel Killed and Wounded in Wars, Conflicts, Terrorist Acts, and Other Hostile Incidents," at www.history.navy.mil/index.html (accessed May 9, 2008). Additional sources and notes are as follows. Mexican War: the figures in parentheses are Beebe and DeBakey (1952, 21). Civil War (North): the figures in parentheses are Beebe and DeBakey (1952, 21). Civil War (South): Confederate losses are uncertain. The figures in parentheses are Beebe and DeBakey (1952, 21); the figures in brackets are Clodfelter (2001, 332). Spanish–American War: figures in parentheses are Beebe and DeBakey (1952, 21). Their estimates shown as for the navy combine the navy and marines. Figures in brackets are Clodfelter (2001, 272). According to Clodfelter, 2,061 Americans died of disease in the zone of combat, and 2,982 in other areas, including stateside ports. The figures for the navy include marines, but exclude the men lost from the explosion of the battleship *Maine*. Altogether 260 men were lost, 232 from the navy, and 28 from the marines (Department of the Navy – Naval Historical Center, www.history.navy.mil/index.html). All other figures are Carter *et al.* (2006, Table Ed1–5). Philippine–American War: the figures in parentheses are Beebe and DeBakey (1952, 21); the figures in brackets are from Clodfelter (2001, 272). World War I: the figures in parentheses are from Beebe and DeBakey (1952, 21). The figures for the army include those for the Air Service. World War II: the figures in parentheses are from Beebe and DeBakey (1952, 21). Cold War: the figures in brackets are from Clodfelter (2001, 570). The figure for died of injuries is Clodfelter's estimate of personnel lost in submarine accidents.

Appendix 3 *The financial costs of US wars in the twentieth century*

	Costs during the period of active conflict (billions of current dollars)	Costs during the period of active conflict in constant dollars (billions of 2008 dollars)	Costs during the period of active conflict as a share of average GDP during the war[a] (%)	Veterans' benefits discounted to the midpoint of the war at 4.5% (billions of 2008 dollars)	Total costs (billions of 2008 dollars)	Total costs as a share of average GDP during the war (%)
Spanish–American War (1898–9)	0.274	6.3	1.46	17.92	24.22	5.6
Philippine–American War (1899–1902)	0.230 (0.211)	4.9	1.05	7.58	12.51	2.6
Turn-of-the-century imperialism (1898–1915)	3.073	60	11.17	25.50	85.58	15.6
World War I (1918–19)	32.020	313	43.00	305.7	618.22	82.3
World War II (1939–47)	320.315	3,291	185.30	1,373	4,664	262.5
Korean War (1950–5)	175.871	1,186	48.24	215.6	1401.77	57.0
Cold War (1948–9, 1956–66, 1975–90)	1,881	5,193	99.66	na	na	na

Vietnam War (1967–74)	382.142	1,697	35.25	554.8	2,251.7	46.7
War against Communism (1948–90)	2,438.634	8,076	169.92	na	na	na
Persian Gulf War (1991)	61.000	89	1.02	371.9	460.5	5.3

Sources and notes: The dates used in preparing this table were based on the periods during which military spending appeared to be elevated by the war. In some cases this perspective produces different dates than would be generated by a focus on political events, such as the signing of peace treaties or casualty figures. In each case GDP and the GDP deflator are from Johnston and Williamson (2010) and veterans' benefits from Edwards (2010, Table 2). [a] Comparing the total cost with average GDP during the war is but one of many ways of compressing an evolving relationship into a single number. An alternative that was used by Friedman (1952) is to compute the share of GDP in each year going to the war effort, and then to sum the shares for the duration of the war. In practice this usually results in a similar estimate. I show the ratio of total spending to average GDP here because it is, hopefully, a more intuitive measure of "war effort." Spanish–American War: Table 3.1. Philippine–American War: Table 4.1. The veterans of the Spanish–American War, the Philippine–American War and the Boxer rebellion were treated together for the purpose of paying compensation and disability payments. To divide the resulting amount between the two wars I used the figures on the number serving from Appendix 1. Turn-of-the-Century Imperialism: Table 4.1. I included with those serving in the Philippine–American War a small allowance for those who served in the Boxer rebellion. World War I: Table 5.4. World War II: Table 6.8. Korean War: I used the sum of spending on defense and international affairs from Economic Report of the President (2010, Table B80) as the basic measure of military spending. These series are for fiscal years, rather than calendar years. Then I computed spending between 1950 and 1955 on the assumption that the share of GDP devoted to the military was the same as in 1991–96. The cost of the war shown here was the difference between the actual and hypothetical values. This calculation, an underestimate, does not include the costs of the draft, the long-run costs of maintaining US forces in South Korea, or war-related expenditures by civilian agencies such as the Office of Price Stability. Cold War: The same method as for the Korean War. Vietnam War: The same method as for the Korean War. The dates for the war used in this table are for years in which federal spending appears to have been substantially affected by the war. US involvement in Vietnam extended over a longer period. War against Communism: In each column the sum of the amounts for the Korean War, the Cold War, and the Vietnam War. Persian Gulf War: Expenditures: US Department of Defense (1992).

Appendix 4 *Sources of federal tax revenues in World War I, World War II, and the Korean War*

	Total tax revenues	Customs	Alcohol and tobacco	Other excise taxes	Income tax	Corporate income tax	Excess profits tax	Estate and gift taxes
Millions of dollars								
Korean War (nominal)	174,423	1,788	12,477	15,144	81,461	55,476	5,623	2,454
Korean War (1950 prices)	159,469	1,635	11,407	13,842	74,465	50,733	5,145	2,243
Korean War increase	26,212	367	764	1,690	19,340	2,944	983	125
WWII (nominal)	178,209	2,327	15,236	11,194	76,431	29,704	40,199	3,118
WWII (1940 prices)	143,475	1,903	12,174	8,870	60,845	23,779	33,388	2,516
WWII increase (1940 prices)	123,727	857	8,476	6,915	56,522	17,346	32,175	1,436
WWI (nominal)	22,744	1,578	2,766	1,535	5,744	3,679	6,908	533
WWI (1916 prices)	15,136	1,035	1,834	943	3,769	2,435	4,786	334
WWI increase (1916 prices)	12,442	395	827	930	3,249	1,920	4,786	334
Percentages of total tax revenues								
Korean War (nominal)	100	1.03	7.15	8.68	46.70	31.81	3.22	1.41
Korean War (1950 prices)	100	1.03	7.15	8.68	46.70	31.81	3.23	1.41

Korean War increase (1950 prices)	100	1.40	2.91	6.45	73.78	11.23	3.75	0.48
WWII (nominal)	100	1.31	8.55	6.28	42.89	16.67	22.56	1.75
WWII (1940 prices)	100	1.33	8.49	6.18	42.41	16.57	23.27	1.75
WWII increase (1940 prices)	100	0.69	6.85	5.59	45.68	14.02	26.01	1.16
WWI (nominal)	100	6.94	12.16	6.75	25.26	16.17	30.37	2.34
WWI (1916 prices)	100	6.84	12.12	6.23	24.90	16.09	31.62	2.21
WWI increase (1916 prices)	100	3.17	6.65	7.48	26.11	15.43	38.47	2.69

Sources and notes: The data are from US Bureau of the Census (1960, series Y259–Y262, Y268, Y270, Y271, Y288, Y289, and Y307). The Korean War was defined as fiscal 1951 through fiscal 1953; WWII as 1941–6; and WWI as 1917–22. The first row for each war shows the sum of all tax revenues, or all revenues from a particular tax, over the war years. The second row for each war expresses the amounts in base year prices using the GDP deflator (Carter *et al.* 2006, series Ca1). The third row for each war is the second row less the base year amounts multiplied by the number of war years. In addition to tax receipts the federal government also received revenues from borrowing and from a number of other sources such as income from government enterprises (the post office, the Panama Canal, and so on), seigniorage, payments from foreign governments, and so on. There are also small errors that arise mainly from differences in accounting periods.

References

Adams, Henry C. 1918. Borrowing as a phase of war financiering. *Annals of the American Academy of Political and Social Science* 75 (Financing the War) (Jan.): 23–30.

Adams, Stephen B. 1997. *Mr. Kaiser goes to Washington: the rise of a government entrepreneur.* The Luther Hartwell Hodges series on business, society, and the state. Chapel Hill: University of North Carolina Press.

Alchian, Armen A., and Reuben A. Kessel. 1959. Redistribution of wealth through inflation. *Science* 130 (3375) (Sep. 4): 535–9.

Alperovitz, Gar. 1995. *The decision to use the atomic bomb and the architecture of an American myth.* New York: A. A. Knopf.

Angrist, Joshua D. 1993. The effect of veterans' benefits on education and earnings. *Industrial and Labor Relations Review* 46 (July): 637–52.

1990a. Lifetime earnings and the Vietnam era draft lottery: evidence from social security administrative records. *American Economic Review* 80 (3) (June): 313–36.

1990b. Lifetime earnings and the Vietnam era draft lottery: evidence from social security administrative records. *American Economic Review* 80 (5) (Dec.): 1284–6.

Auxier, George W. 1940. Middle Western newspapers and the Spanish American War, 1895–1898. *Mississippi Valley Historical Review* 26 (4) (Mar.): 523–34.

1939. The propaganda activities of the Cuban junta in precipitating the Spanish–American War, 1895–1898. *Hispanic American Historical Review* 19 (3) (Aug.): 286–305.

Ayres, Leonard P. 1919. *The war with Germany: a statistical summary.* Washington, DC: Government Printing Office.

Baack, Bennett D., and Edward John Ray. 1985. Special interests and the adoption of the income tax in the United States. *Journal of Economic History* 45 (3) (Sep.): 607–25.

Bailey, Thomas A. 1937. Was the presidential election of 1900 a mandate on imperialism? *Mississippi Valley Historical Review* 24 (1) (June): 43–52.

Baldwin, Hanson Weightman. 1950. *Great mistakes of the war.* New York: Harper.

Balke, Nathan S., and Robert J. Gordon. 1989. The estimation of prewar Gross National Product: methodology and new evidence. *Journal of Political Economy* 97 (1) (Feb.): 38–92.

Ball, John McNickle. 1947. *Reclaimed rubber: the story of an American raw material.* New York: Rubber Reclaimers Association.

Bank, Steven A., Kirk J. Stark, and Joseph J. Thorndike. 2008. *War and taxes*. Washington, DC: Urban Institute Press.

Barro, Robert J. 1989. The neoclassical approach to fiscal policy. In *Modern business cycle theory*, ed. Robert J. Barro, 326–64. Cambridge University Press.

1987. Government spending, interest rates, prices, and budget deficits in the United Kingdom, 1701–1918. *Journal of Monetary Economics* 20 (2) (Sep.): 221–47.

Baruch, Bernard M. 1936. *Taking the profits out of war: a program for industrial mobilization.* New York: Privately printed.

Bedard, Kelly, and Olivier Deschênes. 2006. The long-term impact of military service on health: evidence from World War II and Korean War veterans. *American Economic Review* 96 (1) (Mar.): 176–94.

Beebe, Gilbert Wheeler, and Michael E. DeBakey. 1952. *Battle casualties, incidence, mortality, and logistic considerations*. Springfield, Ill.: Thomas.

Bellamy, Matthew J. 2005. *Profiting the crown: Canada's polymer corporation, 1942–1990.* Montreal and Ithaca: McGill-Queen's University Press.

Bernstein, Barton J. 2003. Reconsidering the "atomic general": Leslie R. Groves. *Journal of Military History* 67 (3) (July): 883–920.

1998. Truman and the A-bomb: targeting noncombatants, using the bomb, and his defending the "decision." *Journal of Military History* 62 (3) (July): 547–70.

1976. *The atomic bomb: the critical issues.* Critical Issues in American History. Boston: Little, Brown.

1975. Roosevelt, Truman, and the atomic bomb, 1941–1945: a reinterpretation. *Political Science Quarterly* 90 (1) (Spring): 23–69.

1966. The Truman administration and the steel strike of 1946. *Journal of American History* 52 (4) (Mar.): 791–803.

Bernstein, Michael A. 1990. American economic expertise from the Great War to the Cold War: some initial observations. *Journal of Economic History* 50 (2) (June): 407–16.

Birchall, Frederick T. 1936. Food curb clouds Reich's Christmas. *New York Times* Dec. 21.

Birtle, Andrew J. 1997. The US army's pacification of Marinduque, Philippine islands, April 1900–April 1901. *Journal of Military History* 61 (2) (Apr.): 255–82.

Bodenger, Robert George. 1971. Soldiers' bonuses: a history of veterans' benefits in the United States, 1776–1967. Ph.D. dissertation, Pennsylvania State University.

Bogart, Ernest Ludlow. 1920. *Direct and indirect costs of the Great World War.* Preliminary Economic Studies of the War 24. 2nd rev. edn. New York: Oxford University Press.

Boot, Max. 2002. *The savage wars of peace: small wars and the rise of American power.* New York: Basic Books.

Bordo, Michael D. 1995. Is there a good case for a new Bretton Woods international monetary system? In Papers and Proceedings of the Hundred and Seventh Annual Meeting of the American Economic Association, Washington, DC, January 6–8, 1995. *American Economic Review* 85 (2) (May): 317–22.

Bordo, Michael D., and Barry J. Eichengreen. 1993. *A retrospective on the Bretton Woods system: lessons for international monetary reform.* National Bureau of Economic Research Project Report. University of Chicago Press.

Boyle, Stanley E. 1961. Government promotion of monopoly power: an examination of the sale of the synthetic rubber industry. *Journal of Industrial Economics* 9 (2) (Apr.): 151–69.

Bradsher, Henry S. 1999. *Afghan Communism and Soviet intervention.* Oxford University Press.

Brandes, Stuart D. 1997. *Warhogs: a history of war profits in America.* Lexington: University Press of Kentucky.

Brodie, Bernard. 1955. Some notes on the evolution of air doctrine. *World Politics* 7 (3) (Apr.): 349–70.

Brookings. 2002. "The Costs of the Manhattan Project," at www.brookings.edu/projects/archive/nucweapons/manhattan.aspx (accessed July 15, 2010).

Burk, Kathleen. 1979. The diplomacy of finance: British financial missions to the United States 1914–1918. *Historical Journal* 22 (2) (June): 351–72.

Cagan, Phillip. 1965. *Determinants and effects of changes in the stock of money, 1875–1960.* New York: National Bureau of Economic Research.

Campagna, Anthony S. 1987. *US national economic policy, 1917–1985.* New York: Praeger.

Card, David, and Thomas Lemieux. 2001. Going to college to avoid the draft: the unintended legacy of the Vietnam War. In Papers and Proceedings of the Hundred Thirteenth Annual Meeting of the American Economic Association. *American Economic Review* 91 (2) (May): 97–102.

Carter, Susan B., Scott Sigmund Gartner, Michael R. Haines, Alan L. Olmstead, Richard Sutch, and Gavin Wright. 2006. *Historical statistics of the United States: earliest times to the present*. Millennial edn. New York: Cambridge University Press.

Caruana, Leonard, and Hugh Rockoff. 2007. An elephant in the garden: the Allies, Spain, and oil in World War II. *European Review of Economic History* 11 (2): 159–87.

2003. A wolfram in sheep's clothing: economic warfare in Spain, 1940–1944. *Journal of Economic History* 63 (1): 100–26.

Chambers, John Whiteclay. 1987. *To raise an army: the draft comes to modern America*. New York: The Free Press; London: Collier Macmillan.

Chandler, Lester V. 1949. Federal Reserve policy and the federal debt. *American Economic Review* 39 (2) (Mar.): 405–29.

Chase, John L. 1955. Unconditional surrender reconsidered. *Political Science Quarterly* 70 (2) (June): 258–79.

Clark, J. M. 1917. The basis of war-time collectivism. *American Economic Review* 7 (4) (Dec.): 772–90.

1931. *The costs of the World War to the American people*. Carnegie Endowment for International Peace. Division of Economics and History: Economic and Social History of the World War, American Series. New Haven and London: Yale University Press, H. Milford, and Oxford University Press.

Clark, Robert Louis, Lee A. Craig, and Jack W. Wilson. 2003. *A history of public sector pensions in the United States*. Philadelphia: University of Pennsylvania Press.

Clayton, James L. 1972. The fiscal cost of the Cold War to the United States: the first 25 years, 1947–1971. *Western Political Quarterly* 25 (3) (Sep.): 375–95.

Clodfelter, Michael. 2001. *Warfare and armed conflicts: a statistical reference to casualty and other figures, 1500–1999*. 2nd edn. Jefferson, N.C.: McFarland.

Collins, William J. 2001. Race, Roosevelt, and wartime production: fair employment in World War II labor markets. *American Economic Review* 91 (1) (Mar.): 272–86.

Copeland, Morris A., Jerome Jacobson, and Herman Lasken. 1945. The WPB index of war production. *Journal of the American Statistical Association* 40 (230) (June): 145–59.

Corum, James S. 1998. The Spanish Civil War: lessons learned and not learned by the Great Powers. *Journal of Military History* 62 (2) (Apr.): 313–34.

Costa, Dora L. 1998. *The evolution of retirement: an American economic history, 1880–1990*. NBER Series on Long-term Factors in Economic Development. University of Chicago Press.

Cotton, Timothy Y. C. 1986. War and American democracy: electoral costs of the last five wars. *Journal of Conflict Resolution* 30 (4) (Dec.): 616–35.

Cowles Commission for Research in Economics, and Alfred Cowles. 1939. *Common-stock indexes*, Vol. III. 2nd edn. Bloomington, Ind.: Principia Press.

Davis, Lance Edwin, and Robert J. Cull. 1994. *International capital markets and American economic growth, 1820–1914*. Cambridge University Press.

Davis, Lance Edwin, and Stanley L. Engerman. 2006. *Naval blockades in peace and war: an economic history since 1750*. Cambridge University Press.

2003. History lessons: sanctions: neither war nor peace. *Journal of Economic Perspectives* 17 (2) (Spring): 187–97.

Davis, Lance Edwin, Robert A. Huttenback, and Susan G. Davis. 1986. *Mammon and the pursuit of empire: the political economy of British imperialism, 1860–1912*. Interdisciplinary Perspectives on Modern History. Cambridge University Press.

De Long, J. Bradford, and Barry J. Eichengreen. 1993. The Marshall Plan: history's most successful structural adjustment program. In *Post-World War II economic reconstruction and its lessons for eastern Europe today*, ed. Rudiger Dornbusch, Wilhelm Nölling, and Richard Layard. Cambridge, Mass.: MIT Press.

De Long, J. Bradford, and Lawrence H. Summers. 1988. How does macroeconomic policy affect output? *Brookings Papers on Economic Activity* (2): 433–80.

Despres, Emile, Albert G. Hart, Milton Friedman, Paul A. Samuelson, and Donald H. Wallace. 1950. The problem of economic instability. *American Economic Review* 40 (4) (Sep.): 501–3, 505–38.

Dewey, Davis Rich. 1931. *Financial history of the United States*. 11th edn. New York and London: Longmans, Green and Co.

Dewhurst, J. Frederic, and Twentieth Century Fund. 1947. *America's needs and resources*. New York: The Twentieth Century Fund.

Dooley, Peter C. 1989. Ricardo and Keynes on war finance. *Atlantic Economic Journal* 17 (3): 21–33.

Dornbusch, Rudiger, Wilhelm Nölling, and P. R. G. Layard. 1993. *Postwar economic reconstruction and lessons for the east today*. Cambridge, Mass.: MIT Press.

Dos Passos, John. 1968. Gold rush down south. In *America at war: the home front, 1941–45*, ed. Richard Polenberg. Englewood Cliffs, NJ: Prentice-Hall.

Dye, Alan. 1998. *Cuban sugar in the age of mass production: technology and the economics of the sugar central, 1899–1929*. Stanford University Press.

Eckstein, A. M. 1991. Is there a "Hobson–Lenin thesis" on late nineteenth-century colonial expansion? *Economic History Review* 44 (2) (May): 297–318.

Economic Report of the President. Washington, DC: Government Printing Office. See US Congress, Joint Economic Committee, 2010 for the formal reference.

Edelstein, Michael. 2001. The size of the US armed forces during World War II: feasibility and war planning. In *Research in Economic History, Vol. XX*, ed. Alexander J. Field, Gregory Clark, and William A. Sundstrom, 47–97. Amsterdam, New York, and London: Elsevier Science and JAI.

2000. War and the American economy in the twentieth century. In *The Cambridge Economic History of the United States, Volume II: The Long Nineteenth Century*, ed. Stanley L. Engerman and Robert E. Gallman, 329–405. Cambridge University Press.

1990. What price Cold War? Military spending and private investment in the US, 1946–1979. *Cambridge Journal of Economics* 14 (4) (Dec.): 421–37.

Edwards, Ryan D. 2010. US war costs: two parts temporary, one part permanent. NBER *Working Paper no. 16108*.

Eichengreen, Barry J. 2011. *Exorbitant privilege: the rise and fall of the dollar and the future of the international monetary system*. Oxford University Press.

1995. *Europe's postwar recovery*. Studies in Monetary and Financial History. Cambridge University Press.

Ellis, Howard W. 1940. German exchange control, 1931–1939: from an emergency measure to a totalitarian institution. *Quarterly Journal of Economics* 54 (4/2) (Aug.): 1–158.

Ellis, John. 1993. *World War II: a statistical survey: the essential facts and figures for all the combatants*. New York: Facts on File.

Eloranta, Jari. 2007. From the great illusion to the Great War: military spending behavior of the great powers, 1870–1913. *European Review of Economic History* 11 (2) (Aug.): 255–83.

Engelbrecht, H. C., and Frank Cleary Hanighen. 1934. *Merchants of death: a study of the international armament industry*. New York: Dodd, Mead & Co.

Ferguson, Niall. 2006. Political risk and the international bond market between the 1848 revolution and the outbreak of the First World War. *Economic History Review* 59 (1): 70–112.

2004. *Empire: the rise and demise of the British world order and the lessons for global power.* New York: Basic Books.

2001. *The cash nexus: money and power in the modern world, 1700–2000.* New York: Basic Books.

1995. Keynes and the German inflation. *English Historical Review* 110 (436) (Apr.): 368–91.

Field, Alexander J. 2008. The impact of the Second World War on US productivity growth. *Economic History Review* 61 (3) (Aug.): 672–94.

Field, James A., Jr. 1978. American imperialism: the worst chapter in almost any book. *American Historical Review* 83 (3) (June): 644–68.

Firestone, John M. 1960. *Federal receipts and expenditures during business cycles, 1879–1958.* Princeton University Press.

Fischer, David Hackett. 2004. *Washington's crossing: pivotal moments in American history.* Oxford University Press.

Fisher, Irving. 1918. How the public should pay for the war. *Annals of the American Academy of Political and Social Science* 78 (Mobilizing America's Resources for the War) (July): 112–17.

Fleisig, Heywood. 1976. War-related debts and the Great Depression. Papers and Proceedings of the Eighty-eighth Annual Meeting of the American Economic Association. *American Economic Review* 66 (2) (May): 52–8.

Flynn, George Q. 1979. *The mess in Washington: manpower mobilization in World War II.* Contributions in American history 76. Westport, Conn.: Greenwood Press.

Freedman, Lawrence, and Efraim Karsh. 1991. How Kuwait was won: strategy in the Gulf War. *International Security* 16 (2) (Autumn): 5–41.

Friedman, Milton. 1967. Why not a volunteer army? *New Individualist Review* 4 (4).

1957. *A theory of the consumption function.* National Bureau of Economic Research General Series 63. Princeton University Press.

1952. Price, income, and monetary changes in three wartime periods. Papers and Proceedings of the Sixty-fourth Annual Meeting of the American Economic Association. *American Economic Review* 42 (2) (May): 612–25.

1951. Comments on monetary policy. *Review of Economics and Statistics* 33 (3) (Aug.): 186–91.

Friedman, Milton, and Anna Jacobson Schwartz. 1982. *Monetary trends in the United States and the United Kingdom: their relation to income, prices, and interest rates, 1867–1975.* National Bureau of Economic Research Monograph. University of Chicago Press.

1970. *Monetary statistics of the United States: estimates, sources, methods.* National Bureau of Economic Research Studies in Business Cycles 20. New York: National Bureau of Economic Research.

1963. *A monetary history of the United States, 1867–1960*. National Bureau of Economic Research Studies in Business Cycles 12. Princeton University Press.

Fulbright, J. William. 1967 [1966]. *The arrogance of power*. New York: Random House.

Galbraith, John Kenneth. 1981. *A life in our times*. Boston: Houghton Mifflin.

1969. *How to control the military*. Garden City, N.Y.: Doubleday.

1952. *A theory of price control*. Cambridge, Mass.: Harvard University Press.

Gareau, Frederick H. 1961. Morgenthau's plan for industrial disarmament in Germany. *Western Political Quarterly* 14 (2) (June): 517–34.

Gates, John Morgan. 1973. *Schoolbooks and Krags; the United States army in the Philippines, 1898–1902*. Contributions in Military History 3. Westport, Conn.: Greenwood Press.

Gaughan, Anthony. 1999. Woodrow Wilson and the rise of militant interventionism in the south. *Journal of Southern History* 65 (4) (Nov.): 771–808.

Gemery, Henry A., and Jan S. Hogendorn. 1993. The microeconomic bases of short-run learning curves: destroyer production in World War II. In *The sinews of war: essays on the economic history of World War II*, ed. Geofrey Mills and Hugh Rockoff, 150–65. Ames, Iowa: Iowa State University Press.

Gilbert, Martin. 1994. *The First World War: a complete history*. New York: H. Holt.

Glasson, William Henry, and David Kinley. 1918. *Federal military pensions in the United States*. New York: Carnegie Endowment for International Peace and Oxford University Press.

Goldin, Claudia D. 1991. The role of World War II in the rise of women's employment. *American Economic Review* 81 (4) (Sep.): 741–56.

1980. War. In *Encyclopedia of American economic history, Vol. III*, ed. Glenn Porter, 935–57. New York: Charles Scribner's Sons.

Goldin, Claudia, and Robert A. Margo. 1992. The great compression: the wage structure in the United States at mid-century. *Quarterly Journal of Economics* 107 (1) (Feb.): 1–34.

Goldsmith, Raymond W. 1946. The power of victory: munitions output in World War II. *Military Affairs* 10 (1) (Spring): 69–80.

Gordon, Robert J. 1969. $45 billion of US private investment has been mislaid. *American Economic Review* 59 (3) (June): 221–38.

Gordon, Robert J., and Robert Krenn. 2010. The end of the Great Depression 1939–41: policy contributions and fiscal multipliers. *NBER Working Paper no. 16380.*

Grant, Ulysses S. 1885. *Personal memoirs of U. S. Grant.* New York: C. L. Webster.

Greenwood, Jeremy, Ananth Seshadri, and Guillaume Vandenbroucke. 2005. *The baby boom and baby bust. American Economic Review* 95 (1) (Mar.): 183–207.

Gregory, Anthony. 2011. "What price war? Afghanistan, Iraq, and the cost of conflict." Independent Policy Report. Oakland, Calif.: The Independent Institute.

Grubb, Farley. 2007. *Ben Franklin and the birth of paper money*, Federal Reserve Bank of Philadelphia and the Library Company of Philadelphia, www.philadelphiafed.org.

Halliday, Fred. 1991. The Gulf War and its aftermath: first reflections. *International Affairs* 67 (2) (Apr.): 223–34.

Harrington, Fred H. 1935. The anti-imperialist movement in the United States, 1898–1900. *Mississippi Valley Historical Review* 22 (2) (Sep.): 211–30.

Harrison, Mark. 1988. Resource mobilization for World War II: the USA, UK, USSR, and Germany, 1938–1945. *Economic History Review* 41 (2) (May): 171–92.

1998. *The Economics of World War II.* Cambridge University Press.

Hartley, Keith, and Todd Sandler. 1995. *Handbook of defense economics.* Handbooks in Economics 12. Amsterdam and New York: Elsevier.

Hawley, Ellis Wayne. 1966. *The New Deal and the problem of monopoly: a study in economic ambivalence.* Princeton University Press.

Hayek, Friedrich A. von. 1976 [1944]. *The road to serfdom.* University of Chicago Press.

Heath, Jim F. 1971. Domestic America during World War II: research opportunities for historians. *Journal of American History* 58 (2) (Sep.): 384–414.

Heller, Walter W. 1965. The future of our fiscal system. *Journal of Business* 38 (3) (July): 235–44.

Herbert, Vernon, and Attilio Bisio. 1985. *Synthetic rubber: a project that had to succeed.* Contributions in Economics and Economic History 63. Westport, Conn.: Greenwood Press.

Hersey, John. 1946. *Hiroshima.* New York: A. A. Knopf.

Hess, Gregory D., and Athanasios Orphanides. 1995. War politics: an economic, rational-voter framework. *American Economic Review* 85 (4) (Sep.): 828–46.

Hewitt, Kenneth. 1983. Place annihilation: area bombing and the fate of urban places. *Annals of the Association of American Geographers* 73 (2) (June): 257–84.

Hickman, Bert G. 1955. *The Korean War and United States economic activity, 1950–1952.* New York: National Bureau of Economic Research.

Higgs, Robert. 2008. Caging the dogs of war: how major US neoimperialist wars end. *Independent Review* 13 (2): 299–312.

1999. From central planning to the market: the American transition, 1945–1947. *Journal of Economic History* 59 (3) (Sep.): 600–23.

1994. The Cold War economy: opportunity costs, ideology, and the politics of crisis. *Explorations in Economic History* 31 (3): 283–312.

1993. Private profit, public risk: institutional antecedents of the modern military procurement system in the rearmament program of 1940–1941. In *The sinews of war: essays on the economic history of World War II*, ed. Geofrey Mills and Hugh Rockoff, 166–98. Ames, Iowa: Iowa State University Press.

1992. Wartime prosperity? A reassessment of the US economy in the 1940s. *Journal of Economic History* 52 (1) (Mar.): 41–60.

1987. *Crisis and Leviathan: critical episodes in the growth of American government*. New York: Oxford University Press.

Hobson, J. A. 1902. *Imperialism: a study*. New York: J. Pott & Company.

1900. *The war in South Africa: its causes and effects*. New York: Macmillan.

Holland, Thomas E. 1969. "Operation Twist" and the movement of interest rates and related economic time series. *International Economic Review* 10 (3) (Oct.): 260–5.

Howard, Frank Atherton. 1947. *Buna rubber, the birth of an industry*. New York: D. Van Nostrand Company.

Hufbauer, Gary Clyde, Kimberly Ann Elliott, and Jeffrey J. Schott. 1990. *Economic sanctions reconsidered: history and current policy*. 2nd edn. Washington, DC: Institute for International Economics.

Hume, David. 1970 [1752]. Of public credit. In *David Hume: writings on economics*, ed. Eugene Rotwein, 90–107. Madison: University of Wisconsin Press.

Hunter, Kenneth H., and Edward L. Hogan. 1950. *War Production Board's steel division's experience with World War II controls particularly under the controlled materials plan*. US Department of Commerce. US Bureau of Foreign and Domestic Commerce, Office of Industry and Commerce, Iron and Steel Division.

Hutchinson, William, and Ricardo Ungo. 2004. Social saving of the Panama Canal. Department of Economics, Vanderbilt University, Working Paper 0423, available at http://search.ebscohost.com/login.aspx?direct=true&db=ecn&AN=0769495&site=ehost-live: http://www.vanderbilt.edu/Econ/wparchive/workpaper/vu04-w23.pdf.

Hyman, Sidney. 1976. *Marriner S. Eccles, private entrepreneur and public servant*. Stanford, Calif.: Graduate School of Business, Stanford University.

Irwin, Douglas A. 2010. Did France cause the Great Depression? *NBER Working Paper no. 16350.*

Janeway, Eliot. 1951. *The struggle for survival: a chronicle of economic mobilization in World War II*. Chronicles of America 53. New Haven: Yale University Press.

Johnson, Marilynn S. 1993. *The second gold rush: Oakland and the east bay in World War II*. Berkeley: University of California Press.

Johnston Louis, and Williamson, Samuel H. 2004. The annual real and nominal GDP for the United States, 1789–present. In Economic History Services, available at www.eh.net/hmit/gdp/ (accessed March 2004).

2010. What was the US GDP then? *In Measuring Worth, 2010*, available at www.measuringworth.org/usgdp/ (accessed February 2, 2011).

Kang, Sung Won, and Hugh Rockoff. 2006. Capitalizing patriotism: the liberty loans of World War I. *NBER Working Paper no. 11919.*

Kant, Immanuel. 1917 [1795]. *Perpetual peace: a philosophical essay*, trans. M. Campbell Smith. London: George Allen and Unwin.

Karnow, Stanley. 1991. *Vietnam, a history*. New York: Penguin.

Keaney, Thomas, and Eliot A. Cohen. 1993. *Gulf War air power survey*. Washington, DC: Office of the Secretary of the Air Force.

Keegan, John. 1999. *The First World War*. New York: A. Knopf.

Kemmerer, E. W. 1905. The establishment of the gold exchange standard in the Philippines. *Quarterly Journal of Economics* 19 (4) (Aug.): 585–609.

Kendrick, John W. 1961. *Productivity trends in the United States*. National Bureau of Economic Research General Series 71. Princeton University Press.

Kennan, George F. 1967. *Memoirs, 1925–1950*. Boston: Little, Brown.

1947. The sources of Soviet conduct. *Foreign Affairs* 25 (4) (July): 566–82.

Kennedy, David M. 1980. *Over here: the First World War and American society*. New York: Oxford University Press.

Keynes, John Maynard. 1964 [1936]. *The general theory of employment, interest and money*. New York: Harcourt, Brace & World.

1940. *How to pay for the war: a radical plan for the Chancellor of the Exchequer*. London: Macmillan.

1923. *A tract on monetary reform*. London: Macmillan.

1922. *A revision of the treaty: being a sequel to the Economic Consequences of the Peace*. London: Macmillan.

1920 [1919]. *The economic consequences of the peace*. New York: Harcourt, Brace and Howe.

Kimball, Warren F. 1976. *Swords or ploughshares?: The Morgenthau plan for defeated Nazi Germany, 1943–1946*. The Americas Alternatives Series. Philadelphia: Lippincott.

Kirshner, Jonathan. 2007. *Appeasing bankers: financial caution on the road to war*. Princeton Studies in International History and Politics. Princeton University Press.

Klein, Burton. 1948. Germany's preparation for war: a re-examination. *American Economic Review* 38 (1) (Mar.): 56–77.

Koh, B. C. 1971. Dilemmas of Korean reunification. *Asian Survey* 11 (5) (May): 475–95.

Koistinen, Paul A. C. 2004. *Arsenal of World War II: the political economy of American warfare, 1940–1945*. Modern War Studies. Lawrence: University Press of Kansas.

1998. *Planning war, pursuing peace: the political economy of American warfare, 1920–1939*. Modern War Studies. Lawrence: University Press of Kansas.

1997. *Mobilizing for modern war: the political economy of American warfare, 1865–1919*. Modern War Studies. Lawrence: University Press of Kansas.

Kuznets, Simon Smith. 1945. *National product in wartime*. New York: National Bureau of Economic Research.

LaFeber, Walter. 1993. *The American search for opportunity, 1865–1913*. Vol. II of *The Cambridge History of American Foreign Relations*. Cambridge University Press.

Larson, Eric V. 1996. *Casualties and consensus: the historical role of casualties in domestic support for US military operations*. Santa Monica, Calif.: Rand.

Lebergott, Stanley. 1980. The returns to US imperialism, 1890–1929. *Journal of Economic History* 40 (2) (June): 229–52.

Lenin, Vladimir Ilyich. 1939 [1916]. *Imperialism, the highest stage of capitalism: a popular outline*. New York: International Publishers.

Lent, George E. 1951. Excess-profits taxation in the United States. *Journal of Political Economy* 59(6) (Dec.): 481–97.

Lewis, Cleona, and Karl T. Schlotterbeck. 1938. *America's stake in international investments*. Washington, DC: The Brookings Institution.

Lieberman, Sanford R. 1983. The evacuation of industry in the Soviet Union during World War II. *Soviet Studies* 35 (1) (Jan.): 90–102.

Linn, Brian McAllister. 2000. *The Philippine War, 1899–1902*. Modern War Studies. Lawrence: University Press of Kansas.

Linton, Calvin Darlington. 1975. *The bicentennial almanac: 200 years of America 1776–1976*. Nashville: T. Nelson.

Longo, W. E., W. Cheadle, A. Fink, R. Kozol, R. DePalma, R. Rege, L. Neumayer, *et al.* 2005. The role of the veterans' affairs medical centers in patient care, surgical education, research and faculty development. *American Journal of Surgery* 190 (5) (Nov.): 662–75.

Lowe, Keith. 2007. *Inferno: the fiery destruction of Hamburg, 1943*. New York: Scribner.

Lutz, H. L. 1930. Inter-Allied debts, reparations, and national policy. *Journal of Political Economy* 38 (1) (Feb.): 29–61.

McCutcheon, John T. 1950. *Drawn from memory, containing many of the author's famous cartoons and sketches*. Indianapolis: Bobbs-Merrill.

MacIsaac, David. 1976. *Strategic bombing in World War Two: the story of the United States Strategic Bombing Survey*. New York: Garland.

McNeill, William Hardy. 1982. *The pursuit of power: technology, armed force, and society since AD 1000*. University of Chicago Press.

Maley, William. 2009. *The Afghanistan wars: twentieth-century wars*. 2nd edn. Basingstoke: Palgrave Macmillan.

Mantoux, Étienne. 1952 [1946]. *The Carthaginian peace; or, the economic consequences of Mr. Keynes*. New York: Charles Scribner's Sons.

Marcosson, Isaac Frederick. 1947. *Colonel Deeds, industrial builder*. New York: Dodd, Mead.

Meeropol, Robert. 2003. *An execution in the family: one son's journey*. New York: St. Martin's Press.

Meeropol, Robert, and Michael Meeropol. 1986. *We are your sons: the legacy of Ethel and Julius Rosenberg*. 2nd edn. Urbana: University of Illinois Press.

Melman, Seymour. 1985. *The permanent war economy: American capitalism in decline*. New York: Simon & Schuster.

Meltzer, Allan H. 2003 *A history of the Federal Reserve, vol. I*. University of Chicago Press.

2009. *A history of the Federal Reserve, vol. II*. University of Chicago Press.

Mill, John Stuart. 1936 [1848]. *Principles of political economy, with some of their applications to social philosophy*, ed. W. J. Ashley. London and New York: Longmans, Green.

Miller, E. T., H. L. Lutz, Edmond E. Lincoln, T. K. Urdahl, and O. M. W. Sprague. 1917. Loans and taxes in war finance: discussion. Papers and Proceedings of the Twenty-ninth Annual Meeting of the American Economic Association. *American Economic Review* 7 (1 Supplement) (Mar.): 214–23.

Miller, Stuart Creighton. 1982. *"Benevolent assimilation": the American conquest of the Philippines, 1899–1903*. New Haven: Yale University Press.

Mills, Geofrey, and Hugh Rockoff. 1987. Compliance with price controls in the United States and the United Kingdom during World War II. *Journal of Economic History* 47 (1) (Mar.): 197–213.

Milne, David. 2007. "Our equivalent of guerrilla warfare": Walt Rostow and the bombing of North Vietnam, 1961–1968. *Journal of Military History* 71 (1) (Jan.): 169–203.

Milward, Alan S. 1984. *The reconstruction of western Europe, 1945–51.* Berkeley: University of California Press.

1977. History of the world economy in the twentieth century, Vol. V: *War, economy, and society, 1939–1945.* Berkeley: University of California Press.

1965. *The German economy at war.* London: University of London, Athlone Press.

Mises, Ludwig von. 1949. *Human action: a treatise on economics.* New Haven: Yale University Press.

Mitchener, Kris James, and Marc Weidenmier. 2008. Trade and empire. *Economic Journal* 118 (533)(11): 1805–34.

2005a. Empire, public goods, and the Roosevelt corollary. *Journal of Economic History* 65 (3): 658–92.

2005b. Supersanctions and sovereign debt repayment. *NBER Working Paper no. 11472.*

Molander, Earl A. 1976. Historical antecedents of military-industrial criticism. *Military Affairs* 40 (2) (Apr.): 59–63.

Morgenthau, Henry, Robert Lester, Charles Edward Smith, Barbara Brown, and Franklin D. Roosevelt Library. 1995. *The Morgenthau diaries.* Research Collections in American Politics. Bethesda, MD: University Publications of America.

Morris, Richard B., and Jeffrey Brandon Morris. 1996. *Encyclopedia of American history.* 7th edn. New York: HarperCollins.

Mulligan, Casey B. 1998. Pecuniary incentives to work in the United States during World War II. *Journal of Political Economy* 106 (5) (Oct.): 1033–77.

Nash, Gerald D. 1959. Herbert Hoover and the origins of the Reconstruction Finance Corporation. *Mississippi Valley Historical Review* 46 (3) (Dec.): 455–68.

Nelson, Donald Marr. 1946. *Arsenal of democracy: the story of American war production.* New York: Harcourt, Brace.

Novick, David, Melvin Anshen, and William Charles Truppner. 1949. *Wartime production controls.* New York: Columbia University Press.

Noyes, Alexander Dana. 1926. *The war period of American finance, 1908–1925.* New York and London: G.P. Putnam's Sons.

Officer, Lawrence H. 2011. Annual wages in the United States: unskilled labor and manufacturing workers, 1774–present. In *Measuring Worth*, available at www.measuringworth.com/uswage (accessed June 6, 2011).

Officer, Lawrence H., and Samuel H. Williamson. 2011. Purchasing power of money in the United States from 1774 to 2010. In *MeasuringWorth*, available at www.measuringworth.com/ppowerus (accessed June 6, 2011).

Ohanian, Lee E. 1997. The macroeconomic effects of war finance in the United States: World War II and the Korean War. *American Economic Review* 87 (1) (Mar.): 23–40.

Oi, Walter Y. 1967. The economic cost of the draft. Papers and Proceedings of the Seventy-ninth Annual Meeting of the American Economic Association. *American Economic Review* 57 (2) (May): 39–62.

O'Neill, William L. 1993. *A democracy at war: America's fight at home and abroad in World War II*. New York: The Free Press.

Overy, R. J. 2010. *War in the Pacific*. Long Island, N.Y.: Osprey Publishing.

1999. *The origins of the Second World War*. Seminar Studies in History. 2nd edn. New York: Longman.

1996. *Why the Allies won*. New York: W.W. Norton.

1980. *The air war, 1939–1945*. New York: Stein and Day.

Parrini, Carl P., and Martin J. Sklar. 1983. New thinking about the market, 1896–1904: some American economists on investment and the theory of surplus capital. *Journal of Economic History* 43 (3) (Sep.): 559–78.

Perez, Louis A., Jr. 1999. Incurring a debt of gratitude: 1898 and the moral sources of United States hegemony in Cuba. *American Historical Review* 104 (2) (Apr.): 356–98.

Pigou, A. C. 1941 [1921]. *The political economy of war*, rev. edn. New York: The Macmillan Company.

Pollack, Sheldon David. 2009. *War, revenue, and state building: financing the development of the American state*. Ithaca: Cornell University Press.

Pratt, Julius W. 1934. American business and the Spanish–American War. *Hispanic American Historical Review* 14 (2) (May): 163–201.

1932. The "large policy" of 1898. *Mississippi Valley Historical Review* 19 (2) (Sep.): 219–42.

Radosh, Ronald, and Joyce Milton. 1997. *The Rosenberg file*, 2nd edn. New Haven: Yale University Press.

Rae, John. 1895. *Life of Adam Smith*. London: Macmillan and Co.

Report of President Truman on the atomic bomb. 1945. *Science* 102 (2642) (Aug. 17): 163–5.

Rhode, Paul W. 2004. After the war boom: reconversion on the Pacific coast, 1943–1949. In *History matters: essays on economic growth, technology, and demographic change*, ed. Timothy W. Guinnane, William A. Sundstrom, and Warren Whatley, 187–220. Stanford University Press.

Rhodes, Benjamin D. 1969. Reassessing "Uncle Shylock": the United States and the French war debt, 1917–1929. *Journal of American History* 55 (4) (Mar.): 787–803.

Rhodes, Richard. 1995. *Dark sun: the making of the hydrogen bomb*. New York: Simon and Schuster.

1986. *The making of the atomic bomb*. New York: Simon and Schuster.

1979. Economic mobilization in wartime Japan: business, bureaucracy, and military in conflict. *Journal of Asian Studies* 38 (4) (Aug.): 689–706.

Robbins, Lionel. 1947. *The economic problem in peace and war: some reflections on objectives and mechanisms*. London: Macmillan.

1939. *The economic causes of war*. London: Jonathan Cape.

Rockoff, Hugh. 2006. Veterans. In *Historical statistics of the United States: earliest times to the present*, ed. Susan B. Carter, Scott Sigmund Gartner, Michael R. Haines, Alan L. Olmstead, Richard Sutch, and Gavin Wright, S340–S349. Cambridge University Press.

2005. Until it's over, over there: the US economy in World War I. In *The economics of World War I*, ed. Stephen Broadberry and Mark Harrison, 310–43. Cambridge University Press.

1998a. The peace dividend in historical perspective. Papers and Proceedings of the Hundred and Tenth Annual Meeting of the American Economic Association. *American Economic Review* 88 (2) (May): 46–50.

1998b. The United States: from ploughshares to swords. In Harrison, ed. *The economics of World War II*, 81–116. Cambridge University Press.

1984. *Drastic measures: a history of wage and price controls in the United States*. Studies in Economic History and Policy. Cambridge University Press.

1981a. Price and wage controls in four wartime periods. *Journal of Economic History* 41 (2) (June): 381–401.

1981b. The response of the giant corporations to wage and price control in World War II. *Journal of Economic History* 41 (1): 123–8.

Romer, Christina D. 1992. What ended the Great Depression? *Journal of Economic History* 52 (4) (Dec.): 757–84.

1989. The prewar business cycle reconsidered: new estimates of Gross National Product, 1869–1908. *Journal of Political Economy* 97 (1) (Feb.): 1–37.

1988. World War I and the postwar depression: a reinterpretation based on alternative estimates of GNP. *Journal of Monetary Economics* 22 (1) (July): 91–115.

Roosevelt, Theodore. 1894. Review of the influence of sea power upon history, 1660–1783, and the influence of sea power upon the French Revolution and empire, 1793–1812 by Captain A.T. Mahan. *Political Science Quarterly* 9 (1) (Mar.): 171–3.

Ross, Myron H. 1966. "Operation Twist": a mistaken policy? *Journal of Political Economy* 74 (2) (Apr.): 195–9.

Rostow, W. W. 2003. *Concept and controversy: sixty years of taking ideas to market*. Austin: University of Texas Press.

1981. *Pre-invasion bombing strategy: General Eisenhower's decision of March 25, 1944*. Ideas and Action Series 1. Austin: University of Texas Press.

Rotwein, Eugene. 1964. Economic concentration and monopoly in Japan. *Journal of Political Economy* 72 (3) (June): 262–77.

Rupp, Leila J. 1978. *Mobilizing women for war: German and American propaganda, 1939–1945*. Princeton University Press.

Russia (Federation), General'nyĭshtab, Lester W. Grau, and Michael A. Gress. 2002. *The Soviet–Afghan War: how a superpower fought and lost*. Modern War Studies. Lawrence: University Press of Kansas.

Safire, William. 2008. *Safire's political dictionary.* Oxford University Press.

Samuel, Lawrence R. 1997. *Pledging allegiance: American identity and the bond drive of World War II*. Washington, DC: Smithsonian Institution Press.

Schaffer, Ronald. 1980. American military ethics in World War II: the bombing of German civilians. *Journal of American History* 67 (2) (Sep.): 318–34.

Schelling, Thomas C. 2006. An astonishing sixty years: the legacy of Hiroshima. *American Economic Review* 96 (4) (Sep.): 929–37.

Schlesinger, Arthur M. Jr. 1986. *The cycles of American history.* Boston: Houghton Mifflin.

Schlesinger, Arthur M., Jr., and John S. Bowman, eds. 1993. *The almanac of American history.* New York: Barnes & Noble.

Schmeckebier, L. F. 1942. Organization of the executive branch of the national government of the United States: changes between November 15, 1941, and March 31, 1942. *American Political Science Review* 36 (3) (June): 482–91.

Schumpeter, Joseph Alois. 1954. *History of economic analysis*. Oxford University Press.

Schwartz, Anna J. 1987. The postwar institutional evolution of the international monetary system. In Anna J. Schwartz, *Money in historical perspective*, 333–63. University of Chicago Press.

Seligman, Edwin R. A. 1918. Loans versus taxes in war finance. *Annals of the American Academy of Political and Social Science* 75 (Financing the War) (Jan.): 52–82.

Severo, Richard, and Lewis Milford. 1989. *The wages of war: when America's soldiers came home: from Valley Forge to Vietnam*. New York: Simon and Schuster.

Shultz, George Pratt, Robert Z. Aliber, and University of Chicago. 1966. *Guidelines, informal controls, and the market place: policy choices in a full employment economy.* Studies in Business 12. University of Chicago Press.

Shultz, William J., and M. R. Caine. 1937. *Financial development of the United States.* New York: Prentice-Hall.

Silber, William L. 2007. *When Washington shut down Wall Street: the great financial crisis of 1914 and the origins of America's monetary supremacy.* Princeton University Press.

Silbey, David. 2007. *A war of frontier and empire: the Philippine–American War, 1899–1902.* New York: Hill and Wang.

Singer, J. David, and Melvin Small. 1972. *The wages of war, 1816–1965: a statistical handbook.* New York: Wiley.

Smith, Adam. 1976 [1759]. *The theory of moral sentiments.* Indianapolis: Liberty Classics.

1976 [1776]. *An inquiry into the nature and causes of the wealth of nations*, eds. R. H. Campbell, Andrew S. Skinner, and William B. Todd. The Glasgow edition of the works and correspondence of Adam Smith 2. Oxford: Clarendon Press.

Smith, George David. 1988. *From monopoly to competition: the transformations of Alcoa, 1888–1986.* Cambridge University Press.

Smith, R. Elberton. 1959. United States army in World War II: The War Department: *The army and economic mobilization.* Washington: Office of the Chief of Military History, Dept. of the Army.

Solo, Robert. 1954. Research and development in the synthetic rubber industry. *Quarterly Journal of Economics* 68 (1) (Feb.): 61–82.

1953. The sale of the synthetic rubber plants. *Journal of Industrial Economics* 2 (1) (Nov.): 32–43.

Speer, Albert. 1970 [1952]. *Inside the Third Reich: memoirs.* New York: Macmillan.

Sprague, O. M. W. 1917. Loans and taxes in war finance. Papers and Proceedings of the Twenty-ninth Annual Meeting of the American Economic Association *American Economic Review* 7 (1, Supplement) (Mar.): 199–213.

1918. The relationship between loans and taxes in war finance. *Annals of the American Academy of Political and Social Science* 75 (Financing the War) (Jan.): 83–9.

Stamp, J. C. 1917. The taxation of excess profits abroad. *Economic Journal* 27 (105) (Mar.): 26–37.

Stanley, Marcus. 2003. College education and the midcentury GI bills. *Quarterly Journal of Economics* 118 (2) (May): 671–708.

Stein, Herbert. 1996. *The fiscal revolution in America: policy in pursuit of reality.* 2nd rev. edn. Washington, DC: AEI Press.

Stiglitz, Joseph, and Linda Bilmes. 2008. *The three trillion dollar war: the true cost of the Iraq War*. New York: W. W. Norton.

Studenski, Paul, and Herman Edward Krooss. 1952. *Financial history of the United States*. New York: McGraw-Hill.

Taft, William Howard. 1912. Cost of occupation of Philippine Islands. Message from the President of the United States, transmitting statement relative to the cost which has accrued to the United States as a result of the occupation of the Philippine Islands. 62nd Congress, 2nd Session, H.Doc. 875, July 19.

Taussig, F. W. 1921. Is market price determinate? *Quarterly Journal of Economics* 35 (3) (May): 394–411.

1919. Price-fixing as seen by a price-fixer. *Quarterly Journal of Economics* 33 (2) (Feb.): 205–41.

Telser, Lester G. 2003. The veterans' bonus of 1936. *Journal of Post Keynesian Economics* 26 (Winter): 227–43.

Temin, Peter. 1969. *The Jacksonian economy*. Norton Essays in American History. New York: Norton.

Toland, John. 1970. *The rising sun: the decline and fall of the Japanese empire, 1936–1945*. New York: Random House.

Tooze, J. Adam. 2007. *The wages of destruction: the making and breaking of the Nazi economy*. New York: Viking Penguin.

Trachtenberg, Marc. 1982. Versailles after sixty years. *Journal of Contemporary History* 17 (3) (July): 487–506.

Truman, Harry S. 1955. *Memoirs*. Garden City, N.Y.: Doubleday.

Turvey, Ralph. 1961. Inflation as a tax in World War II. *Journal of Political Economy* 69 (1) (Feb.): 70–3.

Twentieth Century Fund and James Frederic Dewhurst. 1947. *America's needs and resources: a Twentieth Century Fund survey which includes estimates for 1950 and 1960*. New York: The Twentieth Century Fund.

US Bureau of the Budget. 1972 [1946]. *The United States at war: development and administration of the war program by the federal government*. Franklin K. Lane project on the problems and future of the San Francisco Bay area. New York: DaCapo Press.

US Bureau of the Census. 1960. *Historical statistics of the United States, colonial times to 1957*. Washington, DC: Government Printing Office.

1975. *Historical statistics of the United States*. Washington, DC: US Dept. of Commerce, Bureau of the Census.

US Congress, Joint Economic Committee. 2010. *The 2010 joint economic report: report of the Joint Economic Committee, Congress of the United States, on the 2010 economic report of the president, together with minority views and additional views*. Report/111th congress, 2nd session, House of Representatives, vol. 111–545. Washington, DC: Government Printing Office.

US Department of Defense. 1992. *Conduct of the Persian Gulf War: final report to Congress*. Washington, DC: Dept. of Defense.

US Department of Veterans' Affairs, Research Advisory Committee on Gulf War Veterans' Illnesses. 2008. *Gulf War illness and the health of Gulf War veterans: scientific findings and recommendations*. Washington, DC: Research Advisory Committee on Gulf War Veterans' Illnesses.

US President's Commission on an All-Volunteer Armed Force. 1970. *The report of the president's commission on an all-volunteer armed force*. Washington, DC: Government Printing Office.

US President's Commission on Veterans' Pensions. 1956. *A report on veterans' benefits in the United States, staff report no. I: the historical development of veterans' benefits in the United States*. Printed as US House of Representatives, House Committee print no. 244, 84th cong., 2nd sess.

US Senate. 1902a. *Expenditures in the Philippine islands, etc.* S. doc. 416. 57th cong., 1st sess.

1902b. *Naval expenditures in the Philippines*. S. doc. 372. 57th cong., 1st sess.

1900. *Number of deaths of soldiers in the Philippines*, etc. S. doc. 426. 56th cong., 1st sess.

US Special Committee to Study the Rubber Situation, Bernard M. Baruch Chair. 1942. *Report of the rubber survey committee*. Washington, DC: Government Printing Office.

US Strategic Bombing Survey. 1946a. *The effects of the atomic bombings of Hiroshima and Nagasaki* (June). Washington, DC: Government Printing Office.

1946b. *Summary report (Pacific War)* (July). Washington, DC: Government Printing Office.

1945. *Summary report (European War)*. Washington, DC: Government Printing Office.

US War Production Board. 1942. *Controlled materials plan: November 2, 1942*. Washington, DC: Government Printing Office.

Varg, Paul A. 1968. The myth of the China market, 1890–1914. *American Historical Review* 73 (3) (Feb.): 742–58.

Vedder, Richard K., and Lowell E. Gallaway. 1997. *Out of work: unemployment and government in twentieth-century America*. New York University Press.

Vernon, J. R. 1994. World War II fiscal policies and the end of the Great Depression. *Journal of Economic History* 54 (4) (Dec.): 850–68.

Viner, Jacob. 1920. Who paid for the war? *Journal of Political Economy* 28 (1) (Jan.): 46–76.

Vonnegut, Kurt. 1991 [1968]. *Slaughterhouse-five, or, the children's crusade: a duty-dance with death*. New York: Dell.

Wallich, Henry Christopher. 1955. *Mainsprings of the German revival*. Yale Studies in Economics 5. New Haven: Yale University Press.

Walton, Gary M., and Hugh Rockoff. 2010. *History of the American economy*. 11th edn. Mason, Ohio: South-Western/Cengage.

Warner, John T., and Beth J. Asch. 2001. The record and prospects of the all-volunteer military in the United States. *Journal of Economic Perspectives* 15 (2) (Spring): 169–92.

Weber, Gustavus Adolphus, and Laurence Frederick Schmeckebier. 1934. *The veterans' administration, its history, activities and organization. Institute for Government Research [of the Brookings Institution] Service Monographs of the United States Government* 66. Washington, DC: The Brookings Institution.

Weigley, Russell Frank. 1973. *The American way of war: a history of United States military strategy and policy*. Wars of the United States. New York: Macmillan.

Werrell, Kenneth P. 1986. The strategic bombing of Germany in World War II: costs and accomplishments. *Journal of American History* 73 (3) (Dec.): 702–13.

White, Eugene N. 2001. Making the French pay: the costs and consequences of the Napoleonic reparations. *European Review of Economic History* 5 (3) (Dec.): 337–65.

Wilcox, E. V. 1918. Plan of the Department of Agriculture for handling the farm labor problem. In Papers and Proceedings of the Thirtieth Annual Meeting of the American Economic Association. *American Economic Review* 8 (1, Supplement) (Mar.): 158–70.

Wilkins, Mira. 1970. *The emergence of multinational enterprise: American business abroad from the colonial era to 1914*. Cambridge, Mass.: Harvard University Press.

Williams, Walter L. 1980. United States Indian policy and the debate over Philippine annexation: implications for the origins of American imperialism. *Journal of American History* 66 (4) (Mar.): 810–31.

Williamson, Samuel H. 2008. Five ways to compute the relative value of a US dollar amount, 1790 to present. In *Measuring Worth, 2008*, available at www.measuringworth.com (accessed March 18, 2008).

Wirls, Daniel. 1992. *Buildup: the politics of defense in the Reagan era*. Ithaca: Cornell University Press.

Wolcott, Susan. 1990. Keynes vs. Churchill: British unemployment in the twenties. *Journal of Economic History* 50 (2) (June): 442–4.

Wolf, Ralph F. 1952. Rich man, poor man. *Scientific Monthly* 74 (2) (Feb.): 69–75.

1948. Eighty-eight years of synthetic rubber. *Scientific Monthly* 66 (3) (Mar.): 221–31.

Wooley, John, and Gerhard Peters. 2008. The American presidency project. Available at www.presidency.ucsb.edu/platforms.php (accessed January 14, 2008).

Yasuba, Yasukichi. 1996. Did Japan ever suffer from a shortage of natural resources before World War II? *Journal of Economic History* 56 (3) (Sep.): 543–60.

Zevin, Robert. 1972. An interpretation of American imperialism. *Journal of Economic History* 32 (1) (Mar.): 316–60.

Index